ASTROLOGY FOR YOURSELF

ASTROLOGY

A Workbook for

FOR

Personal Transformation

YOURSELF

HOW TO UNDERSTAND AND INTERPRET
YOUR OWN BIRTH CHART

DOUGLAS BLOCH & DEMETRA GEORGE

Ibis Press
An Imprint of Nicolas-Hays, Inc.
Berwick, Maine

Dedicated to
students of astrology throughout the world
who through their dedication have preserved
the knowledge of this ancient art

This edition published in 2006 by
Ibis Press, an imprint of
Nicolas-Hays, Inc.
P.O. Box 540206
Lake Worth, FL 33454-0206
www.nicolashays.com
Nicolas-Hays and Ibis Press books
are distributed to the trade by
Red Wheel/Weiser, LLC
65 Parker St., Ste. 7
Newburyport, MA 01950-4600
www.redwheelweiser.com

"Thinking of Bying or Selling a House?" reprinted by permission of *The Wall Street Journal* © Dow Jones & Company, Inc.
1986. All rights reserved.

"Physiological Correspondences of the Signs" and "Physiological Correspondences of the Planets" reprinted from *Astrology:*

The Divine Science by Mark Douglas and Marcia Moore, reprinted
by permission of Arcane Publications.

Library of Congress Cataloging-in-Publication Data
George, Demetra, 1946–
    Astrology for yourself.
    Bibliography: p.
    1. Horoscopes. I. Bloch, Douglas, 1949–
II. Title
BF1728.A2G357 1987 133.5'4 86-18966
ISBN 978-0-89254-122-5

Cover design by Kathryn Sky-Peck
Book design: Paula Morrison
Printed in the United States of America by Bang Printing,
Brainerd, Minnesota

20   19   18
10   9   8

The paper used in this publication meets the minimum require-
ments of the American National Standard for Information
Sciences—Permanence of Paper for Printed Library Materials
Z39.48–1992 (R1997).

Table of Contents

The Figures in This Book

The Tables in This Book

The Exercises in This Book

These Programmed Learning Exercises comprise the heart of this book. By completing them you will uncover the meaning of your birth chart and discover the mystery that is you.

Acknowledgements

Many individuals have made valuable contributions to this work written in three stages over a period of eight years.

I first conceived of writing a self-help astrology text in the spring of 1978. That summer, I was able to get the book off its feet, thanks to Kay David who served as my editor and to Dean Price whose Gemini skill with words enabled me to formulate many of the keyword tables that later appeared in *Astrology For Yourself*.

Two years later, I was assisted by Sheila Seitz who donated her editorial feedback and by the encouragement of my friends Stuart Warren and Robert Wheeler. At this point, the book was completed, titled *Beyond Sun Signs*, but no publisher could be found.

The manuscript would have remained unpublished had it not been for my indispensable collaborator, Demetra George, who in October of 1985 suggested the idea of writing an astrological workbook. At that point, I realized that *Beyond Sun Signs* could be rewritten in a workbook format, and hence it metamorphosed into *Astrology For Yourself*.

During the next six hectic months, our progress was aided by the editorial feedback of Nancy Avery, Carolyn Quigley, Jim Markham, and my wife Joan. My work supervisor Brian Bergeron provided me with the flexibility to balance a demanding writing schedule with a full time job.

Finally, my heartfelt thanks go to my parents. They provided a nurturing environment that enabled me to initiate my writing career. But more important, their ongoing support of my decision to embark upon a road less traveled has enabled me to remain true to myself. For allowing me to pursue my own path of self discovery, I will always be grateful.

Douglas Bloch
August 12, 1986
Portland, Oregon

Astrology For Yourself is the culmination of twelve years of teaching the astrological language. During that time I experimented with a variety of graphic forms to assist students in realizing how astrological principles expressed themselves in their personal lives. To all these students I give special thanks for their efforts and feedback in refining the workbook format.

In September of 1985, as I was preparing some new handouts for a beginning astrology class, the concept for this workbook suddenly arrived—literally pouring out of my head. For this inspiration I want to thank Mary Greer for allowing us to take off on *Tarot For Your Self*. Jonathan Saturnen and Dennis Conroy both provided valuable input in clarifying the exercises.

Without Douglas the creation of *Astrology For Yourself* would not have been possible. His hard work, helpful insights and expertise in giving form to our fanciful ideas was essential for the completion of this work.

I also want to extend appreciation to Philip Russell for providing the graphics in the original self-published edition of *Astrology for Yourself,* as well as his help in teaching me about the MacIntosh computer. To my children, Daniel and Reina Frankfort, I offer a mother's gratitude for their patience and understanding during the long hours of writing.

Both Douglas and I give special thanks to our editor Randy Fingland who guided this project along the many steps to its completion.

Finally I give gratitude to the Wisdom Dakinis and the Lady Yeshe Tsogyel for glimpses of the clear light. May this offering of *Astrology For Yourself* benefit all beings.

Demetra George
August 12, 1986
Waldport, Oregon

Introduction

Getting Started

Edmund Halley: *Why do you believe in Astrology?*
Sir Isaac Newton: *I have studied the subject, Mr. Halley. You have not!*

ISAAC NEWTON was no slouch. Many consider him to be endowed with the most brilliant and profound mind ever visited upon a mortal. Yet, despite the incredulity of Halley (the comet man) and his colleagues, Newton actually *believed* in astrology. So did Benjamin Franklin. And Galileo. And Carl Jung. And a host of other historical luminaries. Clearly, there might be something more to this ancient art than the overgeneralized horoscope columns that appear in the daily papers.

But how can one find out for sure if astrology does work? Is it, in the words of one astrologer, "the most accurate and comprehensive means of understanding human personality, behavior change, and growth?" Or is it merely a parlor game? The answer, it seems, may be easily determined if one takes Sir Isaac's advice to heart—*study the subject!*

Which is why we have written *Astrology For Yourself.*

Astrology for Yourself is designed to introduce you to the language/art/science of astrology by walking you through a simple, easy to learn, step-by-step procedure for interpreting your own birth chart. The vehicle for this process is a series of self-directed programmed-learning exercises that will literally enable you to write your own chart interpretation.

Is Astrology For Yourself *For Me?*

Before you begin this book, you definitely want to determine if it was written with you in mind. The answer to this question is a resounding *yes!* if you fall into any of the following categories:

1. You have just obtained a copy of your natal chart *for the first time*, and would like to learn how to interpret it.

2. Perhaps you have just had your chart *interpreted by an astrologer* and would like to pursue the process of self-discovery on your own.

3. You are a *beginning student* who would like to learn about astrology, but don't have the time to take a class.

4. You are at the *intermediate* level and have studied your chart a little (either had it interpreted or have taken a beginning class), but would like to understand it in more depth.

5. You are a *counseling astrologer* who interprets charts for your clients and would like to have a good introductory book to recommend to them.

6. You are an *astrologer* who *teaches classes* and needs a standard textbook to use with your students, one that invites them to participate in the learning process.

7. You are a *professional* astrologer who simply wants to review the fundamentals of your own birth chart. As an example, while proofing the text, we (the authors) discovered a host of new insights about our own birth charts, even though we had been studying them for more than a decade!

If you can identify with any of the above descriptions, then *Astrology For Yourself* was written for you.

What Do I Need to Get Started?

In order to pursue *Astrology For Yourself* beyond Chapter One, you will *need* a personal copy of your **natal birth chart**, preferably one that contains the positions of the four major asteroids and also lists your planetary aspects.

If you already have such a chart, then you can use it. If you don't have your complete birth chart, then you will have to *send away* for it or have an astrologer in your area construct one for you, or you can order an *Astrology For Yourself* computer report. The *address* and *order form* are located in *Appendix D* at the back of the book. If you order your birth chart *now*, you can obtain it within five to seven days, not long at all.

In the meantime, you can complete Chapter One, and while you are waiting for your chart to arrive, to avoid constantly having to turn to the back of the book, you may photocopy Appendices A and B and place them in a separate folder kept next to *Astrology For Yourself*. In this way you can more easily look up the keywords as you complete the exercises. You may elect to follow this procedure if you find it more convenient.

When you are ready, turn to Chapter One where you will be introduced to an astrological friend you have no doubt met—your Sun sign.

How Will I Benefit From *Reading* Astrology For Yourself? ─────

Aside from providing you with a wealth of *knowledge* about your birth chart (and therefore yourself), *Astrology for Yourself* promises to promote *personal growth* and change in your life. Through filling out the workbook, you will gain one or more of the following benefits:

- A basic understanding of your talents, abilities and strengths, and how you can best express them in your life.

- An overall understanding of your life's meaning and purpose.
- Insights into your life's challenges—and how you can transform them into opportunities.
- A deeper and more comprehensive understanding of a variety of important dimensions in your life:
  - Career and Vocational needs
  - Relationship needs
  - Health
  - Finances
  - Child-rearing
  - Your major life cycles—when they will occur and what they mean

────── *Journal Entry* ──────

In the space below, briefly note which of the above topics are most important to you. After completing the book, you will be given the opportunity to chronicle your progress through filling out the questionnaire in Chapter Eight.

_____

_____

_____

_____

_____

_____

_____

_____

_____

_____

_____

_____

_____

_____

_____

_____

_____

_____

_____

_____

_____

_____

Part I

Learning the Basics

I N the following chapters, you are going to learn a new and wonderful language—the language of astrology. If you are a beginning student, here is the place to start. In the following pages, you will discover the letters of the astrological alphabet and will combine those letters into words and words into sentences—sentences that describe the entire spectrum of human personality and behavior.

If you are an intermediate or advanced student, we suggest that you, too, read Part 1 and especially participate in the workbook exercises. Through completing these self-inquiries, you will **fine tune** your understanding of the birth chart and perhaps gain new insights altogether.

Chapter 1

───*Introducing the Zodiac*───

Astrology as a Language of Energy ────────────────

A STROLOGY is a language, art, and science that studies the relationship between the cycles of celestial bodies and the affairs of people on earth. Derived from the Greek roots astron (star) and logos (word or speech), astrology literally means "star talk." The purpose of learning astrology is to better know and understand ourselves and our place in the cosmos. In the following pages, we are going to take you on a journey of self-discovery that only astrology can provide.

If someone were to ask you to describe astrology, you would most likely think of the twelve signs of the Zodiac, popularly known as the "Sun signs." They are listed in Table 1 along with their symbols and corresponding dates. Beside this table, Figure 1 displays the zodiacal signs arranged in their traditional circle format ("Zodiac" is Greek for "circle of animals").

On an energy level, the signs represent the twelve primary energy fields, the formative principles of the universe, or the archetypal patterns. On a psychological level, the signs correspond to twelve basic personality types; and even more specifically, to the twelve basic psychological needs that each and every human being experiences. Table 2 gives a brief overview of these personality traits.

Although everyone has all twelve of these signs somewhere in their chart, each person was born under a specific "Sun sign." In the following exercise, you will learn to determine your own Sun sign.

Table 1: The Signs of the Zodiac

Symbol	Sign	Approximate Dates*
♈	Aries, the Ram	March 21-April 20
♉	Taurus, the Bull	April 21-May 20
♊	Gemini, the Twins	May 21-June 20
♋	Cancer, the Crab	June 21-July 21
♌	Leo, the Lion	July 22-August 22
♍	Virgo, the Virgin	August 23-September 22
♎	Libra, the Scales	September 23-October 22
♏	Scorpio, the Scorpion	October 23-November 21
♐	Sagittarius, the Centaur	November 22-December 20
♑	Capricorn, the Goat	December 21-January 20
♒	Aquarius, the Water Bearer	January 21-February 18
♓	Pisces, the Fish	February 19-March 20

*If you were born on one of the transition dates (known as the cusp), then have a professional astrologer or a birth chart computing service determine your correct sun sign.

Table 2: Zodiacal Essences

Symbol	Sign	Principle	Skillful Application	Unskillful Application
♈	Aries "I am"	Activity	Initiative	Impulsiveness
♉	Taurus "I have"	Manifestation	Productivity	Materialism
♊	Gemini "I think"	Rationality	Intelligence	Superficiality
♋	Cancer "I feel"	Nourishment	Care	Insecurity
♌	Leo "I show"	Creativity	Love	Pride
♍	Virgo "I analyze"	Discrimination	Clarity	Criticism
♎	Libra "I relate"	Balance	Diplomacy	Indecision
♏	Scorpio "I transform"	Death and Rebirth	Regeneration	Abuse of Power
♐	Sagittarius "I seek"	Exploration	Wisdom	Delusion
♑	Capricorn "I utilize"	Order	Accomplishment	Opportunism
♒	Aquarius "I'm different"	Change	Originality	Rebelliousness
♓	Pisces "I imagine"	Unity	Compassion	Martyrdom

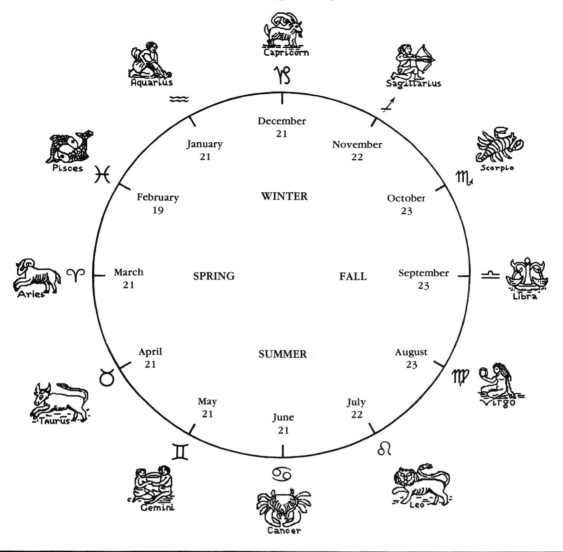

Exercise 1: I Learn My Sun Sign

Using Table 1 and your knowledge of your **Date of Birth**, determine the zodiacal sign under which you were born. Then fill in the sentence below.

My Sun is in the sign of _____.

Now that you know your Sun sign, how can you understand its meaning? One way is to pick up a mass market pop-astrology book and read the paragraphs on your sign. Unfortunately, besides giving you a very superficial description of your sign, these books do not tell *why* each sign means what it does.

In the following pages we are going to examine the Zodiac in a much more meaningful way. We are going to discover the *building blocks* that underlie the Zodiac. These basic principles will provide you with a new and deeper understanding of your Sun sign's attributes.

The Building Blocks of the Zodiac:
——Element, Polarity, Modality, Orientation——

The signs of the Zodiac represent the 12 primary energy patterns of our universe. Each sign, or energy pattern, is a unique combination of the concepts known as polarity, element, and modality.

The Four Elements

Although you may be unaware of it, you are already quite familiar with the astrological language. Consider the following statements:

"He's down to earth."
"She's got her feet on the ground."
"He's as solid as a rock."
"She's all fired up."
"He's too spaced out."
"Her still waters run deep."

You have no doubt used such figures of speech to describe yourself or others at various times. But have you ever pondered their origins? If not, you may be surprised to learn that these and other common expressions are derived from the astrological elements of fire, earth, air and water.

These four elements—Fire-plasma, Air-gases, Earth-solids, and Water-liquids—have been used by all ancient cosmologies (the Greeks, Chinese, Hindus, American Indians, etc.) to describe the basic building blocks of all organic and psychic forms. The symbology of the elements is reflected in the song with the chorus chant of "Earth my body, water my blood, air my breath, fire my spirit." Astrologically, the elements depict four distinct personality temperaments that are basic to human nature.

Fire is the *identity* principle.

Earth is the *material substance* principle.

Air is the *mental* principle.

Water is the *feeling* principle.

It is from these four elements that the twelve signs of the Zodiac are derived. Let us now explore the psychological characteristics of the elements and learn how they are expressed through the signs of the Zodiac. As we describe the elements in detail, you will undoubtedly recognize portraits of yourself, family, friends and co-workers.

The Fire Signs: Identity

*Give me a spark of Nature's fire
That's the learning I desire.*

Robert Burns

The astrological language contains three signs that specifically express the fire principle. They are Aries, Leo, and Sagittarius.

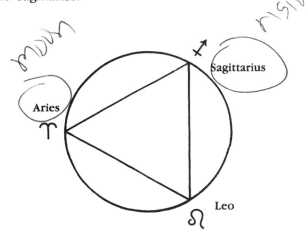

The element of fire corresponds to the active life force, the principle that animates and energizes. Fire represents the energy of spirit. Individuals with an emphasis of fire often express themselves through direct action and inspire others with their visions. Fire seeks to realize its identity.

One of the most important principles of astrology states that any positive principle, when exaggerated, can become negative. Hence, the overly fiery individual can turn assertion into aggression, enthusiasm into fanaticism, or daring into recklessness. Like a fire raging out of control, this person consumes everything in his or her path.

On the other hand, a person deficient in fire lacks energy, zest, and *joie de vivre*. These are the people who need three cups of coffee to get them through the day.

The Air Signs: Social and Mental——

The Breath of Nature
When great nature sighs we hear the winds
Which, noiseless in themselves
Awaken noises from other beings,
Blowing on them.
From every opening
Loud voices sound. Have you not heard
This rush of tones?

Chang Tzu

Three signs of the Zodiac personify the qualities of air. They are Gemini, Libra and Aquarius.

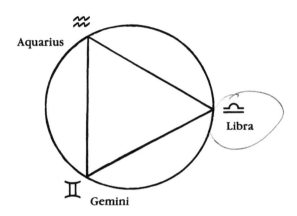

The element of air corresponds to the mental realm of ideas where thoughts become the structures through which energy precipitates and coalesces into form. Air represents the energy of breath. Individuals with an emphasis of air often express themselves by sharing and communicating their ideas to others. Air seeks to make social and intellectual connections.

Too much air produces the "up in the air" or "airhead" individual who cannot ground him- or herself long enough to apply any of his or her marvelous ideas. These people often appear scattered, inconsistent, and indecisive.

Too little air, on the other hand, can lead to a lack of perspective and objectivity in life. Difficulties in learning and poor communication skills may also be the result of a deficiency of this element.

The Earth Signs: Material——————

That I am a part of the earth my feet know
perfectly.

D.H. Lawrence

Three signs of the Zodiac embody the traits of earth. They are Taurus, Virgo, and Capricorn.

The element of earth corresponds to the physical realm where objects are perceived directly by the senses

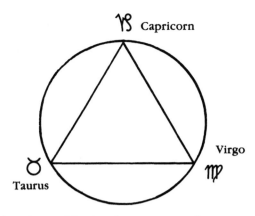

as real and tangible. Earth represents the energy that gives form and substance to creation. Individuals with an emphasis of earth often express themselves by mastering the world of common-sense reality, actualizing their dreams, and supplying their basic survival needs. Earth seeks to provide material substance.

Too much earth in the birth chart produces a "stick in the mud"—the person whose overcautious nature and fear of change prevents him or her from taking risks and breaking out of an old rut.

Too little earth, however, creates an "ungrounded" individual who has difficulties coping with the mundane responsibilities of everyday life. When he or she promises that your book will be returned next week, you can expect to see it the following month. The solid earth person, on the other hand, feels obligated to keep commitments and to fulfill responsibilities.

The Water Signs: Emotional & Soul——

The highest motive is to be like water.
Water is essential to all living things,
Yet, it demands no pay or recognition
Rather it flows humbly to the lowest levels.
Nothing is weaker than water,
Yet, for overcoming what is hard and strong,
Nothing surpasses it.

Lao Tsu

Three signs that best reflect the watery temperament

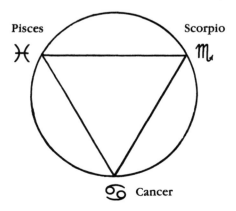

Table 3a: Keywords for the Fire and Air Signs

ATTRIBUTES OF FIRE
Aries   Leo   Sagittarius

Skillful Application	Unskillful Application
radiant, glowing, warm, flaming energetic, creative, fervent, aspiring spontaneous, passionate, daring	hot-headed, rash, impatient, impulsive impetuous, excitable, willful uncontrollable, burns out
assertive, courageous, enterprising self-confident, individualistic independent, free, active	aggressive, pushy, violent, domineering obnoxious, egocentric, overwhelming foolhardy, insensitive
enthusiastic, exuberant, demonstrative inspirational, rapturous, spirited impassioned, optimistic	overzealous, fanatical, manic unrealistic, chases false hopes

ATTRIBUTES OF AIR
Gemini   Libra   Aquarius

Skillful Application	Unskillful Application
mental, intellectual, abstract rational, logical, conceptual theoretical	spacy, ungrounded, intangible insubstantial, ethereal over-intellectual
communicative, social, friendly gregarious, curious, inquisitive, alert	wordy, verbose, loquacious nosy, meddlesome, gossiping
objective, impersonal, impartial dispassionate, unbiased, fair, tolerant unprejudiced, observant	uncaring, detached, unfeeling aloof, distant, removed
clever, witty, versatile	inconsistent, flighty, nervous indecisive, vacillating, superficial

---

are Cancer, Scorpio and Pisces.

The element of water corresponds to the emotional realm of feelings where the subtleties of meaning and interrelatedness are perceived. Water represents the energy and power of unconscious forces that motivate us. Individuals with an emphasis of water often express themselves through their sympathy, compassion, and intuitive awareness. Water seeks emotional and soul understanding.

Overly watery people live on an emotional roller coaster. Calm one day, stormy the next, they are forever turbulent. Such individuals need to bring their undisciplined feelings under their conscious control in order to experience inner peace. Moreover, watery folk may perceive themselves as weak, helpless, and needing protection. Hence, they need to transform these feelings of dependency by tapping into their power and inner strength. If you don't think that water can be powerful, visualize a roaring waterfall or an ocean at high tide.

On the other hand, individuals who lack water can easily become cold and unsympathetic. In order to develop their feeling nature, they often form close ties with watery types.

———Table 3b: Keywords for the Earth and Water Signs———

ATTRIBUTES OF EARTH
Taurus   Virgo   Capricorn

Skillful Application	Unskillful Application
practical, pragmatic, realistic useful, dependable, reliable trustworthy, deliberate, cautious	overly conservative, unenterprising afraid to take risks, security-oriented opportunistic, Machiavellian
grounded, solid, stable, physical tangible, material, substantial structured, corporeal, sensuous	stubborn, rigid, unyielding materialistic, acquisitive, possessive narrow-minded, has tunnel vision
patient, enduring, persevering plodding, persistent, resolute industrious, productive	obstinate, intransigent inflexible, immovable unchangeable, unbending

ATTRIBUTES OF WATER
Cancer   Scorpio   Pisces

Skillful Application	Unskillful Application
nurturing, sustaining, providing protecting, shielding, retiring	overprotective, smothering clinging, needy
feeling, emotional, sensitive empathetic, compassionate, healing	overemotional, maudlin, fearful insecure, thin-skinned, shy
bonding, merging, unifying dissolving, absorptive, impressionable	undefined, chaotic disordered, lacks ego-strength
flowing, receptive, yielding adaptive, amorphous, changing	weak, helpless, powerless dependent, "watered down" victimized, martyred
psychic, deep, hidden mysterious	secretive, deceptive, covert uncommunicative, untruthful

Figure 2: The Element Wheel

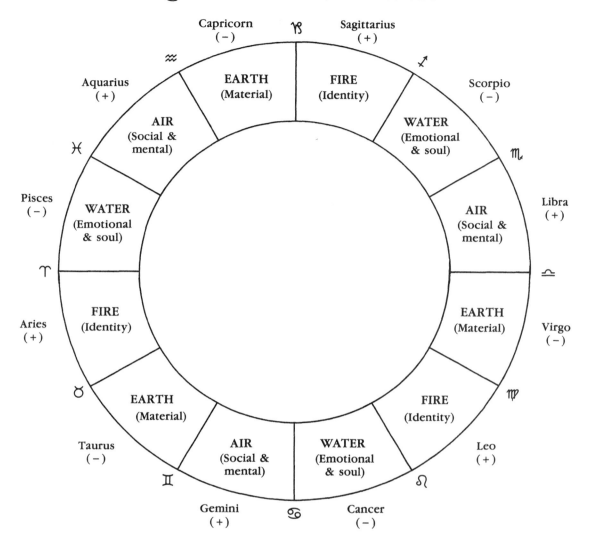

Capricorn (−) ♑
Sagittarius (+) ♐
Aquarius (+) ♒
Scorpio (−) ♏
Pisces (−) ♓
Libra (+) ♎
Aries (+) ♈
Virgo (−) ♍
Taurus (−) ♉
Leo (+) ♌
Gemini (+) ♊
Cancer (−) ♋

EARTH (Material) — Capricorn
FIRE (Identity) — Sagittarius
AIR (Social & mental) — Aquarius
WATER (Emotional & soul) — Scorpio
WATER (Emotional & soul) — Pisces
AIR (Social & mental) — Libra
FIRE (Identity) — Aries
EARTH (Material) — Virgo
EARTH (Material) — Taurus
FIRE (Identity) — Leo
AIR (Social & mental) — Gemini
WATER (Emotional & soul) — Cancer

Exercise 2: My Sun Sign's Element

From the wheel in Figure 2, locate your own Sun sign. Determine which element it falls under. Then turn to Table 3a or 3b, find your element table and locate the keywords that best describe you. Then copy them exactly onto the blank lines below.

My Sun sign's element is _____ .
(see Figure 2)

I apply this energy skillfully when I am _____ ,

or _____ .
(use skillful element keywords from Table 3)

I apply this energy unskillfully when I am _____

or _____ .
(use unskillful element keywords from Table 3)

Did you identify with your element's keywords? In most cases, you should. If you didn't, it is because there are sign and element influences in your chart other than the Sun sign that influence personality. You will learn about them when you interpret your chart in Chapter Three.

The Astrological Polarities

Before we leave the four elements, let us consider for a moment how they interact among themselves. If for example, we take the Fire element and ask "What other element is most compatible with or supportive of it?", what might the answer be? What element literally "feeds" the flames of fire and is necessary for the fire's continued existence? The needed element is Air.

On the other hand if you planted a seed in the parched Earth and wanted an element to nourish the soil so that the seed could grow, which would you pick? The answer is Water, of course.

Thus, we see that Fire and Air can be grouped into one category and Earth and Water into another. What distinguishes these categories from one another? Fire-Air signs are more out-going and self-expressive—pouring forth their energies into the world. Their key-word is **Freedom**.

The Earth-Water signs, on the other hand, are more in-going and self-repressive—magnetizing what they need and conserving their energies within themselves. Their keyword is **Security**.

This distinction is found in all ancient cosmologies which describe the universe as formed by the interplay of two opposing forces or polarities—Light and Dark, Positive and Negative, etc. The ancient Chinese philos-ophers called the active, positive energy pole **Yang**, while the receptive, negatively charged energy pole was named **Yin**.

The Fire and Air signs correspond to the **Yang** pole while the Earth and Water signs correspond to the **Yin** pole as seen in the diagram below.

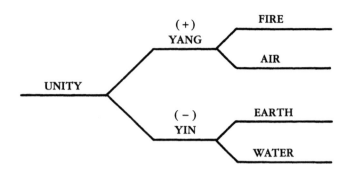

From now on, we will be using the terms Yin and Yang to describe astrological gender, for they have less perjorative connotations than the traditional descriptive phrases of "masculine/feminine" and "positive/negative."

Table 4 provides some keywords that further describe these two opposite energy impulses.

Exercise 3: My Sun Sign's Polarity

By now, you probably know your Sun sign's polarity. If your Sun sign is fire or air, the sign polarity is YANG. If it is earth or water, then the polarity is YIN. Using this information, complete the following sentences.

My Sun sign's polarity is _____.
(Fire or Air = Yang; Earth or Water = Yin)

Two characteristics of this polarity are _____

and _____.
(fill in keywords that fit you from Table 4)

Once again, you have learned a little more about yourself. As we stated in the last exercise, your Sun sign will not always describe you perfectly, but in most cases should be fairly accurate.

YANG

Fire (+)	Air (+)
Aries	Libra
Leo	Aquarius
Sagittarius	Gemini

YIN

Earth (−)	Water (−)
Capricorn	Cancer
Taurus	Scorpio
Virgo	Pisces

EXHALE

active
masculine
day force
extroverted
positive (anode) pole of energy
electric
levity
conscious
logical
individualistic
outgoing
expressive
left-brained

INHALE

receptive
feminine
night force
introverted
negative (cathode) pole of energy
magnetic
gravity
instinctive
intuitive
social-collective
ingoing
receptive
right-brained

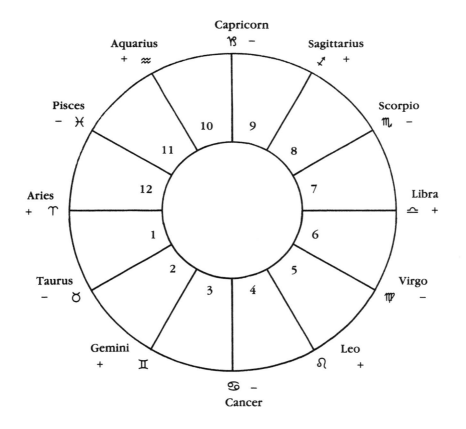

Note that on the above wheel, the (+) and (−) signs alternate. In addition, the fire and air signs are found opposite each other, as is true with the earth and water signs.

The Modalities

Clearly, the four elements describe four distinct personality temperaments. Alone, however, they cannot depict the richness and complexity of the astrological language. Consider for example the fire signs of Aries, Leo, and Sagittarius. Though the signs comprise a common thread (the fire element), each is a unique strand: Aries is the pioneer, Leo is the performer, and Sagittarius the philosopher. These differences arise because each sign manifests its fiery nature through a distinct mode.

The twelve signs of the Zodiac can be divided into three groups called modes or modalities, each of which contains four signs.

The three modalities, known as *cardinal, fixed,* and *mutable,* describe a threefold cyclic process.

The **Cardinal** phase initiates and *generates* energy, and corresponds to the signs Aries, Cancer, Libra, and Capricorn.

The **Fixed** phase stabilizes and *concentrates* energy, and corresponds to the signs Taurus, Leo, Scorpio, and Aquarius.

The **Mutable** phase adapts and *distributes* energy, and corresponds to the signs Gemini, Virgo, Sagittarius and Pisces.

The elements and modalities may be distinguished in the following manner:

The **elements** describe how *energy manifests as* **form**.

The **modalities** depict how *energy manifests as* **movement**—specifically as centrifugal, centripetal, and spiralic patterns.

These patterns can be portrayed through the image of a wheel (Figure 3).

Figure 3: The Modality Wheel

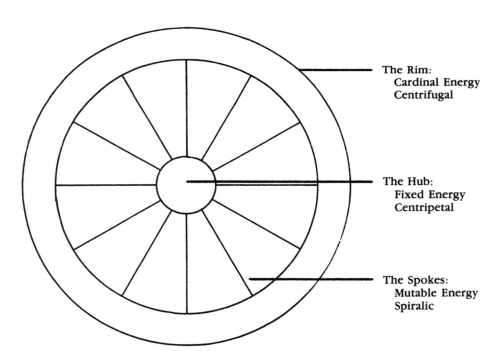

The Rim:
Cardinal Energy
Centrifugal

The Hub:
Fixed Energy
Centripetal

The Spokes:
Mutable Energy
Spiralic

The *cardinal phase* represents *outward*, centrifugal motion corresponding to the *rim*.

The *fixed phase* symbolizes *inward*, centripetal motion corresponding to the *hub*.

The *mutable phase* describes linking, *spiralic* motion corresponding to the *spokes* that join the hub to the rim.

Let us now explore the modalities in greater detail.

Astrology for Yourself

The Cardinal Signs: Initiating Action —

The cardinal modality is expressed in four signs—Aries, Cancer, Libra and Capricorn.

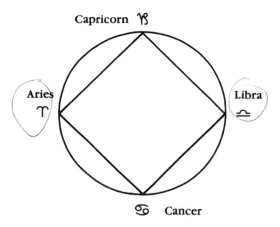

The cardinal signs correspond to centrifugal, radiating energy which moves outward in a definite direction. The essential nature of these signs is to initiate action, start things, get things going.

The person with an exaggeration of the cardinal mode suffers from choosing too many activities and commitments. While these individuals may start a number of projects, they rarely complete them.

With a deficiency of cardinal energy, however, an individual may lack drive, initiative, and the ability to engage in purposeful activity.

The Fixed Signs: Stabilizing Security —

The four fixed signs are Taurus, Leo, Scorpio, and Aquarius.

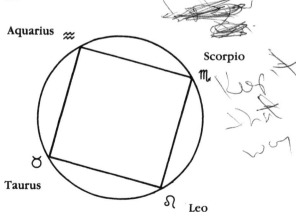

Fixed signs correspond to centripetal radiating energy moving inward toward a center. The essential nature of these signs is to preserve and sustain what was started in the cardinal phase. Whereas cardinal signs start projects, fixed signs finish them; the former act, the latter draw action to them.

Fixed signs exhibit persistence, endurance, and fixity of purpose. When overly fixed, however, they become rigid, stubborn, and unyielding. Hence, their problems are usually chronic, requiring a great deal of time and energy to resolve.

Those who are deficient in the fixed influence often lack concentration, stamina, and perseverance.

The Mutable Signs: Adapting to Learning —

The four mutable signs are Gemini, Virgo, Sagittarius, and Pisces.

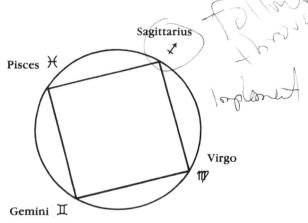

The mutable signs correspond to spiralic patterns of energy. The essential nature of mutable signs is to take what was initiated in cardinal and stabilized in the fixed phase, and adapt these energies to the changing conditions of time and space.

As the spoke of the wheel links the hub to the rim, the mutable person is the perfect go-between, making contacts and connections wherever he or she travels. Contrary to the fixed predecessor, this individual is flexible and adaptable, thriving on change and variety.

Excessively mutable individuals tend to be overly changeable and restless. Hence, they need to focus on a set direction and avoid dissipating their vital force. Mutable types can be high-strung, prone to worry and periodically suffer from nervous exhaustion. Hence, periods of rest and relaxation are necessary to maintain balance.

The immutable person may be likened to the rigid tree that is toppled by a strong gale. Rather he or she should emulate the willow—gracefully yielding to the howling wind and thereby adapting to the forces of change.

Now that we have described the modalities, read over the element-modality wheel in Figure 4.

In addition, review the *keywords* for the modalities in Table 5.

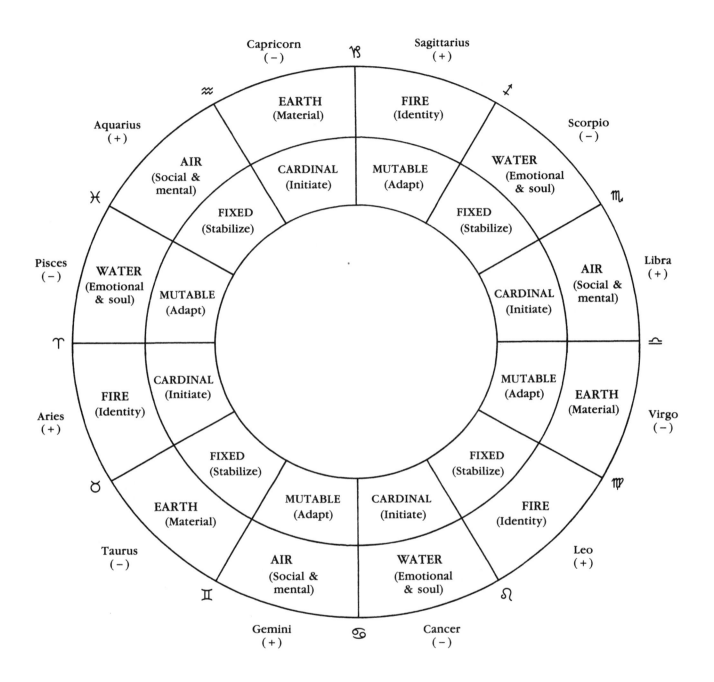

Table 5: Keywords for the Modalities

Qualities of the Cardinal Modality
Aries   Libra   Cancer   Capricorn

Skillful Application
Generating, beginning, doing
initiating, originating, enterprising
active, direct, purposeful

Unskillful Application
Starts but does not finish, impatient
dissatisfied
overactive, overcommitted, forceful

Qualitites of the Fixed Modality
Taurus   Scorpio   Leo   Aquarius

Skillful Application
Concentrating, stabilizing, sustaining
finishing, establishing, preserving
conserving

steadfast, focused, powerful, persistent
constant, determined

Unskillful Application
Stubborn, rigid, resistant to change
stuck, obsessed, overly retentive, inert
habit-bound

Qualities of the Mutable Modality
Gemini   Sagittarius   Virgo   Pisces

Skillful Application
Distributing, adaptable, flexible
adjustable, connecting, linking, mental
adapting, learning, changing
versatile, dual

Unskillful Application
Scattered, unfocused, depleted
dissipated, diffused, distracted
inconsistent, prone to worry, indecisive
restless, unfinishing

Exercise 4: My Sun Sign's Modality

From the wheel in Figure 4, locate your own Sun sign and determine which modality it corresponds to. Then using keyword Table 5 above, complete the following exercise:

My Sun sign's Modality is _____ .
                                                (see Figure 4, page 16)
I apply this energy skillfully when I am _____ ,

_____ or _____ .
                (see Table 5, page 17)
I apply this energy unskillfully when I am _____ or

_____ .
        (see Table 5, page 17)

Once again, do the above keywords fit your personality? In most cases, you should notice a correlation between the keywords you picked and your character traits.

The Building Blocks Summarized

Let us summarize what we have learned about element, polarity and modality by following the evolution of energy from unity to differentiation. Refer to Figure 5 while reading the following passage.

The primordial nature of all substance is unified, whole, and undifferentiated. However, as energy transforms into matter, it takes on the appearance of distinct material forms. The One divides, polarizing itself into Two, which spawns a dualistic reality.

This first division of energy into two is known as **Polarity** (find it in Figure 5). In astrology polarity divides the signs into two groups of opposite energy impulses: Yang (+) charge and Yin (–) charge. The six signs Aries, Gemini, Leo, Libra, Sagittarius, and Aquarius (every other one on the zodiacal wheel) correspond to the positive electrical charge, while the six signs Taurus, Cancer, Virgo, Scorpio, Capricorn and Pisces correspond to the negative electrical charge. This alternating energy pulse regulates the exhale and inhale breath which animates all life.

The next step in the differentiation from the One occurs when each of these two polarities again subdivides to create four basic energy forms (locate this division in Figure 5). These forms of energy are known as the **Elements**: Fire, Air, Earth and Water. Each element corresponds to a group of three signs.

The final classification is that of **Modality**. As *polarity* refers to the electrical *charge* of energy, and

element to the organic *forms* of energy, *modality* describes the *movement* of energy. There exist three basic modes or movements of energy—centrifugal (outward), centripetal (inward), and spiralic. These modalities manifest through the Zodiac as the Cardinal, Fixed, and Mutable signs. Each modality corresponds to a group of four signs.

The meaning of the twelve signs of the Zodiac arise from a *combination* of these principles.

Look now at the bottom of Figure 5 and observe the table formed by the elements (fire, earth, air and water) and the modalities (cardinal, fixed and mutable). Note that when we combine the three modalities, or the movement of energy, with the four elements, or the forms of energy, we create the twelve primary patterns of energy which are called the zodiacal signs. In each elemental column there exists one Cardinal sign, one Fixed sign, and one Mutable sign. Likewise in each modality row, there exists one Fire sign, one Air sign, one Earth sign and one Water sign. Thus each sign is a unique combination of modality and element.

For example, refer to the row of the four Cardinal signs—Aries, Cancer, Libra and Capricorn. Being cardinal, they are all concerned with initiating action. However, because each of these cardinal signs is a *different* element, the element classification determines *what kind* of action is being initiated.

With *Aries,* a cardinal *fire* sign, it is **identity** action

——————*Figure 5: The Building Blocks of the Zodiac*——————

POLARITY:	Energy Charge	(+) Yang ▪ (–) Yin
ELEMENT:	Energy Form	Fire ▪ Air ▪ Earth ▪ Water
MODALITY:	Energy Movement	Cardinal ▪ Fixed ▪ Mutable

UNITY

(+)   (–)

YANG
Exhale Breath

YIN
Inhale Breath

	FIRE	**AIR**	**EARTH**	**WATER**
CARDINAL	♈ Aries	♎ Libra	♑ Capricorn	♋ Cancer
FIXED	♌ Leo	♒ Aquarius	♉ Taurus	♏ Scorpio
MUTABLE	♐ Sagittarius	♊ Gemini	♍ Virgo	♓ Pisces

that is being initiated. This is why Aries symbolizes personal independence and self-awareness.

With *Cancer*, a cardinal *water* sign, it is **emotional** and **soul** action that is being initiated. Hence Cancers have a very active feeling nature.

With *Libra*, a cardinal *air* sign, it is **mental** and **social** action that is being initiated. Thus Librans are focused on establishing partnerships and learning to harmonize with others.

And with *Capricorn*, a cardinal *earth* sign, it is **material** action that is being initiated. Consequently, Capricorns strive to create tangible forms that have a practical use in society.

These interactions of element and mode produce the basic structure of the astrological alphabet—the 12 signs of the Zodiac. To help you to internalize this structure, we would like you to complete Exercise 5.

Exercise 5: The Elements and Modalities Combined

Fill in the table below in the following manner: First write the symbol for each sign, its modality and element (use Figure 4 for this information). Then, using the list we have provided, fill in the mode and element keywords to complete each line. This is done by placing the element keyword in the middle of the modality keyphrase. For example, Aries is a **Cardinal** (Initiating Action) and **Fire** (Identity). To formulate the keyphrase, we place the word "Identity" between "Initiating" and "Action" to form the phrase *Initiating-Identity-Action*. We have placed this combination in the first line of the

table below. Using the same procedure, complete the remaining table.

As an intermediate student, you will gain additional insights into the element-mode-sign relationships through completing this exercise. If you are a beginner and find the keyphrase column difficult to complete, fill in the keywords for the first two columns, under the headings Mode and Element.

An *answer key* to this exercise is located at the end of the chapter.

KEYWORDS

MODALITIES

Cardinal: **Initiating Action**
Aries, Cancer, Libra, Capricorn

Fixed: **Stabilizing Security**
Taurus, Leo, Scorpio, Aquarius

Mutable: **Adapting to Learning**
Gemini, Virgo, Sagittarius, Pisces

ELEMENTS

Fire: **Identity**
Aries, Leo, Sagittarius

Earth: **Material**
Taurus, Virgo, Capricorn

Air: **Mental and Social**
Gemini, Libra, Aquarius

Water: **Emotional and Soul**
Cancer, Scorpio, Pisces

Symbol	Sign	Mode	Element	Keyphrase (Mode, Element, Mode)
♈	Aries	*Cardinal*	*Fire*	*Initiating Identity Action*
♉	Taurus	*Fixed*	*Earth*	*Stabilizing Material Security*
♊	Gemini			
♋	Cancer			
♌	Leo			
♍	Virgo			
♎	Libra			
♏	Scorpio			
♐	Sagittarius			

Symbol	Sign	Mode	Element	Keyphrase (Mode, Element, Mode)
♑	Capricorn			
♒	Aquarius			
♓	Pisces			

The Orientations: How We Meet the World

The astrological orientations provide a final looking glass through which we may view our zodiacal friends. The **orientations** refer to three stages of relationship between the individual and his or her environment.

The unfolding of these three orientations parallels the evolution of the twelve zodiacal signs.

The first stage, the **personal** orientation, begins at infancy. At this time, the newborn is primarily focused on getting personal wants and needs met: food, clothing, warmth, personal contact. It sees itself at the center of a universe whose sole purpose is to assure its well being.

The initial four signs of Aries, Taurus, Gemini and Cancer correspond to the personal phase.

As the child matures, it discovers that other people exist and that they too have legitimate needs. In this **interpersonal** phase, he or she becomes a social individual and learns to interact with a wide variety of individuals.

The signs of Leo, Virgo, Libra and Scorpio are interpersonal in nature.

Finally towards the end of life, the individual enters the **transpersonal** stage and seeks to understand his or her relationship with the universe at large. Ultimately,

he or she must accept his or her physical mortality and find a spiritual connection to the infinite.

The transpersonal signs are the final four signs of the Zodiac—Sagittarius, Capricorn, Aquarius, and Pisces.

Like the elements and modalities, the orientations exhibit both positive and negative applications.

The individual who exaggerates his or her **personal** orientation becomes selfish and egocentric. Those deficient in this perspective, however, experience difficulty in fulfilling their rudimentary survival needs.

The overly **interpersonal** individual may become too other-directed and thereby lose touch with his or her own sense of self. Yet, without this orientation, a person is denied his or her need for human contact.

The person with an emphasis on the **transpersonal** signs may feel totally out of place in the mundane world. So concerned is he or she about discovering the meaning of life, that such practical matters as paying the rent are often neglected. The person without this emphasis, however, experiences no connection to a greater whole and thus lacks a spiritual perspective towards life.

Exercise 6: My Sun Sign's Orientation

Now that you know whether your Sun sign is personal, interpersonal, or transpersonal, use the keywords below to complete the following:

My Sun sign's orientation is _____ .

This indicates that my orientation towards life is _____ .
(fill in the appropriate keyphrase from the listing below)

Personal—focused on personal wants and needs
Interpersonal—social, focused on others
Transpersonal—universal, focused on ideals and abstractions

Do the keywords you have just written seem to describe your outlook? In most cases they will.

A Final Synthesis: Writing
Your Sun Sign Interpretation

The building blocks of the Zodiac—polarity, element, modality, and orientation—are graphically summarized for you in the wheel of Figure 6. Their respective keywords are listed in Table 6.

Using the knowledge contained in this figure and table, you can discover the meaning of each sign of the Zodiac, including your own Sun sign.

By combining the fundamental principles of **Element, Polarity, Modality,** and **Orientation,** the essential principles underlying the twelve signs are born. Now you know why those Sun sign descriptions read the way they do. The multitude of personality traits and characteristics arise from these basic primal energies.

For example, let us say that you were born on March 25, a Sun sign Aries. Our Zodiac wheel reveals that the sign Aries contains the following traits: yang, personal, cardinal fire. No wonder the horoscope column refers to you as "fiery, pioneering, impulsive and self-centered!" And what about your successor, the "steadfast, bull-headed, down-to-earth Taurus?" Are not these the traits of a fixed earth sign?

And so the procession continues. From the "flighty and communicative" Gemini (mutable air) to the "enterprising and practical" Capricorn (cardinal earth), a lawful Zodiac unfolds.

Table 6: Keywords for the Basic Energies

THE FOUR ELEMENTS
Fire—Enthusiastic, energetic, creative, passionate, assertive, freedom-loving
Earth—practical, grounded, sensual, reliable, stable, cautious
Air—mental, communicative, social, detached, abstract, changeable
Water—emotional, feeling, nurturing, hidden, sensitive

THE TWO POLARITIES
Yang—outgoing, expressive, logical, left-brained, "masculine"
Yin—ingoing, receptive, intuitive, right-brained, "feminine"

THE THREE MODALITIES
Cardinal—generating, initiating, active, direct, over-committed
Fixed—concentrating, consolidating, focused, persevering, stubborn
Mutable—distributing, connecting, adaptable, flexible, scattered

THE THREE ORIENTATIONS
Personal—focused on personal wants and needs
Interpersonal—social, focused on others
Transpersonal—universal, focused on ideals and abstractions

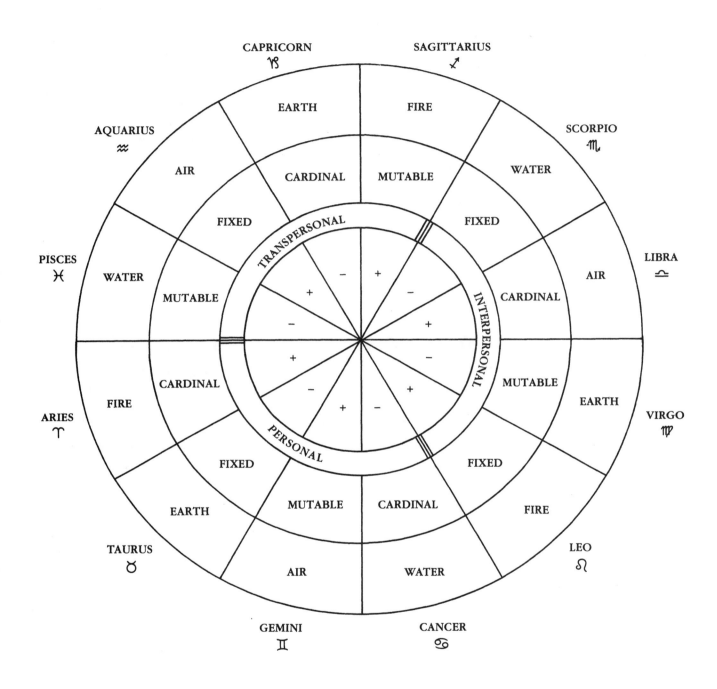

Exercise 7: My Complete Sun Sign Interpretation

This final exercise synthesizes what you have learned in the exercises of this chapter. It will help you to see how these principles define the characteristics of your own Sun sign. Using Figure 6 and the keywords in Table 6, complete the following sentences.

1. My **Sun** is in the sign of _____.

2. My Sun sign's **element** is _____.
   (see Figure 6)
   Two keywords for this element are _____ and _____.
   (use Table 6)

3. My Sun sign's **polarity** is _____.
   (Yang or Yin—see Figure 6)
   Two keywords for this polarity are _____ and _____.
   (use Table 6)

4. My Sun sign's **modality** is _____.
   (see Figure 6)
   Two keywords for this modality are _____ and _____.
   (use Table 6)

5. My Sun sign's **orientation** is _____.
   (see Figure 6)
   A keyphrase for this orientation is _____.
   (use Table 6)

Journal Entry

In the space below, write a short personality description of yourself based upon the keywords you have chosen in the above exercise and throughout the chapter. Let this profile consist of keywords that reflect your Sun sign's element, polarity, modality and orientation. Consider this to be your Sun sign self-portrait.

_____

_____

_____

_____

_____

_____

_____

_____

_____

_____

_____

_____

_____

_____

_____

_____

_____

_____

Examine the words, phrases and sentences that you have just written, both from Exercise 7 and from your journal entry. Do they in fact describe your essential nature very closely? You should find much of what you wrote quite accurate.

Yet, Sun sign astrology does contain a loophole. You may have discovered that your Sun sign description either was **incomplete** or perhaps **contradicted** information you know to be true about yourself. The reason for these **apparent discrepancies** is clear to the seasoned astrologer: The Sun is only *one* of the heavenly bodies that appears in your birth chart.

Here we must make a clear distinction between supermarket "pop astrology" which is merely a Sun sign parlor game, and the comprehensive, scientific approach to astrology which you will learn through this book. In order to paint your true astrological self-portrait, you must go **beyond** your Sun sign and study the influences of the Moon, the eight planets, and the asteroids. This is precisely why an interpretation provided by a professional astrologer is far more **complete** and **accurate** than a reading gleaned from a mass market Sun sign book.

In Chapter Three, "Writing Your Personality Profile," you will follow the good example of the astrological counselor and learn to interpret your **complete** birth chart, using **all** of the letters of the astrological alphabet. But first you must learn to *read* and *identify* the letters. This you will accomplish in Chapter Two.

Answer Key to Exercise 5

Gemini—Mutable Air	Adapting to Mental and Social Learning
Cancer—Cardinal Water	Initiating Emotional and Soul Action
Leo—Fixed Fire	Stabilizing Identity Security
Virgo—Mutable Earth	Adapting to Material Learning
Libra—Cardinal Air	Initiating Mental and Social Action
Scorpio—Fixed Water	Stabilizing Emotional and Soul Security
Sagittarius—Mutable Fire	Adapting to Identity Learning
Capricorn—Cardinal Earth	Initiating Material Action
Aquarius—Fixed Air	Stabilizing Mental and Social Security
Pisces—Mutable Water	Adapting to Emotional and Soul Learning

Further Reading

If you wish to learn more about the topics covered in this chapter, we recommend the following books.

Arroyo, Stephen, *Astrology, Psychology and the Four Elements*
Hodgson, Joan, *Reincarnation Through the Zodiac*
March, Marion and McIvers, Joan, *The Only Way to Learn Astrology, Volume I*

Oken, Alan, *Complete Astrologer*
Rudhyar, Dane, *The Pulse of Life*

Additional resources are located in the bibliography.

Chapter 2

The Structure of the Birth Chart

How to Read Your Birth Chart

IN THIS CHAPTER, you will learn how to locate the planets in your birth chart so that you can interpret them in Chapter Three. Begin by reading over Table 1. It names and identifies the symbols of our astrological alphabet.

The astrological symbols that we have laid out do not exist in a vacuum. They are to be found in the **horoscope** or **birth chart**—an exact replica of our solar system, drawn up for the time of birth. The birth chart is a star map of the positions of the planets at the moment you were born, with you at the center. A birth chart is comprised of an alphabet of three interlocking parts: **signs, houses,** and **planets.** This celestial map is drawn in two dimensions and appears as a circle or wheel as seen in Figure 1—a sample birth chart that has the same basic ingredients as your own.

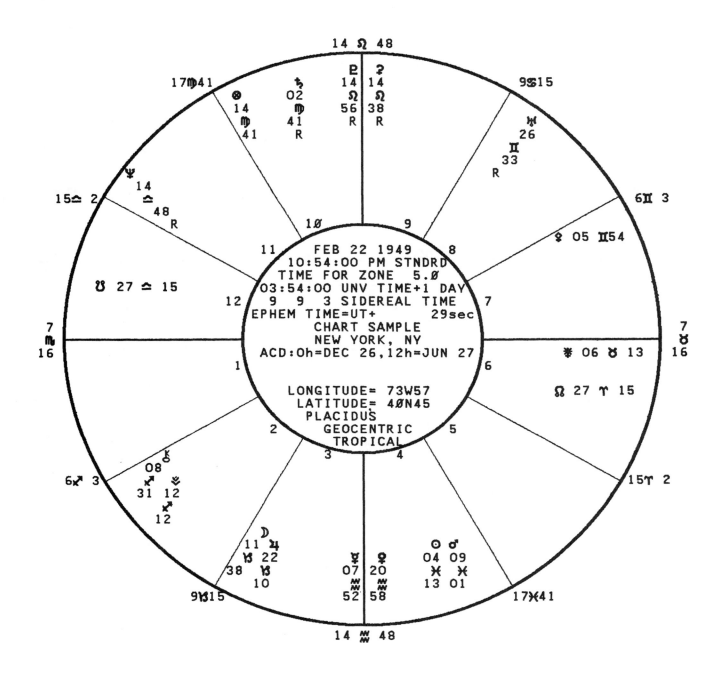

14 ♌ 48

17♍41

9♋15

15♎ 2

6♊ 3

7♏ 16

7♉ 16

6♐ 3

15♈ 2

9♑15

17♓41

14 ♒ 48

♇ 14 ♌ 56 R
☊ 14 ♌ 38 R
♄ 02 ♍ 41 R
⊗ 14 ♍ 41
♆ 14 ♎ 48 R
☋ 27 ♎ 15
⛢ 26 ♊ 33 R
☿ 05 ♊ 54
♃ 06 ♉ 13
☊ 27 ♈ 15
♀ 08 ♐ 31
♇ 12 ♐ 12
☽ 11 ♑ 22
♃ 38 ♑ 10
☿ 07 ♒ 52
♀ 20 ♒ 58
☉ 04 ♓ 13
♂ 09 ♓ 01

FEB 22 1949
10:54:00 PM STNDRD
TIME FOR ZONE   5.0
03:54:00 UNV TIME+1 DAY
9   9   3 SIDEREAL TIME
EPHEM TIME=UT+   29sec
CHART SAMPLE
NEW YORK, NY
ACD:0h=DEC 26,12h=JUN 27

LONGITUDE= 73W57
LATITUDE= 40N45
PLACIDUS
GEOCENTRIC
TROPICAL

Signs

First note the **symbols** of the **signs** of the Zodiac inscribed around the wheel in Figure 1, our sample chart.

ᵀ   ♉   ♊   ♋   ♌   ♍

♎   ♏   ♐   ♑   ♒   ♓

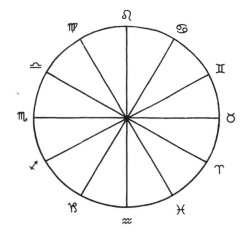

The signs always follow the same order from Aries to Pisces, but the beginning point will differ from chart to chart.

These signs represent twelve universal psychological needs. Everyone has all twelve signs somewhere in their charts, and everyone has all twelve needs somewhere in their lives.

Houses

Next, note that there are twelve sectors of the chart, pieces of the pie numbered 1 to 12. These are called the **houses**. They represent twelve universal departments of life. Think of the houses as fixed and the signs as revolving around them. Depending on the time of day that you were born, you will have different signs on each house.

The sign at the beginning of the first house is also called the Rising sign, or Ascendant. In this birth chart, it is Scorpio (♏). The words "Rising sign" and "Ascendant" are used interchangeably in astrological terminology to signify the same thing.

Rising Sign or Ascendant the sign at the beginning of the 1st house

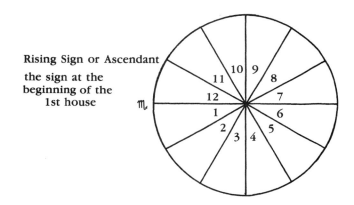

Planets

Finally, the inner wheel contains the symbols for the **planets**, the **asteroids,** and several other points. Note their symbols.

Note that each planet is located in a particular sign and house.

The planets and asteroids symbolize the many aspects of personality.

*The **sign** describes **how** the planetary energy is being expressed, while the **house** position tells us **where** the action is taking place.*

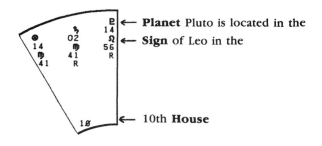

← **Planet** Pluto is located in the

← **Sign** of Leo in the

← 10th **House**

Table 1: A Legend of the Astrological Alphabet

SYMBOL	SIGN		SYMBOL	PLANET
♈	Aries		☉	Sun
♉	Taurus		☽	Moon
♊	Gemini		☿	Mercury
♋	Cancer		♀	Venus
♌	Leo		♂	Mars
♍	Virgo		♃	Jupiter
♎	Libra		♄	Saturn
♏	Scorpio		♅	Uranus
♐	Sagittarius		♆	Neptune
♑	Capricorn		♇ ♇	Pluto
♒	Aquarius		⚷	Chiron
♓	Pisces			

SYMBOL	POINT		SYMBOL	ASTEROID
☊	North Node		⚳	Ceres
☋	South Node		⚴	Pallas
⊗	Part of Fortune		⚶	Vesta
			⚵	Juno

SYMBOL ANGLE

Asc.   Ascendant (the sign on the 1st house)
Desc.   Descendant (the sign on the 7st house)
M.C.   Midheaven (the sign on the 10th house)
I.C.   Imum Coeli (the sign on the 4th house)

How to Locate a Planet's Position

Let us now locate a planetary position in our sample chart. Let's begin with some simple geometry. There are twelve signs in the circle of the Zodiac. Since a circle measures 360 degrees, each sign contains 360 ÷ 12 or 30 degrees. Each degree in turn contains 60 minutes. Thus, when reading the numbers next to the planet, the first number refers to the degree (0 to 29) and the second number represents the minute (0 to 59).

So when you locate a planet's position, the first symbol refers to the glyph of the **planet.** Next comes a number from 0 to 29 which indicates the **degree.** This number is followed by a symbol signifying the zodiacal **sign** (Aries through Pisces), and then a second number indicating the **minute** (0 to 59).

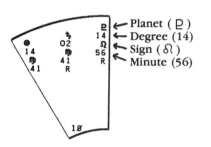

In the preceeding figure the planet Pluto (♇) is located at 14 degrees and 56 minutes of the sign Leo ♌ .

Look now at the Moon (☽). You should find it located in the third house in eleven degrees and thirty-eight minutes of the sign Capricorn (11 ♑ 38).

How about the Sun (☉)? You should locate it in the fourth house in four degrees and thirteen minutes of Pisces (4 ♓ 13).

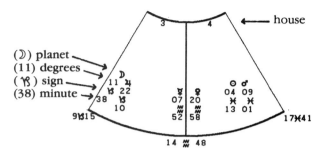

Now try these two exercises to see if you understand how to determine a planet's position. Turn to Figure 1 and locate the planetary positions for:

Uranus: _____ _____ _____ _____
            planet (glyph) degree (number) sign (glyph) minute (number)

Neptune: _____ _____ _____ _____
            planet (glyph) degree (number) sign (glyph) minute (number)

Answers: ♅ 26 ♊ 33 and ♆ 14 ♎ 48

How the Houses are Divided

Now let's see how the houses are divided. Note that each house begins with a specific sign degree. For example, turn to Figure 1 and look at the beginning of the second house (also known as the "cusp" of the house). You should find six degrees and three minutes of Sagittarius (6 ♐ 3) written there.

The concept of signs on the cusps (beginnings) of a house is an issue that often confuses new students. Let us look at this in more detail. The 360 degree circle is equally divided among the 12 zodiacal signs, so that each sign contains exactly 30 degrees. However, each of the twelve houses does not contain exactly 30 degrees. Some houses have less than 30 degrees and some have more than 30 degrees, although the wheel's total degree count is always 360.

In our sample chart the third house begins with 9 ♑ 15 and ends at 14 ♒ 48 at the beginning of the fourth house. What this indicates is that the third house

contains the 9th through 30th degrees of Capricorn and the 0 through 14th degrees of Aquarius. So any planet between 9 ♑ 15 and 29 ♑ 59 will be located in this sector as well as any planet between 0 ♒ 00 and 14 ♒ 48. Likewise the fourth house contains from the 14th to the 30th degree of Aquarius and from 0 to the 17th degree of Pisces.

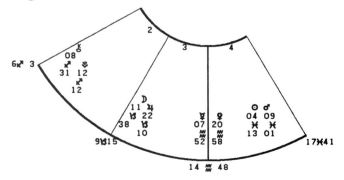

Intercepted Signs

Normally, each successive house will have a new sign. In some charts, however, the same sign may begin two successive houses and another sign may be contained entirely with a house (this is called an "intercepted" sign).

In this chart Aquarius and Leo are the intercepted signs. They are contained within the first and seventh houses. The first house spans from the 20th to the 30th degree of Capricorn, all 30 degrees of Aquarius and from 0 to the 6th degree of Pisces. The seventh house covers the 20th to the 30th degree of Cancer, all 30 degrees of Leo, and from 0 to the 6th degree of Virgo.

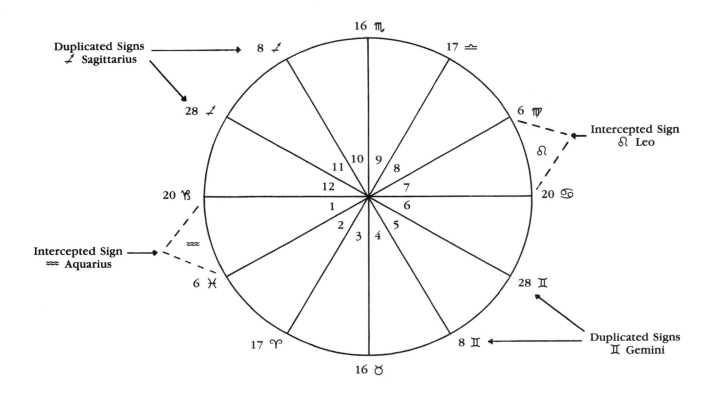

Retrograde Planets

One final notation that should be mentioned is the symbol R or Rx after a planet signifying "retrograde" motion. The specific meaning of retrograde planets as well as intercepted houses will be explained in Chapter Five. It is not unusual to have one or more planets retrograde in your chart.

In our sample chart Figure 1, Pluto ♇ , Saturn ♄, Neptune ♆, Uranus ♅, and Ceres ⚳ are all retrograde. Locate the symbol R after their degree notation.

You should now have a brief overview of the structure of a birth chart. Each birth chart is like a snowflake; no two are alike. Now let's take a look at the unique snowflake that is you.

Reading Your Planets by Sign and House Position

Exercise 1: How to Locate the Planets in My Birth Chart

In this exercise, you will learn to locate each planet, asteroid, and other significant points in *your own birth chart*. Once you determine their positions, you will be writing them down in the table we have provided.

Once again, we remind you that in order to do this exercise and complete the rest of the book, you will need a copy of your own birth chart. If you do not possess your birth chart, please turn to Appendix D to find out how you can obtain it!

If you do have your own birth chart, place it in front of you and turn to Table 1. Begin by finding the symbol for the Sun ☉ in the table. Then turn to your birth chart, locate the Sun's symbol, and determine its sign and house placement, just as you did in the exercises at the beginning of the chapter. The symbol and degree of the sign should be written right next to the Sun as we illustrated in the previous paragraphs. Once you have gathered this information, then fill out sentence 1 in Table 2.

Repeat the same process with the Moon ☽ in your chart and fill out sentence 2. Continue until you have completed all of Table 2. This table will provide you with the basic information required to write your own birth chart interpretation in Chapter Three.

To assist in familiarity with the structure of your birth chart, we have provided a blank wheel on page 33. Right now, transpose the symbols from your own birth chart onto this wheel.

A final note should be made about the position of the south node of the moon ☋ which many chart printouts do not specify. If your chart does not contain your south node, it is located *exactly opposite* the sign and house of your north node. Thus if the north node ☊ were in Aries in the second house, the south node ☋ would be in Libra (Libra is the sign opposite Aries) in the eighth house (the eighth house is opposite the second house).

You can use the diagram below to determine opposite signs and houses. For example, Leo is opposite Aquarius, the fourth house is opposite the tenth house, etc.

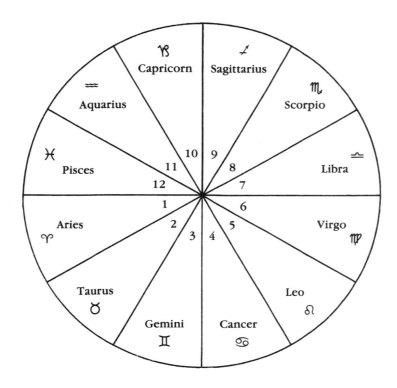

——Table 2: The Positions of Your Astrological Symbols——

Below are listed the sign and house positions of your most important astrological points that you will be referring to in this book. If you are having an astrological consultation, your astrologer should fill this out for you, using your own chart. Otherwise, you can use Exercise 1 to locate the points for yourself.

This completed table will prove indispensible to you as you learn to unravel the mystery of your birth chart.

1. My **Sun** (☉) is in the Sign of _____ in the _____ House.

2. My **Moon** (☽) is in the Sign of _____ in the _____ House.

3. My **Mercury** (☿) is in the Sign of _____ in the _____ House.

4. My **Venus** (♀) is in the Sign of _____ in the _____ House.

5. My **Mars** (♂) is in the Sign of _____ in the _____ House.

6. My **Jupiter** (♃) is in the Sign of _____ in the _____ House.

7. My **Saturn** (♄) is in the Sign of _____ in the _____ House.

8. My **Uranus** (♅) is in the Sign of _____ in the _____ House.

9. My **Neptune** (♆) is in the Sign of _____ in the _____ House.

10. My **Pluto** (♇) is in the Sign of _____ in the _____ House.

11. My **Chiron** (⚷) is in the Sign of _____ in the _____ House.

12. My **Ceres** (⚳) is in the Sign of _____ in the _____ House.

13. My **Pallas** (⚴) is in the Sign of _____ in the _____ House.

14. My **Vesta** (⚶) is in the Sign of _____ in the _____ House.

15. My **Juno** (⚵) is in the Sign of _____ in the _____ House.

16. My Moon's **North Node** (☊) is in the Sign of _____ in the _____ House.

17. My Moon's **South Node** (☋) is in the Sign of _____ in the _____ House.

18. My **Part of Fortune** (⊗) is in the Sign of _____ in the _____ House.

19. My **Ascendant** or **Rising Sign** (ASC) is _____ and is located at the cusp (the beginning) of the first House.

20. My **Descendant** or Setting Sign (DESC) is in the Sign of _____ at the cusp of the seventh House.

21. My **Midheaven** or Medium Coeli (MC) is in the Sign of _____ at the cusp of the tenth House.

22. My **Undersky** or Imum Coeli (IC) is in the Sign of _____ at the cusp of the fourth House.

Throughout the book, you will find that we have provided blank charts and space for notes so that you can practice on your friends and family.

An Overview of the Alphabet:
—Keywords for the Planets, Signs, and Houses—

Your birth chart is composed of three distinct yet inter-related energies—**Planets, Signs,** and **Houses.**

Of these the **Planets** are the most important. In astrological symbolism, the planets represent basic psychological functions or faculties common to all people. The planets are the dynamic, driving, activating energies in the birth chart. In the language of astrology, they are the **verbs,** the active voice that tells us **what** is happening in the birth chart.

The **Signs** of the Zodiac act as filters that color the expression of the planetary energies. They show **how** the planets are expressing themselves.

The astrological **Houses** represent twelve departments of life that serve as fields of experience for the planets. The houses tell us **where** the action is taking place.

For example, if my Sun were in the sign of Aries I would express my basic identity (the Sun) in an impulsive, spontaneous, fiery way (characteristic of Aries). If the Sun were in the fifth house, I would center myself in the areas of my life described by the fifth house (e.g. creative self-expression or children). It is by combining the meanings of the planets, signs and houses in this way that you will write your own birth chart interpretation in Chapter Three.

In the following pages, you will receive an introduction to the meanings of the signs, planets, and houses. Learning their keywords will give you a valuable introduction to the letters of the astrological alphabet. Don't worry about memorizing them, however, as you will be given specific keyword tables to refer to in Chapter Three.

For now, just familiarize yourself with the basic concepts.

My Birth Chart

Transpose the symbols from your own birth chart to this space.

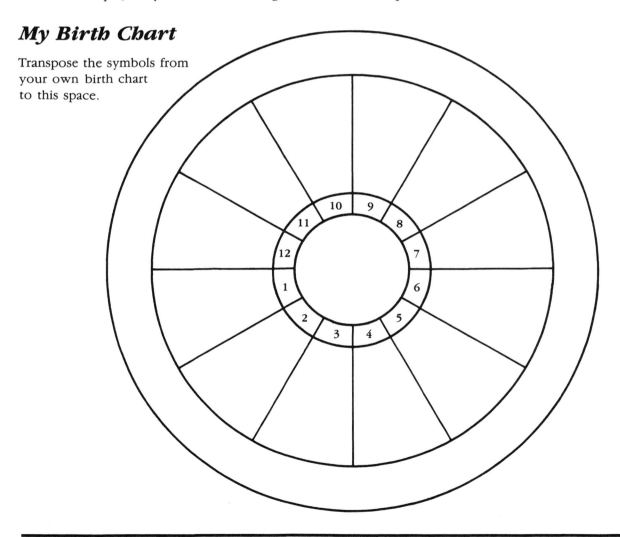

The Astrological Signs

The signs of the Zodiac signify 12 styles of being in the world. Like filters, they color or modify the planetary energies, indicating **how** these energies are being expressed.

Table 3: Sign Keyphrases

ARIES ♈ The Ram
The Sign of the **Pioneer**
A Personal, Cardinal Fire Sign
Fire Image—A Shooting Star
"I am"
Keyphrase: My need to be independent and develop self-awareness

TAURUS ♉ The Bull
The Sign of the **Builder**
A Personal, Fixed Earth Sign
Earth Image—A Copious Garden
"I have"
Keyphrase: My need to be resourceful, productive, and stable

GEMINI ♊ The Twins
The Sign of the **Communicator**
A Personal, Mutable Air Sign
Air Image—A Butterfly
"I think"
Keyphrase: My need to communicate with and learn from others

CANCER ♋ The Crab
The Sign of the **Nurturer**
A Personal, Cardinal Water Sign
Water Image—An Oasis
"I feel"
Keyphrase: My need to give and receive emotional warmth and security

LEO ♌ The Lion
The Sign of the **Performer**
An Interpersonal, Fixed Fire Sign
Fire Image—The Sun
"I show"
Keyphrase: My need to express myself creatively and be appreciated by others

VIRGO ♍ The Virgin
The Sign of the **Analyst**
An Interpersonal, Mutable Earth Sign
Earth Image—A Many-faceted Crystal
"I analyze"
Keyphrase: My need to analyze, discriminate, and function efficiently

LIBRA ♎ The Scales
The Sign of the **Diplomat**
An Interpersonal, Cardinal Air Sign
Air Image—A Rainbow
"I relate"
Keyphrase: My need to cooperate with others and to create balance and harmony in my life

SCORPIO ♏ The Scorpion
The Sign of the **Healer**
An Interpersonal, Fixed Water Sign
Water Image—A Melting Ice Crystal
"I transform"
Keyphrase: My need for deep involvements and intense transformations

SAGITTARIUS ♐ The Centaur
The Sign of the **Explorer**
A Transpersonal, Mutable Fire Sign
Fire Image—The Burning Bush
"I seek"
Keyphrase: My need to explore and expand the horizons of my mind and world

CAPRICORN ♑ The Mountain Goat
The Sign of the **Governor**
A Transpersonal, Cardinal Earth Sign
Earth Image—The Mountain Peak
"I utilize"
Keyphrase: My need for structure, organization, and social accomplishment

AQUARIUS ♒ The Water Bearer
The Sign of the **Reformer**
A Transpersonal, Fixed Air Sign
Air Image—A Flash of Lightning
"I'm different"
Keyphrase: My need to be innovative, original, and to be an agent of change

PISCES ♓ The Fish
The Sign of the **Dreamer**
A Transpersonal, Mutable Water Sign
Water Image—The Ocean
"I imagine"
Keyphrase: My need to commit myself to a dream or ideal and work towards its realization

The Astrological Planets

The planets symbolize basic psychological functions or faculties common to all people. They tell us **what** is happening in the birth chart.

Table 4: Planet Keyphrases

SYMBOL	PLANET	PSYCHOLOGICAL FUNCTION
☉	SUN	My basic identity and conscious purpose
☽	MOON	My emotions, feelings, and daily habits
☿	MERCURY	My capacity to think, speak, learn and reason
♀	VENUS	My capacity to attract people and things that I love and value
♂	MARS	My capacity to act and assert myself based on personal desire
♃	JUPITER	My search for meaning, truth, and ethical values
♄	SATURN	My capacity to create order, form, and discipline in my life
♅	URANUS	My unique individuality and capacity to liberate myself from past limitations
♆	NEPTUNE	My capacity to transcend the finite self through expressing unity with a greater whole
♇ ♇	PLUTO	My capacity to transform and renew myself
⚷	CHIRON	My capacity for holistic understanding
⚳	CERES	My capacity to unconditionally love and nurture myself and others
⚴	PALLAS	My capacity for creative wisdom and original perceptions
⚶	VESTA	My capacity to integrate and focus my energies
⚵	JUNO	My capacity for meaningful relationships

In Table 3 please note that the Sun (a star) and the Moon (a satellite) are categorized as "planets," because they symbolize the same types of psychological functions.

The same holds true of the planetoid Chiron (discovered in 1977) and the four asteroids, Ceres, Pallas, Vesta, and Juno. Discovered in 1801–2, the asteroids were not included in birth charts until 1973 when tables of their positions were published. Since then, a growing number of astrologers have begun to use them in birth chart interpretation. If you don't know the locations of Chiron or the asteroids in your birth chart, you can easily order them (see Appendix D).

Figure 2: The
—Arrangement of the Houses—

The astrological houses act as fields of experience for the expressions of the planetary functions. They indicate **where,** or in what *department of life,* the action is taking place.

At this point, we should mention that the twelve signs and the twelve houses form a *one-to-one correspondence.* That is, the symbolism of Aries corresponds to the meaning of the first house, Taurus to the second house, Gemini to the third house, etc. Consequently, as you understand the signs, the meanings of the houses will fall into place.

Like the twelve signs, the houses can be seen as *phases* or cycles of experience that unfold in an evolutionary sequence, beginning with the birth of self-awareness in the first house and ending with the dissolving of the ego in the twelfth.

The arrangement of these houses is shown pictorially in Figure 2 below.

Their phases and keywords are illustrated in Table 5.

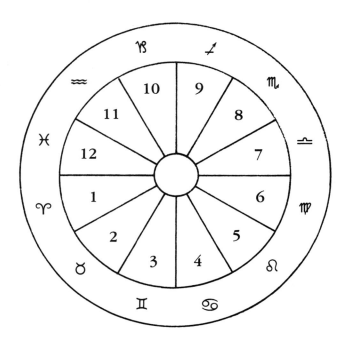

——————Table 5: Keywords for the Astrological Houses——————

HOUSE	PHASE	FIELD OF EXPERIENCE
1	Emergence of Self-Awareness	One's Persona
2	Identification with Substance	Possessions, Resources
3	Relating to the Environment	Mental Activity
4	Personal Integration	Establishing Foundations
5	Externalization of Oneself	Self-Expression
6	Self-Examination	Self-Improvement
7	Relating to Others	Forming Partnerships
8	Merging with Others	Transformation through Relationship
9	Expansion of Awareness	The Search for Meaning
10	Social Participation	Securing a Vocation
11	Social Reform	Social Aspirations and Ideals
12	Ending the Old Cycle and Preparing for the New	Self-Transcendence

Figure 3: The Wheel of the Astrological Houses

The following figure shows the actual structure of the twelve houses as twelve 30 degree segments of a circle. Thematic keywords are written in each house.

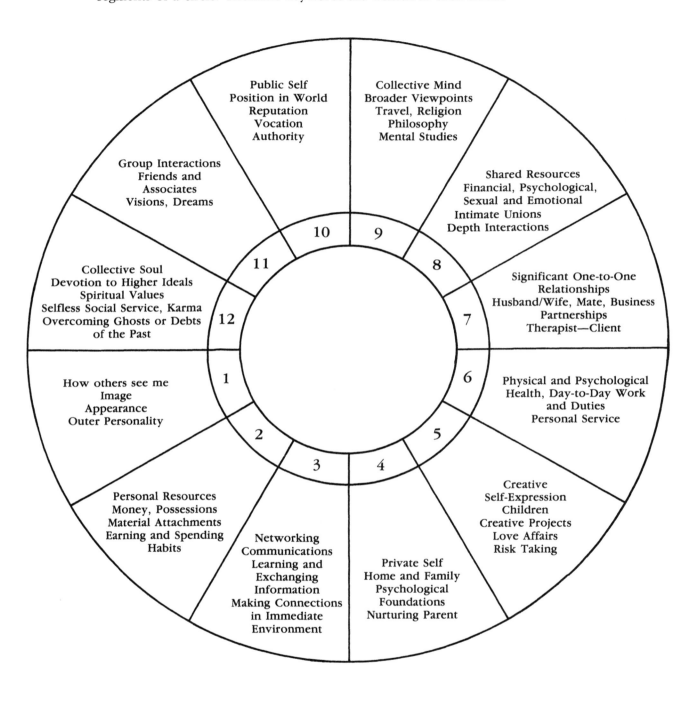

Summary of the Astrological Alphabet

Introduction to Rulerships

From Table 6, next page, and Figure 6, page 22, you should notice that a one-to-one correspondence exists between the planets, signs and houses. Each planet corresponds to a particular sign and house. In astrological tradition, particular importance has been attached to the planet-sign correspondence.

When a planet corresponds to a particular sign, it is said to "**rule**" that sign.

Below are listed the twelve signs and the planets and asteroids that rule them.

SIGN	PLANETARY RULER
Aries	Mars
Taurus	Venus
Gemini	Mercury
Cancer	Moon, Ceres
Leo	Sun, Pallas
Virgo	Mercury, Vesta
Libra	Venus, Juno
Scorpio	Pluto
Sagittarius	Jupiter, Chiron
Capricorn	Saturn
Aquarius	Uranus
Pisces	Neptune

Notice that in Table 6, Aries, Mars and the first house are contained in one sector. This is because each is derived from the same primary or monadic energy. Thus, if you look over the keywords for Mars, Aries and the first house, you will find that a common theme (based on the principles of element, polarity and modality) runs through their meanings.

The same relationship holds true among Taurus, Venus and the second house (in the second sector);

Gemini, Mercury and the third house, etc.

Therefore we can conclude that the astrological alphabet consists of **twelve primary letters**, each of which differentiates into a planet, sign and house.

Finally, Figure 4 is a wheel that summarizes all that we have learned by showing the keywords for each planet, sign and house. The material is listed in tabular form in Table 6.

Further Reading

If you wish to learn more about the topics covered in this chapter, we recommend the following books.

Hall, Manly Palmer, *Astrological Keywords*
Lewi, Grant, *Astrology for the Millions*
Moore, Marcia, *Astrology The Divine Science*

Rudhyar, Dane, *The Astrology of Personality*
Hand, Robert, *Horoscope Symbols*

Additional resources are located in the bibliography.

—Table 6: The Twelve Letters of the Astrological Alphabet—

Sector	Principle	Sign	House	Planet
1	*Cardinal*—Initiating Action *Fire*—Identity	*Aries*—My need to be independent and develop self-awareness	*1st*—How others see me Image, Appearance Outer Personality	*Mars*—My capacity to act and assert myself based on personal desire
2	*Fixed*—Stabilizing Security *Earth*—Material	*Taurus*—My need to be resourceful, productive and stable	*2nd*—My personal resources—Money, Possessions and Material Attachments	*Venus*—My capacity to attract people and things that I love and value
3	*Mutable*—Adapting to Learning *Air*—Mental and Social	*Gemini*—My need to communicate with and learn from others	*3rd*—Making connections in my immediate environment; networking, learning and exchanging information	*Mercury*—My capacity to think, speak, learn and reason
4	*Cardinal*—Initiating Action *Water*—Emotional and Soul	*Cancer*—My need to give and receive emotional warmth and security	*4th*—Home and family Psychological foundations Private Self	*Moon*—My emotions, feelings, and daily habits *Ceres*—My capacity to unconditionally love and nurture myself and others
5	*Fixed*—Stabilizing Security *Fire*—Identity	*Leo*—My need to express myself creatively and be appreciated by others	*5th*—Creative Projects: Children, Love Affairs Risk-taking	*Sun*—My basic identity and conscious purpose *Pallas*—My capacity for creative wisdom and original perceptions
6	*Mutable*—Adapting to Learning *Earth*—Material	*Virgo*—My need to analyze, discriminate and function efficiently	*6th*—Personal integration Physical & psychological health, Day-to-day work & duties, Service	*Vesta*—My capacity to integrate and focus my energies *Mercury*
7	*Cardinal*—Initiating Action *Air*—Mental and Social	*Libra*—My need to cooperate with others and create harmony and balance in my life	*7th*—My significant one-to-one relationships: husband/wife business partners, mates, clients	*Juno*—My capacity for meaningful relationships *Venus*
8	*Fixed*—Stabilizing Security *Water*—Emotional and Soul	*Scorpio*—My need for deep involvements and intense transformations	*8th*—My shared resources: financial, sexual, emotional & psychological intimate unions	*Pluto*—My capacity to transform and renew myself
9	*Mutable*—Adapting to Learning *Fire*—Identity	*Sagittarius*—My need to explore and expand the horizons of my mind & world	*9th*—The collective mind: Broader viewpoints through travel, religion, philosophy & mental studies	*Jupiter*—My search for meaning, truth and ethical values *Chiron*—My capacity for holistic understanding
10	*Cardinal*—Initiating Action *Earth*—Material	*Capricorn*—My need for structure, organization and social accomplishment	*10th*—My public self, position in the world, reputation and vocation	*Saturn*—My capacity to create order, form and discipline in my life
11	*Fixed*—Stabilizing Security *Air*—Mental and Social	*Aquarius*—My need to be innovative, original and create social change	*11th*—My social aspirations Group interactions Friends and Associations	*Uranus*—My capacity to liberate myself from past limitations; my unique individuality
12	*Mutable*—Adapting to Learning *Water*—Emotional and Soul	*Pisces*—My need to commit myself to a dream or ideal & work towards its realization	*12th*—My devotion to higher ideals and spiritual values, social service, collective soul, overcoming ghosts or debts of the past	*Neptune*—My capacity to transcend the finite self through feeling unity with a greater whole

Figure 4: An Astrological Mandala

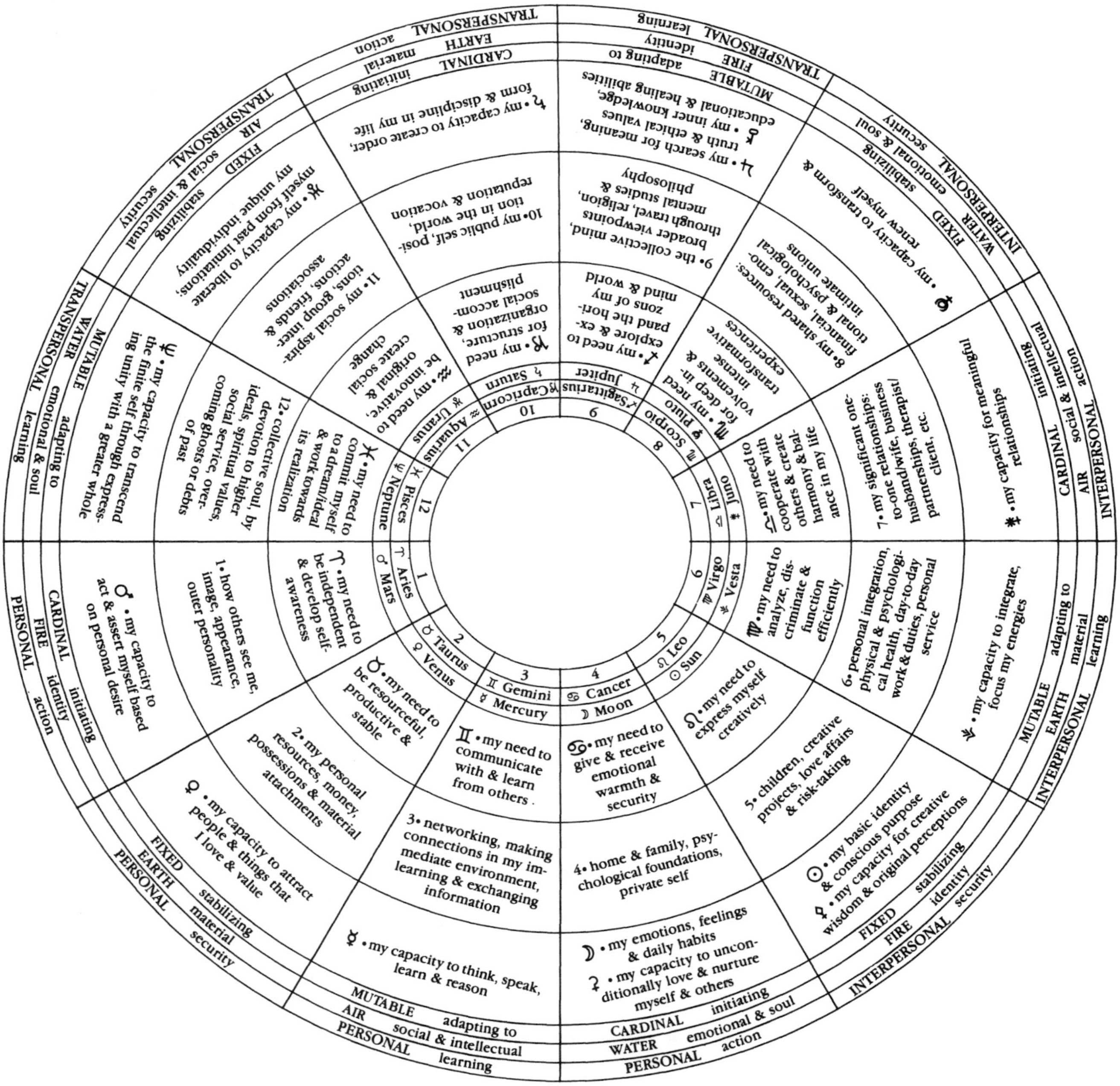

Astrology for Yourself

Chapter 3

Writing Your ———— *Personality Profile* ————

I N CHAPTER ONE, we gave you an understanding of how the signs of the Zodiac are put together so that you could obtain a greater understanding of your own Sun sign. We also pointed out that knowing your Sun sign was only the first step in getting to know yourself.

In Chapter Two, you learned that the Astrological Alphabet consists of three primary colors or principles: planets, signs, and houses.

In Chapter Three, we are going to examine how these colors combine to produce your zodiacal portrait. Although we have provided Journal Entry questions with minimal answering space, you may wish to keep a separate journal or use your own paper to fill in your zodiacal portrait and thereby have it all in a single place for easy reference. Before we begin, let us consider two other significators of your personality: the Moon and Ascendant.

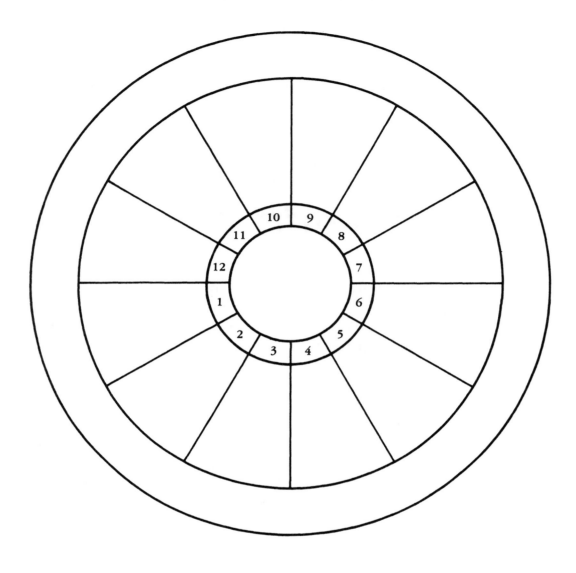

Notes: _____

_____

_____

_____

_____

_____

_____

_____

_____

_____

_____

The Sun, Moon and Ascendant

The Sun, Moon and Ascendant are considered to be the three primary indicators of personality in the birth chart.

The **Sun** represents the essence of who you know yourself to be, your conscious purpose and identity. On an esoteric level the Sun refers to the present—the inherent potential you have to work with in the here and now.

The **Moon** represents the innermost **core** of your being, your private feelings and subconscious habits and attitudes. On an esoteric level the Moon refers to your past—early childhood influences, racial heritage, and past lives.

The **Ascendant**, also called the **Rising sign**, is the sign of the Zodiac that was rising or ascending over the Eastern horizon at the time of your birth. The Ascendant represents the **outer** layer of your being, your mask or persona coloring how you present yourself to the world at large. On an esoteric level the Ascendant refers to the future—your direction of soul growth and unfoldment.

The relationship between the Sun, Moon, and Ascendant is depicted in Figure 1 and Table 1.

Figure 1: The Layers of Personality

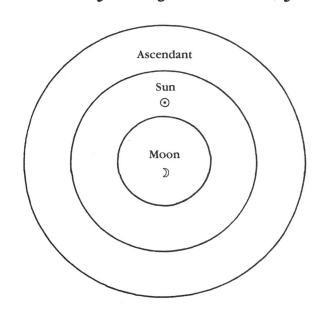

Table 1: The Sun, Moon and Ascendant

1. The Ascendant describes your unique way of being in the world. It shows how you come across in pursuing your Sun's purpose. The Sun sign determines the important decisions you make within, but the Rising sign depicts how those decisions are outwardly expressed.

SUN SIGN	RISING SIGN
Your inner self	Your outer self
How you see yourself	How others see you
Your essence	Your image
Your central core	Your mask or persona
Your purpose or motivation	The vehicle for its expression

2. The Ascendant combines with the Sun and Moon signs to form an astrological trinity that sets the tone for the entire chart. It is only natural that the Sun, Moon, and Ascendant should function as a unit, for the heavenly cycles on which they are based—the **Year**, the **Month**, and the **Day**—govern the rhythms of your earthly existence.

THE SYMBOL	THE CYCLE FROM WHICH IT IS DERIVED
Sun sign	The **Yearly** cycle of the seasons
Moon sign	The **Monthly** cycle of the moon's phases
Rising sign	The **Daily** cycle of the Earth's rotation on its axis

———Exercise 1: I Interpret My Sun, Moon and Ascendant———

Let us now analyze your Sun, Moon, and Rising signs according to polarity, element, mode, and orientation. To begin, look up the positions of your Sun sign, Moon sign, and Rising sign in Table 2, page 32.

My **Sun** (my essence) is in the sign of _____.

My **Moon** (my feelings) is in the sign of _____.

My **Ascendant** (my image) is in the sign of _____.

Now, using Figure 6, page 22 and Keyword Table 6, page 21, fill in the blanks below.

1. **Element Analysis:** Using Figure 6, page 22, look up the elements of your Sun, Moon, and Rising signs.

   My **Sun sign's element** is _____.

(Fire, Earth, Air, or Water)

   My **Moon sign's element** is _____.

   My **Rising sign's element** is _____.

   Analyze the results above. Does any element seem emphasized? Is any lacking? If any element appears more than once, write three of its keywords below, using Table 6, page 21, as your source.

   A. _____ B. _____ C. _____

2. **Polarity Emphasis:** Now look at polarities. You know that Fire and Air comprise the Positive or Yang polarity, while Earth and Water make up the Negative or Yin Polarity. Using this information, complete the following:

   My **Sun sign's polarity** is _____.

(Yang or Yin)

   My **Moon sign's polarity** is _____.

   My **Rising sign's polarity** is _____.

   The polarity that appears most often is _____.

   From Table 6, page 21, two keywords for this polarity are:

   A. _____ B. _____

3. **Modality Emphasis:** Again using Figure 6, page 22 complete the following information:

   My **Sun sign's modality** is _____.

(Cardinal, Fixed, or Mutable)

   My **Moon sign's modality** is _____.

   My **Rising sign's modality** is _____.

   As we did with the elements, if any modality appears more than once, write down three of its keywords from Table 6, page 21, below.

   A. _____ B. _____ C. _____

4. **Orientation Emphasis:** Finally, using Figure 6, page 22, determine the orientations of your Sun, Moon, and Rising signs:

My **Sun sign's orientation** is _____ .
(Personal, Interpersonal, or Transpersonal)

My **Moon sign's orientation** is _____ .

My **Rising sign's orientation** is _____ .

If any orientation comes up more than once, write down its keyphrase from Table 6, page 21, below.

_____

_____

──────────*Journal Entry*──────────

The above exercise should have provided you with more information about your birth chart and therefore about yourself. Did you find the keywords helpful? Did they seem to fit what you know about yourself?

In the space below, in your own words, write a brief **self portrait** that is derived from the insights you have gained about your Sun, Moon and Rising signs.

_____

_____

_____

_____

_____

_____

_____

_____

_____

_____

_____

_____

_____

_____

_____

_____

_____

_____

_____

You have now begun your birth chart interpretation by painting a broad outline of your astrological portrait. The basic picture should be familiar. Yet many details remain to be filled in.

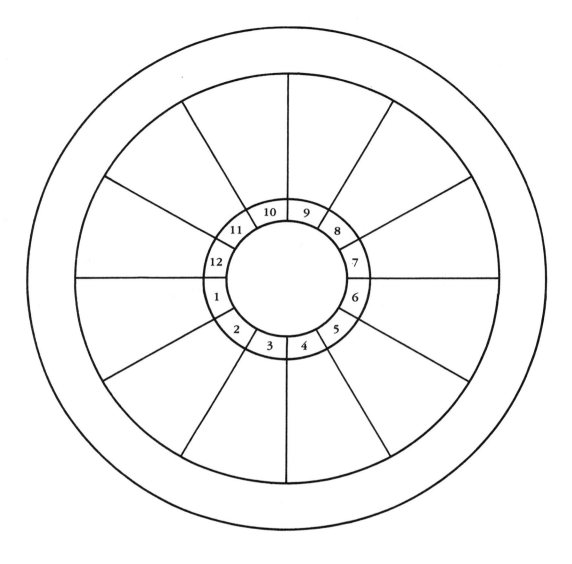

Notes: _____

_____

_____

_____

_____

_____

_____

_____

_____

_____

_____

_____

The Four Angles of the Birth Chart

The Ascendant or Rising sign is one of four extremely important points in the chart known as the astrological **angles**.

The angles are formed by the intersection of the horizontal and vertical axes of the chart (the horizon and the meridian) with the outer circle. These intersections occur at four points—north, south, east and west. These points are called the four astrological **angles:** the Ascendant, Descendant, Medium Coeli, and Imum Coeli, as illustrated in Figure 2.

Figure 2:
The Structure
of the Four Angles

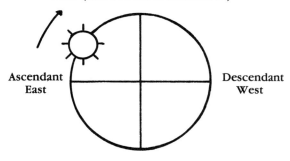

South
M.C. (also known as Midheaven)

Ascendant
East

Descendant
West

I.C. (also known as Undersky)
North

A brief note: The reason that east appears at the left of the diagram is that in the northern hemisphere, where astrology originated, to look at the noonday sun (represented by the Midheaven), you must **face south**. This places west to your right and east to your left.

The angles are extremely important in your birth chart, because they define the basic structure of your life's experiences. As we have described, the **Ascendant** or Rising sign portrays your unique way of being in the world, the vehicle that you use to express your Sun's purpose and motivation. The **Descendant**, or

Setting sign, found directly opposite the Ascendant, shows what you seek in others. It is your "relationship self."

Together, the Ascendant and Descendant symbolize a polarity of **self** (Asc.) versus **other** (Desc.) that describes how you balance your need to be an individual with your need to cooperate with others.

The **M.C.** or Medium Coeli ("point of culmination") represents the most elevated sign in the sky at the time of your birth. Hence it represents how you are seen by society at large—your career, reputation, and stance in the world. This is clearly your "public self." On the other hand, the **I.C.** or Imum Coeli ("the undersky") lies directly opposite the M.C. and represents your personal, "private self."

Together, the M.C. and I.C. create a polarity of **personal integration** (I.C.) versus **social function** (M.C.) that describes how your base of operations supports and reflects your public or professional expression.

Figure 3:
The Meaning of
the Four Angles

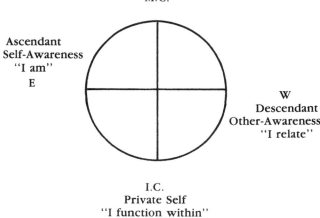

S
"I function in society"
Public Self
M.C.

Ascendant
Self-Awareness
"I am"
E

W
Descendant
Other-Awareness
"I relate"

I.C.
Private Self
"I function within"
N

Now it is time to discover how these four functions operate in your birth chart. On the next page, you will be asked to complete a number of sentences, using keywords from Appendix A. We will talk more about Appendix A in the next exercise. For now, read over the sample analysis and then complete the sentences using the appropriate keywords.

The Angles in My Birth Chart:
Sample Analysis of the Ascendant

Using Figure 1, page 26:

My **Ascendant** is in the sign of _____*Scorpio*_____.
(see Table 2, page 32)

My Ascendant, or Rising sign, describes how I express my personality. Thus, I can best project myself to others by fulfilling:

_____*My need for deep involvements and intense transformations*_____.
(fill in the sign keyphrase from Appendix A)

When I am confident, I tend to project myself in a ___*healing*___, ___*renewing*___,

and ___*magnetic*___ manner.
(choose skillful sign keywords from Appendix A)

However, when I feel unsure of myself or overcompensate,

I may be ___*resentful*___ and ___*suspicious*___.
(choose unskillful sign keywords from Appendix A)

Now, try it yourself.

I Interpret The Angles in My Birth Chart

ASCENDANT "I am"

My **Ascendant** is in the sign of _____.
(see Table 2, page 32)

My Ascendant, or rising sign, describes how I express my persona or outer image. Thus, I can best project myself to others by fulfilling:

_____.
(fill in the sign keyphase from Appendix A)

When I am confident, I tend to project myself in a _____, _____,

and _____ manner.
(choose skillful sign keywords from Appendix A)

However, when I feel unsure of myself or overcompensate,

I may be _____ and _____.
(choose unskillful sign keywords from Appendix A)

DESCENDANT "I relate"

My **Descendant** is in the sign of _____.
(see Table 2, page 32)

In my birth chart, my Descendant sign describes the qualities I seek or need in others (one to one relationships) which often represent my less conscious aspects. Thus, I can attract the partnerships I need by owning and acknowledging my

_____.
(fill in the sign keyphase from Appendix A)

When my partnerships or relationships are in harmony, they tend to be

_____, _____, and _____.
(choose skillful sign keywords from Appendix A)

However when I am projecting my repressed energies onto my significant others, I may

experience them as _____ and _____.
(choose unskillful sign keywords from Appendix A)

M.C. or MEDIUM COELI "I function in society"

My **M.C.** is in the sign of _____.
(see Table 2, page 32)

My M.C., or Midheaven sign, describes how I function in and contribute to society. Thus, I can best be in the world and achieve my professional and career identity by fulfilling:

_____.
(fill in the sign keyphase from Appendix A)

When I am competent, I tend to project myself in the world in a _____,

_____, and _____ manner.
(choose skillful sign keywords from Appendix A)

However, when I feel unsure of myself or out of place, I may be _____

and _____.
(choose unskillful sign words from Appendix A)

I.C. or IMUM COELI "I function within"

My **I.C.,** or Undersky, is in the sign of _____.
(see Table 2, page 32)

My I.C. describes my need for an emotionally secure foundation on which to base my life's operations. Thus, I can best establish a solid home and foundation by fulfilling:

_____.
(fill in the sign keyphase from Appendix A)

When I am secure and grounded, I tend to feel _____, _____,

and _____.
(choose skillful sign keywords from Appendix A)

However when I feel insecure and ungrounded, I may be _____

and _____.
(choose unskillful sign keywords from Appendix A)

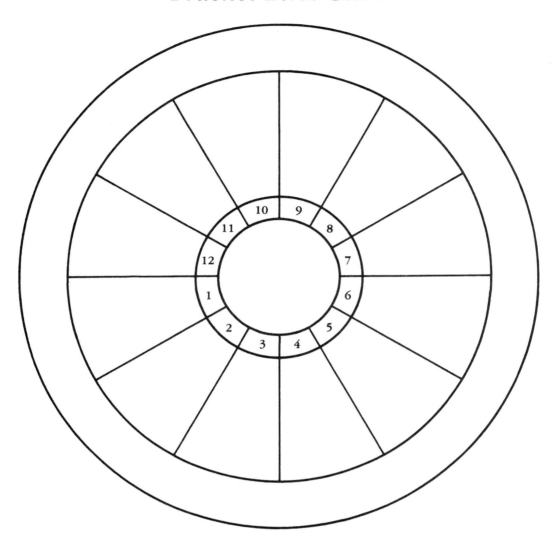

Notes: _____

_____

_____

_____

_____

_____

_____

_____

_____

_____

_____

_____

The Planets in the Birth Chart

How to Interpret the Planets in Your Birth Chart

You are now ready to begin interpreting the effects of each planet, or part of your personality, by analyzing it according to its sign and house position in your birth chart.

Remember that the **planets** are the basic driving energies of the chart. They show **what** is taking place.

The **signs** of the Zodiac act as mediums for the expression of the planetary energies. They show **how** the planetary functions are manifesting.

The **houses,** on the other hand, act as fields of experience for the planetary functions. They indicate **where,** or in what department of life, the planetary action is taking place.

To begin the process of interpreting your planets, refer to Table 2, page 32 to determine the sign and house location of each planet in your chart. Then, fill in the blanks of the programmed text by using the keywords from the sign keywords in Appendix A and the house keywords in Appendix B.

You will be referring to Appendices A and B on a continual basis for the remainder of this book. Our students found that having to constantly turn to the back of the book during each exercise was distracting and caused them to lose their concentration.

First Possibility

One way to remedy this situation is to go to an office supply store and purchase a set of plastic tabs. Label and attach one each to the first page of Appendices A, B and C. Then, whenever you need to refer to an appendix, you can quickly flip to the appropriate tab. Using this procedure, you will gain easy access to the all important keywords that you will need to complete this and future exercises.

Second Possibility

A second way to remedy the situation is to photocopy Appendices A and B, bind them together (with a paper clip, staple or folder) and place them beside your workbook. By doing this, you can gain easy access to the keywords that you will need to complete this and future exercises.

How to Fill Out Part 1

For the first sentence, you will want to look up your planet's sign position in Table 2, page 32.

The planet keyphrase that begins each exercise (in bold letters) represents a distillation of the primary qualities of the planet. Appendix C provides additional planetary keywords. You may wish to read them over in order to see how each planet functions on *all* of its levels.

To complete the next three sentences, simply refer to Appendix A for the appropriate keyphrase and keywords.

How to Fill Out Part 2

Part 2 of each exercise asks you to determine the element of the sign in which the planet is placed. For example, Part 2 of the sample analysis reads "My Sun sign's element is _____." We filled in the element **Water,** because the Sun was in Pisces, and Pisces is a *water* sign.

You will do this with each of your planets. First determine the actual sign that the planet is in (stated in part 1), and then look up that sign's element, using Figure 2, page 11, the element wheel. Then you will circle the keyphrase that is matched with that element in the chart below.

How to Fill Out Part 3

For the first sentence, look up the planet's house position in Table 2, page 32.

In the second sentence, turn to Appendix B to locate the appropriate keywords.

Journal Entry

Although we have provided Journal Entry questions with minimal answering space, you may wish to keep a separate journal or use your own paper to fill in your zodiacal portrait and thereby have it all in a single place for easy reference.

The Meaning of Empty Houses

As you complete the exercise, you will find that some houses are emphasized because they contain a number of planets, while other houses contain none at all. What do these "empty" houses signify? If you think of the birth chart as a large home, each astrological house would correspond to a room in the home. For example, the fourth house (associated with Cancer) could be symbolized by the kitchen, the tenth house (associated with Capricorn) would be the office, the fifth house (associated with Leo) the recreation room, etc. When many planets are positioned in a house, this means that you probably spend a great deal of time in that room. You feel comfortable because you can express yourself easily there.

On the other hand, if a house is empty, you certainly spend time there, as all rooms of the home are a part of your daily living; however, this room is visited less frequently, and does not function as a central focus in your daily activities.

(A note to intermediate students, the theme of the empty house is determined by the sign located on the house cusp. The planet associated with that sign is the key to activating the affairs of the empty house.)

Increasing Your Life's Options Through This Exercise

The sign keywords from Appendix A describe the characteristics and tendencies of the signs of the Zodiac. Though each sign represents a basic mode of energy, this energy can manifest in a range of possible expressions during the course of your life. This is why we have given you such a large number of keywords to choose from.

Although these sign energies are neutral, they can manifest in either **skillful** or **unskillful** ways. For example, if we give two carpenters the same tools and raw materials, one may build a graceful, solid structure while the other may create a rickety shack. Likewise, your birth chart depicts the potential that you have to work with, but your *free will* and the *choices* you make will determine how skillfully you build your life.

This point separates modern astrology from the fortune telling and determinism that characterized much of the practice in the Middle Ages. Unfortunately, many individuals still think of astrology in a deterministic light, not realizing that it actually *increases* rather than restricts our *options*.

Therefore, it is important to realize that if you have been using a certain energy in a way that is creating destructive or unhappy results in your life, you can also choose to express the very same energy in a more positive or constructive manner. It is not a matter of adding something that you do not have, but of better learning how to *use* what is *already available*.

Now let us continue the journey of writing your own birth chart with an *example* that will demonstrate how the process works.

Exercise 3: I Interpret the Planets in My Birth Chart

Sample Planetary Analysis: The Sun

1. My sun is in the sign of ____*Pisces*____. (We are assuming that this person is a Sun sign Pisces).

   My Sun sign represents my purpose, will, and power. I can bext express this potential by _*my need to commit myself to a dream or ideal and work towards its realization*_ .

   (fill in the sign keyphrase from Appendix A)

   When I am using these sign qualities **skillfully**, I tend to be ____*empathetic*____,

   ____*sacrificing*____, or ____*healing*____.

   (choose skillful sign keywords from Appendix A)

   However, when I am using these sign qualities **unskillfully**,

   I may be _____*confused*_____ or _____*chaotic*_____.

   (choose unskillful sign keywords from Appendix A)

2. My Sun sign's element is _____*water*_____.

   (refer to Figure 2, page 11)

   Using the chart below, circle the response that is paired with this element.

SUN SIGN'S ELEMENT	SOUL LESSON I NEED TO LEARN
Fire	Love
Earth	Service
Air	Relating To Others
(Water)	(Peace)

3. My Sun is in the _____*fourth*_____ house.

   (refer to Table 2, page 32)

   Therefore, my basic purpose, will and power are best expressed in these areas of

   my life: ____*home*____ and ____*family*____, ____*personal integration*____.

   (choose house keywords from Appendix B)

Now that you have seen the sample Sun exercise completed, you should be ready to proceed on your own. As you go over each planet, realize that each interpretation you write will not always make perfect sense. In some instances, the sentences you compose may seem a bit awkward or unclear. This is because chart interpretation is a complex art and cannot always be reduced to simple keywords. In most instances, however, the keywords you choose should give you a good feeling for how you are using the planetary energy in your life. And by completing the journal entries at the end of each exercise, you will gain additional insights about how you are expressing the planetary function.

The Sun

The Creator   **Ruler of Leo**   **"I will"**

The **Sun**, planetary ruler of the sign Leo, symbolizes **one's basic identity and conscious purpose**.

As the physical Sun functions as the center of the Solar System, the astrological Sun symbolizes our psychological and spiritual center. It represents our inner life force, vitality, and purpose.

The symbol of the Sun is that of a circle surrounding a point. The circle represents the infinite and unlimited potential of spirit. The dot represents the point where the infinite manifests into finite form. The entire symbol thus depicts the realization of infinite potential through a specific point—the individual.

Hence, the Sun sign signifies our individuality and sense of identity. It enables us to experience a sense of self, to identify with the words "I," and "me." When we are in touch with this solar force and consciously activate it, we declare, "I am a unique **individual** in the world. There is no other like me. I have entered this life with a unique **purpose** and a contribution to make that is mine and mine alone." Thus, the Sun gives us the desire to become more than we are, to grow, and to shine in the world.

If this solar energy is blocked, then our sense of self will be weakened or diminished. When we are not in touch with our Sun, we lack faith and confidence in ourselves. In addition, we find it difficult to integrate our life around a central theme. We drift about, having neither direction nor purpose.

If, on the other hand, the solar energy is excessive, then we may become extremely prideful or boastful. The ego may become too overbearing and dominant, producing an inflated sense of self.

The Sun is the activating, creative force in the birth chart. It is the divine spark residing within each of us. By expressing this creative potential, we truly become co-creators with the Gods and Goddesses.

Physiologically, the Sun rules the human heart, whose biological function exactly parallels that of the heavenly star. For as the physical Sun pulsates life-giving warmth to all living beings on Earth, so too does our inner Sun, the human heart, pump life-giving blood to every cell in the body.

Skillful Expression: purposeful, integrated, creative, self-confident

Unskillful Expression: unintegrated, timid, or self-centered, dominating

The Sun: Keyphrases
- My source, center, will, vitality and life force
- My potential for creative self-expression
- My ability to focus my talents and to realize a life purpose

1. My planet the **Sun** is in the sign of _____.
   (refer to Table 2, page 32)

   My Sun sign represents **my purpose, will, and power**. I can best express this

   potential by fulfilling: _____.
   (fill in the sign keyphrase from Appendix A)

   When I am using these sign qualities **skillfully**, I tend to be _____,

   _____, or _____.
   (choose skillful sign keywords from Appendix A)

   However when I'm using these sign qualities **unskillfully**, I may be _____

   or _____.
   (choose unskillful sign keywords from Appendix A)

2. My Sun sign's element is _____.
   (refer to Figure 2, page 11)

   Using the chart below, circle the response that is paired with this element.

SUN SIGN'S ELEMENT	SOUL LESSON I NEED TO LEARN
Fire	Love
Earth	Service
Air	Relating to Others
Water	Peace

3. My Sun is in the _____ house.
   (refer to Table 2, page 32)

   Therefore, my basic purpose, will and power are best expressed in these areas of
   my life:

   _____ and _____
   (choose house keywords from Appendix B)

Journal Entry

Using the space below write a few sentences on how you are expressing the Sun's energy in your own life. The following questions may serve to stimulate and activate your thinking about the planet.

Do I have a clear sense of my life's purpose and direction? Do I experience my life as a meaningful, integrated whole?

Am I in touch with my will and my power? Do I have a healthy sense of my own self-worth? How am I expressing my creative potential? Do I have creative outlets that I enjoy?

_____

_____

_____

_____

_____

_____

_____

The Moon

The Sustainer   **Ruler of Cancer**   **"I emote"**

The Moon, planetary ruler of the sign Cancer, symbolizes **our emotions, feelings, and daily habit patterns**.

Mythologically, the Moon was personified as the Goddess, and in her triple form she displayed herself as Artemis the new moon, Selene the full moon, and Hecate the dark moon. These symbolized the maiden, mother, and crone phases of a woman's life span. In this way the Moon is the foundation for all of the other feminine planets and asteroids.

As the lunar cycle regulates the woman's menstrual cycle, the Moon is regarded as the source of fertility, birthing, and growth of new life. Thus traditionally the Moon has been a symbol for the mother, family and domestic life, and our emotional needs. The Moon signifies how as adults we define security based on our experience of being nurtured, supported, and protected. While the Sun indicates what we want, the Moon describes what we need—and cannot do without.

The Moon is the primary symbol of the feminine Yin polarity and stands in equal power to the Solar masculine Yang principle. The Moon's function in this relationship is to offer a receptive container in which to give form to the Sun's energy. Esther Harding reflects, "The Yin is said to be of equal power to the Yang because it brings all his stirrings into manifestation." Within each one of us, it is through the vehicle of our Moon personality that we can actualize the potential of our Sun's purpose. Traditional concepts associated with the Moon—our adaptability, emotional responses, daily habit patterns, receptivity, and nurturing matrix—have been based upon the principle that the Moon reflects the light of the Sun.

In the moon's monthly lunation cycle, each evening we see a different face of her phases as she reflects varying amounts of light. Our lunar nature makes us sensitive to the changing conditions of our environment, thereby enabling us to continually adjust our way of relating to the outer world. The Moon's capacity for flexibility in an ever changing reality provides a protected form in which we can unfold our Sun's purpose.

Our responses to these situations are often instinctive, because they are unconscious and based on emotional reactions from early childhood experiences and family training. As the Moon represents the nurturing matrix out of which all life arises, it is most influential in the earliest parts of our life. As young children before seven years of age (when the rational mind is developed) we are emotional sensors, unconsciously absorbing many or our parents' assumptions and attitudes. Here lie the beginnings of our psychological patterns that arise from infantile experiences. This storehouse of dimly remembered emotional perceptions forms our Moon personality. When we feel threatened in our security, this unconscious aspect of ourselves instinctively responds to secure our protection.

It is important to note that the Moon underlies all of the feminine expressions and is more than just a mother symbol. The asteroid Ceres gives additional information about the Moon's specific nurturing relationship between parent and child.

As the ruler of the water sign Cancer, the Moon governs our emotional life and feelings. In the same way the infant does not realize he or she is separate from the mother, the Moon does not recognize separateness. When we merge with the world through feeling, we become "intuitive," and perceive beyond rational knowing. However, when we allow our fluctuating emotions to become excessive, then we ride an emotional roller coaster, at the mercy of our ever changing moods.

Finally, the Moon governs the past. Through the Moon we can access our personal subconscious, racial memory and ancestral heritage.

Physiologically, the Moon rules the body's fluids: lymph, glandular secretions, mother's milk, etc. It also governs the breasts, stomach and the woman's menstrual cycle which corresponds to the twenty-nine-day lunar revolution.

Skillful Expression: nurturing, providing, protective, sensitive, intuitive

Unskillful Expression: overemotional, insecure, fearful, moody

I Interpret the Moon in My Birth Chart

The Moon Keyphrases
• My emotions and feelings • My habit patterns • My inner feminine

1. My planet the **Moon** is in the sign of _____.

    In the birth chart, my Moon sign indicates **how I respond emotionally and meet my security needs.** Thus, I can best fulfill these needs by expressing:

    _____.
    (fill in the sign keyphrase from Appendix A)
    When I am using these sign qualities **skillfully**, I tend to **feel** _____,

    _____, or _____.
    (choose skillful sign keywords from Appendix A)
    However, when I'm using these sign qualities **unskillfully**, I may **feel** _____

    or _____.
    (choose unskillful sign keywords from Appendix A)

2. My Moon sign's element is _____.
    (refer to Figure 2, page 11)
    Using the chart below, circle the response that is paired with this element.

MOON SIGN'S ELEMENT	HOW I EMOTIONALLY RESPOND AND FIND SECURITY
Fire	Warmly, impulsively, and energetically Security is found through self-expression
Earth	Cautiously, pragmatically, and sensually Security is found in form and structure
Air	Intellectually, communicatively, and detachedly Security is found in the world of ideas
Water	In a nurturing, feeling and flowing manner Security is found through emotional intimacy

3. My Moon is in the _____ house.
    (refer to Table 2, page 32)
    Therefore, my feelings, emotional responses, and habit patterns are best expressed in these areas of my life:

    _____ and _____.
    (choose house keywords from Appendix B)

Journal Entry

Using the space below write a few sentences on how you are expressing the Moon's energy in your own life. The following questions may serve to stimulate and activate your thinking about the planet.

How do I experience my feelings and moods? Can I easily share my feelings with others? Are there times when I let my moods run my life?

How do I experience my own inner feminine? Do I accept my intuitions and hunches as valid?

What habit patterns have I developed that aid and support my lifestyle? What habits and conditioning would I like to change?

In what ways does my Moon personality facilitate the expression of my Sun's purpose?

_____

_____

_____

_____

Mercury

The Messenger   **Ruler of Gemini and Virgo**   **"I think"**

Mercury, planetary ruler of the signs Gemini and Virgo, symbolizes **our capacity to think, speak, learn and reason.**

In Greek mythology, Mercury was portrayed as Hermes, the winged messenger god. The swiftest of the Gods, Hermes/Mercury delivered messages throughout the land with great speed and alacrity. In his hand he carried the caduceus, a staff of two snakes intertwined about a vertical rod, a symbol of the power of knowledge.

From the above symbolism, it is clear that Mercury, planet of the intellect, epitomizes the air element and rules Gemini. In its association with Gemini, Mercury governs the intellect, rational mind, speech and language.

Aside from being a messenger, Hermes was a marvelous orator, writer and teacher. Likewise, Mercury types are excellent communicators and often earn their living by using the gift of speech.

In human development, Mercury rules the ages between seven and thirteen. Sigmund Freud called this period the latent stage, a time when the child's energies could be fully channeled into **learning.** During this period which focuses on the elementary school experience, the child does indeed develop the Mercury functions. He or she learns to read and write, to think symbolically; and acquires a great deal of knowledge about the world. This is why many educators believe that the primary education lays the foundation for future learning and mental development.

When the Mercury function is not working properly, problems in learning or communication may develop. One such example is portrayed by the so called "learning disorders" which affect a number of children.

Physiologically, Mercury rules the central nervous system. This communication network consists of billions of interconnected cells which carry messages to and from the brain much like an electronic switching network. Mercury also rules the respiratory system, including the lungs, bronchi, windpipe and nose.

Skillful Expression: communicative, intelligent, rational, clever

Unskillful Expression: overintellectual, restless, overtalkative, cunning

Mercury Keyphrases
- My reasoning mind
- My ability to formulate concepts and ideas
- My ability to communicate them to others

1. My planet **Mercury** is in the sign of _____.

   In the birth chart, my Mercury sign shows **how I acquire knowledge, formulate concepts, and communicate them to others.** Thus, I can best communicate and use my rational mind by fulfilling:

   _____.
   (fill in the sign keyphrase from Appendix A)

   When I am using these sign qualities **skillfully**, I tend to **communicate** in a

   _____, _____, or _____ manner.
   (choose skillful sign keywords from Appendix A)

   However, when I'm using these sign qualities **unskillfully**, I may **communicate** in a

   _____ or _____ manner.
   (choose unskillful sign keywords from Appendix A)

2. My Mercury sign's element is _____.
   (refer to Figure 1, page 11)

   Using the chart below, circle the response that is paired with this element.

MERCURY'S ELEMENT	HOW I THINK AND COMMUNICATE
Fire	Inspiringly and independently
Earth	Concretely and pragmatically
Air	Logically and theoretically
Water	Intuitively and imaginatively

3. My Mercury is in the _____ house.
   (refer to Table 2, page 32)

   Therefore, my capacity for learning and communication is best expressed in these areas of my life:

   _____ and _____.
   (choose house keywords from Appendix B)

Journal Entry

Using the space below write a few sentences on how you are expressing Mercury's energy in your own life. The following questions may serve to stimulate and activate your thinking about the planet.

How do I relate to the world of the mind? Do I see myself as primarily a "mental" individual?

What is my style of communication? Do I prefer to communicate in a verbal or nonverbal manner?

What is my approach to learning? Do I enjoy adding to my knowledge? Do I like to learn from books, or do I prefer to learn by doing?

_____
_____
_____
_____
_____
_____

Venus

Goddess of Love and Beauty   **Ruler of Taurus and Libra**   **"I Harmonize"**

Venus, planetary ruler of the signs Libra and Taurus, symbolizes the **capacity to attract the people and things we love and value.**

Venus represents the core essence of the feminine nature. Through her powers of divine beauty and magnetic desirability she ignites the spark of the creative process. She is the wellspring of the feminine vital force which begets and renews life.

Venus was known to the Greeks as Aphrodite, Goddess of Love and Beauty. In her earlier Asiatic origins, she was also worshipped as a nature goddess and primal mother of all on-going creation.

As the embodiment of grace, harmony and loveliness, Venus cultivates beauty through the arts and social graces. She endows a natural elegance and refined aesthetic sense. Those individuals under her patronage are the artists and musicians of the Zodiac, expressing balance and harmony through color, line, proportion, modulation, melody and rhythm. In Venus' world, beauty of form and harmony of living heal and uplift the human soul. When the Venus principle is exaggerated, it can lead to overindulgence of the senses, laziness, and abhorrence of hard work.

Venus also symbolizes our personal magnetism, and how we draw to ourselves what we love and value. In her rulership of the Earth sign Taurus, she attracts sensual pleasure—material substance, money, and the good life. Through her, we determine what we appreciate.

In her association with the air sign Libra, Venus governs our social urge—the need to interact and join with others. In love and friendship, Venus signifies what turns us on and how we turn others on. Venus reveals the way we express our affections and feelings for others, how we give of ourselves to them.

Traditional astrology associates Venus with mates or marriage partners. However, mythological Venus did not honor her marriage vows, and had many lovers, gods and mortals alike. She served as the goddess who taught the lessons of sexuality, desirability, taking responsibility for the affections we arouse in others, as well as sorrow, loss, rejection, and impermanence in love. Thus, while Venus represents the principle of attraction, it is the asteroid Juno, Goddess of Marriage, that gives more specific information about our capacity to sustain ongoing relationships. Venus is our social urge to interact with others, but not necessarily to bond with them for a long time. She indicates how women express their own sensuality, like a flower alluring a bee. And to the extent that men project their "anima" or feminine aspect, Venus for them is the image of their ideal woman.

Physiologically, Venus rules the female sex organs, the body's glands, the venous return of blood, the throat (through Taurus), and the kidneys (through Libra).

Skillful Expression: beautiful, refined, harmonizing, graceful, artistic

Unskillful Expression: self-indulgent, vain, oversensuous, lazy

I Interpret Venus in My Birth Chart

Venus Keyphrases
- My need for interaction with others
- What turns me on; what I find attractive
- Aesthetics, charm, refinement, good taste, artistic interests

1. My planet **Venus** is in the sign of _____.

   In the birth chart, my Venus indicates **how I relate to others and express my aesthetic sensibility.** Thus, I can best attract people and the things that I love and value by fulfilling:

   _____.
   (fill in the sign keyphrase from Appendix A)

   When I am using these sign qualities **skillfully**, I tend to **interact** in a

   _____ , _____ , or _____ manner when
   (choose skillful sign keywords from Appendix A)

   seeking unions with others.

   However, when I'm using these sign qualities **unskillfully**, I may **interact** in a

   _____ or _____ manner.
   (choose unskillful sign keywords from Appendix A)

2. My Venus sign's element is _____.
   (refer to Figure 1, page 11)

   Using the chart below, circle the response that is paired with this element.

VENUS' ELEMENT	WHAT I SEEK IN MY INTERACTIONS WITH OTHERS
Fire	Excitement and adventure; passion and romance
Earth	Sensuality and practicality; comfort and stability
Air	Thoughts and ideas; mental interactions
Water	Feeling and sentiment; emotional bonding

3. My Venus is in the _____ house.
   (refer to Table 2, page 32)

   Therefore, my capacity for love, beauty and harmony is best expressed in these areas of my life:

   _____ and _____.
   (choose house keywords from Appendix B)

Journal Entry

Using the space below write a few sentences on how you are expressing Venus' energy in your own life. The following questions may serve to stimulate and activate your thinking about the planet.

How do I relate to my social urge? Am I primarily a "people-person?" How much time do I spend relating to others versus in my own company?

What types of people or things "turn me on?" What am I most attracted to?

How much personal responsibility do I accept for the pain and rejection I experience in my personal interactions?

How important is beauty and harmony in my life? Do I seek out aesthetically pleasing environments? Am I engaged in any artistic endeavors?

_____

_____

_____

_____

Mars

The Warrior   Ruler of Aries   "I act"

Mars, planetary ruler of Aries and Scorpio, symbolizes the **capacity to act and assert ourselves based upon personal desire.**

Known as Ares to the Greeks, Mars gained his reputation as the Roman God of War. In the birth chart, Mars functions as the right hand man of the Sun. The Sun formulates our goals; Mars pursues them. He proclaims, "I want and I will get. No obstacles are too great, no enemies too strong. I will overcome them all." Hence those of us who respond to the vibrations of Mars possess the energy, drive and ambition to accomplish whatever we desire.

Through Mars we learn to act as independent and self-sufficient beings and to **project** ourselves into the world. Mars gives us the courage to stand up for our rights, to assert ourselves and to express anger when necessary. The proper channeling of this assertive energy can produce great accomplishments, courageous deeds, or athletic achievements.

However, when the power of Mars goes unchecked, it manifests as reckless aggression, violence, and war. The prevalence of violence in the world today indicates that one of humanity's greatest challenges lies in learning to redirect its Mars' energies into more constructive outlets.

Mars also represents our capacity for physical passion and desire for sexual gratification. This sexual orientation expresses itself through the masculine desire to thrust, penetrate and eject its seed. Mars' inherent phallic nature is depicted by its symbol ♂ which resembles an erect penis. Individuals with a strong Mars invariably possess strong sexual desires. Their challenge lies in learning to constructively apply this powerful creative force.

In today's Mars-dominated world, two Martian phallic symbols assume great importance: the missile and the warhead. The current proliferation of these destructive weapons is another example of the imbalance of Mars' energy on the planet. When the masculine and feminine energies of Mars and Venus come into balance, then much of the warring and devastating forces will abate.

Physiologically, the fiery Mars rules the muscular system, the blood (specifically the red, oxygen-carrying hemoglobin), the male sexual organs, and the adrenal glands. People who repress their Mars' function often experience a deficiency in one of these bodily functions and complain of having too little energy or drive in their daily lives.

Skillful Expression: courageous, assertive, enterprising, decisive

Unskillful Expression: aggressive, violent, selfish, coarse

Mars Keyphrases

- My ability to project myself in the world; my personal drive
- My level of activity and energy
- My assertive and potentially aggressive urges
- My sexuality

1. My planet **Mars** is in the sign of _____ .
   In the birth chart, my Mars sign describes **how I assert myself and pursue my wants and desires.** Thus, I can best project myself, forge ahead, and get what I

   want by fulfilling: _____ .
   (fill in the sign keyphrase from Appendix A)
   When I am using these sign qualities **skillfully**, I tend to **act** in a _____ ,

   _____ , or _____ manner.
   (choose skillful sign keywords from Appendix A)
   However when I'm using these sign qualities **unskillfully**, I may **act** in a

   _____ or _____ manner.
   (choose unskillful sign keywords from Appendix A)

2. My Mars sign's element is _____ .
   (refer to Figure 1, page 11)
   Using the chart below, circle the response that is paired with this element.

MARS' ELEMENT	HOW I ASSERT AND PROJECT MYSELF
Fire	Energetically and directly
Earth	Conservatively and patiently
Air	Communicatively and abstractly
Water	Indirectly and empathetically

3. My Mars is in the _____ house.
   (refer to Table 2, page 32)
   Therefore, my capacity to assert myself, forge ahead, and get what I want is best

   expressed in these areas of my life: _____ and

   _____ .
   (choose house keywords from Appendix B)

Journal Entry

Using the space below write a few sentences on how you are expressing Mars' energy in your own life. The following questions may serve to stimulate and activate your thinking about the planet.

How do I express my assertive urge? Can I stand up for myself without becoming aggressive?

When I want something in my life, am I able to "go for it" or do I hold back and hesitate?

How do I deal with my anger? Do I get it off my chest immediately or hold it in until it explodes at a later date?

How do I experience my sexuality? How do I integrate my desire nature with my love nature?

_____

_____

_____

_____

_____

♃
Jupiter

Principle of Improvement   **Ruler of Sagittarius**   **"I expand"**

Jupiter, planetary ruler of Sagittarius, symbolizes **our search for meaning, truth, and ethical values.**

Jupiter is the largest planet in the Solar System, spinning so fast that it bulges at the equator. As Zeus in Greek Mythology, he ruled the world from atop Mt. Olympus. Jupiter symbolizes the principle of increase and expansion. While Mars directs its fiery energy in one direction ♂, Jupiter expands like a balloon, in all directions ♃.

Jupiter enlarges awareness through seeking a broader vision of reality—a vision gained through exploring the realms of philosophy, religion, ethics, higher education, and foreign travel. Jupiter's placement in the birth chart shows how we express our highmindedness and ethical principles.

The planet of joviality, Jupiter instills faith and hope in the souls of men and women. Through the workings of Jupiter, the entrepreneur dreams of the future business, the patient expresses optimism about an ultimate recovery and the parent envisions a better life for the child.

Throughout the centuries, Jupiter has been called "the great benefic," the bringer of good fortune, benevolence, abundance and prosperity. Perhaps this is because good fortune usually arises from maintaining a confident and optimistic attitude. It is the Jupiter function within that produces the positive expectation that later materializes in "good fortune."

Of course, Jupiter can become overoptimisitic and inspire false hope. This is where Jupiter's outlook needs to be tempered with a bit of realism and practicality. Another unskillful expression of Jupiter arises from exaggeration and excess. The faults of Jupiter are depicted by the phrase, "too much of a good thing can be bad for you." Too much food results in obesity; too much faith produces poor judgment; too much travel leads to rootlessness; too much good fortune may lead to taking things for granted. Therefore, heavenly justice decrees that Jupiter be followed by Saturn, the planet of limitation.

Physiologically, Jupiter rules the process of growth and preservation. While Mars provides the energy for growth, Jupiter rules the activity itself. Jupiter also governs the body's largest gland, the liver. An enlarged liver is a sure sign of overindulgence, especially of alcohol.

Skillful Expression: benevolent, broadminded, generous, optimistic

Unskillful Expression: excessive, exaggerative, misjudging, pompous

I Interpret Jupiter in My Birth Chart

Jupiter Keyphrases
- My desire to improve and enrich my life
- My need to look to the future and expand my horizons
- My benevolence, generosity and optimistic outlook

1. My planet **Jupiter** is in the sign of _____.

   In the birth chart, my Jupiter sign indicates **how I seek meaning in my life and expand my horizons.** I can best express these potentials by fulfilling:

   _____.
   (fill in the sign keyphrase from Appendix A)

   When I am using these sign qualities **skillfully,** I tend to **expand my horizons** in a

   _____, _____, or _____ manner.
   (choose skillful sign keywords from Appendix A)

   However, when I'm using these sign qualities **unskillfully,** I may be

   _____ or _____.
   (choose unskillful sign keywords from Appendix A)

2. My Jupiter sign's element is _____.
   (refer to Figure 1, page 11)

   Using the chart below, circle the response that is paired with this element.

JUPITER'S ELEMENT	HOW I FIND MEANING	HOW I EXPAND MY AWARENESS
Fire	Through self-expression	Through new adventures
Earth	In concrete reality	By building new forms
Air	Through teaching others	By discovering new ideas
Water	Through emotional closeness	By exploring the hidden

3. My Jupiter is in the _____ house.
   (refer to Table 2, page 32)

   Therefore, my search for truth, meaning, and personal growth is best expressed in these areas of my life:

   _____ and _____.
   (choose house keywords from Appendix B)

Journal Entry

Using the space below write a few sentences on how you are expressing Jupiter's energy in your own life. The following questions may serve to stimulate and activate your thinking about the planet.

How am I attempting to expand my awareness beyond my mundane concerns? Am I constantly growing?

Where do I look for meaning in my life? Do I have a philosophy or faith that helps me to develop a sense of purpose?

What do I want to do in a big way without becoming excessive?

_____

_____

_____

_____

_____

_____

♄ Saturn

The Teacher   Ruler of Capricorn   "I Manifest"

Saturn, planetary ruler of the sign Capricorn, symbolizes **the capacity to create order, form, and discipline in one's life.**

Saturn, the last planet to be seen with the naked eye, is primarily known for the beautiful rings that encircle its equator. These rings express in physical form Saturn's primary function—limitation.

The manner in which Saturn teaches us discipline is analogous to the way that a parent disciplines his or her child. Initially, the parent may set the child's limits by confining play to the back yard. If the child stays within these boundaries, he is given permission to play next door. Now, however, he has new limits; he may not cross the street to visit Johnny. If he follows these rules, he will soon be allowed to visit his friend. As the process unfolds, each time the child assumes new responsibilities, he gains additional freedoms. Yet, if at any time he oversteps the limits that his parents have set, he is quickly punished by being restricted to his original surroundings.

This story illustrates Saturn's most important lesson: Spiritual growth occurs through the fulfillment of earthly responsibilities and obligations. Through being faithful to the needs of Saturn—raising a family, holding a job, keeping commitments—we learn more about life than any book can teach. If, however, we overstep our boundaries *or* neglect our responsibilities, then we experience the subsequent limitation. These limitations can manifest as restrictions, blockages, frustrations, crystallized conditions, unresolved fears and inhibitions.

Saturn's position in the chart, by house and sign, often points to the areas where these feelings of limitation are most strongly felt. Yet, Saturn also promises that if we confront these problems head on, we will ultimately transform our inadequacies into our greatest assets.

Saturn's symbol is depicted by the cross of matter over the semicircle of the soul. Hence, Saturn governs the need to learn the lessons of the physical plane. These lessons are given to us by Saturn's most important law—the law of karma. On the physical plane, this law states that every action produces an equal but opposite reaction, or "what goes around comes around."

Saturn, therefore, metes out perfect, impersonal justice to all. It tests us every step of our lives, leaving no room for escapism, self-deception, or wishful thinking. Through Saturn's workings, we get **exactly** what we deserve, no more and no less.

In its skillful expression, Saturn's energy enables us to take our ideals and translate them into concrete forms and structures that maintain and support our lives. Often this takes time and discipline, so we learn patience, to wait. In mythology, Saturn was depicted as the Greek Kronos, God of Time and Cycles. Saturn gives all we have earned and worked for in the fullness of time. Like a slowly ripening tree, we slowly grow to maturity when we are ready to bear the fruits of success and accomplishment.

Saturn uses time to assist us in another way. In our story, the child needed time to prove his sense of responsibility. Likewise, many of our greatest lessons can only be learned over time, through repeated experiences.

In conclusion, Saturn teaches that the purpose of life is growth through experience. Saturn's path is not always easy, for sometimes our most valuable lessons are also the most painful. However, in working through our lessons, like the child, we gain the freedom to progress to higher stages of development. If Jupiter provides us with the faith that all will work out for the best, then Saturn teaches us how, through our own efforts, we can turn that vision into a reality.

Physiologically, Saturn rules the sytems that provide the body with its form and structure. These include the skeletal system, the skin, teeth, joints and knees. Saturn also governs the gall bladder, spleen and hearing organs.

Saturnine illnesses are structural disorders caused by blockages or crystallization occurring over time. Examples include rheumatism, arthritis, and arteriosclerosis. Saturnine individuals are also prone to the emotional stresses of worry, depression, despondency and gloom. Hence, they should seek out cheerful companions and environments that will facilitate a more positive outlook on life.

Skillful Expression: responsible, disciplined, grounded, thorough, patient

Unskillful Expression: fearful, inhibited, pessimistic, depressed, controlling

I Interpret Saturn in My Birth Chart

Saturn Keyphrases
- My ability to create form and structure in my life
- The fears, insecurities and inhibitions I need to overcome
- Universal laws: time, karma, gravity, cycles, old age

1. My planet **Saturn** is in the sign of _____.

   In the birth chart, my Saturn sign indicates **how I can limit, define, and focus myself.** Thus, I can best create order, form, structure, and discipline in my life by fulfilling:

   _____.
   (fill in the sign keyphrase from Appendix A)

   When I am using these sign qualities **skillfully**, I tend to define myself as

   _____, _____, or _____.
   (choose skillful sign keywords from Appendix A)

   However, when I'm using these sign qualities **unskillfully**, I tend to feel inhibited, blocked, restricted in my life. Consequently, I may feel

   _____ or _____.
   (choose unskillful sign keywords from Appendix A)

2. My Saturn sign's element is _____.
   (refer to Figure 1, page 11)

   Using the chart below, circle the response that is paired with this element.

SATURN'S ELEMENT	THE AREA OF GREATEST RESTRICTION THAT NEEDS TO BE RESTRUCTURED
Fire	My creative expression and belief in myself
Earth	My ability to function in the mundane world
Air	My mental faculties and communication skills
Water	My need to give and receive nurturance and to find emotional security

3. My Saturn is in the _____ house.
   (refer to Table 2, page 32)

   Because Saturn is the great Teacher, important lessons in my life may come to me in these areas of my life:

   _____ and _____.
   (choose house keywords from Appendix B)

Journal Entry

Using the space below write a few sentences on how you are expressing Saturn's energy in your own life. The following questions may serve to stimulate and activate your thinking about the planet.

Where do my major responsibilities lie? Do I accept or resist them?

Where do I need to exercise self-control, discipline and order in my life?

What aspects of myself or my environment do I experience as lacking or limiting? How can I bring fulfillment to these areas?

_____

_____

_____

_____

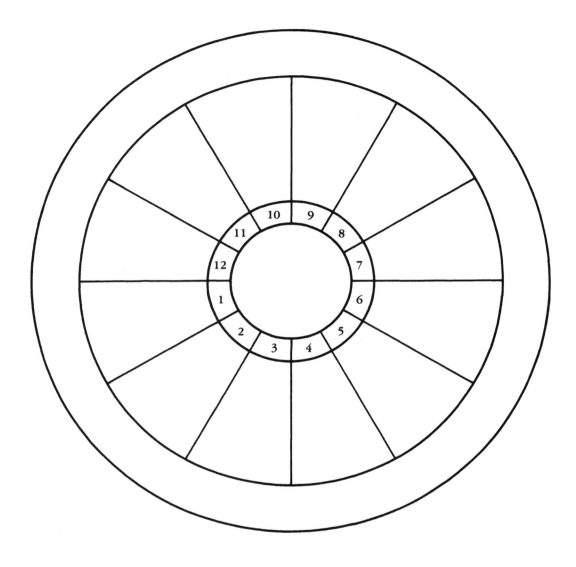

Notes: _____

_____

_____

_____

_____

_____

_____

_____

_____

_____

_____

_____

The Trans-Saturnian Planets:
Ambassadors of the Galaxy

Our waking consciousness is but only a special type of consciousness, whilst all around it, parted from us by the filmiest of screens, there lies forms of consciousness entirely different.

We may go through life without suspecting their existence. But apply the requisite stimulus and at a touch they are there in all their completeness.

William James

The final three planets we are about to consider, Uranus, Neptune and Pluto, are also known as the Trans-Saturnian planets. Until recently, Saturn, the most distant planet to be seen with the naked eye, defined the limits of humanity's spiritual and earthly vision. Then, on March 13, 1781, amateur astronomer William Herschel sighted Uranus. Suddenly, Saturn's limits were shattered and a new vista opened for both astronomy and astrology.

Uranus, Neptune and Pluto are William James' "requisite stimuli" that liberate us from Saturn's finite awareness. Uranus shatters Saturn's limits, Neptune dissolves them, and Pluto transforms them. Because these planets link us to a more transcendent consciousness, astrologer Dane Rudhyar named them "the ambassadors of the galaxy."

These ambassadors are also called the "higher octave" planets because they function at a higher level of vibration than the personal planets. For example, the mentally brilliant and intuitive Uranus functions as the higher octave of Mercury. The universal love of Neptune expresses the higher octave of Venus' personal love. And Pluto transforms the lower passion and desire of Mars. These relationships and correspondences will be explained in greater detail in the coming pages.

The recent discovery of the higher octave planets (Neptune was sighted in 1846, Pluto in 1930) symbolizes the manner in which human evolution has accelerated over the past two centuries. Since Uranus was discovered in 1781, humanity has radically transformed its conception of itself and its relationship to planet Earth. This transformation further accelerated when Pluto entered its own sign of Scorpio in 1984. Over the next two decades, the rapid rate of political, economic and social change will increase even faster.

Aside from affecting global trends, Uranus, Neptune and Pluto play a major role in directing individual development. Their location in the birth chart shows how and where we can experience a more universal awareness.

Because these planets move so slowly, they tend to stay in one sign for many years, and thus affect **generations** of people.

PLANET	ORBIT THROUGH THE ZODIAC	AVERAGE TIME IN EACH SIGN
Uranus	84 years	7 years
Neptune	165 years	14 years
Pluto	248 years	21 years

For example, individuals born between July 1939 through October 1956 all have Pluto in Leo in their birth charts. This generation's destiny was to undergo a transformation (Pluto) in their creative expression (Leo) as we witnessed in the 1960s and 70s. The previous Pluto in Cancer generation (1912–1939) had to face a completely different set of issues—the undermining (Pluto) of their security (Cancer) by the First World War and the Great Depression.

As you interpret the outer planets in your chart, realize that their sign positions will be shared by most people in your generation. Their **house** positions, however, which are determined by the time of day one is born, are different for each person. Thus, while twenty people may be born with Pluto in Leo, each will have Pluto placed in a unique house.

Therefore, pay particular attention to *the houses* in which your outer planets are located. It is in these areas of your life that you will be called to experience a more universal and transcendent reality.

Uranus

The Awakener   **Ruler of Aquarius**   **"I liberate"**

Uranus, planetary ruler of the sign Aquarius, signifies **our unique individuality** and **the capacity to liberate ourselves from past limitations.**

The discovery of Uranus by the astronomer William Herschel on March 13, 1781 came as a complete surprise to both the astronomical and astrological worlds. Since the beginning of time, the planet Saturn had defined the border of the Solar System. Now, miraculously, that boundary was transcended and a new universe opened up.

Astrologers were greatly excited about the discovery of Uranus. Since they had no previous experience of putting the planet in birth charts, they discerned the planet's meaning by observing the events associated with its discovery:

- In 1776, the American Revolution began.
- In 1789, the French Revolution broke out.
- In 1785, the first flight in a hot air balloon enabled us to escape the pull of gravity (ruled by Saturn).
- In 1787, Uranium was discovered.
- In 1800, Herschel discovered infra-red rays and extended our awareness of light beyond the visible spectrum.

Subsequent decades witnessed new scientific discoveries and inventions, the application of electricity, and the advent of the Industrial Revolution.

Based upon the discovery of Uranus and these revolutionary events, astrologers named Uranus "the great awakener." In liberating us from Saturn's limitations, Uranus sweeps away the old and brings in the new.

As the planet of change, Uranus acts in a sudden, electric and often unpredictable manner. As the higher octave or vibration of Mercury, Uranus rules speeded-up thought. While Mercury deduces that A implies B implies C implies D . . . Z, the Uranian mind instantly perceives that A implies Z. Like lightning, Uranian revelations come from out of the blue in sudden flashes and brilliant insights.

Uranus represents the principle of deviation. Not only does it deviate from its mathematically predicted orbit, it also rolls on its belly during rotation. How bizarre! Likewise, Uranian individuals are known for their unorthodox behavior. In deviating from what is "normal" they may become rebels, revolutionaries, eccentrics, geniuses or inventors. One such example is William Herschel, who personified the qualities of the planet he discovered. A true genius, Herschel was a musician by profession and studied mathematics, astronomy and language as "mere hobbies."

Above all, the Uranian individual is a law unto him– or herself, standing alone and apart from the masses. This Uranian **individuality** is beautifully summed up in the words of Henry David Thoreau, a man who lived out the archetype:

> *If a man does not keep pace with his companions, perhaps it is because he hears a different drummer. Let him step to the music which he hears, however measured or far away.*

Though Uranus rebels against Saturn's limits, their natures are by no means incompatible. Without Saturn's realism and prudery, Uranian change becomes chaotic and destructive. When Uranus works with Saturn, change occurs in a meaningful way.

Thus, the innovative painter first learns the laws of perspective (Saturn) and then breaks them (Uranus). The candle spends time hardening in its Saturnian mold before it gains liberation. Uranus' freedom is predicated upon Saturn's discipline; the two are inseparable. As Uranian inventor Thomas Edison put it, "Genius is 1% inspiration (Uranus) and 99% perspiration (Saturn)."

In the birth chart, Uranus indicates how and where we can create meaningful change in our lives. It also shows how and where we can best express our individuality and uniqueness. Its unskillful expressions can lead to blind rebellion, antisocial behavior, fanaticism, or erratic and inconsistent behavior. In these situations, a bit of Saturnian constraint and order can correct the imbalance.

Physiologically, Uranus rules the electrical impulses that travel through the body's nerves. Uranian individuals have highly sensitive nervous systems and are prone to nervous tension and subsequent exhaustion. Illnesses associated with Uranus appear suddenly, unexpectedly and without apparent cause.

Skillful Expression: brilliant, original, inventive, progressive, innovative

Unskillful Expression: erratic, unreliable, rebellious, deviant, antisocial

Uranus Keyphrases
- The awakener, illuminator, liberator, rebel, radical, revolutionary
- My unique, unorthodox, unconventional, eccentric and "genius" self
- My capacity for freedom and independence

1. My planet **Uranus** is in the sign of _____.

   My Uranus sign indicates **how I can best express my uniqueness and originality** which I can do by fulfilling:

   _____.
   (fill in the sign keyphrase from Appendix A)

   When I am using these sign qualities **skillfully**, I tend to express my uniqueness in a

   _____, _____, or _____ manner.
   (choose skillful sign keywords from Appendix A)

   However, when I'm using these sign qualities **unskillfully**, I may be

   _____ or _____.
   (choose unskillful sign keywords from Appendix A)

2. My Uranus sign's element is _____.
   (refer to Figure 1, page 11)

   Using the chart below, circle the response that is paired with this element.

URANUS' ELEMENT	HOW I EXPRESS MY UNIQUENESS	WHERE I NEED TO CHANGE
Fire	Spontaneously, freely	In my creativity
Earth	Tangibly, practically	In my attachment to things
Air	Mentally, verbally	In my thoughts and ideas
Water	Emotionally, mysteriously	In my feelings

3. My Uranus is in the _____ house.
   (refer to Table 2, page 32)

   Therefore, my unconventionality will most likely manifest in these areas of my life:

   _____ and _____.
   (choose house keywords from Appendix B)

─────Journal Entry─────

Using the space below write a few sentences on how you are expressing Uranus' energy in your own life. The following questions may serve to stimulate and activate your thinking about the planet.

In what aspects of my life do I need to experience independence, freedom, and liberation from boundaries and restrictions?

How do I respond to change? Do I welcome or fear it?

How do I express my originality and uniqueness as a person? Do I feel comfortable when I stand out from the crowd?

In what areas of my life am I most unconventional?

_____

_____

_____

_____

_____

_____

Neptune

The Mystic   **Ruler of Pisces**   **"I unify"**

Neptune, planetary ruler of the sign Pisces, symbolizes **the capacity to transcend the finite self through experiencing unity with a greater whole.**

The discovery of Neptune was truly a remarkable event. Years before its sighting, its existence had been hypothesized as the cause of Uranus' inexplicable eccentricity. Subsequently, English astronomer John Adams and the French Urbain Jean Leverrier simultaneously calculated Neptune's position. On the eve of September 23, 1846, Leverrier sighted the new planet in the exact location he had predicted. After a period of confusion about who should gain credit for the discovery, the body was named after Neptune, God of the Sea.

As with Uranus, astrologers looked to world events to provide clues to Neptune's inner meaning:

• In the 1840s, mesmerism and hypnotism came into widespread use.

• In 1844, nitrous oxide became the first anaesthetic to be used in medicine. By the time of Neptune's discovery, ether and chloroform were also in use.

• In 1848, the spiritualist movement was born in the United States and England. A host of mystical movements soon followed: Transcendentalism (1850s), the Bahai Faith (1863), Jehovah's Witnesses (1871), Christian Science (1875) and Theosophy (1871).

• In 1848, Marx and Engels published *The Communist Manifesto*, a doctrine of political and social idealism.

Thus, like Uranus, Neptune's discovery reflected humanity's entrance into new dimensions of reality. Instead of **shattering** Saturn's limits, however, Neptune, the cosmic solvent, dissolves Saturn's limitations in its oceanic waters. As the falling raindrop unites with the sea, so Neptune seeks to lose itself by merging with a greater whole. This inner longing, so difficult to achieve on the physical plane, is most often sought through an artistic or spiritual experience that momentarily allows the Neptunian individual to transcend his or her earthly bondage. Hence, Neptune represents the higher octave or more subtle expression of the planet Venus. If Venus symbolizes personal love, Neptune symbolizes universal love and beauty; while Venus harmonizes with another person, Neptune symphonizes with the cosmos.

Such experiences may also produce inspirational works of poetry, art and music such as the choral masterpiece *The Messiah* which was written in a reverie by the Piscean composer Handel.

The glyph of Neptune resembles the Greek letter psi Ψ, now used as the logo for the field of parapsychology. Like the psychic, the Neptunian individual is supremely sensitive to the supersensible worlds. He or she is the tuning fork, the clear channel, the perfect receptor, who can receive information from other planes of consciousness. Thus, many clairvoyants and mediums contain Neptune prominently in their birth charts. One such example is Edgar Cayce, the Sleeping Prophet, born with the Sun, Mercury, Venus and Saturn in Neptune's sign Pisces.

Having such extreme sensitivity, the impressionable Neptunian soul can easily go astray. Like a psychic sponge, he or she identifies with every passing thought or feeling. Such bombardment clouds the vision and hampers the powers of discrimination. As the line separating reality from illusion grows more nebulous, the Neptunian person is often shrouded in a fog of chaos and unreality. What is the antidote for this confusion? It lies with our old friend Saturn who represents the "reality principle." Thus, Saturn's grounding and stabilizing vibrations can bring the lost Neptunian soul "down to earth" and turn him or her into the practical dreamer.

In the birth chart, Neptune depicts how and where we seek to express our highest ideals so that we can make the world a more loving and beautiful place.

Physiologically, Neptune is associated with the pineal gland, also known as the "third eye." According to spiritual teachings, the opening of this center gives one access to psychic and clairvoyant abilities.

Diseases of Neptune are often of a mysterious nature. At times, they are caused by phobias or vague fears of the unknown. Psychotic disturbances where the individual "loses touch with reality" and various forms of drug addiction are also linked to the misapplication of the Neptunian vibration.

Skillful Expression: idealistic, intuitive, psychic, inspirational, healing

Unskillful Expression: confused, escapist, hypersensitive, deluded, ungrounded

Neptune Keyphrases
* My need to transcend my finite self and merge with a greater whole
* My intuitive, impressionable, psychic, telepathic self
* The part of me that is a dreamer, visionary, utopian, healer, artist, savior or martyr

1. My planet **Neptune** is in the sign of _____.

   In the birth chart, my Neptune sign indicates **how I formulate my dreams and ideals.** Thus, I can best express my idealism and mystical yearnings by fulfilling:

   _____.
   (fill in the sign keyphrase from Appendix A)
   When I'm using these sign qualities **skillfully**, I tend to be_____,

   _____, or _____.
   (choose skillful sign keywords from Appendix A)
   However, when I'm using these sign qualities **unskillfully**, I may be

   _____ or _____.
   (choose unskillful sign keywords from Appendix A)

2. My Neptune sign's element is _____.
   (refer to Figure 1, page 11)
   Using the chart below, circle the response that is paired with this element.

NEPTUNE'S ELEMENT	HOW I EXPRESS MY IDEALS AND DREAMS
Fire	Through inspiration and ecstacy
Earth	Through applying them in a concrete manner
Air	Through communicating them to others
Water	Through empathy and compassion towards suffering

3. My Neptune is in the _____ house.
   (refer to Table 2, page 32)
   Therefore, my need to merge with a greater whole and experience transcendence is best expressed in these areas of my life: _____

   and _____.
   (choose house keywords from Appendix B)

————Journal Entry————

Using the space below write a few sentences on how you are expressing Neptune's energy in your own life. The following questions may serve to stimulate and activate your thinking about the planet.

How do I define my dreams and highest spiritual ideals? How am I going about making my dreams come true?

How and where can I best fulfill my need to feel a part of a greater whole?

In what situations do I feel confused, chaotic and uncertain? When I am confused, how do I restore clarity and order to the situation?

Do situations come up where I feel like a victim or martyr? If so, how can I empower myself and take charge of my experience?

_____

_____

_____

_____

_____

Pluto

Pluto, planetary ruler of the sign Scorpio, symbolizes **the capacity for self-transformation and self-renewal.**

The existence of Pluto was first suspected when astronomers noticed a slight gravitational pull affecting the orbit of Neptune. The research of astronomer Percival Lowell led to its eventual sighting on February 18, 1930. The official discovery was announced on March 13, Lowell's 75th birthday and the 149th anniversary of the discovery of Uranus.

Though Lowell had named the newcomer "planet X," scientists at his observatory requested suggestions for a new name. The first letter received was sent by an eleven year old English girl who proposed the name Pluto. It was immediately accepted.

Pluto was first sighted as it passed through the sign of Cancer, symbol of our basic security needs. Astrologers soon correlated its appearance with the following events:

• In 1914 as Pluto entered Cancer, World War I began, forever destroying the old social and political order of the 19th century.

• In 1929 a global depression destroyed the economic security of millions and forever altered the international economic system.

• During the 1930s, the birth of modern depth psychology plunged humanity into the investigation of the unconscious mind. This was also the era of gangsters and racketeering.

• When Pluto entered Leo in 1939, Fascism spread throughout Europe as dictators sought to control and manipulate the masses.

• In August 1945, the detonation of the first atomic bomb initiated the Nuclear Age.

From the above events which reveal the destructive properties of Pluto, we can understand why many astrologers first viewed the planet in an adverse light. Pluto, however, clearly possesses a redeeming side. To understand the workings of Pluto, imagine that its glyph symbolizes a flower encapsulating its seed. Before the seed can produce new life, it must first fall to the ground and die. Next, it lies buried in the soil, hidden from the light of day. In that state it undergoes a mysterious transmutation. With the passage of time, a new seedling pokes its head through the soil; a new plant has been born.

Thus, while Uranus shatters form in a flash of lightning and Neptune slowly dissolves it, Pluto penetrates to the core of an object and permanently transforms it. Metaphors for this process include the metamorphosis of the caterpillar into a butterfly, the death and resurrection of Christ, and the alchemical transmutation of lead into gold.

From the above examples, we can see that the Plutonian process is irreversible. The butterfly cannot return to being a caterpillar; similarly the person who undergoes a Plutonian experience emerges as a fundamentally different person. He or she will *never* be the same again.

In penetrating nature's innermost secrets, Pluto uncovers her creative and destructive forces. Thus, depending on his or her *level of evolution*, the Plutonian individual may become the black magician or the spiritual healer, the dictator or the religious saint. Pluto's darker side has manifested through the Mafia, Hell's Angels, the "family" of Charles Manson, himself a Scorpio, the use of torture, the manipulation of the masses through propaganda, and Plutonium 235. The latter, a byproduct of nuclear power, has a half life of 225,000 years and is one of the most toxic substances on Earth.

As for its positive applications, Pluto governs the regenerative force which manifests in physical and psychological healings. In the healing process, the patient first brings up and eliminates all toxins from his or her system, be they physical, emotional or mental. Then, the healing power of nature takes over. Those born with Pluto prominent in their charts possess an intuitive knowledge of this process which they often use to heal themselves, and then others.

In the birth chart, Pluto indicates how and where one may undergo transformative experiences. Unskillful expressions of Pluto's energy occur when the process focuses solely on the destructive part of the death–rebirth process. Yet, when the transformative process is allowed to fulfill itself, then the soul's dark night is a necessary prelude to the dawning of a glorious rebirth.

Physiologically, Pluto governs the process of catabolism and anabolism, the continual death and rebirth of bodily cells. Through this process, we receive a new set of skin cells every 24 hours, a new blood stream every 120 days, and a completely new body every 7 years.

Pluto's regenerative influence also manifests through the sexual union. While Mars rules sexual desire, Pluto (the higher vibration of Mars) governs the orgasm and the subsequent conception that creates new life!

Diseases of Pluto occur through autointoxication, the poisoning of the body through the slow build up of physical toxins (radiation, carcinogens, etc.) or psychological ones (e.g., hatred and resentment). The dis-ease of cancer seems to be particularly related to Pluto. Pluto also rules genetic mutations which by altering the DNA code can permanently transform the make up of the species.

Skillful Expression: transforming, renewing, regenerating, healing

Unskillful Expression: destructive, manipulative, controlling, vindictive

---

I Interpret Pluto in My Birth Chart

Pluto Keyphrases
- My experience of both death and rebirth, destruction and renewal
- Whatever is unseen, invisible, hidden, subterranean
- My need to bring what is buried and hidden up into the light of day

1. My planet **Pluto** is in the sign of _____.

   In the birth chart, my Pluto sign shows **how I undergo transformation and renewal.** Thus, my capacity to transform and renew myself will express itself through:

   _____.
   (fill in the sign keyphrase from Appendix A)
   When I'm using these sign qualities **skillfully**, I tend to be

   _____, _____, or _____.
   (choose skillful sign keywords from Appendix A)
   However, when I'm using these sign qualities **unskillfully**, I may be

   _____ or _____.
   (choose unskillful sign keywords from Appendix A)

2. My Pluto sign's element is _____.
   (refer to Figure 1, page 11)
   Using the chart below, circle the response that is paired with this element.

PLUTO'S ELEMENT	HOW I TRANSFORM MYSELF AND OTHERS
Fire	Through my creative self-expression
Earth	Through my work and accomplishments
Air	Through my ideas and communications
Water	Through my emotions and feelings

3. My Pluto is in the _____ house.
   (refer to Table 2, page 32)
   Therefore, the areas of my life in which I experience the greatest change and transformation are:

   _____ and _____.
   (choose house keywords from Appendix B)

Journal Entry

Using the space below write a few sentences on how you are expressing Pluto's energy in your own life. The following questions may serve to stimulate and activate your thinking about the planet.

In what areas of my life have I undergone a complete "death and rebirth" experience? What has been destroyed? What was reborn? Do I feel permanently changed by the experiences?

How do I experience the need to let go of old and outmoded aspects of my life? When I am asked to let go, do I accept the process or hold on tightly?

In what areas do I wish to penetrate and probe below the surface and get to the core of the matter?

_____

_____

_____

_____

_____

_____

_____

_____

_____

_____

_____

_____

The Asteroids and Chiron

Thousands of starlike bodies known as the asteroids orbit in our Solar System between Mars and Jupiter. Although Bode's Law in 1792 predicted the existence of a planet in this gap, the first of these bodies was not discovered until 1801. On New Years Day, the Italian astronomer Father Guissepe Piazzi spotted a new planet which he named Ceres after the guardian divinity of his native Sicily. The next few years saw the discovery of many other new asteroids including Pallas, Juno and Vesta. Chiron, traveling between Saturn and Uranus, was sighted in 1977 by Charles Kowal.

As new bodies are recognized in space, their archetypal principles are awakened in the human psyche. Since the discovery and use of the asteroids, many aspects of our culture and thinking have undergone rapid change. Like the outer planets Uranus, Neptune and Pluto, the themes of the asteroids can provide a context in which to understand how and why these changes are taking place.

The first four asteroids, named after four great goddesses of antiquity, heralded the activation of feminine consciousness in both men and women. The publication of the first asteroid goddess ephemeris in 1973 mirrored the emergence of a women's movement. Previous to this time the only significators of the feminine in traditional astrology were the Moon and Venus; and the only socially acceptable roles for women were Moon as mother and Venus as mate. As new feminine archetypes Ceres, Pallas, Vesta and Juno became available in astrological symbology, new aspects of feminine expression fully entered into the consciousness of humanity. Consequently, society saw the widespread entrance of women into the fields of politics, the arts, education, sports and other professions. It also marked a time of the rediscovery of women's history and the revival of the Goddess in women's spirituality.

Men also participated in this change by starting to acknowledge their intuitive and feeling selves. Rejecting the macho and breadwinner stereotypes, they became involved in the birthing and raising of their children, and entered into traditional women's careers such as nurses, house husbands, and secretaries. The homosexual movement was another forefront of men's liberation where the expression of the feminine polarity surfaced in many men.

Finally, on a level that goes beyond male and female, the upsurge of the feminine has become the foundation of the general consciousness expansion movement. During the last decade we have witnessed an emergence of right-brain feminine polarity functions in the disciplines of holistic health, education, therapy, and increased psychic awareness.

When placed in the birth chart, the asteroids and Chiron provide a depth and fine tuning that is simply not available through using the traditional ten planets. Situated between Mars and Jupiter, the asteroids function as the transformers between the energy systems of the lower and higher octave planets. The asteroids directly correspond to the psychological issues and transformative crises that men and women are now experiencing on a mass level due to the current activation of these new archetypal principles.

Chiron

The Centaur   **Associated with the sign Sagittarius**

Chiron, the **Centaur**, represents the principle of **holistic knowledge.**

Chiron, an enigmatic messenger to our Solar System, was discovered in 1977 in an orbit between Saturn and Uranus. Astronomers theorize that Chiron was not always part of our Solar System, and at some point in the future will return to his origins in the galaxy. While the asteroids function as transformers between the inner personal planets and the outer social-collective planets, Chiron acts as a bridge between our collective mind and the galactic dimensions. Chiron is our link to communicating with intelligences outside of our conscious reality and planetary system.

Mythologically Chiron was a centaur—half man, half horse associated with shamanic legends of shape-shifters. He came from the nature kingdom of elemental spirits to the human kingdom to give humanity teachings in healing and education. He taught how to communicate to our bodies on the cellular level and to the nature realms in order to extract healing cures from our dreams and from herbs, trees, precious stones and metals, and animal symbols. Chiron's current influence in contemporary society can be seen in the revival of shamanistic lore, and the introduction of holistic health and education techniques that are revolutionizing modern medicine.

Chiron is also the Wounded Healer, and speaks to healing the wounded parts of ourselves. This process enables us to assist others through their healing crises. In empathizing with the pain of others, Chiron deepens our spiritual understanding of the laws of nature.

In *The Mythic Tarot*, Liz Greene associates Chiron with the Hierophant Key as the inner spiritual teacher. One of the keynotes of the coming Aquarian Age is for humanity to cease relying upon the authority of the external teacher and to discover the voice of the inner teacher. Situated in the Solar System between Saturn, the outer teacher of the establishment, and Uranus, the voice of intuition, Chiron is present whenever we undergo a spiritual crisis where our inner intuition urges us to question orthodox dogma.

In order to relieve Chiron's agony from his incurable wound from a poisoned arrow, Jupiter released him from his human immortality. He returned Chiron to his galactic origins by transforming him into the constellation of Sagittarius—half horse, half man. In the constellation, Chiron aims an arrow into the sky which points to 27½ degrees of Sagittarius—the galactic center of the universe. Chiron's activation in our psyche at this time is to prepare humanity for contact with orders of intelligence beyond the human realms. His message is that through the nature kingdom we can find a key that will enable us to communicate beyond our current three dimensional reality.

In chart analysis Chiron is an indicator of holistic perceptions in healing and education. The Chiron personality is wise, grounded in practical reality, and challenges established and limited views. The unskillful expressions of Chiron can manifest as narrow and fragmented understanding, reliance upon dogma and authority, and self-doubt or spiritual unrest.

Skillful Expression: healing, teaching, knowing, holistic

Unskillful Expression: scattered, diffused, ungrounded

I Interpret Chiron in My Birth Chart

Chiron Keyphrases

- Bridge or link between the known and unknown
- Healing and wholemaking, holistic health, integrating mind and body, intuition and instinct
- The maverick, an independent who does not conform to any group or dogma
- Personal questing, the wounded healer, the inner or outer teacher

1. My planetoid **Chiron** is in the sign of _____.

   In the birth chart, my Chiron sign indicates **how I express my educational and healing instincts.** Thus, I can best realize my capacity for holistic knowledge by fulfilling:

   _____
   (fill in the sign keyphrase from Appendix A)
   When I'm using these sign qualities **skillfully,** I tend to express my holistic knowledge
   in a _____ , _____ ,

   and _____ manner.
   (choose skillful sign keywords from Appendix A)
   However, when I'm using these sign qualities **unskillfully,** I may express my knowl-

   edge in a _____ and _____ manner.
   (choose unskillful sign keywords from Appendix A)

2. My Chiron sign's element is _____.
   (refer to Figure 1, page 11)
   Using the chart below, circle the response that is paired with this element.

CHIRON'S ELEMENT	HOW I TEACH AND HEAL
Fire	Through inspiring with visions; energy healing
Earth	Through developing practical and useful techniques; physical healing
Air	Through communicating higher ideas; mental healing
Water	Through nurturing; emotional healing and taking on others' suffering

3. My Chiron is in the _____ house.
   (refer to Table 2, page 32)
   Therefore, my educational and healing abilities will most likely manifest in these areas
   of my life: _____ and _____ .
   (choose house keywords from Appendix B)

Journal Entry

Using the space below write a few sentences on how you are expressing Chiron's energy in your own life. The following questions may serve to stimulate and activate your thinking about the planetoid.

How have I been wounded? What aspects of myself need healing?

How can I best teach others to heal themselves? To what extent do I listen to my "teacher within?"

_____

_____

_____

_____

_____

Ceres

The Great Mother   **Associated with the Signs Cancer, Virgo, and Taurus**

Ceres, The Great Mother and Goddess of Agriculture, represents **our capactiy to unconditionally love and nurture ourselves and others** as the basis for self-worth and acceptance of others. She uses the feminine creative energy to birth and sustain new life forms.

The asteroid goddess Ceres, Great Mother of ancient cultures, presides over the fertility of the Earth and the procreation of her peoples. In her relationship as mother, Ceres represents the principle of the unconditional love that nourishes and sustains life. She symbolizes both the need to care for others and ourselves, as well as the consequences of neglecting what we have given life. Because of Ceres excessive attachment to her daughter that led to Persephone's abduction, this asteroid points to our experiences of repreated loss until we learn the lessons of sharing and the need to let go.

A number of contemporary psychological and societal issues are associated with the entrance of Ceres into our awareness. To begin with, the rise of the number of single parent families, mostly headed by mothers, is rapidly becoming the class of the new poor. Both men and women are coping with the problems of child custody, child support payments, visitation rights, integrating stepparents and stepchildren into already existing families, working mothers' needs for suitable daycare facilities, and birth control. Here Ceres is being felt as a need to secure a source of unconditional love in today's world of fragmenting family structures where children and parents experience separation and loss from one another.

Associated with the element of **Earth,** the Suit of Pentacles and the Empress Key in the Tarot, Ceres symbolizes getting into our bodies. In today's world many individuals are obsessed with a need for nurturing themselves in the face of insecure feelings over body-image and self-esteem. Our relationship with our mother involves deep feelings of self-love and self-hate and can result in such extreme eating disorders as anexoria and bulemia which are currently a source of deep anguish for many individuals. The belief that we have to starve ourselves in order to be beautiful insidiously undermines the self-esteem of many women to whom compulsive dieting has become a way of life. The rumbling of the asteroid goddess Ceres in the psyche is bringing to light the causes and cures for these painful experiences.

Ceres is a significator of the responsibilities between parents and children. Incubating in the culture of M-TV children are becoming sexually active at much earlier ages. The soaring rate of teen pregnancies, as well as massive disclosures about child incest and molestation are causing many parents to question the quality of protection and guidance they have given their children. On the other end of the spectrum, the plight of our elderly parents facing increased lifespan and decreased societal function has raised many emotional issues in their children concerning parental obligation and guilt.

As Earth Goddess, Ceres is evidenced in the growing concern by environmentalists for the preservation of the Earth's natural resources and wildlife. Many individuals are joining forces in protesting the contamination of her soil, water and atmosphere, and the destruction of forests. These encroaching deserts prevent agricultural production and contribute to worldwide starvation and famine.

As humanity unfolds in this next cycle of evolution, Ceres tells us to share—to share our children, our food, our resources, our loved ones. There is more than enough for everyone, and then some, when we transform our grasping into generosity. Ceres also speaks to formulating personal and global policies that encourage, support and sustain the fertile Earth and her inhabitants.

Astrologically, Ceres points to how we face the issues of self-esteem, the relationship to our parents and children, food, dependency, attachment, loss, separation, mother complexes, rejection, grief, sharing, work and productivity.

In the birth chart, Ceres describes how and where we experience the need to nurture and be nurtured.

Skillful Expression: nurturing, providing, productive, sharing, fertile

Unskillful Expression: overprotective, overattached, compulsive, deprived, self-rejecting

Ceres Keyphrases
- Giving and receiving of nurturance; providing and caring for others
- Unconditional self-love and self-regard
- Family relationships, nurturing others through food, nutrition, cultivation of the land

1. My asteroid **Ceres** is in the sign of _____.

   In the birth chart, my Ceres sign indicates **how I give and receive nurturance** and develop self-worth. Thus, my capacity to fully love and nurture myself *and* others can best be expressed by fulfilling:

   _____.
   (fill in the sign keyphrase from Appendix A)
   When I'm using these sign qualities **skillfully,** I tend to **nurture** in a

   _____, _____, or _____ manner.
   (choose skillful sign keywords from Appendix A)
   However, when I'm using these sign qualities **unskillfully,** I may **nurture** in a

   _____ or _____ manner.
   (choose unskillful sign keywords from Appendix A)

2. My Ceres sign's element is _____.
   (refer to Figure 1, page 11)
   Using the chart below, circle the response that is paired with this element.

CERES' ELEMENT	WHAT NURTURES ME (AND HOW I NURTURE)
Fire	Praise and encouragement
Earth	Stability and structure
Air	Relating and communicating
Water	Sympathy and understanding

3. My Ceres is in the _____ house.
   (refer to Table 2, page 32)
   Therefore, my nurturing function can best be expressed in these areas of my life:

   _____ and _____.
   (choose house keywords from Appendix B)

Journal Entry

Using the space below write a few sentences on how you are expressing Ceres' energy in your own life. The following questions may serve to stimulate and activate your thinking about the asteroid.

How do I express my capacity to nurture and be productive?

How do I feel about my self-worth, especially the issues that are connected to food and love dependencies as they contribute to my self-image?

What instructive behavior patterns influence my family relationships—as a child to my parents and as a parent to my children?

How does my overattachment and insecurity make it more difficult for me to experience loss and rejection?

_____

_____

_____

_____

_____

_____

_____

Pallas

The Warrior Queen   **Associated with the Signs Leo, Libra and Aquarius**

Pallas Athene, The Warrior Queen and Goddess of Wisdom, represents **one's capacity for creative wisdom and original perceptions.** Pallas utilizes the feminine creative energy to give birth to ideas.

As Pallas Athene sprang from the head of her father Jupiter, she represents the capacity to give birth to our ideas. The proliferation of teachings on creative visualization, the power to create our own reality, and personal responsibility for the conditions of our lives are some of the manifestations of Pallas awakening in our psyche.

Associated with the element air, the Suit of Swords and the Justice Key in the Tarot, and the yellow ray of intellect, she symbolizes getting into our heads. As the prototype of the artistically creative and intelligent woman, Pallas mirrors our desire to strive for excellence in a chosen field of creative expression. Mythologically Pallas was made to deny her femininity in order to exercise her wisdom, courage and creative abilities. The artificial separation between being intelligent and being a ''real woman'' lies at the root of the modern day conflict women feel in choosing between career goals and relationship needs. As women writers put it, we are being forced to choose between books (Pallas) and babies (Ceres).

As Ceres signifies the mother-child relationship, Pallas was the goddess who sacrificed her connection to the mother in order to initiate women into the rites of the father-daughter relationship. Many of the psychological complexes described in the bestselling book *The Wounded Woman: Healing the Father-Daughter Relationship* are mirrored in the unfoldment of the Pallas archetype in the human psyche.

Pallas themes also activate uncertainties over our sexual identity. This asteroid goddess points to the balancing of male-female polarities within oneself and the movement towards an androgenous orientation. She suggests a path of transformation whereby we can utilize and release the thrust of our sexual energy into formulating visions and realizing accomplishments.

In mythology, Pallas Athene's wisdom ray of creative intelligence expressed itself in three primary areas of human activity—the **arts, healing** and **political activism.**

In Classical Greece, Pallas served as patroness of artisans and craftspeople. She also taught the practical arts and crafts that enabled humanity to develop a more civilized culture.

In her healing work, Pallas participated in work associated with Hygeia, Goddess of Miraculous Healing. In the birth chart, Pallas gravitates to working with holistic health techniques that integrate whole patterns of the psyche. She also governs all mental healing techniques—visualization, meditation, affirmation, guided imagery and hypnosis.

As warrior queen, Pallas played the role of the protectress who defended people and the state in times of war. Astrologically, then, Pallas symbolizes a femininely defined quality of heroism, bravery, courage and sensible toughness. In the birth chart, she can describe the political activist, feminist, or champion of oppressed minorities.

As humanity approaches a quantum leap in consciousness, Pallas Athene brings us a new awareness of how we perceive reality. She speaks to taking responsibility for our actions and illumines our faculties of clear thought, impartial judgment, and courage to stand behind our ethical principles. Most of all, she urges us to recognize that intelligence can arise from a feminine, as well as masculine source. This understanding enables us to reconcile the unnecessary separation between our love nature and our mental-creative wisdom.

Astrologically, Pallas themes point to how we face the issues of learning, creativity, realization, accomplishment, sublimating sexual energy into creative outlets, alienation from relationships, father complexes, competition, and the fruits or fears of success.

In the birth chart Pallas describes how and where our **mental-creative** urges are expressed.

Skillful Expression: intelligent, creative, original, resourceful

Unskillful Expression: fearing success, calculating, austere, expedient

Pallas Keyphrases
- Intelligence, wisdom, whole pattern perception, healing
- Social concern, political involvements, women's liberation, diplomacy
- The need to integrate the mental and the nurturing sides of ourselves

1. My asteroid **Pallas** is in the sign of _____.

   In the birth chart, my Pallas sign describes **how I express my capacity for creative intelligence and original perceptions.** This can best be done by fulfilling:

   _____.
   (fill in the sign keyphrase from Appendix A)
   When I'm using these sign qualities **skillfully**, my **perceptions** may be

   _____, _____, or _____.
   (choose skillful sign keywords from Appendix A)
   However, when I'm using these sign qualities **unskillfully**, my **perceptions** may be

   _____ or _____.
   (choose unskillful sign keywords from Appendix A)

2. My Pallas sign's element is _____.
   (refer to Figure 1, page 11)
   Using the chart below, circle the response that is paired with this element.

PALLAS' ELEMENT	HOW I EXPRESS MY CREATIVE INTELLIGENCE
Fire	By becoming inspired and formulating visions
Earth	By creating new forms and structures
Air	By developing new ideas and theories
Water	By becoming psychic and intuitive

3. My Pallas is in the _____ house.
   (refer to Table 2, page 32)
   Therefore, my creative intelligence and original perceptions can best be expressed

   in these areas of my life: _____ and

   _____.
   (choose house keywords from Appendix B)

——————Journal Entry——————

Using the space below write a few sentences on how you are expressing Pallas' energy in your own life. The following questions may serve to stimulate and activate your thinking about the asteroid.

How do I express my creative wisdom? Do I feel any sense of control or responsibility for my reality?

What factors have influenced my relationship to my father and my mental self-esteem?

Do I experience a lack of distinction between the male-female differences within myself which manifests as an androgenous orientation?

How do I respond to the social conditioning that intelligence is not a desirable quality in women?

_____

_____

_____

_____

_____

_____

Vesta

Vesta, Priestess of the Flame and Goddess of the Vestal Virgins, represents **our capacity to integrate and focus our energies, and experience wholeness of self.** Vesta utilizes the feminine creative energy for personal regeneration and dedication to specific goals and aspirations.

Vesta, Virgin guardian of the sacred flame, represents the fire of spirit. She holds the teachings of "renewing our virginity," becoming **whole** within ourselves, and tells of a path of inner transformation whereby we can cleanse, repair, and revitalize our bodies and reintegrate our emotions with our minds. Thus the activation of Vesta in our consciousness corresponds with the increase of psychological and physical healing therapies.

Vesta is associated with the element of fire, and with the Suit of Wands, High Priestess and Hermit Keys in the Tarot. In pre-Hellenic times Vesta was associated with unmarried temple priestesses, who acted as channels for the descent of the Moon Goddesses during sacred sexual rites. By Roman times Vesta evolved into the chaste Vestal Virgins who foreswore their sexuality for spiritual commitment. Thus, Vesta can point to a sublimation of the outer-directed sexual force into self-renewal and the pursuit of personal and spiritual aspirations. At the same time, her disassociation of sexuality from spirituality lies at the root of our difficulties and fears in sexual expression.

Because of a current morality that promotes a madonna-whore distinction, confusion arises between the extremes of sexual denial and sexual freedom. Vesta is connected to the recent sexual liberation revolution, as well as its backlash seen in the spread of sexual diseases which are leading to increased fear and alienation from intimate interactions. Her emergence corresponds to the moral health issues that surround the sexual interactions of single people.

Vesta speaks of deepening the relationship with our own soul and spirit. Her themes encompass our search for deeper meaning in the midst of unsatisfying traditional religious creeds. Consequently she corresponds to the recent growth of the psychic arts and occult sciences, Goddess worship and widespread dissemination of ancient spiritual paths. Vesta governs spiritual disciplines which refine our psychic and telepathic channels, and physical disciplines which purify the temples of our bodies.

Vesta was revered as eldest sister and presided over the communities of sisterhoods and brotherhoods. Her presence corresponds to the development of various support groups in contemporary society including meditation groups, men and women's consciousness groups, ritual circles, psychological group therapy, Alcoholics Anonymous and Weight Watchers.

Vesta stands holding a lamp of the eternal flame lighting the path as humanity hurls into a new age. She assists us in focusing our energies as we commit ourselves to inner work on integrating the power of ourselves, and outwardly dedicating this power to fulfilling a vision. For those who live alone by choice or necessity, she is the recognition that "alone" can be a precious friend and ally. Vesta points to perfecting the self as preparation for participation in the group mind.

Astrologically Vesta indicates how we face the issues of personal integration, work, devotion, spiritual practice, commitment, sacrifice, aloneness, solitude, alienation from personal relationships, and a range of sexual complexes based on denial and fear of intimacy.

In the birth chart Vesta describes our style of self-identification, focus and devotion, and where we are able to commit ourselves to work for a worthy goal.

Skillful Expression: focused, integrated, self-identified, committed, sacred

Unskillful Expression: sexually alienated, inhibited, overworked, repressed, narrow-minded

I Interpret Vesta in My Birth Chart

Vesta Keyphrases
- The capacity for personal integration through a variety of disciplines
- Sexual liberation, sexual fears, guilt and inadequacies
- Spiritual devotion, channeling of the kundalini energy

1. My asteroid **Vesta** is in the sign of _____.

   In the birth chart, my Vesta sign symbolizes **how I commit myself to a work or ideal.** Thus, my capacity to integrate and focus my energies can best be met by

   fulfilling: _____.
   (fill in the sign keyphrase from Appendix A)
   When I am using these sign qualities **skillfully**, I tend to **focus myself** in a

   _____, _____, or _____.
   (choose skillful sign keywords from Appendix A)
   However, when I'm using these sign qualities **unskillfully**, my **focus** may be

   _____ or _____.
   (choose unskillful sign keywords from Appendix A)

2. My Vesta sign's element is _____.
   (refer to Figure 1, page 11)
   Using the chart below, circle the response that is paired with this element.

VESTA'S ELEMENT	HOW I INTEGRATE AND FOCUS MYSELF
Fire	Through becoming inspired to create
Earth	Through developing a physical discipline
Air	Through learning and sharing ideas
Water	Through merging and bonding

3. My Vesta is in the _____ house.
   (refer to Table 2, page 32)
   Therefore, my desire to dedicate and commit myself to a worthy goal can best be

   expressed in these areas of my life: _____

   and _____.
   (choose house keywords from Appendix B)

Journal Entry

Using the space below write a few sentences on how you are expressing Vesta's energy in your own life. The following questions may serve to stimulate and activate your thinking about the asteroid.

What spiritual path or discipline can I utilize to facilitate the overall integration of my physical, mental, and emotional bodies?

In what ways do I pull back my energy from others in order to focus on my own visions and needs? How do I "renew my virginity," that is, replenish my vital force?

How is my sexual expression influenced by social moral values? Do I fear and repress my openness to intimacy and sexuality? Or, do I resist the confinement of monogamous relationships?

_____
_____
_____
_____
_____

Juno

The Divine Consort **Associated with the Signs of Libra and Scorpio**

Juno, The Divine Consort and Goddess of Marriage, **represents our capacity for meaningful relationships.** She utilizes the feminine creative energy to foster relationships and develop awareness and sensitivity to others.

Juno, known to the ancient Greeks as the goddess Hera of the moon phases and woman's cycles, married Jupiter, King of the Heavens and initiated women into the rites of marriage. She symbolizes the movement away from the self-containment of Vesta and towards the consummation of union with the other. Her activation in the psyche is causing a revolution in the traditional forms of marriage.

Individuals experience her pressure in their lives as the inability to participate in the old and outmoded relationship roles. High divorce rates point to our dissatisfaction with what these roles have produced. The high frequency of remarriage, nevertheless, tells us that most people continue to desire intimacy within committed relationships. Juno is telling us not to end our relationships, but to reframe them. This redefining of the relationships is evidenced by the growing number of persons living together without the sanctification of legal marriage, as well as the coming out of lesbian and gay couples.

Associated with the element of water and the Suit of Cups in the Tarot, Juno opens us up to the world of emotions within our primary relationships. While Venus is the key to what turns us on and what we are magnetically drawn to, Juno tells us what we need in the day–to–day and year–to–year interactions of constancy with another person. When these needs for intimacy and depth are thwarted or denied, Juno rages and grieves over the failure of the prince and princess to live happily ever after, as she did in her marriage with Jupiter.

When in this state, Juno must choose between continuing the relationship, even if all her ideals are not realized, and ending a form that has become hollow and meaningless. The decision she makes must depend on the individual circumstances of the relationship.

As Triple Moon Goddess, Juno ruled over the entire female reproductive cycle and used the menstrual cycle to measure the orderly passage of time. Her presence can be seen in the educational networks assisting women in reclaiming power in the health care of their bodies. The ideas in the bestselling book *Our Bodies, Our Selves* which elucidates issues such as sexuality, fertility, childbearing, and menopause have become the seed ground for the widespread formation of many women's health collectives.

As classical Juno found herself, via marriage, stripped of her powers, she acts as a universal symbol for the classes of powerless individuals. Modern Juno can be seen in social, economic and political reforms for abused women and children, victims' rights, the plight of displaced homemakers, minorities and the disabled.

Realizing that the old marriage roles cannot contain fulfilling relationships, Juno urges the creation of new forms for partnership. She points us to a path of transforming the inner bride and bridegroom so that honesty, intimacy and depth can be realized in conscious unions. She knows that the general state of warfare that exists on a collective political level is related to individual warfare within relationships. And so beyond personal happiness, but for planetary well-being, Juno symbolizes the urgency to regenerate the images and attitudes which govern interactions between masculine and feminine.

Astrologically, Juno points to how we face the issues of compatibility, relationship commitments, receptivity to others, mutual sharing and trust, jealousy, possessiveness, and power struggles.

In the birth chart Juno describes how and where we experience our needs for relationship and intimacy.

Skillful Expression: sharing, supportive, faithful, intimate, equal, refined

Unskillful Expression: jealous, possessive, vindictive, victimized, unequal

Juno Keyphrases
- The capacity for committed and equal relationship
- The possibility for inequality, power struggles, possessiveness, etc.
- The powerless—minorities, the elderly, abused children, battered wives, etc.

1. My asteroid **Juno** is in the sign of _____.

   In the birth chart, my Juno sign shows **how I express my capacity for meaningful relationships.** This can be done by fulfilling:

   _____.
   (fill in the sign keyphrase from Appendix A)
   When I am using these sign qualities **skillfully**, I may **relate** to a partner who is

   _____, _____, or _____.
   (choose skillful sign keywords from Appendix A)
   However, when I'm using these sign qualities **unskillfully**, I may **relate** to a partner who is _____ or _____.
   (choose unskillful sign keywords from Appendix A)

2. My Juno sign's element is _____.
   (refer to Figure 1, page 11)
   Using the chart below, circle the response that is paired with this element.

JUNO'S ELEMENT	WHAT I NEED IN AN INTIMATE, COMMITTED RELATIONSHIP
Fire	Shared visions, independence, passion
Earth	Stability, consistency, sensuality, comfort
Air	A meeting of the minds, verbal exchange
Water	Emotional rapport and support, understanding

3. My Juno is in the _____ house.
   (refer to Table 2, page 32)
   Therefore, my relationship needs can best be expressed and met in these areas of

   my life: _____ and _____.
   (choose house keywords from Appendix B)

Journal Entry

Using the space below write a few sentences on how you are expressing Juno's energy in your own life. The following questions may serve to stimulate and activate your thinking about the asteroid.

What are my needs for intimate and meaningful commitment in my ongoing relationships? What kinds of neurotic responses erupt when these needs are thwarted or denied?

What situations produce the most stress in my relationship interactions?

To what extent do I draw partners to me who reflect back to me an unexpressed aspect of my own personality?

_____

_____

_____

_____

_____

_____

Table 2: New Asteroid Keyphrases

ASTEROID		KEYPHRASE
Psyche	⚡	My capacity to be psychically sensitive to another person
Eros	♡	My capacity for vitality and passion
Lilith	⚸	My capacity to constructively release my repressed anger and to resolve conflict
Toro	♉	My capacity to use and control power
Sappho	⚵	My capacity for romantic and artistic sensitivity
Amor	◊	My capacity for spiritual or platonic love and compassion
Pandora	▽	My capacity for curiosity which initiates change
Icarus	▽	My capacity for liberation and risk-taking
Diana	☽	My capacity for survival and self-protection
Hidalgo	⌇	My capacity for self-assertion in defense of my principles
Urania	Ⱥ	My capacity for inspired knowledge

The New Asteroids in the Birth Chart

Optional for the Beginner

The new asteroids which we are presenting in this section are no less important in their influence than any of the other planets or asteroids. However, ephemerides or tables listing their zodiacal positions have been available for less than a decade. Consequently, in order to formulate a *tentative keyphrase* for these asteroids' meanings and functions, we have used preliminary observations and the mythological principle inherent in the archetype. Thus, these suggested interpretations are still quite *experimental* in nature.

If you are a beginning student, you may find this section too overwhelming to assimilate with all the other information. If this is the case, *regard it as optional* and go on with the remaining lessons. You can come back to it later. If you are an intermediate or advanced student, we encourage you to plunge right in and fine tune your chart interpretation. If an asteroid is **conjunct** or **opposing** a **planet** or on an **angle** (use a 3 degree orb), pay special attention to its influence in that area.

We hope you enjoy this exciting journey into a pioneering field of astrological research. Send us your comments and observations. It is only by synthesizing all of our perceptions that we can arrive at a deeper understanding of how these new planetary bodies are functioning in our psyche and society. Our address is located in Appendix E.

Further information and **ephemerides** of these new asteroids can be found in **Asteroid Goddesses** (order form is located in Appendix D). Other sources of current research include CAO Times publications by Al Morrison and *Expanding Astrology's Universe* by Zipporah Dobyns. In addition, you may have the positions of your minor asteroids calculated by Astro Computing Services whose address is provided in Appendix D.

Once you obtain the ACS computer chart, the new asteroids will be listed on page two. Below we have reproduced a sample listing. Note that for this workbook, you will skip over the first four and concentrate on the eleven remaining asteroids. The keyphrases and symbols of these eleven asteroids are listed in Table 2, page 88. After reading Table 2, you can write your asteroid interpretations by completing the programmed learning text in the pages that follow.

ASTEROID	LONGITUDE SIGN DEG MIN	HOUSE	DECLIN	LATITUDE	DIS AU	SPEED MIN SEC
DUDU	Can Ø 34.2R	8	35-N-5Ø	12-N-23	2.95	Ø -43
DEMBWSKA	Vir 12 23.ØR	1Ø	15-N-49	9-N-39	2.15	-12 32
PITTSBRG	Leo 1 56.4R	9	21-N-24	1-N-42	1.93	-9 7
FRIGGA	Aqu 8 1.3	3	19-S-52	1-S-4Ø	3.67	24 8
PSYCHE	Cpr 19 2Ø.4	3	19-S-59	2-N- 5	3.56	21 5Ø
URANIA	Aqu 15 3.2	4	16-S-21	Ø-S- 2	3.22	3Ø 1
PANDORA	Cpr Ø 11.Ø	2	29-S-12	5-S-46	3.21	18 57
SAPPHO	Ari 27 13.5	6	9-N- 5	1-S-3Ø	2.4Ø	32 48
EROS	Cpr 8 3Ø.2	2	3Ø-S-43	7-S-33	1.91	35 2Ø
HIDALGO	Tau 13 43.1	7	5Ø-N-42	37-N-13	2.Ø4	34 24
LILITH	Vir 11 4.6R	1Ø	Ø-S-31	8-S-34	1.71	-14 7
AMOR	Pic 14 56.7	4	5-S-38	Ø-N-19	3.5Ø	25 9
ICARUS	Aqu 29 47.2	4	21-S-48	1Ø-S-59	2.17	42 28
TORO	Lib 19 21.2R	12	26-S- 9	2Ø-S-13	Ø.72	-2Ø 25
DIANA	Cpr 12 46.6	3	29-S-35	6-S-47	3.53	19 8

Exercise 4:
I Interpret the New Asteroids in My Birth Chart

Pages 90-101 present information on the New Asteroids. Once you have read the explanation at the top of the page, fill out the blanks as called for and you will reach an understanding of how these New Asteroids pertain to you in the birth chart.

Psyche

Psyche, the butterfly maiden, represents the **principle of psychic sensitivity** to another person.

Psyche symbolizes the capacity for heightened awareness of the mind and feelings of another which can lead to yearning for mystic soul-mate union. Psyche's process is a refinement of personal love toward psychic attunement and bonding, which can then use the conscious relationship as a path to spiritual illumination. The Psyche personality is depicted by deep, intuitive communication. The extreme expression of Psyche can manifest as blocked psychic awareness, insensitivity to others, and an inability to sustain personal relationships.

Keyphrase: My capacity to be psychically sensitive to another person

1. My asteroid **Psyche** is in the sign of _____.

   In the birth chart, my Psyche sign describes how I am psychically attuned to the minds and feelings of others. Thus, I can best express this sensitivity by fulfilling:

   _____.
   (fill in the sign keyphrase from Appendix A)
   When I am using these sign qualities **skillfully**, I tend to express my sensitivity in a

   _____, _____, or _____ manner.
   (choose skillful sign keywords from Appendix A)
   However, when I'm using these sign qualities **unskillfully**, I may express my sensi-

   tivity in a _____ or _____ manner.
   (choose unskillful sign keywords from Appendix A)

2. My Psyche sign's element is _____.
   (refer to Figure 1, page 11)
   Using the chart below, circle the response that is paired with this element.

PSYCHE'S ELEMENT	HOW I EXPERIENCE PSYCHIC SENSITIVITY
Fire	Through visions, inspirations and intuitions
Earth	Through the physical manifestation of form and substance, knowing through my senses
Air	Through mental telepathy—sending and receiving thoughts
Water	Through empathy, feeling within myself another person's emotions

3. My Psyche is in the _____ house.
   (refer to Table 2, page 32)
   Therefore, my psychic bondings with others will most likely manifest in these areas

   of my life: _____ and _____.
   (choose house keywords from Appendix B)

Journal Entry

To what extent am I psychically sensitive to the minds and feelings of others? Does this awareness influence my behavior towards them?

What challenges or difficulties do I encounter if or when I try to "fine tune" my relationships? Do these attempts ever result in feeling even more unfulfilled and alone in my yearning for ideal union?

_____

_____

_____

_____

Eros

Eros, God of Erotic Love, represents the **principle of vitality and passion.**

Eros can refine the unconscious instinctual sexual drive and use the erotic energy to illuminate and energize relationships and creative work. Eros is the powerful emotional force that motivates us toward consummating our desires and visions. Eros is an indicator of what "turns you on," sexual attraction and preference, as well as what keeps you going—the source of vital energy. The extreme expression of Eros can manifest as blocked sexuality or low physical drive.

Keyphrase: My capacity for vitality and passion

1. My asteroid **Eros** is in the sign of _____.

   In the birth chart, my Eros sign shows what "turns me on" in the pursuit of my desires. I can best express my capacity for passion and vitality by fulfilling:

   _____.
   (fill in the sign keyphrase from Appendix A)
   When I am using these sign qualities **skillfully**, I tend to express my passion in a

   _____, _____, or _____ manner.
   (choose skillful sign keywords from Appendix A)
   However, when I'm using these sign qualities **unskillfully**, I may be

   _____ or _____.
   (choose unskillful sign keywords from Appendix A)

2. My Eros sign's element is _____.
   (refer to Figure 1, page 11)
   Using the chart below, circle the response that is paired with this element.

EROS' ELEMENT	HOW I EXPRESS MY PASSION
Fire	Through visions, adventure and spontaneity
Earth	Through sensual interaction and productivity
Air	Through mental stimulation
Water	Through empathy, nurturing and mystery

3. My Eros is in the _____ house.
   (refer to Table 2, page 32)
   Therefore, my passion, vitality, and sexual urges will most likely manifest in these areas of my life:

   _____ and _____.
   (choose house keywords from Appendix B)

Journal Entry

How do I express my passion, not only sexual passion, but also passion in pursuit of a vision conceived by desires?

What activities stimulate my "juices"—my vital life/sex/creative forces?

_____

_____

_____

_____

_____

Lilith

Lilith, Goddess of the Night, represents the principle of **personal power and conflict resolution.**

As the first mate of Adam in the Garden of Eden, Lilith left him, choosing exile and isolation rather than domination and subjugation. Lilith symbolizes the capacity to constructively release repressed anger and resolve conflict. In chart analysis Lilith can be an indicator of making choices between personal autonomy and consensus negotiation. The extreme expressions of Lilith can manifest as emotional rage, sexual fear, rejection, or violence, violation, and the inability to reach agreement.

Keyphrase: My capacity to constructively release my anger and resolve conflict

1. My asteroid Lilith is in the sign of _____.

   In the birth chart, my Lilith sign indicates how I use my power to maintain my autonomy and to resolve conflict. Thus, I can best express my capacity to transform repressed anger and negotiate agreement by fulfilling:

   _____.
   (fill in sign keyphrase from Appendix A)
   When I am using these sign qualities **skillfully**, I tend to express this power in a

   _____, _____, and _____ manner.
   (choose skillful sign keywords from Appendix A)
   However, when I'm using these sign qualities **unskillfully**, I may use this power in a

   _____ or _____ manner.
   (choose unskillful sign keywords from Appendix A)

2. My Lilith sign's element is _____.
   (refer to Figure 1, page 11)
   Using the chart below, circle the response that is paired with this element.

LILITH'S ELEMENT	HOW I RESOLVE CONFLICT
Fire	Through being frank and out-front
Earth	Through learning to share resources
Air	Through negotiation and compromise
Water	Through forgiveness

3. My Lilith is in the _____ house.
   (refer to Table 2, page 32)
   Therefore, my attempts in conflict resolution where sex, anger, or autonomy are involved will most likely manifest in these areas of my life:

   _____ and _____
   (choose house keywords from Appendix B)

Journal Entry

Where and how does my rage over injustice in interpersonal relations ignite my anger toward others?

In what ways do I express that anger, or do I withdraw from the conflict of a confrontation? Do I use sex as a tool of power or control?

What methods can I employ to resolve conflict which will enable me to continue a relationship and not break it off?

_____

_____

_____

Toro

Toro, symbol of the bull, represents the **principle of the power of boundless strength.**

Toro describes how we use and control power, and represents the potential to transform raw instinctive desire into focused and controlled power. Toro also shows how we confront and handle the onslaught of negative energies that we experience either from without or within our own minds. Toro indicates strength, forcefulness and power. The extreme expressions of Toro can manifest as violent and destructive actions, or paranoia and victimization.

Keyphrase: My capacity to use and control power

1. My asteroid Toro is in the sign of _____ .

   In the birth chart, my Toro sign shows how I use my personal power to attract or avert negative energies. Thus, I can best develop strength and confidence by fulfilling:

   _____
   (fill in the sign keyphrase from Appendix A)
   When I'm using these sign qualities **skillfully**, I tend to express my power in a

   _____, _____ , and _____ manner.
   (choose skillful sign keywords from Appendix A)
   However, when I'm using these sign qualities **unskillfully**, I may be

   _____ or _____ .
   (choose unskillful sign keywords from Appendix A)

2. My Toro sign's element is _____ .
   (refer to Figure 1, page 11)
   Using the chart below, circle the response that is paired with this element.

TORO'S ELEMENT	HOW I EXPRESS MY POWER
Fire	Through direct action
Earth	Through material pressure (money is power)
Air	Through verbal persuasion
Water	Indirectly and subtly

3. My Toro is in the _____ house.
   (refer to Table 2, page 32)
   Therefore, my strength and power (or lack of it) will most likely manifest in these areas of my life:

   _____ and _____ .
   (choose house keywords from Appendix B)

Journal Entry

To what extent do I acknowledge my power? Do I use it to benefit myself at the expense of others' well-being? To what extent are power struggles an issue in my life?

Do I deny my capacity for power and become a victim, attracting assaults from others?

In what ways do my inner fears and insecurities contribute to my aggressive and defensive behavior patterns?

_____

_____

_____

_____

Sappho

Sappho, a Sixth Century B.C. Greek poetess, represents the **principle of romantic and artistic sensitivity.**

Sappho's poetry evokes all of the emotions, both ecstatic and painful, associated with sexuality. Sappho spoke of a variety of loves—single and multiple, conjugal and nonconjugal, heterosexual and lesbian, and maternal. Sappho taught the need to honor the healing power of love in whatever form it presents itself. Sappho is an indicator of sensuality, sexuality, sexual preference, romantic, poetic and artistic sensitivity. The unskillful expressions of Sappho can manifest as emotional difficulties in love and sexuality.

Keyphrase: My capacity for romantic and artistic sensitivity

1. My asteroid Sappho is in the sign of _____.

   In the birth chart, my Sappho sign shows how I express my feelings associated with my sexual encounters or artistic sensibilities. Thus I can best express my capacity for romantic and artistic sensitivity by fulfilling:

   _____
   (fill in sign keyphrase from Appendix A)
   When I am using these sign qualities **skillfully**, I tend to express my sensitivity in a

   _____ , and _____ manner.
   (choose skillful sign keywords from Appendix A)
   However, when I'm using these sign qualities **unskillfully**, I may express my sensitivity in a _____ or

   _____ manner.
   (choose unskillful sign keywords from Appendix A)

2. My Sappho sign's element is _____.
   (refer to Figure 1, page 11)
   Using the chart below, circle the response that is paired with this element.

SAPPHO'S ELEMENT	HOW I EXPRESS MY ROMANTIC AND ARTISTIC SENSITIVITY
Fire	Through passion and inspired vision
Earth	Through physical sensuality and appreciation of the natural world
Air	Through mental stimulation and communication
Water	Through the subtlety of feeling and merging

3. My Sappho is in the _____ house.
   (refer to Table 2, page 32)
   Therefore, my capacity for romantic and artistic sensitivity will most likely manifest in these areas of my life:

   _____ and _____
   (choose house keywords from Appendix B)

Journal Entry

How do I express and cope with the feelings which follow my sexual encounters?

Can I respond to feelings of love between people which go beyond stereotyped roles?

Is my romantic sensitivity a factor in my sexual preference?

How do I support and contribute to feminine arts and education?

_____

_____

Amor

Amor, Roman God of Love, represents the principle of **platonic love and compassion.**

Amor symbolizes a state of loving as opposed to "being in love." Amor expresses a loving kindness that is given without judgment or expectation of return.

Amor is an indicator of good will toward others, pure motivation, and selfless service. The unskillful expression of Amor can suggest difficulties in expressing one's compassionate and empathic nature.

Keyphrase: My capacity for spiritual or platonic love and compassion

1. My asteroid Amor is in the sign of _____.

   In the birth chart, my Amor sign indicates how I show loving kindness and universal love towards others. Thus I can best express my capacity for spiritual love and compassion by fulfilling:

   _____
   (fill in sign keyphrase from Appendix A)

   When I am using these sign qualities **skillfully,** I tend to express loving kindness in a

   _____, and _____ manner.
   (choose skillful sign keywords from Appendix A)

   However, when I'm using these sign qualities **unskillfully,** I may express a lack of

   kindness in a _____ or

   _____ manner.
   (choose unskillful sign keywords from Appendix A)

2. My Amor sign's element is _____.
   (refer to Figure 1, page 11)

   Using the chart below, circle the response that is paired with this element.

AMOR'S ELEMENT	HOW I EXPRESS LOVING KINDNESS
Fire	Through encouragement and inspiration
Earth	Through providing material resources and physical support
Air	Through talking and communicating
Water	Through nurturing and sympathy

3. My Amor is in the _____ house.
   (refer to Table 2, page 32)

   Therefore, my compassion and pure love will most likely manifest in these areas of my life:

   _____ and _____
   (choose house keywords from Appendix B)

Journal Entry

To what extent am I able to express loving kindness and good will towards another?

   Can I rejoice in the good fortunes of others?

   Which of my experiences have motivated a selfless desire within me to benefit beings?

   _____

   _____

   _____

   _____

Pandora

Pandora, a beautiful mortal who opened a forbidden box, represents **the principle of curiosity that initiates change.**

Pandora operates as an agent of change, inviting the unexpected and opening up new possibilities. Pandora brings to light what was previously hidden. Pandora is an indicator of innovation, unexpected discovery, controversy and unorthodox actions. The unskillful expression of Pandora can manifest as meddling and inconsiderate or destructive exposure.

Keyphrase: My capacity for curiosity which initiates change

1. My asteroid Pandora is in the sign of _____.

   In the birth chart, my Pandora sign shows how my curiosity stirs up and uncovers situations. Thus I can best initiate change by fulfilling:

   _____
   (fill in sign keyphrase from Appendix A)
   When I am using these sign qualities **skillfully**, I tend to express my curiosity in a

   _____, and _____ manner.
   (choose skillful sign keywords from Appendix A)
   However, when I'm using these sign qualities **unskillfully**, I may express my curiosity

   in a _____ and

   _____manner.
   (choose unskillful sign keywords from Appendix A)

2. My Pandora sign's element is _____.
   (refer to Figure 1, page 11)
   Using the chart below, circle the response that is paired with this element.

PANDORA'S ELEMENT	**HOW I STIR UP SITUATIONS AND INITIATE CHANGE**
Fire	By frank and direct action
Earth	By challenging the status quo
Air	By communicating controversial issues
Water	By arousing the depths of feeling

3. My Pandora is in the _____ house.
   (refer to Table 2, page 32)
   Therefore, my curiosity and change initiating activities will most likely manifest in these areas of my life:

   _____ and _____
   (choose house keywords from Appendix B)

Journal Entry

To what extent do I allow my curiosity to lead me into new situations?

What happens when I zero in on "hot spots" and uncover hidden knowledge?

Do my unorthodox questions and actions get me into trouble, i.e., arouse others' irritation?

_____

_____

_____

_____

_____

Icarus

Icarus, the winged youth who flew towards the Sun, represents **the principle of liberation**; the most direct, yet most dangerous path to freedom

Icarus points to the necessity of maintaining self-discipline and mindfulness during free flight to avoid extremes which result in disaster. Icarus can function as physical freedom from confining situations, psychological freedom from social conditioning, and spiritual freedom from samsara, i.e., the repeating earthly cycles of birth and death, brought about by karma. In chart analysis the Icarus personality rebels against restriction and continually tests and attempts to go beyond his or her limits—with varying degrees of success. The extremism inherent in Icarus can manifest as recklessness, overreach, or fear of flight.

Keyphrase: My capacity for liberation and risk-taking

1. My asteroid Icarus is in the sign of _____.

   In the birth chart, my Icarus sign indicates how I free myself from confining situations. Thus I can best express my capacity to liberate myself by fulfilling:

   _____
   (fill in sign keyphrase from Appendix A)

   When I am using these sign qualities **skillfully**, I tend to express my freedom urges

   in a _____, and _____ manner.
   (choose skillful sign keywords from Appendix A)

   However, when I'm using these sign qualities in an **unskillful** manner, I may express my freedom urges in a _____ or

   _____, manner.
   (choose unskillful sign keywords from Appendix A)

2. My Icarus sign's element is _____.
   (refer to Figure 1, page 11)

   Using the chart below, circle the response that is paired with this element.

ICARUS' ELEMENT	**HOW I ACT TO FREE MYSELF**
Fire	Through diving ahead into new situations
Earth	Through breaking down old structures and creating new forms
Air	Through changing my old limiting ideas
Water	Through releasing negative feelings and finding inner peace

3. My Icarus is in the _____ house.
   (refer to Table 2, page 32)

   Therefore, my desire for freedom and risk-taking will most likely manifest in these areas of my life:

   _____ and _____
   (choose house keywords from Appendix B)

Journal Entry

What situations activate my desire to take risks in order to free myself from confining circumstances? Do I leap from the frying pan into the fire?

To what extent can I exercise mindfulness and self-discipline over these flights of freedom in order to prevent recklessness and disaster?

_____

_____

_____

Diana

Diana, Goddess of Untamed Nature, represents the principle of **survival and self-protection.**

Diana signifies the wisdom that comes from an instinctual understanding of nature and natural laws. She functions as a protectress of all that is young and vulnerable (including one's own inviolate essence) and wrathfully promotes the attributes of strength and independence.

In chart analysis Diana indicates a personality that is private, self-identified, strong, and concerned with survival. The unskillful expressions of Diana can manifest as fear of intimacy and being overly harsh with oneself and others.

Keyphrase: My capacity for survival and self-protection

1. My asteroid Diana is in the sign of _____.

In the birth chart, my Diana sign shows how I instinctively pull inward and protect myself. Thus, I can best express my capacity for survival, self-defense and independence by fulfilling:

_____.
(fill in sign keyphrase from Appendix A)

When I am using these sign qualities **skillfully**, I tend to express my protective instincts in a _____, _____, and _____ manner.
(choose skillful sign keywords from Appendix A)

However, when I'm using these sign qualities **unskillfully,** I may express my protective instincts in a _____ or _____ manner.
(choose unskillful sign keywords from Appendix A)

2. My Diana sign's element is _____.
(refer to Figure 1, page 11)

Using the chart below, circle the response that is paired with this element.

DIANA'S ELEMENT	HOW I PROTECT MYSELF AND LOVED ONES
Fire	Through direct and courageous action
Earth	Through my practical knowhow and common sense
Air	Through my verbal and mental abilities
Water	Through indirect or nonviolent resistence

3. My Diana is in the _____ house.
(refer to Table 2, page 32)

Therefore, my instincts for privacy, self-protection and independence will most likely manifest in these areas of my life:

_____ and _____.
(choose house keywords from Appendix B)

Journal Entry

How do I protect the young and vulnerable aspects of myself from violation by others? How do these defenses serve to isolate me from others?

Am I frozen in an adolescence identity, "maiden" or "puer", and fear deep and ongoing intimacy with others?

To what extent do I rely upon my instincts and connections with animals and nature for survival cues?

_____

_____

_____

Hidalgo

Hidalgo, Mexican revolutionary and priest, represents the **principle of protecting and fighting for one's beliefs.**

Hidalgo provides the courage and conviction to act on one's beliefs. Hidalgo uses the form of protest to challenge the authority of any kind of established dogma, as in the current movement of Liberation Theology.

In chart analysis the Hidalgo personality is characterized by an assertive, rugged, willful, or rebellious nature that strongly defends one's principles. The extreme expressions of Hidalgo can manifest as fanaticism, self-righteousness and narrow-minded obsession.

Keyphrase: My capacity for self-assertion in defense of my principles

1. My asteroid Hidalgo is in the sign of _____.

   In the birth chart, my Hidalgo sign signifies how I assert myself in the defense of my principles. Thus, I can best express my capacity to act on my beliefs by fulfilling:

   _____.
   (fill in sign keyphrase from Appendix A)
   When I'm using these sign qualities **skillfully,** I tend to express my defensive urge in a

   _____, and _____ manner.
   (choose skillful sign keywords from Appendix A)
   However, when I'm using these sign qualities **unskillfully,** I may express my defensive urges in a _____ or _____ manner.
   (choose unskillful sign keywords from Appendix A)

2. My Hidalgo sign's element is _____.
   (refer to Figure 1, page 11)
   Using the chart below, circle the response that is paired with this element.

HIDALGO'S ELEMENT	HOW I ACT UPON AND DEFEND MY PRINCIPLES
Fire	By direct action and inspiring others with a vision
Earth	By demonstrating pragmatic and realistic solutions
Air	By communicating and disseminating information
Water	By arousing sympathy and compassion

3. My Hidalgo is in the _____ house.
   (refer to Table 2, page 32)
   Therefore, my assertiveness in what I believe will most likely manifest in these areas of my life:

   _____ and _____.
   (choose house keywords from Appendix B)

Journal Entry

Do I have the courage to put my beliefs into action? How do my principles influence my behavior?

What situations stimulate my activist tendencies to resist authority and dogmatic views?

_____

_____

_____

_____

_____

Urania

Urania, Heavenly Muse, represents the **principle of inspired knowledge.**

As the muse serves as a source of divine inspiration, Urania in our psyche symbolizes insight and truth gained through meditation. Urania is a deep thinker who uses her mental astuteness to probe both macrocosm and microcosm. Urania is associated with astrology, astronomy, music theory, the pure sciences and numbers. The unskillful expression of Urania can manifest as blocked access to intuition and insight.

Keyphrase: My capacity for inspired knowledge

1. My asteroid Urania is in the sign of _____.

   In the birth chart, my Urania sign indicates how I bring insight into my rational understanding. Thus, I can best express my capacity for inspired knowledge by fulfilling:

   _____.
   (fill in sign keyphrase from Appendix A)
   When I'm using these sign qualities **skillfully,** I tend to express my inspirations in a

   _____, _____, and _____ manner.
   (choose skillful sign keywords from Appendix A)
   However, when I'm using these sign qualities **unskillfully,** I may express my inspirations in a _____ or _____ manner.
   (choose unskillful sign keywords from Appendix A)

2. My Urania sign's element is _____.
   (refer to Figure 1, page 11)
   Using the chart below, circle the response that is paired with this element.

URANIA'S ELEMENT	HOW I EXPERIENCE INSIGHTS
Fire	Through visions
Earth	Through nature and the senses
Air	Through ideas
Water	Through feelings

3. My Urania is in the _____ house.
   (refer to Table 2, page 32)
   Therefore, my inspirational experiences will most likely manifest in these areas of my life:

   _____ and _____.
   (choose house keywords from Appendix B)

Journal Entry

To what extent am I able to access my intuition and insight to gain inspired visions?
What methods (meditation, etc.) can I utilize to open my channels to higher wisdom from the subtle planes?

_____

_____

_____

_____

_____

_____

Go back now to the beginning of these exercises and read over your responses. You should be impressed by the wealth of information you have compiled about yourself. To gain this information, many people send away for computer generated readings. But here you have done it on your own! And what's more, you can use this same process to interpret the birth charts of your friends and loved ones.

In the next chapter, you will use the same keyword system to determine your astrological potentials in work and love.

Further Reading

If you wish to learn more about the topics covered in this chapter, we recommend the following books.

Bacher, Elman, *Studies in Astrology,* Volumes 1–4

Dobyns, Zipporah, *The Astrologer's Casebook*

George, Demetra, *Asteroid Goddesses*

Greene, Liz, *Saturn: A New Look at an Old Devil*

Marks, Tracy, *The Art of Chart Synthesis*

Mayo, Jeff, *The Planets and Human Behavior*

Pottenger, Maritha, *Complete Horoscope Interpretation*

Additional resources are located in the bibliography.

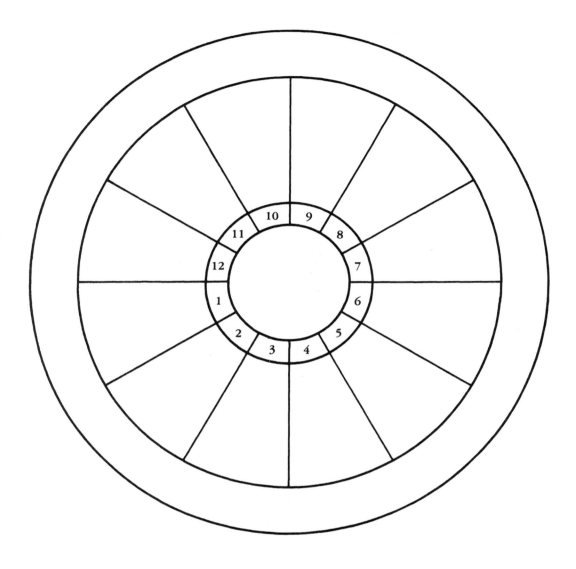

Notes: _____

_____

_____

_____

_____

_____

_____

_____

_____

_____

_____

Chapter 4

—Work Signs and Love Signs—

AS A RULE, people consult astrologers for the same reason they consult any counselor—because they seek guidance about a specific concern in their lives. And as any practicing astrologer will verify, the two major areas of concern for most individuals are **work** and **love**. Sigmund Freud recognized this in his psychoanalytic practice when he defined the major issues in his patients' lives as "Liebe und Arbeit" (love and work).

The purpose of this chapter is to show you how to interpret the themes of work and love in your own birth chart. By completing the programmed learning exercises that follow, you will gain a basic understanding of your birth chart's *career* and *love* potential.

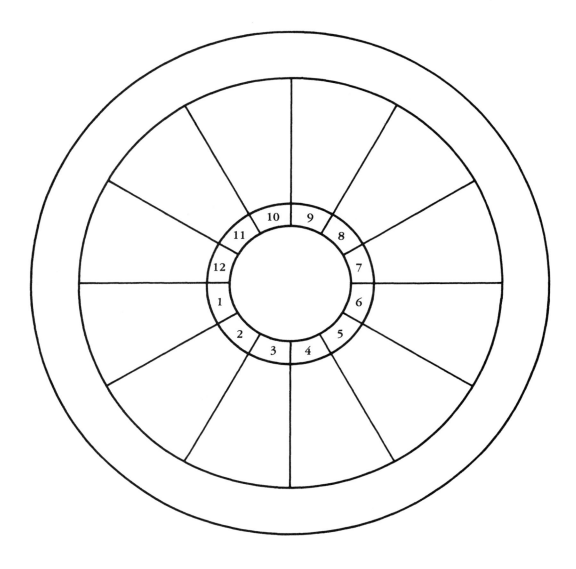

Notes: _____

_____

_____

_____

_____

_____

_____

_____

_____

_____

_____

_____

Astrology and Your Vocation

"Work is love made visible."

Kahlil Gibran

What can your birth chart tell you about your work life? While it cannot target a specific career, it can point out your vocational needs that you bring to work as well as your talents and abilities that can be best expressed in a societal way. Once you have an understanding of your vocational needs and talents, you will have a much greater chance of creating a fulfilling work life.

An understanding of your chart's vocational potential can be accomplished in a variety of ways. The starting-off point is your Sun sign. Because the Sun represents your conscious purpose, will, and creative potential, its sign needs will be a major factor in discovering your life's work.

One way to understand the signs' vocational needs is through examining the needs of the elements. For example:

Fire signs are drawn to vocations that offer adventure, challenge, independence, and the opportunity to create one's own destiny.

Earth signs are more interested in careers that provide stability, security, a steady income, and the opportunity to produce tangible results.

Air signs gravitate toward careers that involve work with people, variety, and the opportunity to communicate and share ideas.

Water signs are best suited for vocations that involve nurturing, healing, the use of imagination, and create settings that provide a sense of belonging.

Over the centuries, astrologers compiled a list of vocations that correspond to the twelve signs of the Zodiac. One such collection is contained in Table 1, page 106. After you have read over the careers associated with your Sun sign, complete Exercise 1 below.

Sun Sign Careers

Exercise 1: My Sun Sign's Vocational Potential

Sample Analysis

My **Sun** is in the sign of _____*Pisces*_____.

(fill in your Sun sign)
Three careers associated with this sign that I am drawn to are: ____*Priests*____,
_____*Artists*_____, and _____*Nurses*_____.
(fill in vocational sign keywords from Table 1)

Your Turn

My **Sun** is in the sign of _____.

(fill in your Sun sign)
Three careers associated with this sign that I am drawn to are: _____,
_____, and _____.
(fill in vocational sign keywords from Table 1)

Aries—Vocations that require independence, daring and the pioneering spirit: entrepreneurs, pioneers in any field, idea people, those who initiate new projects, troubleshooters, directors, adventurers, executives.

Firemen or fire fighters, forest rangers, engineers (metallurgical), members of the armed forces, firearms experts, police officers, machinists, mechanics, iron and steel workers, locksmiths, welders, athletics that involve speed and daring, race car drivers, contact sports, boxers, dancers, movement therapists, physical education instructors, surgeons.

Taurus—Vocations dealing with the earth and substance: farmers, ranchers, agriculture instructors, landscape architects, gardeners, rock collectors (semi-precious gems), builders, carpenters, building contractors, concrete pourers, chiropractors, massage therapists, computer programmers.

Occupations involved with money and finance: bankers, bank tellers, stock brokers, financiers, money managers, investment advisors, securities analysts, treasurers, economists.

Artists, sculptors, jewelers, pottery makers, fashion designers, tailors, florists, musicians, singers, voice teachers, throat specialists.

Gemini—Vocations involved with communication or transportation: authors, proofreaders, ad copywriters, screenplay writers, editors, reporters, teachers, lecturers, linguists, speech therapists, librarians, bookstore owners, publishers, magazine employees, radio operators or disc jockeys, television producers, telephone operators or repair persons, telemarketers, stationery store owners, journalists, salespeople, printers, book distributors, clerks, office workers, secretaries, typists, typesetters.

Messengers, mail carriers, taxi drivers, bus drivers, railway employees, plane pilots, accountants, jacks-of-all-trades. Can engage in two or more occupations at once.

Cancer—Vocations that nurture: physically or emotionally (especially through food): caterers, restaurant owners, chefs, cooks, bakers, waiters and waitresses, confectioners, dairy farmers, grocers, food distributors, nutritionists.

Social workers, counselors, psychics, nurses, family therapists, preschool teachers, children's writers, caretakers, water-related occupations, plumbers, swimmers, lifeguards, fishermen.

All careers dealing with the home: realtors, landlords, hotel managers, innkeepers, homemakers, governesses, maids, laundry workers.

Leo—Performers of all types: actors and actressses, playwrights, entertainers, dancers, singers, musicians, movie stars, circus performers, jugglers, clowns, sports figures, teachers (good teachers are entertainers), amusement park owners, speculators, gamblers.

Leaders of all types: executives, managers, government officials, politicians, foremen, judges, athletes, salespeople, the profession of selling, promoters, diamond and precious metal brokers, gold workers, heart specialists, all vocations involving children.

Virgo—Vocations dealing with analysis, detail and technical expertise: statisticians, accountants, bookkeepers, computer programmers, teachers of technical subjects, stenographers, critics, inspectors of all types, draftsmen, graphic artists, technical illustrators, craftspeople, specialists.

Health occupations and the social services, mental health workers, therapists, psychiatrists, psychoanalysts, social workers, employment counselors, nurses, doctors, massage therapists, respiratory technicians, dental hygienists, dentists, secretaries, office managers, food service workers, waiters and waitresses, dieticians, nutritionists, veterinarians, zoologists, sanitation workers, janitors, public health officials, house cleaners, butlers.

Libra—Vocations that pursue balance, harmony and justice: negotiators and counselors of all types, marriage counselors, wedding-related businesses, diplomats, labor arbitrators, judges, lawyers, managers, salespeople.

Occupations dealing with beauty: artists, architects, painters, illustrators, photographers, fashion designers, fashion industry workers, milliners, color consultants, clothing store owners or salespeople, beauticians, hairdressers, cosmeticians, interior and exterior decorators, cosmetic manufacturers and dealers, jewelers, florists, candy makers.

Scorpio—Vocations that focus on uncovering hidden secrets: researchers, muckraking journalists, investigators, detectives, physicists, occultists, those who work behind the scenes, espionage agents, vice squad workers, psychics, astrologers, all matters dealing with death, funeral home directors, morticians, cemetery workers, insurance salespeople, soldiers, those working under the earth, undertakers.

Those who work as healers: all medical practitioners, physicians, nurses, psychiatrists, psychologists, surgeons, pharmacists, pathologists, past-life investigators, hospice workers, chemists, music therapists, musicians.

Sagittarius—Vocations dealing with exploration, travel and adventure: explorers, astronomers, travel agents, airline employees, flight attendants, astronauts, import-export agents, foreign correspondents, language interpreters, traveling salespeople, promoters, customs officers, athletes of all types, archers, sporting goods manufacturers, horse trainers, breeders and jockeys.

Occupations dealing with higher knowledge: philosophers, college professors, ministers, theologians, missionaries, preachers, orators, publishers, metaphysical writers, philanthropists, lawyers.

Capricorn—Vocations dealing with administering and organizing: administrators of all types, managers, business owners, executives, government officials, politicians, judges, manufacturers, coordinators, principals at schools, wardens, disciplinarians, buyers, consultants, vocational counselors.

Occupations that work with form and structure: architects, contractors, builders, carpenters, civil and industrial engineers, economists, chiropractors, orthopedic specialists, osteopaths, miners, landowners, mountain climbers.

Aquarius—Vocations dealing with progress and invention: inventors, scientists, educators, researchers, astrologers, social workers, psychologists, futurists, humanitarians, social reformers, United Nations workers, employees of world relief organizations, future-oriented occupations, astronauts, airplane pilots, aviators, parachutists, hang glider pilots, solar energy researchers, physicists, radio and television technicians, electricians, electrical engineers.

Pisces—Vocations of a spiritual, healing or artistic nature: religious workers, priests, monks, nuns, sisters of mercy, rabbis, clairvoyants, mediums, charity workers, prison workers.

Physicians, faith healers, psychic healers, nurses, hospital workers, psychiatrists, psychologists, hypnotists, anesthesiologists, podiatrists.

Poets, musicians, writers (inspirational, fantasy, metaphysical, science fiction), actors, dancers, painters, artists, entertainers, comedians, singers, filmmakers.

Water-related activities, fishermen, sailors, sea captains, divers, swimmers, lifeguards, marine scientists, oceanographers, bartenders, oil industry workers.

Now that you have understood your Sun sign's vocational needs, it is time to go beyond the Sun sign level and look into the rest of the chart. To do this, you will examine the specific houses of the birth chart that correspond to your work life.

The Work Houses

When we think of work, we think of a means of offering a practical service which will provide us with money so that we can support ourselves in the mundane world. In this sense, work is a **practical** or **earthy** endeavor. Thus we will look at the **earth houses,** those that correspond to the earth signs of Taurus, Virgo, and Capricorn. Since Taurus, Virgo, and Capricorn are the second, sixth and tenth signs of the Zodiac, the earth houses are numbers 2, 6 and 10 as seen in the figure.

Let us now examine each of these houses in your birth chart and the effects they have on your career potential.

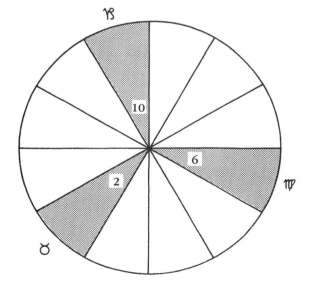

—Figure 1: The Work Houses—

——Exercise 2: My Midheaven and My Vocational Potential——

The Midheaven is the sign that is located at the beginning of the tenth house. Earlier, you located the sign on your Midheaven and wrote it down in Table 2, page 32. You also wrote about its sign needs in Exercise 2, page 49.

The Midheaven symbolizes your social or public role in the world. It depicts the contribution you wish to make to your community that forms the basis of your social reputation and status. Along with your Sun sign, it is a valuable indicator of long term career choices.

The following exercise will enable you to identify those special talents and gifts that you wish to share with the world.

1. My M.C. or Midheaven sign is in the sign of _____.
   (see Table 2, page 32)
   Three vocations associated with this sign that I am drawn to are _____,
   _____ and _____.
   (see Table 1, page 106)

2. My M.C. describes how I function in and contribute to society. Thus, I can best be in the world and achieve my professional and career identity by fulfilling

   _____.
   (fill in the sign keyphrase from Appendix A)
   When I am competent, I tend to project myself in the world in a _____,
   _____, and _____manner.
   (choose skillful sign keywords from Appendix A)
   However when I feel unsure of myself or out of place, I may be _____
   and _____.
   (choose unskillful sign keywords)

3. My Midheaven sign's element is _____.
   (see Figure 2, page 11)

Using this information, circle this element's keyphrase in the table below.

ELEMENT	WHAT I WISH TO BE RECOGNIZED FOR
Fire	My creative and inspirational accomplishments
Earth	My practical and tangible accomplishments
Air	My intellectual and social accomplishments
Water	My emotional and nurturing accomplishments (caring for others, etc.)

Not only the Midheaven, but the tenth house as a whole corresponds to the department of life known as "career and professional standing." Thus, planets located in the tenth house will show which of your personality functions are seeking expression in your vocational activities. For example, if you have Mercury in the tenth house, then your communication and learning skills will be actively expressed in your career.

To determine which (if any) planets are located in your tenth house, look at your birth chart, or turn to Table 2, page 32, where each planet's house position is listed. Then fill out the table below, using Appendix C to find the planetary keyphrases.

10TH HOUSE PLANET	WHAT I WANT TO EXPRESS IN MY CAREER AND BE KNOWN FOR
1. _____	_____
2. _____	_____
3. _____	_____
4. _____	_____
5. _____	_____

Remember that *how* the above planetary capacities are expressed will be determined by their sign placements, which you located and described in Exercise 2, page 48. For example, if you have the Moon in the tenth house, you may want to be a nurturer in your career. But if the Moon is in **Gemini** (an air sign), you will want to nurture through your *ideas* (writing, etc.); if the Moon were in **Cancer** (a water sign), you would want to nurture through your *emotions* (counseling others, perhaps). Thus, in interpreting your planets in the work houses, pay special attention to their sign positions.

Exercise 3: The Sixth House and My Work Potential

The next vocational indicator we will discuss is the sign on the cusp (the beginning) of your sixth house. Essentially, the sixth house depicts the routine responsibilities, duties, and obligations of your job. It is your "working environment" as opposed to your career title (the tenth house). The sign on the cusp of the sixth house describes your basic *approach* to these daily job activities.

For example, a stock broker with Libra at the Midheaven and Gemini on the sixth house may be recognized as a fine counselor (tenth house Libra), but his daily work involves a substantial amount of paperwork and phone work (sixth house Gemini).

Turn now to your own chart and locate the sign that begins your sixth house. It is located just below your descendent. In Figure 1, page 26, the sixth house sign is Aries (♈). Once you have located your sixth house sign, complete the following sentences.

1. The sign on my 6th house cusp is _____ .
   (see Table 2, page 32)

   My 6th house sign describes what I need in the daily routines of my working environment. I best achieve them by fulfilling:

   _____
   (fill in the sign keyphrase from Appendix A)
   Therefore, in my daily work environment, I need to be _____ ,

   _____ , and _____ .
   (choose skillful sign keywords from Appendix A)
   However, when I am not getting my needs met, I may become _____

   _____ and _____ .
   (choose unskillful sign keywords from Appendix A)

2. My sixth house sign's element is _____ .
   (see Figure 2, page 11)

Using this information, circle the element's need in the table below.

ELEMENT	WHAT I NEED FROM MY WORKING ENVIRONMENT
Fire	The freedom to pursue my goals and ideals
Earth	Structured activities that produce tangible results
Air	Contact with people, mental stimulation, and variety
Water	The opportunity to give and receive nurturance

Finally, planets in the sixth house show personality functions that are seeking expression in your job's daily activities. From your own chart or Table 2, page 32, locate your sixth house planets and list them below with their corresponding keyphrases from Appendix C.

6TH HOUSE PLANET	WHAT I WISH TO EXPRESS IN MY WORKING ROUTINE
1. _____	_____
2. _____	_____
3. _____	_____
4. _____	_____
5. _____	_____

Exercise 4: The Second House
and My Resources and Talents

Let us now turn to our final work indicator—the second house. Traditionally, the second house describes one's resources, possessions and assets. While we are accustomed to thinking of resources/possessions in material terms, they may also be mental, emotional, or spiritual in nature. Thus, in thinking about your career, view the second house as describing those talents, strengths and abilities that you may use as resources in fulfilling your social role in the community.

The sign on the second house cusp describes the exact nature of those career resources. Look now at your birth chart and locate the sign that begins your second house. It is located just below the Ascendant. In Figure 1, page 26, the second house sign is Sagittarius. Once you have located your sign, fill in the following sentence.

1. The sign on my 2nd house cusp is _____.
   (see Table 2, page 32)

   The sign on my 2nd house describes the nature of my career talents and resources. I can best attract these resources by fulfilling:

   _____.

   When I am successfully generating these resources, I am _____

   _____ and _____.
   (choose skillful sign keywords from Appendix A)

   However, when I am experiencing lack or limitation in my resources, my attitude

   towards my resources may be _____

   and _____.
   (choose unskillful sign keywords from Appendix A)

2. My 2nd house sign's element is _____.
   (see Figure 2, page 11)

   Using this information, circle this element's resources in the table below.

ELEMENT	THE TYPES OF CAREER RESOURCES THAT I POSSESS
Fire	Inspirational resources: my ability to create new visions and goals
Earth	Material resources: my ability to produce tangible results
Air	Mental resources: my ability to use ideas and to communicate
Water	Emotional resources: my ability to nurture and to use my imagination

Planets in your second house describe those personality functions that can help you to develop your resources. Look now at your birth chart or Table 2, page 32, to determine the planets that fall in your second house. Then, list them below with their planet keyphrases which are located in Appendix C.

SECOND HOUSE PLANET	WHAT I CAN USE TO DEVELOP MY EARNING POTENTIAL
1. _____	_____
2. _____	_____
3. _____	_____
4. _____	_____
5. _____	_____

This concludes our section on vocational astrology. By now you should have a clearer idea of what your vocational needs and talents are. Realize that this analysis is only an introduction. In more advanced interpretation, you would consider the "planetary rulers" of the second, sixth and tenth houses and look to their sign, house, and aspect configurations. If you wish a more detailed analysis of your vocational potential, we would recommend reading a vocational astrology book from the bibliography, taking a class in vocational astrology, or consulting a professional astrologer.

Journal Entry: Vocation

To help you synthesize the information you have learned about your vocational needs, review the material you have just completed. Then drawing on examples from your own life experiences, consider and answer the following questions.

Are you aware of what your vocational needs are? Are you expressing them?

_____

_____

_____

_____

_____

_____

_____

_____

Are you meeting your vocational needs in your current work? Have you in the past?

_____

_____

_____

_____

_____

_____

_____

_____

Do your vocational needs match your current job, training, and education?

_____

_____

_____

_____

_____

_____

_____

_____

If you truly followed your heart's desire, what work would you most like to pursue?

_____

_____

_____

_____

_____

_____

_____

_____

_____

Astrology and Your Relationships

Perhaps the most often asked question that astrologers receive is "What signs do I best get along with?" Once again, this type of question is evidence of the "Sun sign" mentality that pervades the public's approach to astrology. For as you will learn, there are a number of factors that determine compatibility between birth charts. But before we talk about them, let us first briefly define two terms—"relationship" and "compatibility."

When most of us use the term "relationship," we are usually referring to a "primary" or marital partnership. In the study of chart compatibility, however, the term "relationship" can be applied to any meaningful human interaction. These include:

Wife—Husband; Parent—Child; Teacher—Student; Friend—Friend; Lover—Lover; Employer—Employee; Business Partners, etc.

Thus, if you are involved in any of the above relationships, you can apply the principles of astrological compatibility to them.

As for "compatibility," we are first going to define it in terms of **Element** interactions. From your work with polarities in Chapter One, you should recall that the **Fire** and **Air** signs harmonize to form the **Yang** polarity, while the **Earth** and **Water** signs blend to form the **Yin** polarity. In relationship studies, we have found that the Yang signs primarily need **freedom** and the ability to participate in shared creativity and independence while the Yin signs desire **security** and closeness, specifically emotional and material security. Table 2 depicts these differing needs.

Table 2: The Signs' Needs in Relationships

YANG SIGNS (FREEDOM AND INDEPENDENCE)		YIN SIGNS (STABILITY AND SECURITY)	
Fire CREATIVE	Aries Leo Sagittarius	**Earth** MATERIAL	Taurus Virgo Capricorn
Air MENTAL	Gemini Libra Aquarius	**Water** EMOTIONAL	Cancer Scorpio Pisces

My Birth Chart's Love Potential

> The meeting of two personalities
> Is like the contact of two substances.
> If there is any reaction, both are transformed.
> C.G. Jung

According to Table 2, the energy of Cancer is likely to flow and harmonize with that of Pisces, because Pisces is the same element (water) and has the same types of needs in a relationship. In the relationship between Cancer and the fire sign Aries, the needs are very different and the energies will have a greater tendency to clash. Consequently, water–water combinations tend to be more harmonious than water–fire ones.

At this point, you may be asking yourself, "What signs are most compatible with my own?" without asking a far more important question—"What are *my own*

needs in a relationship?" For once you understand what you need and want in a partnership, then you can go forth and seek it. But, unless you know what you are looking for, how can you expect to find it?

In your birth chart, a number of significant points describe what you are seeking in a partnership. These relationship indicators are described in the following:

1. **The Sun** shows your basic will, motivation, and purpose which you will want to match with your partner's.

2. **The Moon** depicts the types of emotional needs that you bring to a relationship. It also governs your daily habits and routines which become extremely significant if you are living with your partner.

3. **The Ascendant** manifests as your outer garment; is important in determining physical attraction be-

tween people.

4. **Mercury** shows the style in which you communicate with another.

5. **Venus** indicates what "turns you on," what you find appealing in others.

6. **Juno** describes what you need in a committed, long-term relationship. Your marriage partner should have some of the qualities of the sign where your Juno is placed.

7. **The Descendant,** like Juno, depicts the qualities you seek in a long term partnership; also shows what you may project onto a partner.

8. **Mars** shows how you and your partner can work together. It also describes sexual attraction and sources of possible conflict.

Exercise 5: I Define My Needs in a Relationship

In Chapter Three, you interpreted these planets and points in your chart. Now you will use their sign positions to generate an overview of your relationship needs.

Complete the following sentences, using Table 2, page 32, to locate the sign positions, and Table 2, page 113, to determine their element and polarity.

1. My **Sun** is in the sign of _____. The sign's element is _____;
(see Table 2, page 32) *(see Table 2, page 113)*
(fire, earth, air or water). Its polarity is _____ (Yin or Yang).

2. My **Moon** is in the sign of _____. The sign's element is _____.

Its polarity is _____.

3. My **Ascendant** is in the sign of _____. The sign's element is _____.

Its polarity is _____.

4. My **Mercury** is in the sign of _____. The sign's element is _____.

Its polarity is _____.

5. My **Venus** is in the sign of _____. The sign's element is _____.

Its polarity is _____.

6. My **Juno** is in the sign of _____. The sign's element is _____.

Its polarity is _____.

7. My **Descendant** is in the sign of _____. The sign's element is _____.

Its polarity is _____.

8. My **Mars** is in the sign of _____. The sign's element is _____.

Its polarity is _____.

Now count the occurrences of Yin and Yang above.

Of the eight points listed, _____ are in the Yin signs and _____ are in Yang signs.

The **more represented polarity** is _____.

This indicates that in my relationships **I most often prefer** _____
(write "freedom and independence" if Yang was the predominant polarity; "stability and security" if it was Yin).

Next, count the number of times each element appeared and write it next to the element name in the table below.

ELEMENT	MY COUNT	RELATIONSHIP NEEDS
Fire	_____	Shared visions, independence, passion
Earth	_____	Stability, consistency, sensuality, comfort
Air	_____	Meeting of the minds, verbal exchange
Water	_____	Emotional rapport and support, understanding

Exercise 6: I Determine
My Compatibility With Another

In this exercise, we are simply going to take your relationship needs that you defined in Exercise 5 and compare them with those of another person. In order to do this, you will need a copy of your partner's birth chart. (If you don't have one and don't know how to obtain one, turn to Appendix D.) Realize that your ''partner'' can be anyone with whom you have a close relationship—spouse, friend, parent, child, teacher, business associate, etc.

Once you have your partner's birth chart, then locate the positions of the planets, just as you did with your own in Table 2, page 32. We are going to compare your relationship points according to how they relate through their signs' elements.

Part 1: My Partner's Needs in a Relationship

Fill in the following sentences for your partner, just as you did for yourself.

1. My **partner's Sun** is in the sign of _____. The sign's element is _____. Its polarity is _____.

2. My **partner's Moon** is in the sign of _____. The sign's element is _____. Its polarity is _____.

3. My **partner's Ascendant** is in the sign of _____. The sign's element is _____. Its polarity is _____.

4. My **partner's Mercury** is in the sign of _____. The sign's element is _____. Its polarity is _____.

5. My **partner's Venus** is in the sign of _____. The sign's element is _____. Its polarity is _____.

6. My **partner's Juno** is in the sign of _____. The sign's element is _____. Its polarity is _____.

7. My **partner's Descendant** is in the sign of _____. The sign's element is _____. Its polarity is _____.

8. My **partner's Mars** is in the sign of _____. The sign's element is _____. Its polarity is _____.

Now count the occurrences of Yin and Yang above.

Of the eight points listed, _____ are in the Yin signs and _____ are in Yang signs.

My partner's **most represented polarity** is _____.

This indicates that in his or her relationships **my partner most often prefers**

_____ (write ''freedom and independence '' if Yang was the predominant polarity; ''stability and security'' if it was Yin).

Next, count the number of times each element appeared and write it next to the element name in the table below.

ELEMENT	MY COUNT	MY PARTNER'S COUNT	RELATIONSHIP NEEDS
Fire	_____	_____	Shared visions, independence, passion
Earth	_____	_____	Stability, consistency, sensuality, comfort
Air	_____	_____	Meeting of the minds, verbal exchange
Water	_____	_____	Emotional rapport and support, understanding

Study the above comparison closely, for it will reveal the basic elemental compatibility between the charts. In the next section, we will refine this process.

—Journal Entry—

Now compare your most emphasized elements with those of your partner. Are they of the same polarity (Fire-Air or Earth-Water)? If they are, then a basic temperamental compatibility exists. Your relationship needs are most likely in harmony.

Do you have one element or polarity emphasized that is not shared by your partner, or vice versa? If so, this could be a source of conflict *or* a source of complementarity.

In the space below, take a moment and write down the insights you have gained about your relationship from comparing your element emphasis with that of your partner's.

_____

_____

_____

_____

_____

_____

_____

_____

_____

_____

_____

_____

_____

_____

_____

_____

_____

_____

_____

Table 3: Element Combinations

Fire—Fire
Skillful: Our fire signs share energy and enthusiasm.
Unskillful: Our imbalanced Fire produces competition, conflict, and burnout.

Fire—Earth
Skillful: Earth's practicality grounds Fire's inspiration.
Unskillful: Earth's conservatism conflicts with Fire's need for adventure.

Fire—Air
Skillful: Air's ideas feed the flames of Fire's creativity.
Unskillful: There may be too much theory and not enough application.

Fire—Water
Skillful: Water's sensitivity balances Fire's intensity. Fire's courage assists Water's timidity.
Unskillful: Water's need for closeness and bonding conflicts with Fire's need for freedom and independence.

Earth—Earth
Skillful: Our earth signs enhance practicality and productivity.
Unskillful: Our imbalanced Earth produces conservatism, boredom, and resistance to change.

Earth—Air
Skillful: Earth applies Air's ideas in a useful way; pragmatism balances theory.

Unskillful: Earth's desire for consistency conflicts with Air's need for change.

Earth—Water
Skillful: Earth provides a structure to stabilize Water's emotions; Water nurture's Earth and gives it life.
Unskillful: Too much comfort prevents growth and keeps the partnership "stuck in the mud."

Air—Air
Skillful: Our Air signs delight in commmunicating (talking) with each other.
Unskillful: Our imbalanced Air can keep the relationship overly intellectual and ungrounded.

Air—Water
Skillful: Air's intellect gives perspective to Water's emotions; Water teaches Air how to feel.
Unskillful: Air's logic conflicts with Water's feelings; Air's detachment can't satisfy Water's need to emotionally connect.

Water—Water
Skillful: Our water signs can nurture, support, encourage, and heal each other.
Unskillful: Our imbalanced water may cause us to become overemotional, hypersensitive to each other, too dependent, and afraid to take risks.

Part 2: I Compare
My Needs With My Partner's Needs

By now you should realize that certain temperaments naturally adjust to each other (Fire to Air; Earth to Water). Yet, we must always bear in mind that the astrological energies are essentially **neutral**; it is **how we apply them** that makes the difference. Thus, there are positive and negative virtues of *any* two element combinations. Table 3 demonstrates this by providing skillful and unskillful interpretations of each of the element interactions. (Read the interpretations carefully, for you will be using them in your next exercise.)

In reviewing this table, a point to bear in mind is that the terms *"harmony"* and *"disharmony"* are not necessarily synonymous with "desirable" and "undesirable" or good and bad. Just as too many trines can produce an overly comfortable life where the individual is not challenged to do his best, a relationship that has too many "favorable" aspects can become placid and stagnant. On the other hand, when differences occur between two charts, the partners can learn from and balance each other.

Thus, we have found that the best types of relationships contain a **balance** of so called "easy" and "difficult" element compatibilities.

Now, using the keywords in Table 3 complete the sentences below. Let's start with a **sample exercise.**

---

1. My Sun is in the sign of _____*Pisces*_____. Its element is _____*Water*_____.

   My partner's Sun is in the sign of _____*Scorpio*_____. Its element is _____*Water*_____.
   (see Table 2, page 113)

   When we choose to use these energies skillfully, our goals and purposes may combine in the following manner:

   _____*Our water signs can nurture, support, and heal each other*_____
   (fill in skillful element-element keyphrase from Table 3, page 117)

   When we choose to combine these energies unskillfully, then our goals and purposes may combine as follows:

   _____*We may become overemotional, hypersensitive, and afraid to take risks*_____
   (choose unskillful element-element keyphrase from Table 3, page 117)

Now that you have seen how this exercise works, try it out for yourself and your partner. Using Table 3, complete the following sentences.

1. My **Sun** is in the sign of _____. Its element is _____.
   (see Table 2, page 32)   *(see Table 2, page 113)*

   My **partner's Sun** is in the sign of _____. Its element is _____.
   (see Table 2, page 32)   *(see Table 2, page 113)*

   When we choose to use these energies **skillfully**, our goals and purposes may combine in the following manner:

   _____
   (fill in skillful element-element keyphrase from Table 3, page 117)

   When we choose to combine these energies **unskillfully**, then our goals and purposes may combine as follows:

   _____
   (fill in unskillful element-element keyphrase from Table 3, page 117)

2. My **Moon** is in the sign of _____. Its element is _____.

   My **partner's Moon** is in the sign of _____. Its element is _____.

   When we choose to use these energies **skillfully**, our feelings and daily habit patterns may combine in the following manner:

   _____

   When we choose to combine these energies **unskillfully**, then our feelings and daily habit patterns may combine as follows:

   _____

3. My **Ascendant** is in the sign of _____. Its element is _____.

   My **partner's Ascendant** is in the sign of _____. Its element is _____.

   When we choose to use these energies **skillfully**, our outer personalities may combine in the following manner:

   _____

   When we choose to combine these energies **unskillfully**, then our outer personalities may combine as follows:

   _____

4. My **Mercury** is in the sign of _____. Its element is _____.

   My **partner's Mercury** is in the sign of _____. Its element is _____.

   When we choose to use these energies **skillfully**, our styles of communication may combine in the following manner:

   _____

When we choose to combine these energies **unskillfully**, then our styles of communication may combine as follows:

_____ .

5. My **Venus** is in the sign of _____ . Its element is _____ .

My **partner's Venus** is in the sign of _____ . Its element is _____ .

When we choose to use these energies **skillfully**, our styles of loving may combine in the following manner:

_____ .

When we choose to combine these energies **unskillfully**, then our styles of loving may combine as follows:

_____ .

6. My **Juno** is in the sign of _____ . Its element is _____ .

My **partner's Juno** is in the sign of _____ . Its element is _____ .

When we choose to use these energies **skillfully**, our needs for a committed relationship may combine in the following manner:

_____ .

When we choose to combine these energies **unskillfully**, then our needs for a committed relationship may combine as follows:

_____ .

7. My **Descendant** is in the sign of _____ . Its element is _____ .

My **partner's Descendant** is in the sign of _____ . Its element is _____ .

When we choose to use these energies **skillfully**, our needs for a balanced partnership may combine in the following manner:

_____ .

When we choose to combine these energies **unskillfully**, then our needs for a balanced partnership may combine as follows:

_____ .

8. My **Mars** is in the sign of _____ . Its element is _____ .

My **partner's Mars** is in the sign of _____ . Its element is _____ .

When we choose to use these energies **skillfully**, our physical desires and method of resolving conflict may combine in the following manner:

_____ .

When we choose to combine these energies **unskillfully**, then our physical desires and method of resolving conflict may combine as follows:

_____ .

Journal Entry: Relationship

To help you synthesize the information you have learned about yourself and your relationship needs, review the material you have just completed. Then drawing on examples from your own life experiences, consider and answer the following questions.

Am I aware of and expressing my relationship needs? Am I getting them met now? Was I in my previous relationships?

_____

_____

_____

_____

_____

If I don't have a current primary partner, in what ways am I expressing my needs for relating? Am I getting these needs met?

_____

_____

_____

_____

_____

As I look at my past, have I been honest with myself in expressing what my real needs were in a relationship? Or have I denied, ignored, or allowed others to invalidate these needs?

_____

_____

_____

_____

_____

As I look at my partner's needs as I have defined them in the exercises, do they correspond to what I know about him or her? Have I been sensitive to my partner's needs? Am I able to respond? Does my partner recognize and express his or her needs?

_____

_____

_____

_____

_____

_____

_____

Do my partner's needs match my needs?   As I look at the element table in Exercise 6, in which areas do we share needs and which areas are exclusive to each of us?

_____

_____

_____

_____

_____

In what areas of my relationship am I using my skillful element combinations? In which areas am I using the unskillful ones?

_____

_____

_____

_____

_____

Based on a new understanding of my partner's needs, how can I be more sensitive to them? For example: If my partner has Moon in Air, I can talk more. If my partner has Moon in Water, I can be more affectionate. If my partner has Moon in Fire, I can respect his/her freedom. If my partner has Moon in Earth, I can be more practical.

_____

_____

_____

_____

_____

Figure 2: Comparison of Two Charts

Chart Sample
New York,NY
FEB 22 1949 22h 54m 0s
ZONE 5.0 STANDARD TIME
NATAL CHART

(CHART 1)   WITH   (CHART 2)

Joan
Lebanon,OR
OCT 27 1953 13h 2m 0s
ZONE 8.0 STANDARD TIME
NATAL CHART

CHART 2 PLANETS IN CHART 1 Placidus HOUSES

CHART 1 PLANETS IN CHART 2 Placidus HOUSES

*** ASPECTS BETWEEN THE TWO SETS OF PLANETS ***
CHART 1 PLANETS ACROSS (Tropical ZODIAC), CHART 2 DOWN (Tropical ZODIAC)

Aspect Symbol	♂	⚺	⚹	⚼	□	△	⚻	□q	Bq	⅋	180 Parallels
Degree	0	30	45	60	72	90	120	135	144	150	180
	20	11	21	15	10	29	34	9	7	16	17 18

Total Number of Mutual Aspects:

Weighted Contact Strength between the two charts— .428

Grand Total—214

Compatibility and Connectedness

Compatibility

After completing this section, you should have a beginning idea of how you and your partner's birth charts interact. The next step would be to take **each planet** and asteroid in **your birth chart** and **compare** it to each planet and asteroid in your **partner's**. This is what the professional astrologer would do for you if you went to him or her for a *relationship reading*.

Obviously, such a detailed analysis would be beyond the scope of this work. However, we would like to give you a *brief example* of what such a comparison looks like so that you can pursue the analysis on your own.

Figure 2 shows an aspectarian between the charts of Joan and Douglas. We won't be covering aspects until Chapter Six, so if you are a beginner you can skim over this section. If you understand the meaning of aspects, then take a look at the aspectarian. Notice that Douglas' planets are arranged horizontally and Joan's planets are arranged on the vertical. Now look to Douglas' Sun column on the left and start to move down. Directly below it and to the right of Joan's Sun is the symbol for trine (△). (The numbers simply represent the degree and minute of the trine aspect.) This tells us that Douglas' Sun is in a trine aspect to Joan's Sun.

Thus, in this instance, Douglas' **purpose and will** (the Sun) **harmonize** (the trine) with Joan's **purpose and will** (her Sun).

Continue now down the Sun column until you come to the next symbol, that of the square (□) which is located to the right of Joan's Mercury. Thus, Douglas' **Sun** is in a **square** aspect to Joan's **Mercury**. And so on for the complete aspectarian.

Connectedness

One of my friends calls me about once a month saying, "I just met Mr. Right, born June 30, 1944. His Moon is in the same sign as mine, and his Sun trines my Sun. Aren't we compatible? Do you think he might be The One?"

Aside from compatibility, there exists a *second* perspective on chart comparison—the idea of being **connected.** Using the method of chart comparison you just learned, you may discover that you are very compatible with someone, but unless you are also connected, you probably will not be able to sustain an ongoing relationship. On the other hand you may be incompatible, but if you are connected—then a long term relationship (for better or worse) will most likely ensue.

How do you determine this quality of connected-ness? In order to be connected to someone, you must have one of your planets or angles (the Ascendant, Descendant, M.C. or I.C.) in the same or opposite degree as one of their planets or angles. From an energy perspective, the reasoning behind this theory is that **each** of the 360 degrees of the Zodiac vibrates to a **particular frequency.** Because of the law of magnetism, you will be attracted to those individuals who have planets (denoting parts of personality) that resonate to the same frequencies as your own. Because each pair of opposite degrees signifies the two poles of the same energy line, either degree will work.

In determining if planets are connected, we use a small range of + or − 2 degrees. For example, if your Sun is at 5 degrees of Scorpio and your partner's Venus is 3, 4, 5, 6 or 7 degrees of Scorpio, the Sun and Venus are connected. Similarly, if your partner's Venus were located at 3-7 degrees of Taurus (opposite Scorpio) your Sun and Venus would again be connected.

To determine your contact points with another person, simply begin with Aries. Note if you have any planets in Aries, and then see if you partner has any planets in Aries or Libra within 2 degrees of your planet. Then proceed to Taurus-Scorpio, and so on for the other sign polarities (Gemini-Sagittarius, Cancer-Capricorn, Leo-Aquarius and Virgo-Pisces). List these connections and you will have an excellent overview of your major areas of interaction with another person.

These contact points are the *glue* or *bonding* that holds the relationship together. The more of these contact points that you share, the more connected you are. The planets involved will also indicate the nature of your relationship. *Moon* or *Ceres* contacts signify *emotional,* nurturing, or parental interactions; *Juno, Venus* and *Mars* point to *sexual* or *mating* relationships; *Saturn* can indicate *parental* or *authority* figures involved in relationships, etc.

Once a connection has been clearly established, the ensuing relationship will be flowing or stressful, depending on the nature of the planets involved. If the connected planets have a natural affinity (e.g. Venus and the Moon), the interaction will be easier than if a more volatile planetary connection is established (e.g. the fiery Mars and the changeable Uranus).

For those who consider the reincarnation model, it is further suggested that these connections represent karmic contact points. The planets involved indicate what kinds of relationships you had in previous lives, whose karma, or unresolved issues, are now being further enacted in this current life. For example, Moon or Ceres contacts indicate a parent-child interaction. In the current life you may be involved in a husband-wife relationship, but if there exists a strong Moon-Ceres connection, it will be the nurturing, dependency, and parental themes that will become major issues.

Other connections may signify the following: Juno contacts may portray previous marriage partners or mates. Venus and Mars contacts indicate prior sexual connections. Jupiter and Mercury contacts could show prior teacher-student interactions. Moreover, advanced astrological research suggests that sign contacts can point to the historical time period or geographical location in which a relationship took place.

As you can see, there is far more to chart compari-son than the question that began this section, "What sign do I best get along with?" The art of chart comparisons (known in astrology as **"Synastry"**) is a deep, revealing, and highly valuable study. We hope that you have received an informative introduction to this art, and that through the exercises you have identified your important relationship needs and how they compare with those of the significant others in your life.

Volume II in this series *Astrology For Ourselves: The Relationship Compatibility Workbook* will cover these topics and many more in greater detail.

Further Reading: 4

If you wish to learn more about the topics covered in this chapter, we recommend the following books.

Relationship Astrology

Arroyo, Stephen, *Relationships and Life Cycles*
Davison, Ronald, *Synastry*
Goodman, Linda, *Linda Goodman's Love Signs*
Greene, Liz, *Relating, Star Signs for Lovers*

Additional resources are located in the bibliography.

Sargent, Lois H., *How to Handle Your Human Relations*
Townley, John, *Planets in Love*

Vocational Astrology

Wickenburg, Joanne, *In Search of a Fulfilling Career*

Part II

─── *Digging Deeper* ───

A T THIS JUNCTURE, you have been introduced to the basics of the astrological language: the planets, signs and houses. In Chapter One, you learned the building blocks of the signs of the Zodiac, and interpreted your own Sun sign according to these principles. In Chapter Two, you read your chart and were introduced to the planets and houses along with their meanings. In Chapter Three, you interpreted each of your planets according to its sign and house position. You also picked up more about the mythology of each of the planets. In Chapter Four, you found out how the birth chart provides valuable insights into your work and love life.

In the introduction, we stated that several levels of students would be drawn to using *Astrology For Yourself*. If you are on the intermediate level, i.e., you have had some prior exposure to astrology, then much of the material in these chapters might have served as a review. If this is the case, then we encourage you to plunge into the next few chapters.

If however, you began this book without any knowledge of astrology, then you might already feel a bit overwhelmed by the wealth of material that has been presented. For you we recommend that before exposing yourself to additional information, much of which will be quite technical, you spend some time **reviewing what you have just learned.**

To accomplish this, obtain a birth chart of someone you know extremely well such as a member of the family or a close friend. Then, on separate sheets of paper, go back and interpret the chart by completing the programmed learning exercises in Chapters One through Four. We guarantee that by the time you have finished, the information that may now seem a bit vague will become much more clear and familiar. You might even want to pick a third chart and review the exercises once again. The more you do so, the more grounded you will be in the basics. And with that solid foundation, you can easily learn the finer points of interpretation that will be presented in the subsequent chapters.

Whenever you feel ready, begin work on Chapter Five.

Chapter 5

—The Birth Chart As a Whole—

NOW THAT YOU HAVE LEARNED about yourself through the planets, you are ready to explore additional ways of understanding your birth chart. In this chapter, we will look at five new factors—hemisphere emphasis, the moon's nodes, the moon's phases, retrograde planets and intercepted signs.

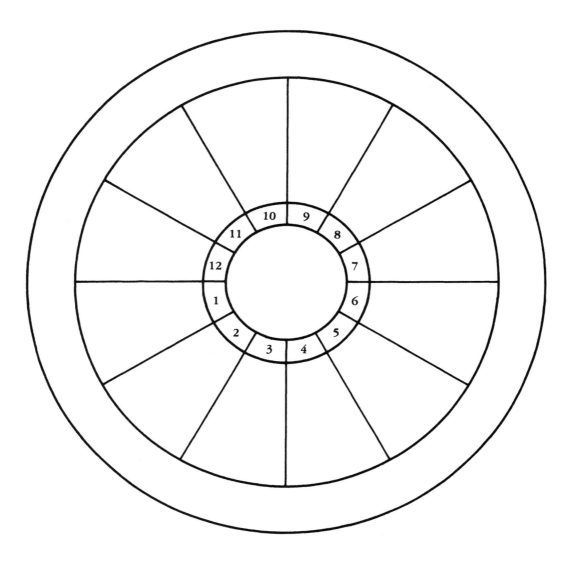

Notes: _____

_____

_____

_____

_____

_____

_____

_____

_____

_____

_____

_____

Hemisphere Emphasis

The birth chart is a map of the positions of the planets at the time and place you were born. Symbolically you are at the center of the circle and at the center of your universe.

The Horizon

The horizontal axis which divides the chart between north and south is called the horizon. If you could recreate the skies at the moment of your birth, the planets above the horizon in the chart would be the ones you could see in the sky directly overhead. The planets below the horizon in the chart would be the ones on the other side of the earth's surface.

The horizon represents a line of awareness.

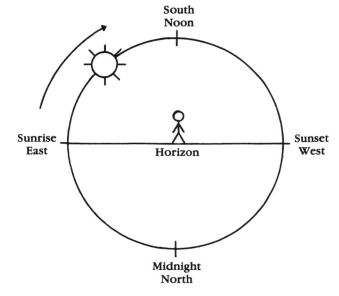

The Meridian

The vertical axis dividing the chart from east to west is called the meridian. Again, if you could recreate the skies at the moment of your birth, the planets on the left of the meridian would be rising in the eastern sky. The planets on the right of the meridian would be setting in the western sky.

The meridian represents a line of concrete experience.

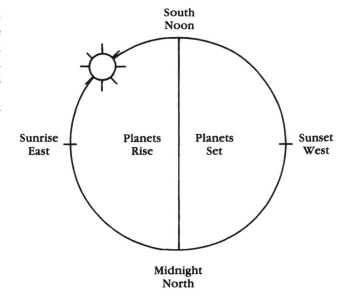

The Outer-Public vs. The Inner-Private Realm

The planets above the horizon, in the upper hemisphere, whose rays symbolically reach us directly through the air, represent parts of our personalities that receive information in an outer, objective or conscious manner.

The planets below the horizon, in the lower hemisphere, whose rays symbolically have to go through the surface of the earth in order to reach us, represent parts of our personalities that receive information in an inner, subjective or subconscious manner.

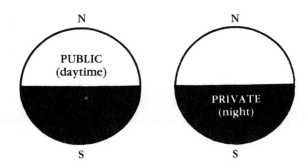

The Active vs. The Responsive Realm

The planets on the left side of the meridian, in the rising hemisphere, represent the active and assertive parts of our personalities. Here is where we sow karmic seeds.

The planets on the right side of the meridian, in the setting hemisphere, represent the receptive and responsive parts of our personalities. Here is where we reap karmic fruits.

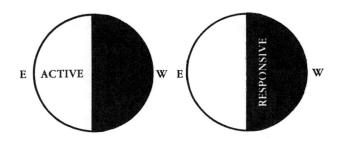

Synthesis

By adding up the number of planets in each sector, you can get a good idea of how you operate on the subjective-objective and the active-responsive scales. Using the keywords from Table 1, you will construct sentences that help to describe your own experiences of these areas.

Table 1: Hemisphere Keywords

UPPER HEMISPHERE
Objective:
outer awareness
extroverted
conscious
public-social

LOWER HEMISPHERE
Subjective:
inner awareness
introverted
subconscious
personal-private

RISING HEMISPHERE
Awareness of self:
active
independent
karma-making
self-motivated

SETTING HEMISPHERE
Awareness of others:
receptive
interdependent
karma-reaping
other-directed

Exercise 1: Am I Primarily Public or Private?

To find out, count the number of planets (the ten planets, Chiron and four asteroids) in your chart that fall above the horizon and below the horizon, and fill in the blanks below.

1. I have _____ (number of) planets in the upper hemisphere of outer awareness.

These planets signify the more extroverted parts of my personality, or my social-objective self. They indicate how I tend to act outside of myself and take part in activities in the outer world. (Review Chapter Three to determine the exact meanings of these planets.)

2. I have _____ (number of) planets in the lower hemisphere of inner awareness.

These planets signify the more introverted (though not necessarily shy or withdrawn) parts of my personality, or my personal-subjective self. They indicate how I tend to be self-involved and live within my private world.

The hemisphere that contains the most planets is the _____ hemisphere.

This tells me that I function primarily as _____

and _____ .
(use hemisphere keywords from Table 1)

Exercise 2: Am I Primarily Active or Responsive?

To find out, count the planets (the ten planets, Chiron and four asteroids) in your chart that fall in the rising and setting hemispheres, and fill in the sentences below.

1. I have _____ (number of) planets in the rising hemisphere of self-directed activity.

These planets signify how I am self-sufficient and tend to make my own choices in life. They indicate the experiences that will enable me to take direct action and make my own decisions.

2. I have _____ (number of) planets in the setting hemisphere of other-directed response.

These planets signify how I am dependent on my surroundings and others for self-determination. They indicate the experiences that will enable me to be sensitive and responsive to the needs and wishes of others.

The hemisphere that contains the most planets is the _____ hemisphere.

This tells me that I function primarily as _____

and _____ .
(use hemisphere keywords from Table 1)

The above exercises should give you a general overview of where you fall on the subjective-objective and self-other scales. Bear in mind, however, that this information **must be integrated** with the rest of the chart. For example, if your subjective hemisphere is strong, but your Sun, Moon, and Ascendant are in the extrovert fire signs, the latter will exert a definite outgoing influence on the personality. Therefore, hemisphere analysis should be used only as a *general overview* and **not** as a final determination of character.

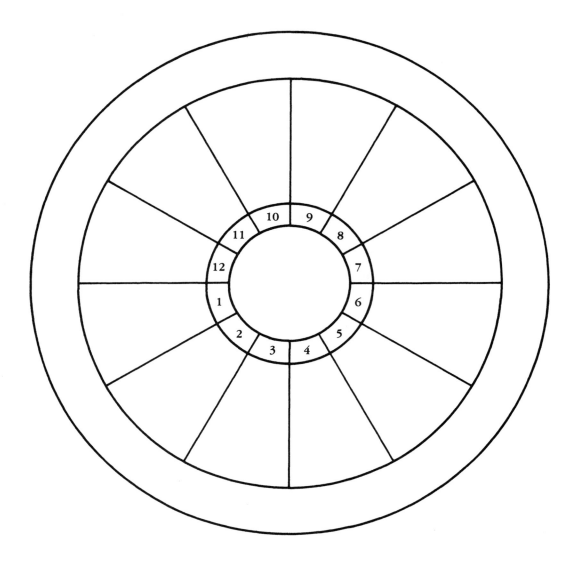

Notes: _____

_____

_____

_____

_____

_____

_____

_____

_____

_____

_____

_____

Two other astrological symbols that will appear in your birth chart are the North and South Nodes of the Moon. Like the angles, the nodes are not physical bodies but points in space. The nodal orbits arise from the intersection of the Moon's orbit with the plane of the ecliptic (the path of the Sun and planets as they appear to revolve around the earth). The north or ascending node (☊) shows where the Moon crosses the Sun's path from south to north. The south or descending node (☋) conversely is formed when the Moon travels from a northerly to southerly celestial latitude. The nodes are referred to in Chinese astrology as the dragon's head (north node) and the dragon's tail (south node).

In the birth chart, the north node is a symbol of spiritual power and integration. It depicts the future and represents how new learning experiences can lead to personal growth.

The south node, lying directly opposite, points to our base of operation—the sum total of knowledge that we have carried over from the past. As a symbol of the past, the south node represents a resource, innate talent, or ability with which we have been born, and it often expresses itself at an early age. Thus, we can use our south node skills to enhance our lives and make a contribution to others and to society, as seen in Table 2.

Our strength comes from what we carry over from the past. Because south node functioning seems so natural, easy, and comfortable, we are vulnerable to overemphasizing these qualities and thus can get stuck there. Eventually we may become bored, limited, stunted in our growth, and depleted of energy.

The nodes after all represent a **polarity**. Problems arise when we remain fixated in the South's Nodes realm and avoid the path of future development depicted by the North Node's sign and house position. For the polarity to remain **balanced**, both sides must be equally represented. Thus, it is suggested that you use your south node as a base of operation while moving forward into the path of future growth depicted by the north node. Table 3 shows how this can occur.

Exercise 3: The Meaning of the Nodes in My Chart

Use Table 2, page 32, to determine the location of the nodes in your birth chart. Then fill out the following sentences.

1) My south node (☋) is in the sign of _____ and in the _____ house.
(see Table 2, page 32)

Thus, an innate talent, resource or ability that I have is my _____ and
(fill in sign keywords from Table 2, page 134)

my_____.
(fill in house keywords from Table 2, page 134)

*Please note that the same keyphrases are used for both sign and house position (e.g., Aries/1st house, Taurus/2nd house). For example, in the sample chart on page 26, the south node is in Libra in the 12th house. Thus, one's innate talent would be the capacity to share and relate to others (Table 2 keywords for *Libra*) and the ability to use empathy and compassion to perceive the unity in all things (Table 2 keywords for the *12th house*).

Finally, if you wish to choose from a list of more descriptive house keywords, you can use those provided in Appendix B.

2) Because the south node is so natural and familiar to me, there is a tendency to overemphasize this part of myself. If this overemphasis occurs, I may experience

_____
(fill in sign keywords from the left column of Table 3, page 134)

and_____.
(ill in house keywords from the left column of Table 4, page 135)

3) My north node (☊) is in the sign of _____ and in the _____ house (see Table 2, page 32). This sign and house position represents my direction toward future growth. The new attitudes of the north node are needed to balance the qualities of the south node. When this balance is provided I can _____
(fill in sign keywords from the right column of Table 3, page 134)

and_____.
(fill in house keywords from the right column of Table 4, page 135)

South Node	Innate Talent or Ability
♈ Aries / 1st house	Functioning as an independent individual
♉ Taurus / 2nd house	Connecting to the material world and its resources
♊ Gemini / 3rd house	Gathering information and effectively communicating it to others
♋ Cancer / 4th house	Nurturing and expressing feelings
♌ Leo / 5th house	Expressing myself and being creative
♍ Virgo / 6th house	Perfecting and refining form
♎ Libra / 7th house	Sharing and relating to others
♏ Scorpio / 8th house	Perceiving the secret working behind manifest form
♐ Sagittarius / 9th house	Seeing systems holistically, understanding how the parts fit into the whole
♑ Capricorn / 10th house	Translating ideals into reality
♒ Aquarius / 11th house	Serving a larger group or humanitarian purpose; originality
♓ Pisces / 12th house	Using empathy and compassion to perceive unity in all things

Table 3: The Nodes in the Signs

South Node	Overemphasis	North Node	Balance Provided
Aries	Overemphasis on self and own independence	Libra	Understand the importance of others.
Taurus	Attachment to material form; resistance to change	Scorpio	Destroy old forms and make way for the new.
Gemini	Overemphasis on facts; immersion in trivia	Sagittarius	Understand how the facts fit into a large whole.
Cancer	Being at the mercy of others; overinvolvement with family	Capricorn	Use self-discipline to direct my emotions so that I can function in the objective world.
Leo	Excessive pride, elitism and self-importance	Aquarius	Develop an altruistic, humanitarian outlook.
Virgo	Emphasis on functionality and efficiency; being judgmental	Pisces	Trust the universe; learn compassion.
Libra	Overdependency on others	Aries	Build self-reliance
Scorpio	Going to extremes; excessive emotional highs and lows	Taurus	Maintain calmness and stability.
Sagittarius	Involvement in abstract, overly impractical concerns	Gemini	Bring abstract ideas into everyday reality.
Capricorn	Excessive ambition; fear of vulnerability	Cancer	Learn to unconditionally accept myself and my feelings.
Aquarius	Excessive detachment; being too erratic and inconsistent	Leo	Develop warmth; relate in a more personal way.
Pisces	Excessive escapism; lack of realism; victimization	Virgo	Learn the skills to function in the world and develop discrimination.

South Node	Overemphasis	North Node	Balance Provided
1st house	Overemphasis on self	7th house	Learn how to cooperate with others
2nd house	Measuring one's value in terms of wealth; overfocus on possessions	8th house	Share physical and emotional resources
3rd house	Too narrow a focus on facts; limited world view	9th house	Develop a broader, wider-ranging perspective
4th house	Overemphasis on family matters; reluctance to leave the home	10th house	Learn how to express myself in the objective world
5th house	Excessive focus on entertainment, speculation or personal concerns	11th house	Focus on group endeavors and community concerns
6th house	Overemphasis on day-to-day routines and responsibilities	12th house	Develop a spiritual world view and practice
7th house	Excessive dependency on others	1st house	Develop a stronger sense of self
8th house	Too much emotional intensity or psychological processing; financial or emotional reliance on others	2nd house	Be grounded in the physical and financial world through the ue of resources and talents
9th house	Involvement in abstract, impractical concerns; excessive education or travel	3rd house	Bring abstract ideas down to earth; focus on the part as well as the whole
10th house	Excessive ambition; too much attachment to reputation	4th house	Create a foundation of self-love and self-acceptance
11th house	Too much emphasis on groups compared to personal concerns; excessive idealism	5th house	Develop warmth and creativity; relate to others in a more personal way
12th house	Excessive desire to retreat from the world and avoid facing reality	6th house	Learn the skills to function in the daily world and be at ease with mundane responsibilities

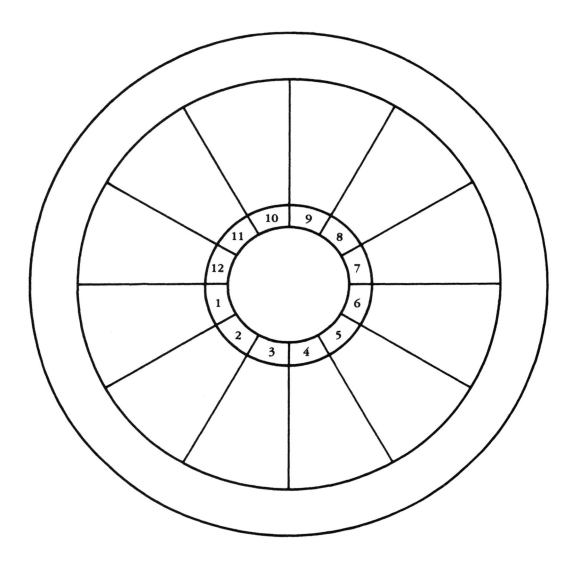

Notes: _____

_____

_____

_____

_____

_____

_____

_____

_____

_____

_____

_____

The Part of Fortune and Moon Phases

The Part of Fortune

The last of the specific symbols in your chart that we will cover is the Part of Fortune. The Part of Fortune is not a heavenly body, but a point in space. Its location is derived from the positions of the Sun, Moon and Ascendant and is a synthesis of these three most sensitive points of personality. The Part of Fortune also indicates how and where you most easily express your Moon Phase purpose (which we will learn about in the next section).

The Part of Fortune focuses the power of the Sun's purpose and the Moon's feelings through the personality of the Ascendant. Consequently, it symbolizes a point of integration—one where we can achieve happiness by being easily able to express our purpose through our natural personality. Thus, according to astrological tradition the Part of Fortune is an indicator of luck—i.e. "good fortune."

The **sign** of the Part of Fortune indicates *how* or which attitudes can facilitate this expression.

The **house** placement signifies *where* or through which activities this fortune can be instinctively realized.

Exercise 4: The Part of Fortune in My Birth Chart

To determine how the part of Fortune is operating in your birth chart, look up its position in Table 2, page 32, and use the appendix keywords to complete the following sentences.

My **Part of Fortune** (⊗) is in the sign of _____ and in the _____ house.

I can most easily integrate my Sun, Moon and Ascendant's needs by fulfilling:

_____ .
(fill in sign keyphrase from Appendix A)

I also can experience the greatest ease of functioning in these areas of my life:

_____ , _____ , and _____ .
(choose house keywords from Appendix B)

When I am skillful in these activities I tend to be _____ ,

_____ , and _____ .
(choose skillful sign keywords from Appendix A)

However, when I am confused or unfocused I may be _____

or _____ .
(choose unskillful sign keywords from Appendix A)

The Meaning of the Moon Phase

As the Moon orbits around the earth each month, it reflects the changing relationship between itself and the Sun. This **Soli-Lunar** relationship or Sun-Moon Phase can be expressed as the angle formed between the Sun and Moon and is used to calculate the Part of Fortune.

The 28-day lunation cycle is subdivided into 8 moon phases, beginning at the New Moon, increasing in light until the cycle culminates at the Full Moon; and then as the Moon wanes and decreases in light ending at the Dark Moon. Each phase lasts about three and a half days.

The phase of the Moon during which you were born is an important significator of personality because it shows the relationship between your Sun and Moon at the time of your birth. This relationship between your solar conscious nature and your lunar subconscious nature indicates the larger overall purpose in your life. The Moon phase points to how your personality can actualize this purpose.

The lunation cycle also describes the birth, growth and development of all organic processes. The New Moon corresponds to the planting and germination of the seed. During the Crescent Moon phase the vital force of the plant breaks through the seed casing and sends its first shoots above the ground. The First Quarter phase correlates to the roots system, and the Gibbous phase to the leaves and stems. The Full Moon phase is the flower of the cycle, and the Disseminating Moon phase is the fruit.

Then as the Moon continues to wane in light, the Last Quarter phase symbolizes the decompositon of the fruit back into the Balsamic phase seed pod. Your birth moon phase can indicate the symbolic point of your function and purpose within a larger cyclic process. For those who consider the reincarnation model, it is proposed that we incarnate successively into each moon phase during a 8-fold cycle of lifetimes in the development of a particular experience or lesson.

Each month when your own Moon phase recurs, you will feel more sensitized to its meaning. This is an extremely fertile period for you each month, not only on a physical level (it has been found that a woman can conceive a child at this time), but also on a mental, creative, or spiritual level. Seeds that you plant find fertile soil for their growth and development.

Turn now to Exercise 5 and learn how your Moon phase will shed more light upon your astrological profile.

Figure 1: The Lunation Cycle

MOON PHASES

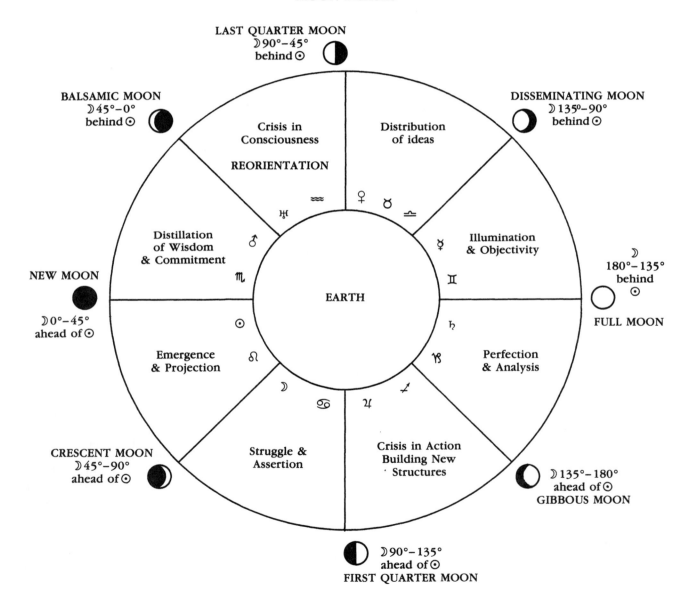

PHASE 1: NEW MOON—EMERGENCE	Initiating a new cycle. Projection of personality and plunging into new experiences in spontaneous and in-stinctive ways.
PHASE 2: CRESCENT MOON—STRUGGLE	Struggling away from the inertia and dependencies of past conditions and mobilizing resources to assert self in a forward direction.
PHASE 3: FIRST QUARTER MOON—ACTION	Taking direct action and managing energy released from crisis situations. Tearing down old structures, building new ones.
PHASE 4: GIBBOUS MOON—PERFECTION	Analyzing self-expression, perfecting techniques and forms. Introspection and questing for revelation.
PHASE 5: FULL MOON—ILLUMINATION	Infusing meaning and content into life structures. Searching for the ideal, fulfillment through relationship.
PHASE 6: DISSEMINATING MOON—DISTRIBUTION	The synthesis and dissemination of ideas. Sharing and communicating what you have learned from experiences so they may be of value.
PHASE 7: LAST QUARTER MOON—REORIENTATION	Crisis in consciousness. Turning away from old accomplishments and following new inspirations. Difficulty in externalizing until complete change occurs.
PHASE 8: BALSAMIC MOON—DISTILLATION	Distilling wisdom essence from entire cycle as legacy for others. The completion of karma. Transformation. Commitment to the future.

————— *Exercise 5: The Moon Phase in My Birth Chart*—————

To discover the meaning of the Moon phase in your birth chart, determine your own Moon phase by following the instructions provided right after this exercise. Then using the keyphrases in Table 5, fill in the following sentence.

My **Sun/Moon phase** is_____, indicating that my larger
(fill in one of the eight phases)

life purpose is_____

_____.
(fill in keyphrase from Table 5)

In order to synthesize the things you have learned about yourself through the Moon Phase, Part of Fortune, and Moon's Nodes, review the material you have just completed. Then in your own words, try to distill experiences from your life that illustrate these concepts.

How does my Moon Phase help me to understand the ways I can best actualize (the Moon) my larger purpose (the Sun)?

_____

_____

_____

_____

In what ways (sign) and in what areas (house) can I most easily express this purpose (Part of Fortune)?

_____

_____

_____

_____

What experiences and attitudes will foster future growth and development toward my larger life purpose (North Node of Moon)?

_____

_____

_____

_____

How and where am I vulnerable in allowing past habitual attitudes to limit and drain my capacity to expand towards growth and potential (South Node of Moon)?

_____

_____

_____

_____

How to Determine Your Moon Phase

Essentially, there are two methods of determining your Moon Phase. A simplified way to determine your Moon Phase can be used if you have a chart print out from Astro Computing Services. If you have an ACS chart, on the left hand side about ⅓ down the page you will see ☉/☽ ANGLE = some number.

If this number is:

0.00–45.00, your Moon Phase is New Moon
45.01–90.00, your Moon Phase is Crescent Moon
90.01–135.00, your Moon Phase is First Quarter Moon
135.01–180.00, your Moon Phase is Gibbous Moon
180.01–225.00, your Moon Phase is Full Moon
225.01–270.00, your Moon Phase is Disseminating Moon
270.01–315.00, your Moon Phase is Last Quarter Moon
315.01–360.00, your Moon Phase is Balsamic Moon

In the reproduction below, we see that ☉/☽ ANGLE = 307.42 or the Last Quarter.

Sample Chart

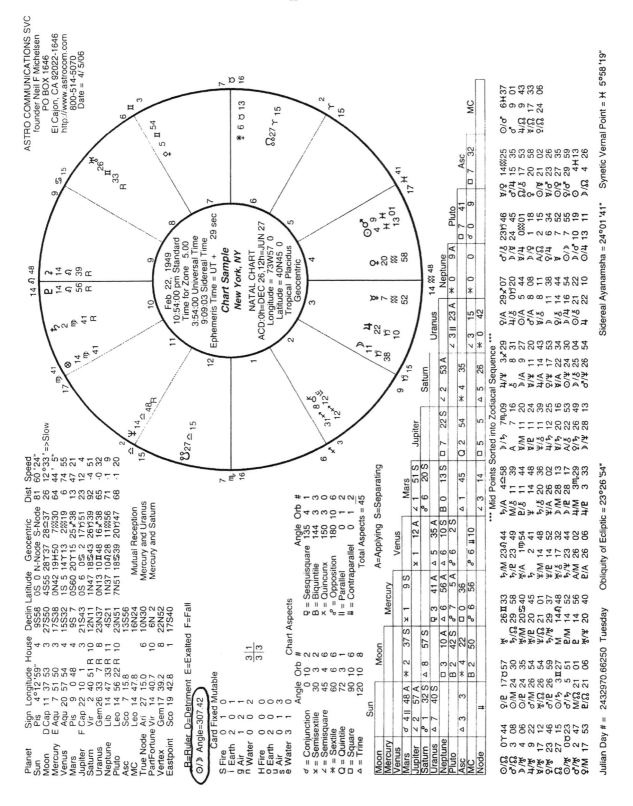

If you are using a different type of chart, you can find your Moon Phase by assembling a Moon Phase and Aspect Wheel. You might want to construct it in any case, as you will be using it for a number of exercises in Chapter Six.

Instructions for Assembling Your Moon Phase and Aspect Wheel

To begin, **cut out** or **photocopy** Figures 3 and 4. You will be needing to cut and paste these diagrams to form your own measuring instrument.

Begin by cutting out the smaller circle, Figure 3. Place it in the center of the larger circle, Figure 4. Align the centers and connect them with a paper fastener so that the inner wheel turns inside the outer wheel. Mounting and pasting these wheels on lightweight cardboard

will make your wheel more durable.

To determine your Moon Phase, rotate the black arrow on the inner wheel to the sign and degree of your Sun. For example, if your *Sun were in 13 degrees of Leo*, you would place the arrow as indicated in the sample moon phase wheel in Figure 2.

Next, holding the wheel in place, locate with your finger the sign and degree of your Moon. In our figure, the *Moon is in 10 degrees of Gemini*. Then point your finger toward the center of the wheel; it will be pointing towards your correct Moon Phase.

Suppose that the Sun were still at 13 degrees of Leo and the *Moon were at 20 degrees of Aries*. What would be the Moon Phase? The answer shown in Figure 2 is the Disseminating Moon Phase. Now proceed to determine your own Moon Phase!

Figure 2: Sample Moon Phase Wheel

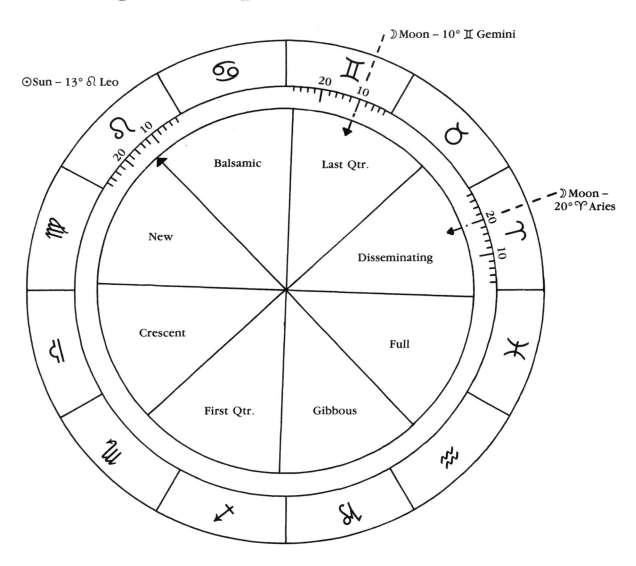

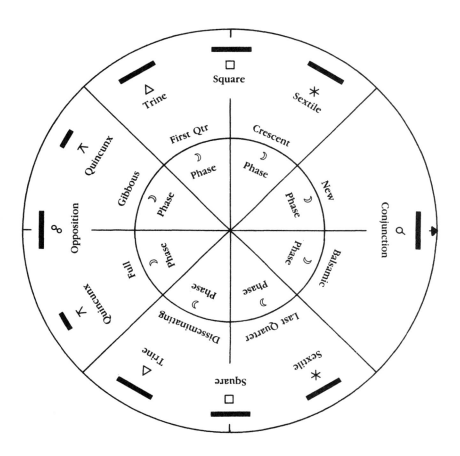

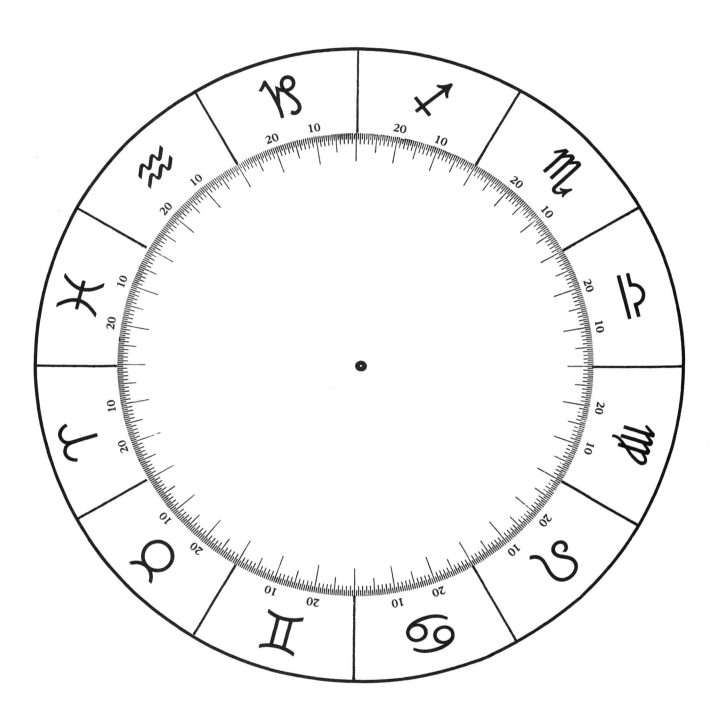

Retrograde Planets and Intercepted Signs

Not every chart has a retrograde planet or intercepted signs and planets. Therefore not every person will be filling out the following exercises. However do read these sections over so that you can gain an appreciation of the subtleties of personality differences.

Retrograde Planets

In your chart you may notice the small notation R or Rx after a planet's position. This refers to the astrological concept of "retrograde" and indicates that the planet was moving in retrograde or an apparent backward motion at the time of your birth.

We use the word "apparent," because planets do not actually move backwards in their orbits. However due to the variations in orbital speeds during certain times of the year, it seems as if a planet is moving backwards from the earth's point of view. There exists a psychological correspondence to this phenomenon.

To illustrate with an analogy, if you are sitting in a stationary train and another train speeds by, you may feel as if you are moving backwards and experience a lurching sensation in your stomach. In reality you have not moved, but the effect you experience is real. In the same way, when a planet is moving retrograde at the time of your birth, you will experience that planetary function in a different way than if it was in direct motion.

There exist many misinterpretations of retrograde planets, the primary one being that planetary function is reversed, inhibited, or repressed in some way. For example Mercury (our capacity to think, speak, learn and reason) retrograde implies an inability to learn or communicate easily. While this is sometimes true, you may also get just the opposite—the precocious or overly loquacious individual who talks continuously about everything. What retrograde actually indicates is that you are using this planetary function at the **extreme ranges** of its expression. So Mercury retrograde can indicate the mystic who has turned his or her thought processes inward, as well as the dynamic and charismatic spokesperson.

Imagine a bell curve of normal population distribution. If you have a planet that is retrograde, you will be expressing the extreme ranges, not the norm, of that planet's functioning as illustrated below.

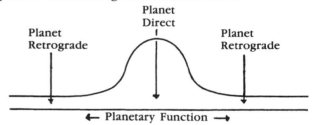

When a planet is direct, you will express its function like the norm of how most other people do. When the planet is retrograde, you will express that planetary function in a much different way than most others do; a way that is more specialized and **unique** to your own individuality.

Exercise 6:
I Locate and Interpret My Retrograde Planets

Look at your birth chart and locate any planets that are retrograde. You may have none, one or several. Review what you wrote about this planet in Chapter Three, your Personality Profile. Consider how you are using this personality function in your own unique way, and write your thoughts in the space below.

A note here to the advanced student. If a planet was retrograde at your birth, it may go direct by progression during your lifetime. Check the ephemeris for the year it goes direct, and you will experience a polarity change in that part of your personality.

Retrograde Planet **The Unique Way That I Express This Planetary Function**

1. _____   _____

2. _____   _____

3. _____   _____

Retrograde Planet	The Unique Way That I Express This Planetary Function
4. _____	_____
5. _____	_____
6. _____	_____

Intercepted Signs and Planets

Intercepted signs are those signs which do not appear on the cusp or beginning of a house, but are contained entirely within a house.

In most hand-drawn and computer charts the intercepted sign is placed outside the wheel in the middle of the house in which it is contained. This is illustrated in the Figure 5 below in which Leo and Aquarius are the intercepted signs.

Figure 5: Intercepted Signs

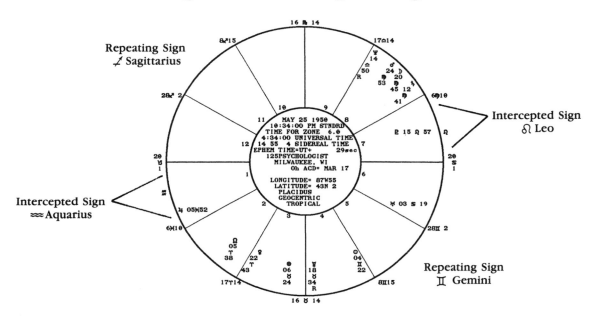

Notice that the signs Gemini and Sagittarius each appear at the beginning of two consecutive houses. If your chart does not have the intercepted signs identified outside the wheel, you will know of their existence if any sign appears on two consecutive house cusps.

There exist varied interpretations of what intercepts signify. You may have difficulty in consciously recognizing and using the way these sign qualities function in the areas of your life activities as designated by the house position. These sign needs may operate beneath the surface of conscious awareness and can thereby bring confusion or a sense of inadequacy in coping with the house activities. You may also experience challenges in expressing the parts of your personality represented by the planets in these intercepted signs.

Some theories propose that intercepted planets refer to unconscious or prior-life painful memories of experiences that would be too difficult to integrate into the personality on a conscious level. Other theories suggest that the energies of intercepted planets are held in reserve during the first part of a person's lifetime (like a reserve tank of fuel). Then in the later part of life, the intercepts "open up" (during major transits), and the individual has vital, vibrant and unused stores of energy to direct toward life goals.

Exercise 7: I Locate and Interpret
My Intercepted Signs and Planets

Look to your chart to determine if you have any intercepted signs. They will always be a pair of opposite signs, i.e. Aries-Libra, Taurus-Scorpio, etc.

The sign polarity of _____ and _____ is intercepted in my chart.

These intercepted signs are in the _____ and _____ houses in my chart.

The following planets are located in these intercepted signs:

_____, _____, _____.

If you have found that your chart *does contain* intercepted signs, then complete the following sentences.

My first intercepted sign is _____ in the _____ house.

I may have challenges in consciously expressing

_____
(fill in sign need from Appendix A)

in this area of my life activities:

_____.
(choose house keywords from Appendix B)

My opposite intercepted sign is _____ in the _____ house.

I may have challenges in consciously expressing

_____
(fill in sign need from Appendix A)

in this area of my life activities:

_____.
(choose house keywords from Appendix B)

If you have any planets in these intercepted signs, list these planets and their keyphrases from Appendix C. You may not have conscious access to the full power of these parts of your personality until the later part of your life.

Planet	**Personality Function**
1. _____	_____
2. _____	_____
3. _____	_____
4. _____	_____
5. _____	_____
6. _____	_____

Journal Entry

To help you synthesize the information you learned about your retrograde planets and intercepted signs, review the material you have just completed. Then drawing on examples from your own life experiences, consider and answer the following questions.

What aspects of myself am I expressing in ways that are different from the norm or mass consciousness, and more unique to my own individuality? (Retrograde planets)

_____

_____

_____

_____

Can I now perceive my individuality in these areas as not being weird, inadequate or hyperactive? In what ways can I express my individuality in a positive and skillful manner?

_____

_____

_____

_____

Does a knowledge of my intercepted signs and houses enable me to recognize those areas where I am not fully aware of my motivations and ways that I operate? What steps can I take to bring these latent functions into the open?

_____

_____

_____

_____

We hope that these exercises in Chapter Five have enabled you to gain deep and useful insights into your inner psychological workings. In Chapter Six we will continue our investigation by examining how your birth chart can shed light on your **planetary patterns.**

Further Reading

If you wish to learn more about the topics covered in this chapter, we recommend the following books.

Moon's Nodes

Schulman, Martin, *Karmic Astrology: The Moon's Nodes and Reincarnation*

Moon Phases

Robertson, Marc, *Not a Sign in the Sky*
Rudhyar, Dane, *The Lunation Cycle*

Retrograde Planets

Jinni and Joanne, *The Digested Astrologer*
Jinni and Joanne, *The Spiral of Life*

Additional resources are located in the bibliography.

Chapter 6

Planetary Patterns
(Optional for Beginners)

I N THIS CHAPTER, we explore one of the most important dimensions of astrology—how the planets interact with each other. Because the planets are the dynamic energies of the birth chart, their interactions comprise a significant part of the total birth chart interpretation.

Planetary interactions occur in two ways—through the astrological **aspects** and through planetary **transits.** These two studies are usually taught at the end of astrological courses because they form the most advanced and complex patterns in the astrological language.

For this reason, we recommend this chapter for *intermediate* or *advanced* students. If you are a beginning student, you may certainly proceed. If, however, you encounter difficulty with some of the exercises, skim them over and take a class on astrology, or use an astrological tutor to supplement the material covered in this chapter.

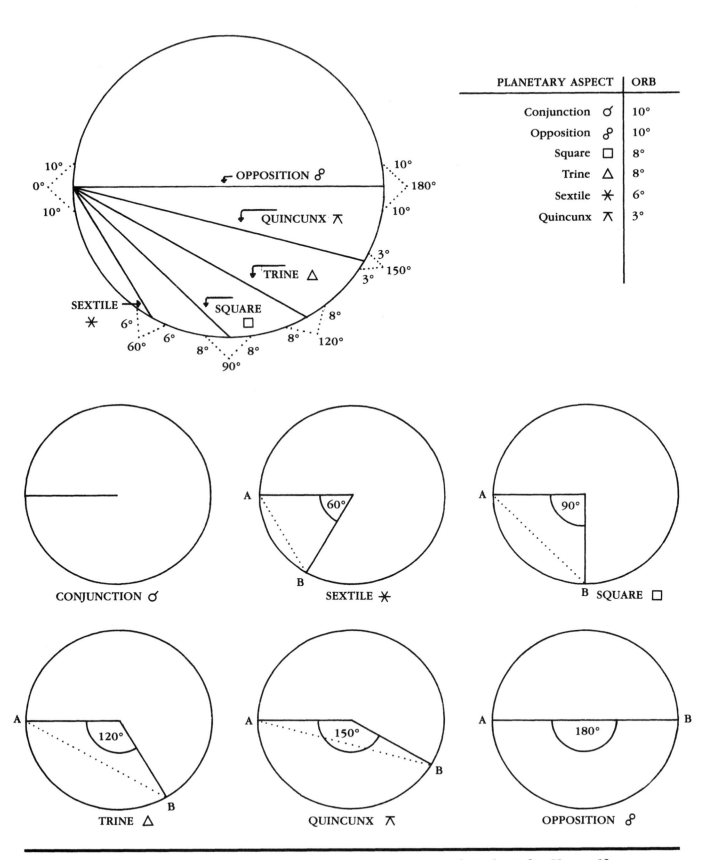

PLANETARY ASPECT		ORB
Conjunction	♂	10°
Opposition	☍	10°
Square	□	8°
Trine	△	8°
Sextile	✳	6°
Quincunx	⚻	3°

CONJUNCTION ♂

SEXTILE ✳

SQUARE □

TRINE △

QUINCUNX ⚻

OPPOSITION ☍

The Planetary Aspects

We are now ready to return to our old friends, the planets.

In Chapter Three, you discovered how each of your planetary energies was modified through being in a particular sign and house. Interpreting these sign and house positions provided you with a wealth of information about yourself.

Yet even more important than the planetary relationships to the signs and houses is their relationship *to each other!* The planets are the dynamic active principles in the birth chart. They represent the many "people" or "sub-personalities" that reside in your psyche. Therefore, how they *interact* among themselves has a major impact on your personality and your well being.

Astrologers call these planetary relationships the planetary **aspects.** You may have heard of terms such as trine, square, opposition, or noticed colored lines in the inner circle of your birth chart. The terms refer to the names of aspects, and the colored lines indicate each aspect relationship.

In the birth chart, the aspects are determined by a very simple method—measuring the **geometric angles** that the planets form with one another. These angular distances are found by dividing the 360 degree circle by whole numbers, i.e. 2, 3, 4, and 6. To keep matters simple, we are only going to be concerned with angular relationships that are multiples of 30 degrees.

When two planets are at certain specified distances from one another, they are said to form an aspect. The aspect describes a particular kind of interaction or relationship that the planets share with one another.

Figure 1 graphically displays the aspects and their degrees.

How to Locate the Aspects in the Birth Chart

In order to interpret the aspects in your chart, you first must determine what they are. This involves looking them up in your **aspectarian.** A sample aspectarian from Astro Computing Services is shown in Figure 2 below. If you already have your own birth chart, the aspectarian may look a bit different and may use aspect symbols instead of the names.

For your reference, we have listed the aspect symbols along with their corresponding abbreviation.

(σ) = CON = Conjunction
($*$) = SXT = Sextile
($\square$) = SQU = Square
($\triangle$) = TRI = Trine
(π) = QNX = Quincunx
($\mathcal{S}$) = OPP = Opposition

Figure 2: A Sample Aspectarian

```
ASPECTS  ANGLE ORB  #              ANGLE ORB  #
CON=Conjunction   Ø  1Ø  2   TRI=Trine       12Ø 1Ø  8
SSX=Semisextile  3Ø   3  2   SQQ=Sesquiquad  135  4  1
SSQ=Semi-Square  45   4  6   BQT=Biquintile  144  3  3
SXT=Sextile      6Ø   6  6   QCX=Quincunx    15Ø  3  Ø
QTL=Quintile     72   3  1   OPP=Opposition  18Ø 1Ø  6
SQR=Square       9Ø  1Ø  6   / =Parallel or   Ø   1  3
A=Applying  S=Separating   I =Contraparallel
              SUN                  TOTAL ASPECTS = 44
```

	SUN	MOON	MERCURY	VENUS	MARS	JUPITER	SATURN	URANUS	NEPTUNE	PLUTO	ASC	MC
MOON												
MERC												
VENU												
MARS	CON 4/48A	SXT 2 37S	SSX 1 09S									
JUPI	SSQ 2 57A			SSX 1 12A	SSQ 1 51S							
SATU	OPP 1 32S	TRI 8 57S			OPP 6 20S							
URAN	TRI 7 40S		SQQ 3 41A	TRI 5 35A								
NEPT		SQR 3 10A	TRI 6 56A	TRI 6 10S	BQT 0 13S	SQR 7 22S	SSQ 2 53A					
PLUT		BQT 2 42S	OPP 7 05A	OPP 6 02S			SSQ 3/23A	SXT 0 09A				
ASC	TRI 3 03	SXT 4 22	SQR 0 36		TRI 1 45	QTL 2 54	SXT 4 35			SQR 7 41		
MC		BQT 2 50	OPP 6 56	OPP 6 11O				SSQ 3 15	SXT 0 00	CON 0 09	SQR 7 32	
NODE					SSQ 3 15	SQR 5 05	TRI 5 25	SXT 0 42				

Aspectarian Viewing Instructions

The aspectarian in the Astro Computing Services computer chart printout calculates thirteen different aspects. However for the purposes of *Astrology For Yourself,* you will be using *only* the *six major* aspects—the conjunction, sextile, square, trine, quincunx and opposition.

In the legend above the aspectarian, the first column is entitled **Aspects,** and gives the name abbreviations and the aspects' names, e.g. CON = Conjunction.

The next column entitled **Angle** refers to the number of degrees, an angular distance, that determines the aspect. For example, SXT = Sextile = 60 indicates that when two planets are 60 degrees apart, they have a sextile relationship.

The third column entitled **Orb** indicates the range of how many degrees plus or minus on either side of the exact angle still constitutes an aspect relationship. ACS uses a 10 degree orb for the conjunction, square, trine and opposition; a 6 degree orb for the sextile; and a 3 degree orb for the quincunx. These orbs are somewhat arbitrary. Some astrologers and chart casting services use smaller orbs while others may use larger orbs.

So while an exact sextile is 60 degrees, planets that are plus or minus a range of 6 degrees on either side of 60 degrees, or 54–66 degrees apart, also qualify for a sextile relationship. In general, the **closer** two planets are to the exact degree of the aspect, the more **powerful** the relationship. However very sensitive individuals respond to aspects with wide or larger orbs, while others may not relate to aspects energies having small orbs. Thus, there do not exist clear-cut definitives on this issue of aspects and orbs.

The final column (#) tells how many times your chart contains that particular aspect.

Two more notations located under the legend are A = Applying and S = Separating. An applying aspect indicates that the faster moving planet is approaching the slower moving planet. A separating aspect signifies that the faster moving planet is leaving or moving away from the slower moving planet. Event oriented schools of astrology believe that applying aspects are more powerful than separating ones. However, psychological approaches to astrology reveal potent influences in the separating aspects as well.

Now take a look at the aspectarian itself.

You will be looking for only the following aspect abbreviations: CON, SXT, SQU, TRI, QCX, OPP. The number after the name abbreviation indicates the actual orb distance of the planets in your chart—the number of degrees from the exact aspect. A or S signifies applying or separating aspect.

You will determine the aspects for Sun through Pluto. Do not include the ASC (Ascendant), MC (Midheaven) or Node. For the asteroid aspects, turn to page 2 of your computer printout from ACS (if you have one), and follow the same directions.

Note that the aspectarian in Figure 2 is a grid that has both columns and rows intersecting to form a number of boxes. Now, let's say you want to locate the aspect between the Sun and Mars. The first column to the left should have the word SUN at the top. Once you have found it, run down the column until you arrive next to the word MARS. What appears in the box? The abbreviation for conjunction (CON). This tells us that in the birth chart, the Sun is in a conjunction aspect to Mars.

Now look up one box so that you are located next to the abbreviation for Venus (VENU). Notice that this box is empty, meaning that no aspect exists between the Sun and Venus at the time of birth. The same holds

true for the Mercury and the Moon as you can see.

On the other hand, if you look two boxes down from Mars in the space next to Saturn (SATU), you will find the abbreviation for opposition (OPP). This tells us that the Sun is in opposition, or 180 degrees from Saturn. (We skipped over the aspect to Jupiter because it is not one of the six we are considering).

Now move one column over to the right that is headed by the Moon. If we move down the column, we see that no aspects are made until we come to the box that is located in the row headed by Mars. In this box, we see the abbreviation for sextile (SXT). This tells us that the Moon is in a sextile or 60 degree aspect to Mars. The SXT 2 37S means that the aspect is separating and has an orb of two degrees and thirty-seven minutes.

So far, we have looked at the aspectarian for the planets. If you have a chart form from Astro Computing Services, page 2 contains an aspectarian for Chiron and the four Asteroids. It appears in Figure 2a.

———————Figure 2a: The Asteroid Aspectarian———————

```
              *** CHART ASPECTS ***

           *CERES*    *PALLAS*   *JUNO*     *VESTA*    *CHIRON*
SUN    - --   -    SQR 1 41A  SXT 2 00A  SQR 7 59A  SQR 4 18
MOON   BQT 2 59S  BQT 0 16A  TRI 5 25S  SSX 0 34A  - --   -
MERC   OPP 6 47A/TRI 1 58S  SQR 1 38S  SXT 4 20A/SXT 0 39
VENU   OPP 6 19S  - --   -    /- --   -    QTL 0 27
MARS   - --   -    SQR 3 07S  SXT 2 47S  SQR 3 11A  SQR 0 30
JUPI   - --   -    SQQ 1 16A  - --   -    - --   -    SSQ 1 21
SATU   - --   -    SQR 3 13S  TRI 3 33S  SQR 9 31S  SQR 5 50
URAN   SSQ 3 05A  - --   -    - --   -    - --   -    - --   -
NEPT   SXT 0 09S  TRI 8 54A  - --   -    SXT 2 36A  - --   -
PLUT   CON 0 18S  QTL 2 57S  SQR 8 43A  TRI 2 45A  TRI 6 25
ASC    SQR 7 23   QCX 1 22   OPP 1 02   - --   -    SSX 1 15
MC     CON 0 09  I- --   -    SQR 8 34  ITRI 2 36   TRI 6 17
NODE   - --   -    - --   -    CON 8 58  SQQ 0 04  SQQ 3 44
CHIR   TRI 6 07  /OPP 2 38  QCX 2 18   CON 3 41  - --   -
CERE   - --   -    - --   -    SQR 8 25A  TRI 2 27A  TRI 6 07
PALL   - --   -    - --   -    SSX 0 20S  OPP 6 18A/OPP 2 38
JUNO   SQR 8 25A  SSX 0 20S  - --   -    BQT 0 02S  QCX 2 18
VEST   TRI 2 27A  OPP 6 18A  BQT 0 02S  - --   -    CON 3 41
```

Basically, you read this aspectarian in the same way as the previous one—by rows and columns. For example, if we find **Ceres** at the top of the leftmost column and look down three spaces opposite Mercury, we find the abbreviation for the opposition (OPP), signifying that Ceres and Mercury form an opposition aspect.

Now turn to Figure 2 and Figure 2a and determine the remaining major aspects (CON, SXT, SQU, TRI, QCX, OPP). Proceed down each column, just as we did before, and locate each of the aspects. Then, write your

answers in the table we have provided on the next page. Periodically, check your answers with those listed in the answer key at the end of the section.

If you find that you are getting the hang of it by the twentieth aspect and don't want to take the time to complete the entire exercise, that's OK.

By filling out this exercise, you will be able to take the next step and locate the aspects in your own birth chart.

	PLANET A	ASPECT	PLANET B
1.			
2.			
3.			
4.			
5.			
6.			
7.			
8.			
9.			
10.			
11.			
12.			
13.			
14.			
15.			
16.			
17.			
18.			
19.			
20.			
21.			
22.			
23.			
24.			
25.			
26.			
27.			
28.			
29.			
30.			
31.			
32.			
33.			
34.			
35.			
36.			
37.			
38.			
39.			
40.			
41.			
42.			
43.			
44.			
45.			
46.			
47.			
48.			

──────Exercise 2: Locating the Aspects in My Birth Chart──────

Turn now to the aspectarian that comes with your birth chart. Find the Sun column at the far left and run your finger down until you encounter the first major aspect (CON, SXT, SQU, TRI, QNX or OPP). When you locate it, write it down in Table 1, My Planetary Aspects. Put the Sun in the Planet A column and the aspecting planet in the Planet B column, just as it was laid out in the answer key to Exercise 1.

When you have completed entering the first aspect, continue down the Sun column, locate and enter each new aspect that you find. When you have come to the planet Pluto, move over to the Moon's column and repeat the process. Then move to Mercury's column,

Venus, Mars, Jupiter, Saturn, Uranus, Neptune and Pluto. Most planets will have one or more aspects, but some planets may not have any aspects.

After you have completed the Pluto aspects, turn to page 2 of the Astro Computing Services printout (if you have one) and locate the asteroid aspectarian. Starting with Ceres, look down the column and identify the major aspects just as you did in Exercise 1. Then continue with Pallas, Juno, Vesta and Chiron until you have written down all of the aspects in Table 1.

To remind you of the aspect symbols and names, we have provided a key at the beginning of the Table.

──────Table 1: My Planetary Aspects──────

ASPECT NAME	SYMBOL	ABBREVIATION
Conjunction	☌	CON
Sextile	⚹	SXT
Square	☐	SQU
Trine	△	TRI
Quincunx	⚻	QNX
Opposition	☍	OPP

	PLANET A	ASPECT	PLANET B
1.			
2.			
3.			
4.			
5.			
6.			
7.			
8.			
9.			
10.			
11.			
12.			
13.			
14.			
15.			
16.			
17.			
18.			
19.			
20.			
21.			
22.			
23.			
24.			
25.			

If you find more aspects, you can continue this list on a separate sheet of your own.

Interpreting Planetary Aspects

As we have already mentioned, aspects indicate the nature of the interactions among the various parts of your personality. They show who is connected to whom, and how easy or difficult that relationship is.

Table 3 at the end of the chapter lists the major aspects and their keyphrases. We are also listing it below for your convenience.

Table 3: Aspect Keyphrases

ASPECT	SYMBOL	ANGLE	KEYPHRASE
Conjunction	☌	0	merges with (positively or negatively), unconsciously identifies with.
Sextile	✳	60 or 2 Signs	productively combines with, facilitates the expression of.
Square	□	90 or 3 Signs	produces stress with, creates dynamic tension with.
Trine	△	120 or 4 Signs	easily combines with, harmonizes with, creatively interacts with.
Quincunx	⚻	150 or 5 Signs	contradicts, creates paradox with, forces adjustment with.
Opposition	☍	180 or 6 Signs	opposes or creates tension with, needs to balance with.

ASPECT	POTENTIAL
Conjunction	Potential for intensified *Strength through Unification*
Sextile	Potential for *Building a New Talent*
Square	Potential for *Productivity through Focus of Energy*
Trine	Potential for *Creative Expression*
Quincunx	Potential for *Transformation through Adjustment*
Opposition	Potential for *Integration through Balance*

By refering to this table, you will see that some aspects (the trine and sextile) are considered to be harmonious or easy, and are referred to as the "soft aspects." Others (the square, quincunx, and opposition) are more difficult or challenging and are called the "hard aspects." The conjunction is considered neutral.

What this means is that if two or more of your planets are in a conjunct, sextile or trine aspect relationship, those parts of your personality symbolized by the planets will probably operate in a harmonious or agreeable manner. However, if two or more of your planets are in a square, quincunx, or opposition aspect, you may experience conflict or tension between those parts of your personality.

Let us take an example. You wake up one morning feeling ill, tired and congested. You have the Sun in Taurus in the fourth house. The Sun has a sextile aspect to the Moon in Cancer in the sixth house, and the Sun also has an opposition aspect to Saturn in the tenth house.

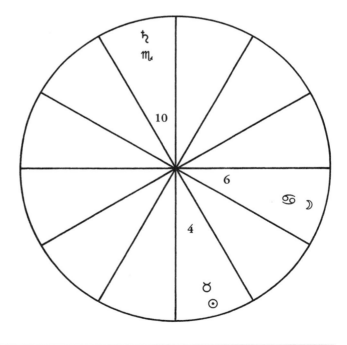

The Sun, or your basic identity, naturally wants to stay at home (fourth house is the area of the home). Because of the Sun's harmonious sextile aspect to the Moon, your Moon's feelings are in total agreement. Moreover, your feelings urge you to nurture yourself (Cancer) with rest, teas and good food in order to improve your health (sixth house). However you may experience resistance to this idea from Saturn who is in opposition to the Sun. The Saturnian hard-working and responsible part of your personality might insist that you get up and go to work. Your boss is depending on you to be there for an important business client—the results of which will influence a possible promotion (tenth house).

How will you resolve this dilemma? Through this example you can see that the way a planet operates is not only influenced by its sign and house position (that is, the Sun is in Taurus in the fourth house), but also by the aspect relationships it has to the other planets (the Sun sextiles the Moon and opposes Saturn). While the hard or difficult aspects present a challenge, they also contain the potential for resolving the problem which results in learning and growth. The opposition aspect between the Sun and Saturn in our example suggests the need to balance and integrate these two parts of your personality. Perhaps one solution might be to get up and meet with the business client, and then take the rest of the day off—thereby satisfying both of the conflicting needs. Can you think of other solutions to this problem?

Let us look at another example to further illustrate this concept of the resolution of challenging aspects. If you have Neptune opposing Saturn in your chart, you might experience a conflict between your dreams and ideals (Neptune) with your sense of pragmatic reality (Saturn). Some possible ways that you might express this aspect is squandering your resources on unrealistic ventures, escaping and avoiding your responsibilities, or denying the validity of spiritual or artistic values in your life. However the potential inherent in the opposition aspects is integration through considering and balancing both sides of the apparent conflict. Thus, when skillfully applied, this aspect could result in the ability to turn your dreams into reality, or give a transcendent meaning to everyday responsibilities.

Before enlightenment: Chop wood, carry water
After enlightenment: Chop wood, carry water

Resolving Challenging Aspects ───────

The birth chart never presents a problem that you are unable to resolve, so that no difficult aspect is ever permanent. The key to the solution is learning how to integrate and satisfy *all* of your varying needs through a skillful application of the planetary energies. This often means taking a stressful aspect and finding a way to express its productive qualities.

For example, you may experience the **square** aspect as a conflict between parts of your personality, but this aspect can produce the greatest *productivity* through its dynamic tension. Visualize the image of a hydroelectric dam which stores water under great pressure in order to generate electricity to do work. Here you have an excellent example of how the square aspect can operate.

Likewise the **quincunx** aspect can be felt as irritation between two parts of your personality that are totally out of synchronization with each other. However the purpose of the quincunx is to create *transformation* through analyzing, adjusting and fine-tuning the personality functions.

The **opposition** aspect may create a tug-of-war between two opposing factors, but when you can allot equal time and value to both sides, you will come into a state of *balance and integration*.

The **conjunction** *can go either way* depending upon the planets involved. They can unify their energies to yield the strength and power of a well-coordinated team, or they can compete with or ignore one another. The keyword here is *intensification*. For example, Moon conjunct Saturn can be experienced as emotional (Moon) depth (Saturn), or as emotional inhibition, depending on how skillfully you are expressing the energies.

The **trine** aspect facilitates a harmonious, creative, and easy flow between the parts of your personality. It may indicate inherent talents and abilities.

The **sextile** aspect presents opportunities which if acted upon can produce the talents and benefits of the trine aspect.

It should be mentioned that although the *sextile* and *trine* aspects are considered *easy*, if you do not exert any effort or initiative, these aspects can rapidly become *passive* and *lazy*. It is usually the hard aspects with their discomfort that produces the need for change that activates the "easy" aspects in the chart.

With all of this in mind, let us now look at two sample delineations which will illustrate the format that you will use to interpret your own aspects.

Because of the many variables that need to be synthesized, interpreting aspects is perhaps the most troublesome procedure that confronts beginning students. We have designed a format that will help you to break down this complicated planetary sentence into its component parts. What is involved is first determining the meaning of a planet in a particular sign and house (Ceres in Leo in the ninth house); then integrating the meaning of the aspect (easy or challenging) in relationship to a second planet in a particular sign and house (Neptune in Libra in the twelfth house).

The first sample aspect analysis is on the following page. Briefly read it over and then turn to the explanation that follows.

1. My planet A __Ceres__ in the sign of __Leo__ in the __9th__ house is in __Sextile__ aspect to my planet B __Neptune__ in the sign of __Libra__ in the __12th__ house.

2. **PLANET A** __Ceres__ → **PLANET A's SIGN** __Leo__ → **PLANET A's HOUSE** __9__
   Keyphrase (App.C): **what** Keyphrase (App.A): **how** Keywords (App.B): **where**

   My capacity to love and *By creatively expressing* *Through the search*

   nurture myself and others *myself and being appreciated* *for higher meaning*

3. **ASPECT** __Sextile__
   ⬍ Aspect keyphrase (Table 3, p.163) __Productively combines with__

4. **PLANET B** __Neptune__ → **PLANET B's SIGN** __Libra__ → **PLANET B's HOUSE** __12__
   Keyphrase (App.C): **what** Keyphrase (App.A): **how** Keywords (App.B): **where**

   My capacity to transcend *By cooperating with others* *Through universal*

   my finite self through *and creating balance and* *visions and service*

   unity with a greater whole *harmony in my life* *to others*

5. If the above aspect is "easy" (a conjunction, sextile or trine), I may be __nurturing__, __productive__, __idealistic__, and __sensitive__.
   (choose 2 skillful keywords for planet A and 2 for planet B from Table 4, page 163)

6. If the above aspect is "difficult" (a conjunction, square, quincunx, or opposition), then I may have chosen to be _____, _____, _____, and _____.
   (choose 2 unskillful keywords for planet A and 2 for planet B from Table 4, page 163)

6a. If I answered section 6 above, then my challenge is to change the stressful aspects between the two planets into a positive one. I can resolve this problem by realizing the potential for _____.
   (fill in aspect potential from Table 3, page 163)

   Thus I can express the planet's skillful qualities by being _____ and _____.
   (choose a skillful keyword for each planet from Table 4, page 163)

7. *Optional:* In your own words, try to compose one or two sentences that synthesize all of the above ideas.

   I can best nurture myself and others (Ceres) by engaging in creative expression

   (Leo) in the areas of higher education and philosophy (9th house). This function

   productively combines with (the sextile) my ability to transcend my finite self

   (Neptune) by cooperating with others (Libra) in creative partnerships (Leo-Libra) to

   offer universal visions as a service to the larger society (12th house).

In the first example we wrote the interpretation for the aspect—Ceres in Leo in the ninth house, sextile Neptune in Libra in the twelfth house. The following sentences will explain how we used the aspect form to create a simple yet powerful interpretation.

1. In the first sentence on the sample worksheet, we entered planet A (**Ceres**)—the name of the planet and its sign and house positions. Then we entered the name of the aspect (**Sextile**) and the same information for planet B (**Neptune**).

2. We then looked up the keyphrase for planet A (**Ceres**), the keyphrase for planet A's sign (**Leo**), and the keywords for planet A's house (**Ninth**). These are located in Appendices C, A and B, respectively. You should now have an idea of how planet A (in and of itself) functions in this chart. However, as we mentioned before, planet A is also influenced by its aspect relationships to other planets.

3. In this section we filled in the aspect name (**Sextile**), and aspect keyphrase located in Table 3, p.163.

4. In this part we looked up and filled in planet B's (**Neptune's**) keyphrases and keywords for its sign (**Libra**) and house (**Twelfth**) as we did for planet A.

5. Here, we simply filled in the skillful planet keywords for Ceres and Neptune as the sextile is an "easy" aspect.

6. Note also that the **Conjunction** can be either easy or difficult. You must decide that for yourself based on how smoothly the basic planetary energies combine. For example a Mars-Saturn conjunction will be more difficult to integrate than a Venus-Jupiter.

After completing this sample aspect analysis, we can integrate the complete meaning of the planetary aspect relationship. This can be done in two ways—looking at what we have written horizontally or vertically. Initially reading the keyphrases **vertically** will be easier.

So first look at the meaning of **planet A** (Ceres) (remembering the planets indicate *what*), and see if the Ceres function operates in an easy or difficult manner (indicated by the aspect keyphrase) with **planet B** (Neptune). In this case, the relationship is harmonious, as the Ceres function productively combines with (sextiles) that of Neptune.

Next, do the same with the relationship between the **sign** (*how*) **keyphrases** of planet A versus planet B (Leo and Libra).

Finally, use the aspect keyphrase to combine the **house** (*where*) **keywords** of planet A and planet B (the ninth and twelfth houses).

You should now have a greater understanding of all the issues involved. In interpreting the aspect from a **horizontal** perspective, you can see how the **total meaning** of planet A (planet—*who* or *what*, sign—*how*, and house—*where*) interfaces by aspect relationship (easy or difficult) with the total meaning of planet B.

The exercise concludes in parts 5 and 6, where we have supplied additional sentences to demonstrate how skillfully or unskillfully you are using the planetary energies. As we have stressed elsewhere in this book, if you are having difficulty expressing the skillful application of a planetary energy, the resolution of the problem lies in activating the positive potential of the very same energy.

Finally, part 7 gives you the opportunity to write a brief summary of the interaction in your own words.

We don't want to confuse you even more, but one more important idea should be mentioned. Ultimately the way you determine how a planet operates is by considering and integrating the meanings of **all** the aspect relationships that planet has. For example, according to the sample aspectarian, the Sun is in opposition to Saturn in Virgo in the tenth house, *and* it trines Uranus, *and* it is conjunct Mars, *and* it trines the Ascendant. This is where the science of astrology becomes the art of astrology. For right now, just understand one aspect at a time. As you continue to study aspect interpretation, the advanced synthesis will come in its own time.

You will be refering to Appendix C for the planet keyphrase. Appendix C also contains additional information about the meanings of each planet. Look over these other keywords in order to gain a more expanded view of how the planet, or corresponding part of your personality, can operate. If any of these keywords seem particularly relevant to you, include them in your interpretations.

Appendix A contains the keyphrases for the signs, and Appendix B the keywords for the houses. Tables 3 and 4 can be located on page 163.

Now turn to page 164 and read over Example 2. This will give you the opportunity to view one more completed aspects form. Note again how the interactions can be read vertically. For example, the opposition aspect can be seen working through the planets (**Sun vs. Saturn**), the signs (**Pisces vs. Virgo**), or through the houses (**the Fourth vs. Tenth**).

The opposition aspect is especially interesting because it usually involves opposing signs which *both* **complement** and **contrast** each other. Rather than identify with one pole or the other, the key to resolving a sign opposition is to **integrate** the two sides, for each sign *needs* its opposite in order to be *balanced* and *complete*.

Therefore, when you have an opposition, besides comparing the planetary keywords, you can also interpret the aspect by using the keywords of the opposing signs. Table 2 presents the keywords for each sign polarity. You can use these keywords as an aid in interpreting the sign polarities that are activated by any oppositions in your own birth chart.

For example, in Example 2 where the Sun-Saturn opposition is occuring in the signs of Pisces and Virgo, the individual must balance the **Pisces-Virgo polarity**—by having *both* skepticism and faith, discrimination and belief, etc.

Finally, after you have completed the two sample aspect interpretations, turn to Table 1 and locate your first listed aspect. It will be between the Sun and some other planet. (If your Sun makes no aspects, then you will start with the Moon.) Using these two as planet A and planet B, fill in the first blank aspect page that follows. Then move to your second aspect and complete the second blank aspect page.

Continue with each aspect listed in Table 1 until you have completed them all. We have provided ten formatted pages for you. If you need more, simply photocopy additional copies of one of the blank forms. When you are done, you have a rich and varied portrayal of the major themes of your birth chart.

——— Table 2: The Sign Polarities ———

ARIES	LIBRA	TAURUS	SCORPIO
Independence	Interdependence	Formation	Transformation
Self	Other	Generation	Regeneration
Me	You	Anabolism	Catabolism
I	Thou	Building up	Breaking down
Action	Interaction	Nature's appearance	Nature's secrets
Competition	Cooperation	Sensuality	Sexuality
Conquest	Compromise		
Aggression	Diplomacy		
War	Peace		

GEMINI	SAGITTARIUS	CANCER	CAPRICORN
Knowledge	Wisdom	Home	Society
Intellect	Understanding	Private self	Public self
Concrete facts	Abstract thought	Inner softness	Outer shell
Nearsighted	Farsighted	Nurturance	Accomplishment
Student	Teacher	Family	Career
Ideas	Ideals	Response	Responsibility
Short journeys	Long journeys		

LEO	AQUARIUS	VIRGO	PISCES
Personal love	Impersonal love	Skepticism	Belief
Romance (filia)	Friendship (agape)	Doubt	Faith
Passion	Detachment	Criticism	Compassion
Monarchy	Democracy	Science	Mysticism
The King/Queen	The People	The many	The one
Center	Circumference	The parts	The whole
Actor	His/her audience	Differentiated	Undifferentiated
The lion	The unicorn	Separateness	Togetherness
		Dividing	Merging

Table 3: Aspect Keyphrases

ASPECT	SYMBOL	ANGLE	KEYPHRASE
Conjunction	♂	0	merges with (positively or negatively), unconsciously identifies with.
Sextile	✶	60 or 2 Signs	productively combines with, facilitates the expression of.
Square	□	90 or 3 Signs	produces stress with, creates dynamic tension with.
Trine	△	120 or 4 Signs	easily combines with, harmonizes with, creatively interacts with.
Quincunx	⚻	150 or 5 Signs	contradicts, creates paradox with, forces adjustment with.
Opposition	☍	180 or 6 Signs	opposes or creates tension with, needs to balance with.

ASPECT	POTENTIAL
Conjunction	Potential for intensified *Strength through Unification*
Sextile	Potential for *Building a New Talent*
Square	Potential for *Productivity through Focus of Energy*
Trine	Potential for *Creative Expression*
Quincunx	Potential for *Transformation through Adjustment*
Opposition	Potential for *Integration through Balance*

Table 4: Planet Keywords

SKILLFUL APPLICATION	PLANET	UNSKILLFUL APPLICATION
Purposeful, Independent, Creative, Self-Assured	Sun	Self-Centered, Unintegrated, Dominating, Timid
Nurturing, Intuitive, Sensitive, Imaginative	Moon	Overemotional, Inconsistent, Moody, Restless
Inquisitive, Communicative, Eloquent, Clever	Mercury	Indecisive, Nervous, Worrisome, Having Poor Learning or Communication Skills
Cooperative, Artistic, Social, Refined	Venus	Self-Indulgent, Vain, Oversensuous, Indolent
Energetic, Courageous, Enterprising, Decisive	Mars	Aggressive, Impulsive, Non-Cooperative, Coarse
Benevolent, Expansive, Optimistic, Broad-Minded	Jupiter	Excessive, Exaggerative, Misjudging, Pompous
Reliable, Industrious, Disciplined, Thorough, Patient	Saturn	Fearful, Inhibited, Pessimistic, Depressed, Controlling
Original, Inventive, Innovative, Progressive	Uranus	Erratic, Unreliable, Rebellious, Fanatical
Inspiring, Idealistic, Artistically Sensitive, Devotional, Empathetic	Neptune	Chaotic, Confused, Hyper-Sensitive, Escapist
Transforming, Intense, Penetrating, Healing	Pluto	Suspicious, Morbid, Repressed, Destructive
Teaching, Guiding, Healing, Wise	Chiron	Scattered, Ignorant, Wounding
Nurturing, Providing, Sharing, Productive	Ceres	Overprotective, Judgmental, Over-Attached, Self-Rejecting
Intelligent, Creative, Confident, Victorious	Pallas	Expedient, Ruthless, Fearing Success, Ignorant
Focused, Integrated, Self-Identified, Devoted	Vesta	Alienated, Inhibited, Overworked, Repressed, Narrow-Minded
Cooperative, Supportive, Sharing, Loyal, Intimate, Fair	Juno	Jealous, Possessive, Vindictive, Victimized, Unequal

1. My planet A _Sun_ in the sign of _Pisces_ in the _4th_ house is in _Opposition_ aspect to my planet B _Saturn_ in the sign of _Virgo_ in the _10th_ house.

2. **PLANET A** _Sun_ → **PLANET A's SIGN** _Pisces_ → **PLANET A's HOUSE** _4_
   Keyphrase (App.C): **what** ... Keyphrase (App.A): **how** ... Keywords (App.B): **where**

   My basic identity and ... _By commiting myself_ ... _In my home, family_

   conscious purpose ... _to a dream or ideal_ ... _and private life_

3. **ASPECT** _Opposition_
   Aspect keyphrase (Table 3) _Creates tension, needs to balance with_

4. **PLANET B** _Saturn_ → **PLANET B's SIGN** _Virgo_ → **PLANET B's HOUSE** _10_
   Keyphrase (App.C): **what** ... Keyphrase (App.A): **how** ... Keywords (App.B): **where**

   My capacity to create order, ... _By analyzing, discriminating,_ ... _In my profession_

   form and discipline in my life ... _and functioning efficiently_ ... _and public life_

5. If the above aspect is "easy" (a conjunction, sextile or trine), I may be

   _____ , _____ , _____

   and _____ .
   (choose 2 skillful keywords for planet A and 2 for planet B from Table 4, page 163)

6. If the above aspect is "difficult" (a conjunction, square, quincunx, or opposition),
   then I may have chosen to be _timid_ , _unintegrated_ , _fearful_ , and _depressed_ .
   (choose 2 unskillful keywords for planet A and 2 for planet B from Table 4, page 163)

6a. If I answered section 6 above, then my challenge is to change the stressful aspects
   between the two planets into a positive one. I can resolve this problem by realizing
   the potential for _integration through balance_ . Thus I can express the planets' skillful
   (fill in aspect potential from Table 3, page 163)
   qualities by being _purposeful_ and _disciplined_ .
   (choose a skillful keyword for each planet from Table 4, page 163)

7. _Optional:_ In your own words, try to compose one or two sentences that synthesize
   all of the above ideas.

   My idealistic and sensitive basic self (Sun in Pisces) _functions best in my private_

   life and family (4th house). _However, in order to achieve balance and a sense of_

   wholeness (the opposition), _I also need to utilize my analytical capacity to create_

   form and discipline (Saturn in Virgo), _recognition and success, in my public life_

   and profession (10th house).

Exercise 3: Interpreting My Planetary Aspects

1. My planet A _____ in the sign of _____ in

   the _____ house is in _____ aspect to my

   planet B _____ in the sign of _____

   in the _____ house.

2. **PLANET A** _____ → **PLANET A's SIGN** _____ → **PLANET A's HOUSE** _____
   Keyphrase (App.C): **what**   Keyphrase (App.A): **how**   Keywords (App.B): **where**

   _____   _____   _____

   _____   _____   _____

   _____   _____   _____

   _____   _____   _____

   ⇕ 3. **ASPECT KEYPHRASE** (Table 3, p.163)_____   ⇕

4. **PLANET B** _____ → **PLANET B's SIGN** _____ → **PLANET B's HOUSE** _____
   Keyphrase (App.C): **what**   Keyphrase (App.A): **how**   Keywords (App.B): **where**

   _____   _____   _____

   _____   _____   _____

   _____   _____   _____

   _____   _____   _____

5. If the above aspect is "easy" (a conjunction, sextile or trine), I may be

   _____ , _____ , _____

   and _____ .
   (choose 2 skillful keywords for planet A and 2 for planet B from Table 4, page 163)

6. If the above aspect is "difficult" (a conjunction, square, quincunx, or opposition),

   then I may have chosen to be _____ , _____ ,

   _____ and _____ .
   (choose 2 unskillful keywords for planet A and 2 for planet B from Table 4, page 163)

6a. If I answered section 6 above, then my challenge is to change the stressful aspects

   between the two planets into a positive one. I can resolve this problem by realizing

   the potential for _____ .
   (fill in aspect potential from Table 3, page 163)

   By resolving the conflict, I can express the planet's skillful qualities by being

   _____ and _____ .
   (choose a skillful keyword for each planet from Table 4, page 163)

7. *Optional:* In your own words, try to compose one or two sentences that synthesize
   all of the above ideas.

   _____

   _____

   _____

———Exercise 3: Interpreting My Planetary Aspects———

1. My planet A _____ in the sign of _____ in

   the _____ house is in _____ aspect to my

   planet B _____ in the sign of _____

   in the _____ house.

2. **PLANET A** _____ → **PLANET A's SIGN** _____ → **PLANET A's HOUSE** _____
   Keyphrase (App.C): **what**   Keyphrase (App.A): **how**   Keywords (App.B): **where**

   _____   _____   _____
   _____   _____   _____
   _____   _____   _____
   _____   _____   _____

   ↕   3. **ASPECT KEYPHRASE** (Table 3) _____   ↕

4. **PLANET B** _____ → **PLANET B's SIGN** _____ → **PLANET B's HOUSE** _____
   Keyphrase (App.C): **what**   Keyphrase (App.A): **how**   Keywords (App.B): **where**

   _____   _____   _____
   _____   _____   _____
   _____   _____   _____
   _____   _____   _____

5. If the above aspect is "easy" (a conjunction, sextile or trine), I may be

   _____ , _____ , _____

   and _____ .
   <small>(choose 2 skillful keywords for planet A and 2 for planet B from Table 4, page 163)</small>

6. If the above aspect is "difficult" (a conjunction, square, quincunx, or opposition),

   then I may have chosen to be _____ , _____ ,

   _____ and _____ .
   <small>(choose 2 unskillful keywords for planet A and 2 for planet B from Table 4, page 163)</small>

6a. If I answered section 6 above, then my challenge is to change the stressful aspects

   between the two planets into a positive one. I can resolve this problem by realizing

   the potential for _____ .
   <small>(fill in aspect potential from Table 3, page 163)</small>

   By resolving the conflict, I can express the planet's skillful qualities by being

   _____ and _____ .
   <small>(choose a skillful keyword for each planet from Table 4, page 163)</small>

7. *Optional:* In your own words, try to compose one or two sentences that synthesize
   all of the above ideas.

   _____
   _____
   _____

Exercise 3: Interpreting My Planetary Aspects

1. My planet A _____ in the sign of _____ in the _____ house is in _____ aspect to my planet B _____ in the sign of _____ in the _____ house.

2. **PLANET A** _____ → **PLANET A's SIGN** _____ → **PLANET A's HOUSE** _____
Keyphrase (App.C): **what**   Keyphrase (App.A): **how**   Keywords (App.B): **where**

_____   _____   _____

_____   _____   _____

_____   _____   _____

_____   _____   _____

↕   3. **ASPECT KEYPHRASE** (Table 3) ↑_____↓   ↕

4. **PLANET B** _____ → **PLANET B's SIGN** _____ → **PLANET B's HOUSE** _____
Keyphrase (App.C): **what**   Keyphrase (App.A): **how**   Keywords (App.B): **where**

_____   _____   _____

_____   _____   _____

_____   _____   _____

_____   _____   _____

5. If the above aspect is "easy" (a conjunction, sextile or trine), I may be

_____ , _____ , _____ and _____ .
(choose 2 skillful keywords for planet A and 2 for planet B from Table 4, page 163)

6. If the above aspect is "difficult" (a conjunction, square, quincunx, or opposition), then I may have chosen to be _____ , _____ , _____ and _____ .
(choose 2 unskillful keywords for planet A and 2 for planet B from Table 4, page 163)

6a. If I answered section 6 above, then my challenge is to change the stressful aspects between the two planets into a positive one. I can resolve this problem by realizing the potential for _____ .
(fill in aspect potential from Table 3, page 163)

By resolving the conflict, I can express the planet's skillful qualities by being

_____ and _____ .
(choose a skillful keyword for each planet from Table 4, page 163)

7. *Optional:* In your own words, try to compose one or two sentences that synthesize all of the above ideas.

_____

_____

_____

Exercise 3: Interpreting My Planetary Aspects

1. My planet A _____ in the sign of _____ in the _____ house is in _____ aspect to my planet B _____ in the sign of _____ in the _____ house.

2. **PLANET A** _____ → **PLANET A's SIGN** _____ → **PLANET A's HOUSE** _____
   Keyphrase (App.C): **what**   Keyphrase (App.A): **how**   Keywords (App.B): **where**

   _____   _____   _____
   _____   _____   _____
   _____   _____   _____
   _____   _____   _____

   ↕   3. **ASPECT KEYPHRASE** (Table 3) _____   ↑↓   ↕

4. **PLANET B** _____ → **PLANET B's SIGN** _____ → **PLANET B's HOUSE** _____
   Keyphrase (App.C): **what**   Keyphrase (App.A): **how**   Keywords (App.B): **where**

   _____   _____   _____
   _____   _____   _____
   _____   _____   _____
   _____   _____   _____

5. If the above aspect is "easy" (a conjunction, sextile or trine), I may be

   _____ , _____ , _____

   and _____ .
   (choose 2 skillful keywords for planet A and 2 for planet B from Table 4, page 163)

6. If the above aspect is "difficult" (a conjunction, square, quincunx, or opposition), then I may have chosen to be _____ , _____ ,

   _____ and _____ .
   (choose 2 unskillful keywords for planet A and 2 for planet B from Table 4, page 163)

6a. If I answered section 6 above, then my challenge is to change the stressful aspects between the two planets into a positive one. I can resolve this problem by realizing the potential for _____ .
   (fill in aspect potential from Table 3, page 163)

   By resolving the conflict, I can express the planet's skillful qualities by being

   _____ and _____ .
   (choose a skillful keyword for each planet from Table 4, page 163)

7. *Optional:* In your own words, try to compose one or two sentences that synthesize all of the above ideas.

   _____
   _____
   _____

Exercise 3: Interpreting My Planetary Aspects

1. My planet A _____ in the sign of _____ in

   the _____ house is in _____ aspect to my

   planet B _____ in the sign of _____

   in the _____ house.

2. **PLANET A** _____ → **PLANET A's SIGN** _____ → **PLANET A's HOUSE** _____
   Keyphrase (App.C): **what**   Keyphrase (App.A): **how**   Keywords (App.B): **where**

   _____   _____   _____

   _____   _____   _____

   _____   _____   _____

   _____   _____   _____

   ↕   3. **ASPECT KEYPHRASE** (Table 3) _____   ↕

4. **PLANET B** _____ → **PLANET B's SIGN** _____ → **PLANET B's HOUSE** _____
   Keyphrase (App.C): **what**   Keyphrase (App.A): **how**   Keywords (App.B): **where**

   _____   _____   _____

   _____   _____   _____

   _____   _____   _____

   _____   _____   _____

5. If the above aspect is "easy" (a conjunction, sextile or trine), I may be

   _____ , _____ , _____

   and _____ .
   <small>(choose 2 skillful keywords for planet A and 2 for planet B from Table 4, page 163)</small>

6. If the above aspect is "difficult" (a conjunction, square, quincunx, or opposition),

   then I may have chosen to be _____ , _____ ,

   _____ and _____ .
   <small>(choose 2 unskillful keywords for planet A and 2 for planet B from Table 4, page 163)</small>

6a. If I answered section 6 above, then my challenge is to change the stressful aspects

   between the two planets into a positive one. I can resolve this problem by realizing

   the potential for _____ .
   <small>(fill in aspect potential from Table 3, page 163)</small>

   By resolving the conflict, I can express the planet's skillful qualities by being

   _____ and _____ .
   <small>(choose a skillful keyword for each planet from Table 4, page 163)</small>

7. *Optional:* In your own words, try to compose one or two sentences that synthesize
   all of the above ideas.

   _____

   _____

   _____

Exercise 3: Interpreting My Planetary Aspects

1. My planet A _____ in the sign of _____ in

   the _____ house is in _____ aspect to my

   planet B _____ in the sign of _____

   in the _____ house.

2. **PLANET A** _____ → **PLANET A's SIGN** _____ → **PLANET A's HOUSE** _____
   Keyphrase (App.C): **what**   Keyphrase (App.A): **how**   Keywords (App.B): **where**

   _____   _____   _____

   _____   _____   _____

   _____   _____   _____

   _____   _____   _____

   ↕   3. **ASPECT KEYPHRASE** (Table 3) _____   ↑↓   ↕

4. **PLANET B** _____ → **PLANET B's SIGN** _____ → **PLANET B's HOUSE** _____
   Keyphrase (App.C): **what**   Keyphrase (App.A): **how**   Keywords (App.B): **where**

   _____   _____   _____

   _____   _____   _____

   _____   _____   _____

   _____   _____   _____

5. If the above aspect is "easy" (a conjunction, sextile or trine), I may be

   _____ , _____ , _____

   and _____.
       <small>(choose 2 skillful keywords for planet A and 2 for planet B from Table 4, page 163)</small>

6. If the above aspect is "difficult" (a conjunction, square, quincunx, or opposition),

   then I may have chosen to be _____ , _____ ,

   _____ and _____.
                            <small>(choose 2 unskillful keywords for planet A and 2 for planet B from Table 4, page 163)</small>

6a. If I answered section 6 above, then my challenge is to change the stressful aspects

   between the two planets into a positive one. I can resolve this problem by realizing

   the potential for _____.
                     <small>(fill in aspect potential from Table 3, page 163)</small>

   By resolving the conflict, I can express the planet's skillful qualities by being

   _____ and _____.
                         <small>(choose a skillful keyword for each planet from Table 4, page 163)</small>

7. *Optional:* In your own words, try to compose one or two sentences that synthesize
   all of the above ideas.

   _____

   _____

   _____

Exercise 3: Interpreting My Planetary Aspects

1. My planet A _____ in the sign of _____ in
   the _____ house is in _____ aspect to my
   planet B _____ in the sign of _____
   in the _____ house.

2. **PLANET A** _____ → **PLANET A's SIGN** _____ → **PLANET A's HOUSE** _____
   Keyphrase (App.C): **what**   Keyphrase (App.A): **how**   Keywords (App.B): **where**

   _____   _____   _____

   _____   _____   _____

   _____   _____   _____

   _____   _____   _____

   ↕   3. **ASPECT KEYPHRASE** (Table 3) _____   ↕

4. **PLANET B** _____ → **PLANET B's SIGN** _____ → **PLANET B's HOUSE** _____
   Keyphrase (App.C): **what**   Keyphrase (App.A): **how**   Keywords (App.B): **where**

   _____   _____   _____

   _____   _____   _____

   _____   _____   _____

   _____   _____   _____

5. If the above aspect is "easy" (a conjunction, sextile or trine), I may be

   _____ , _____ , _____

   and _____ .
   (choose 2 skillful keywords for planet A and 2 for planet B from Table 4, page 163)

6. If the above aspect is "difficult" (a conjunction, square, quincunx, or opposition),
   then I may have chosen to be _____ , _____ ,
   _____ and _____ .
   (choose 2 unskillful keywords for planet A and 2 for planet B from Table 4, page 163)

6a. If I answered section 6 above, then my challenge is to change the stressful aspects
    between the two planets into a positive one. I can resolve this problem by realizing
    the potential for _____ .
    (fill in aspect potential from Table 3, page 163)

    By resolving the conflict, I can express the planet's skillful qualities by being

    _____ and _____ .
    (choose a skillful keyword for each planet from Table 4, page 163)

7. _Optional:_ In your own words, try to compose one or two sentences that synthesize
   all of the above ideas.

   _____

   _____

   _____

Exercise 3: Interpreting My Planetary Aspects

1. My planet A _____ in the sign of _____ in
   the _____ house is in _____ aspect to my
   planet B _____ in the sign of _____
   in the _____ house.

2. **PLANET A** _____ → **PLANET A's SIGN** _____ → **PLANET A's HOUSE** _____
   Keyphrase (App.C): **what**   Keyphrase (App.A): **how**   Keywords (App.B): **where**

   _____   _____   _____

   _____   _____   _____

   _____   _____   _____

   _____   _____   _____

   ↕   3. **ASPECT KEYPHRASE** (Table 3) _____   ↕

4. **PLANET B** _____ → **PLANET B's SIGN** _____ → **PLANET B's HOUSE** _____
   Keyphrase (App.C): **what**   Keyphrase (App.A): **how**   Keywords (App.B): **where**

   _____   _____   _____

   _____   _____   _____

   _____   _____   _____

   _____   _____   _____

5. If the above aspect is "easy" (a conjunction, sextile or trine), I may be
   _____ , _____ , _____
   and _____ .
   (choose 2 skillful keywords for planet A and 2 for planet B from Table 4, page 163)

6. If the above aspect is "difficult" (a conjunction, square, quincunx, or opposition),
   then I may have chosen to be _____ , _____ ,
   _____ and _____ .
   (choose 2 unskillful keywords for planet A and 2 for planet B from Table 4, page 163)

6a. If I answered section 6 above, then my challenge is to change the stressful aspects
    between the two planets into a positive one. I can resolve this problem by realizing
    the potential for _____ .
    (fill in aspect potential from Table 3, page 163)
    By resolving the conflict, I can express the planet's skillful qualities by being
    _____ and _____ .
    (choose a skillful keyword for each planet from Table 4, page 163)

7. *Optional:* In your own words, try to compose one or two sentences that synthesize
   all of the above ideas.

   _____

   _____

   _____

Exercise 3: Interpreting My Planetary Aspects

1. My planet A _____ in the sign of _____ in

   the _____ house is in _____ aspect to my

   planet B _____ in the sign of _____

   in the _____ house.

2. **PLANET A** _____ →   **PLANET A's SIGN** _____ →   **PLANET A's HOUSE** _____
   Keyphrase (App.C): **what**   Keyphrase (App.A): **how**   Keywords (App.B): **where**

   _____   _____   _____

   _____   _____   _____

   _____   _____   _____

   _____   _____   _____

   ↕   3. **ASPECT KEYPHRASE** (Table 3) _____   ↕

4. **PLANET B** _____ →   **PLANET B's SIGN** _____ →   **PLANET B's HOUSE** _____
   Keyphrase (App.C): **what**   Keyphrase (App.A): **how**   Keywords (App.B): **where**

   _____   _____   _____

   _____   _____   _____

   _____   _____   _____

   _____   _____   _____

5. If the above aspect is "easy" (a conjunction, sextile or trine), I may be

   _____ , _____ , _____

   and _____ .
   (choose 2 skillful keywords for planet A and 2 for planet B from Table 4, page 163)

6. If the above aspect is "difficult" (a conjunction, square, quincunx, or opposition),

   then I may have chosen to be _____ , _____ ,

   _____ and _____ .
   (choose 2 unskillful keywords for planet A and 2 for planet B from Table 4, page 163)

6a. If I answered section 6 above, then my challenge is to change the stressful aspects

   between the two planets into a positive one. I can resolve this problem by realizing

   the potential for _____ .
   (fill in aspect potential from Table 3, page 163)

   By resolving the conflict, I can express the planet's skillful qualities by being

   _____ and _____ .
   (choose a skillful keyword for each planet from Table 4, page 163)

7. *Optional:* In your own words, try to compose one or two sentences that synthesize
   all of the above ideas.

   _____

   _____

   _____

ASPECTARIAN 1: PLANET ASPECTS

1. Sun *Conjunct* Mars
2. Sun *Opposition* Saturn
3. Sun *Trine* Uranus
4. Moon *Sextile* Mars
5. Moon *Square* Neptune
6. Mercury *Trine* Neptune
7. Mercury *Opposition* Pluto
8. Venus *Trine* Uranus
9. Venus *Trine* Neptune
10. Venus *Opposition* Pluto
11. Mars *Opposition* Saturn
12. Jupiter *Square* Neptune
13. Neptune *Sextile* Pluto

ASPECTARIAN 2: ASTEROID-PLANET ASPECTS

14. Ceres *Opposition* Mercury
15. Ceres *Opposition* Venus
16. Ceres *Sextile* Neptune
17. Ceres *Conjunct* Pluto
18. Ceres *Trine* Chiron
19. Ceres *Trine* Vesta
20. Pallas *Square* Sun
21. Pallas *Trine* Mercury
22. Pallas *Square* Mars
23. Pallas *Square* Saturn
24. Pallas *Opposition* Chiron
25. Pallas *Opposition* Vesta
26. Juno *Sextile* Sun
27. Juno *Trine* Moon
28. Juno *Square* Mercury
29. Juno *Sextile* Mars
30. Juno *Trine* Saturn
31. Juno *Quincunx* Chiron

32. Vesta *Square* Sun
33. Vesta *Sextile* Mercury
34. Vesta *Square* Mars
35. Vesta *Sextile* Neptune
36. Vesta *Trine* Pluto
37. Vesta *Conjunct* Chiron
38. Vesta *Trine* Ceres
39. Vesta *Opposition* Pallas
40. Chiron *Square* Sun
41. Chiron *Sextile* Mercury
42. Chiron *Square* Mars
43. Chiron *Square* Saturn
44. Chiron *Trine* Pluto
45. Chiron *Trine* Ceres
46. Chiron *Opposition* Pallas
47. Chiron *Quincunx* Juno
48. Chiron *Conjunct* Vesta

You may have found other aspects not listed above.

Note:

Because of the way this aspectarian is constructed, there exist duplications of the same aspect. For example, **Aspect** 18—Ceres *Trine* Chiron is the same aspect as 45—Chiron *Trine* Ceres, just as the equations a = b and b = a are identical.

Other duplications are: 19 = 38, 24 = 46, 25 = 39, 31 = 47, and 37 = 48.

You will find similar duplications in your own chart. Please make note of them so that you do not duplicate them and interpret the sample aspect twice when you write your interpretations in Exercise 3.

Astrological Timing

"To everything there is a season
And a time to every purpose under heaven."
Ecclesiastes, iii, 1–2

"The readiness is all."
Shakespeare

An issue that astrologers face, perhaps more than any other profession, is that of **timing**. The Biblical adage states. "To everything there is a season and a time to every purpose under heaven." Using the principles of astrological timing, astrologers can determine the best time to initiate a new cycle (starting a business, buying a home, getting married, etc.) or when a current cycle will end. Many clients consult astrological counseling in the midst of major life changes, seeking clarity and perspective about what is occurring. By understanding their transits, they gain important information on the nature and duration of their current life cycle.

The study of cyclic behavior is perhaps one of astrology's most important contributions to the study of the human psyche. Astrology, of course, is not the only discipline that studies cycles. The phenomenon of cycles is built into the fabric of creation, and virtually every science is aware of them. There is even a research center that does nothing but chronicle and interpret cyclic activity.

Where astrology makes its unique contribution is in documenting the cyclic nature of *human development.* Psychologists such as Freud and Erikson and journalist Gail Sheehy (author of *Passages*) have written down their observations on the stages of human unfoldment. Astrological literature, however, provides the most *complete* and *precise* information on these "cycles of the psyche."

How does all this affect you? After all, the title of this book is *Astrology for Yourself.* Let us begin with your natal birth chart—the blueprint of your talents and abilities, a statement of your life's intentions. Your birth chart's intention is not to remain unexpressed. By the application of your will and freedom of choice, your celestial potential can manifest when "the time is ripe." Change and growth occur when preparation (the blueprint of your birth chart) meets opportunity (the outer conditions).

The two most frequently used methods of astrological timing are called **transits** and **progressions**. These timing systems of astrology indicate, in the words of Dane Rudhyar, the schedule for the unfoldment of the birth potential over time. Let's explore them now.

Astrological Transits

According to astrology, the *outer conditions* that stimulate these *times of growth* are symbolized by the astrological transits. The word "transition" was perhaps derived from the astrological word "transit." Hence, transits correspond to periods of change in our lives.

Simply defined, transits are the current positions of the planets in the sky as they interact with your birth chart. For example, let's assume that I was born on October 27, with the Sun in 4 degrees of Scorpio. Now today, December 20, 1985, Pluto's current position in the sky is also at 4 degrees of Scorpio. I would therefore say that Pluto is "transiting" or passing over my Sun in Scorpio. This would mean that certain experiences represented by Pluto are being brought to bear upon my solar consciousness.

The natal chart shows the positions of the planets when you were born. After your birth, these planets don't stand still, but continue in their orbits around the sun. As they pass over the degrees occupied by the natal planets, they activate those planetary functions. It becomes time for these parts of personality to walk out on stage and speak their lines. This is why each planetary function comes to the foreground at certain times of your life and not at others.

Because we measure transits by seeing how a planet in the heavens interacts with a planet in the birth chart, it may appear that the transits are "doing something" to us. This would imply a cause-effect relationship, with the transit causing certain events in our lives to occur. Fortunately, this is not the case. It is our philosophy that you are the **creator** of your universe, and therefore you are "at cause" in your life. Thus, we see transits as those experiences that you have drawn to yourself, caused by your own prior choices. As contemporary astrologers are fond of saying, "Events don't happen to you; you happen to events." Or as the great English astrologer Alan Leo put it, *"character is destiny."*

The types of opportunities that astrological transits bring depend specifically on the nature of the transiting planet. The more important life changes are signified by the outer planets (Mars through Pluto). Because they move more slowly through the skies, their transiting periods take longer to occur, last longer when they do occur (up to three years), and thus produce more profound changes. The inner planets, on the other hand, move more rapidly, and their effects are more transitory: here today, gone tomorrow. Thus, they chronicle events of a more temporary nature.

Table 5 (below) summarizes the meanings of the outer planet transits. The planetary period refers to the time it takes the planet to make one revolution around the Sun. It is also the time it takes to make a complete revolution around the wheel of your birth chart.

As you can see, each transit has a potential skillful and unskillful manifestation. Times of change are times of upheaval. The outer planet transits often challenge and disrupt your existing structures and most cherished beliefs. If you resist the flow of change, pain and discomfort will be intensified. Thus, when you receive an outer planet transit, try to let go and have faith that what is happening is for the highest good.

For more information on progressions, see Appendix G, page 249.

Table 5: The Transiting Planets

PLANET	PLANETARY PERIOD	NORMAL TRANSIT DURATION	OPPORTUNITY PROVIDED
Mars	2 years	1 month	The opportunity to take action and strive for what I want. In the process, conflict and strife may arise.
Jupiter	12 years	3 months	The opportunity to expand my horizons and experience abundance. In the process, things may become excessive and exaggerated.
Saturn	29½ years	18 months	The opportunity to focus, define and manifest what I want. In the process, I may have to come out of denial and face reality.
Uranus	84 years	2 years	The opportunity to free myself from past limitations. In the process, existing structures may be shattered.
Neptune	164 years	3 years	The opportunity to experience a greater spiritual perspective and sensivity. In the process, existing structures may be dissolved.
Pluto	248 years	3 years	The opportunity to transform and regenerate an area of my life. In the process, existing structures may be destroyed.

Now that you know what transits are and what their significance is in your birth chart, you are probably asking, "How do I locate them in my own chart?" In order to keep track of the positions of the planets in the heavens, early astrologers had to calculate the positions themselves. Today, however, you can refer directly to planetary tables known as "Ephemerides." Figure 3 depicts a sample page of a planetary Ephemeris for the month of February 1986.

Look first across the top of the page. Note that the planets are listed from left to right—Sun, Moon, Mercury, Venus, Mars, Jupiter, Saturn, Uranus, Neptune, and Pluto. Now look at the leftmost column headed by the word "Day." The 28 days of February are listed down the column. Now find day 1 and look just to the right under the Sun column. You should see the nota-tion 12≈19 49, which tells you that the Sun was located in 12 degrees, 12 minutes and 49 seconds of Aquarius on that day (February 1, 1986). You know that the sign is Aquarius, because it is the first sign that you come to as you look up the column. Now look over to the Moon column; you should see 3 ♏ 17 38, or 3 degrees, 17 minutes and 38 seconds of Scorpio. The remaining columns show only degrees and minutes. Thus, Mercury is in 12 degrees Aquarius and 39 minutes (12≈39), Venus is in 15 degrees Aquarius, 24 minutes (15≈24), etc.

Now it's your turn. Direct your attention to the day of February 6 whose column is marked for you. In the spaces below, write in the transiting positions for the planets for that day.

PLANET	DEGREE AND MINUTE OF ITS SIGN POSITION
☉ Sun	*17° 24' 08" of Aquarius ≈*
☽ Moon	
☿ Mercury	
♀ Venus	
♂ Mars	
♃ Jupiter	
♄ Saturn	
♅ Uranus	
♆ Neptune	
♇ Pluto	

How was that? Were you able to read the Ephemeris without difficulty? It should have been pretty straightforward. To verify your results, check your answers with the answer key at the end of the chapter.

Figure 3: A Sample Page From an Ephemeris

Day	☉	☽	☿	♀	♂	♃	♄	♅	♆	♇
1	12≈19 49	3♏17 38	12≈39	15≈24	29♏33	25≈25	7♐59	21♐08	4♑42	7♏21
2	13 20 43	17 19 02	14 24	16 40	0♐08	25 39	8 03	21 11	4 44	7 21
3	14 21 35	1♐27 12	16 09	17 55	0 44	25 53	8 08	21 13	4 46	7 21
4	15 22 27	15 41 05	17 54	19 10	1 19	26 07	8 12	21 16	4 48	7 21
5	16 23 18	29 58 30	19 41	20 26	1 54	26 22	8 16	21 18	4 50	7 21
6	17 24 08	14♑15 50	21 28	21 41	2 30	26 36	8 20	21 21	4 51	7 22
7	18 24 56	28 28 18	23 15	22 56	3 05	26 50	8 24	21 23	4 53	7 22
8	19 25 44	12≈30 32	25 04	24 12	3 40	27 05	8 27	21 25	4 55	7 22
9	20 26 30	26 17 30	26 52	25 27	4 15	27 19	8 31	21 28	4 57	7R 22
10	21 27 16	9✕45 15	28 41	26 42	4 50	27 33	8 35	21 30	4 58	7 22
11	22 27 59	22 51 41	0✕30	27 57	5 25	27 48	8 38	21 32	5 00	7 22
12	23 28 41	5♈36 37	2 19	29 12	6 00	28 02	8 42	21 34	5 02	7 21
13	24 29 22	18 01 49	4 09	0✕28	6 35	28 17	8 45	21 36	5 03	7 21
14	25 30 01	0♉10 34	5 58	1 43	7 10	28 31	8 48	21 39	5 05	7 21
15	26 30 38	12 07 18	7 46	2 58	7 44	28 45	8 51	21 41	5 07	7 21
16	27 31 13	23 57 10	9 34	4 13	8 19	29 00	8 54	21 43	5 08	7 21
17	28 31 47	5♊45 38	11 21	5 28	8 54	29 14	8 57	21 45	5 10	7 20
18	29 32 19	17 38 09	13 07	6 43	9 28	29 29	9 00	21 47	5 11	7 20
19	0✕32 50	29 39 50	14 51	7 58	10 03	29 43	9 03	21 48	5 13	7 20
20	1 33 18	11♋55 06	16 32	9 13	10 37	29 58	9 06	21 50	5 14	7 '19
21	2 33 45	24 27 20	18 11	10 28	11 11	0✕12	9 09	21 52	5 16	7 19
22	3 34 10	7♌18 36	19 47	11 43	11 45	0 26	9 11	21 54	5 17	7 18
23	4 34 33	20 29 22	21 19	12 58	12 20	0 41	9 13	21 55	5 18	7 18
24	5 34 54	3♍58 30	22 47	14 13	12 54	0 55	9 16	21 57	5 20	7 17
25	6 35 13	17 43 26	24 09	15 28	13 28	1 10	9 18	21 59	5 21	7 17
26	7 35 31	1≏40 36	25 26	16 43	14 02	1 24	9 20	22 00	5 22	7 16
27	8 35 48	15 46 03	26 37	17 58	14 35	1 38	9 22	22 02	5 24	7 16
28	9 36 02	29 56 04	27 41	19 13	15 09	1 53	9 24	22 03	5 25	7 15

Looking at Transits in a Birth Chart

Turn now to Figure 5. It should look very familiar, for it is Figure 1, page 26, the birth chart you used when you learned to locate the planets. Here it is again, but with one major addition. The transiting planets that you looked up in the Ephemeris in the last exercise are now positioned outside the rim of the chart. Thus, we can now see the positions of the planets on February 6, 1986, and *compare them to their original positions* in the birth chart. For example, note that the transiting Moon, in 14 degrees Capricorn, 15 minutes, is almost in the same location as the natal (original) position which was in 11 degrees Capricorn, 38 minutes. If we wanted to form an *aspect* relationship between them we would say that the Transiting Moon is *conjunct* the Natal Moon, or in shorthand, t. ☽ ☌ n. ☽ . Look now to the left of the chart, to the beginning of the first house. The Ascendant of the birth chart is 7 degrees Scorpio, 16 minutes. The transiting Pluto, written outside the wheel is 7 degrees Scorpio, 21 minutes. Thus, we can say that Transiting Pluto is *conjunct* the Natal Ascendant.

As you can see, the conjunctions are easy to spot, but what about the other aspects—the sextile (60), square (90), trine (120), quincunx (150), and opposition (180)? Here you must rely on the moon phase aspect wheel that you used in Chapter Five, or send away for a complete transit report (see Appendix D).

How to Use the Moon Phase-Aspect Wheel to Determine Transiting Aspects

For these instructions, we will be referring to Figure 4 below.

To determine a transiting aspect to **your own chart,** first take your own Moon Phase wheel and insert **your** 10 planets, Chiron, and 4 asteroids on the outer wheel next to the appropriate degrees. You can copy the planetary degrees either from the planets within the chart or from their listings in the upper left hand corner of the Astro Computing Services chart. This is illustrated in Figure 4 where we have copied the Sun and Venus onto the wheel at 4 degrees Pisces and 21 degrees Aquarius.

The next step is to determine the sign and **degree** of the **transiting planet,** in this case Mars, which is in 2 degrees Sagittarius 30 minutes. Next we *rotate the arrow* of the inner wheel and point it to that degree and minute.

Then, holding the wheel in place, we locate the sign and **degree** of the **natal planet,** in this case the Sun ☉ in 4 degrees Pisces and 13 minutes.

Now notice the black bars located around the outer edge of the inner wheel, each of which has an aspect name and symbol. If the natal planet lies above one of

Figure 4: Sample Moon Phase Wheel

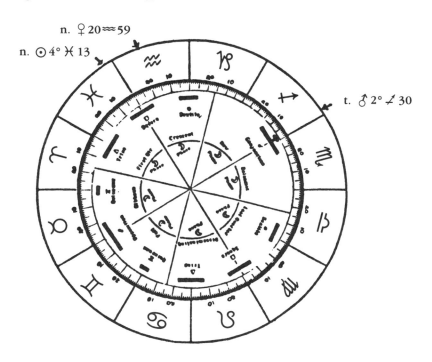

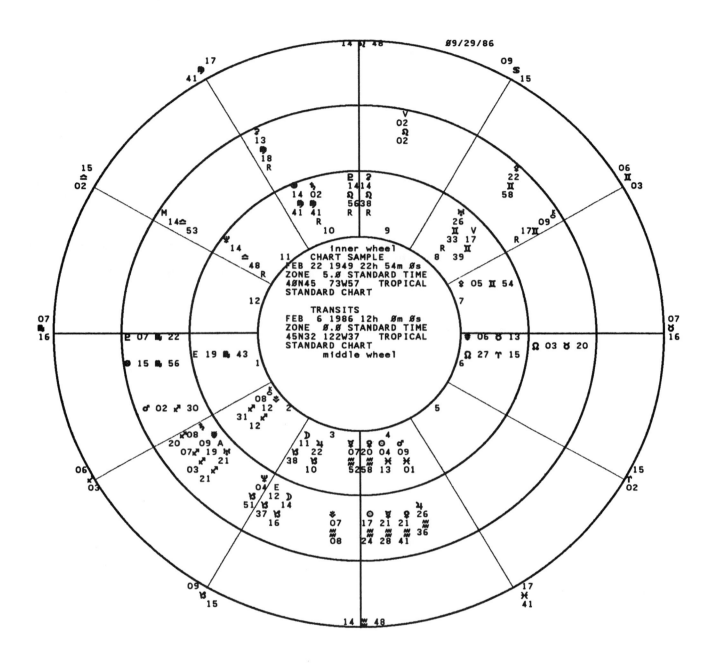

these aspect bars, then it forms the corresponding aspect to the transiting planet. Notice that in Figure 4, the square (□) bar lies below the Sun, telling us that a **square aspect** is formed between **transiting Mars** and the **natal Sun.**

Finally, look at natal Venus (♀) which is located in 20 degrees Aquarius 59 minutes. Note that it lies above an empty space as opposed to a black bar. This signifies that no aspect exists between it and transiting Mars.

This method of calculating the aspects takes time to do and takes practice to get used to. A simpler alternative might be to write to a local chart service company and have them send you a printout of the transiting aspects (see Appendix D). In any event, you should get in the habit of reading a daily ephemeris so that you can at least spot the important *transiting conjunc-* *tions* as they occur in your birth chart.

Below we have begun our list of the transits to the natal chart in Figure 5. See if you can use the moon phase aspect wheel to calculate the remaining aspects between the transiting planets (Mars through Pluto) and the natal planets. In doing this exercise, you should probably not mark up your moon phase wheel since you want to put your own natal planets on it. Instead, write the planets from Figure 5 in *very light pencil* so that you can erase them when you do your own.

We realize that this is a fairly complex exercise, and so if you cannot complete it, simply look up the answers at the end of the chapter and follow along. If this topic seems too advanced right now, we would suggest that you either take a class on astrological transits or have a professional astrologer explain the process in person.

————Exercise 5: A Look at Transits in a Birth Chart————

TRANSITING PLANET	ASPECT FORMED	NATAL PLANET
1. Pluto	Conjunct	Ascendant
2. Mars	Square	Sun
3. Mars		
4. Mars		
5. Mars		
6. Jupiter		
7. Jupiter		
8. Saturn		
9. Saturn		
10. Saturn		
11. Saturn		
12. Uranus		
13. Uranus		
14. Neptune		
15. Neptune		
16. Pluto		
17. Pluto		
18. Pluto		

Interpreting the Transits in the Birth Chart————————

In order to complete this exercise, you will first need to determine what transits are occurring and the aspects they are making to your natal planets. As we mentioned earlier, the transits of the outer planets, Mars through Pluto, correspond to the most important times of change; thus we are going to focus on their transits.

————————*Exercise 6: I Locate My Important Transits*————————

Pick a specific time in your life when something **extremely eventful** occurred—e.g. a marriage, major move, career change, death or separation from a loved one, birth of a child, etc. This event can either be the present day or a specific time in the past. Any significant life change is going to last anywhere from a number of months to a number of years. Once you have decided on such a period, pick a **specific day** that falls somewhere in **the middle** of your transition.

On the date you have picked, use the Ephemeris in Appendix F to determine the locations of Mars through Pluto on that day. Then compute the aspects they form to your natal planets and asteroids. You can either follow the process you used in Exercise 5, or if it was too advanced, you can receive a transit printout from a chart computing service (see Appendix D). Once you have determined the aspects, write them in the table below, just as you did in Exercise 5.

Date of the Transit: Month_____   Day_____   Year_____

TRANSITING PLANET	ASPECT FORMED	NATAL PLANET
1. _____	_____	_____
2. _____	_____	_____
3. _____	_____	_____
4. _____	_____	_____
5. _____	_____	_____
6. _____	_____	_____
7. _____	_____	_____
8. _____	_____	_____
9. _____	_____	_____
10. _____	_____	_____

How to Determine the Relative Importance of Each Transit

Now that you have located a number of transiting aspects for a particular time in your life, how do you tell which are the most significant? Not all of the transits in your birth chart will have the same importance or impact. The transits making **hard aspects** (conjunction, square, and opposition) tend to be associated with outer **events,** while the soft aspects (sextile and trine) denote a state of being or potential opportunities.

A transiting planet making a **conjunction** is the **most powerful,** followed by the opposition and then the square. The closer to the exact degree a transiting planet is to the natal planet, the more powerful the effect.

A question often asked by students is, How close does a transit have to be before you begin to feel its effect? There are several issues to consider in answering this question. In general, we use a 5 degree orb before and 2 degree orb after the exact aspect. But this will vary with both the individual and the transiting planet. The first consideration is the relative sensitivity of the individual to the vibrations of the transiting planet. If a person is very sensitive, he or she will experience the influence while the transiting planet is many degrees away from forming a close orb. For those persons who are not tuned into the planetary energy, the transiting planet may have to form an almost exact aspect before anything is noticed.

The **second** consideration is the transiting planet itself and its rate of speed. Here it is necessary that one has a sense of the normal transit duration in terms of its orbital speed as indicated in Table 5. For example, because Mars and Jupiter move more rapidly around the Sun and the chart, when they are within a 5 degree approaching orb to the natal planet, it may only be a few weeks or a month before they form an exact aspect. But with Neptune and Pluto, planets that move much more slowly, 5 degrees away may indicate that several years will pass before the aspect is exact.

The **third** consideration is to be aware that one should not look to the specific day the transit becomes exact for something to happen. Instead look at that general period of life, at least six months to a year, to determine the effect of a transit. In some cases it may be only in retrospect that one realizes a profound change has occurred.

The **last** important consideration in determining the importance and duration of the transits has to do with retrograde motion. The outer planets have regular and frequent periods of retrograde motion. What this means in terms of the transits is that a transiting planet may pass over a natal planet, then turn retrograde and pass over it a second time in backward motion, and then turn direct again and pass over it a third time be-

fore the contact is finally completed.

The first passage may bring the situation that needs adjustment into focus.

The retrograde passage may bring a time of readjustment and reorientation.

The final direct passage will often coincide with the resolution.

This duration may take up to several years. So one must look through many pages in the ephemeris to determine the entire scope of the transit.

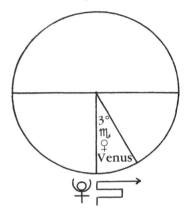

The above diagram is an illustration of a Pluto transit moving direct and retrograde over a natal planet. The duration of the transit lasted for around one year, from the Fall of 1984 to Fall, 1985.

Look in the ephemeris for November 1984: The Pluto transit passed over natal Venus at 3 degrees of Scorpio (first passage).

Pluto continued moving to 4 degrees of Scorpio, and then turned retrograde. As Pluto traveled backwards, it contacted natal Venus again during April and May of 1985 (second passage).

When Pluto turned direct again, it made its final pass over Venus in September of 1985.

In summation

1. Prioritize the transiting planets in order of aspect importance. Conjunction first, opposition second, square third, trine fourth, quincunx fifth and sextile sixth.

2. Consider the speed and duration of each transiting planet. Mars and Jupiter will pass quicker and you can use larger orbs for when their influence begins. Use smaller orbs and a longer time period with Uranus, Neptune and Pluto in accessing their peak effects. Do not forget that these guidelines will vary with individual sensitivity.

3. Keep in mind the stages of the transit when retrograde passes are involved and check the ephemeris for these three (and occasionally five) periods.

4. Look at the **general time period**, and not the specific day.

Table 6: Transiting Planet Keywords

PLANET	OPPORTUNITY PROVIDED
Mars	The opportunity to take action and strive for what I want
Jupiter	The opportunity to expand my horizons and experience abundance
Saturn	The opportunity to focus, define and manifest what I want
Uranus	The opportunity to free myself from past limitations
Neptune	The opportunity to experience a greater spiritual perspective and sensitivity
Pluto	The opportunity to transform and regenerate an area of my life

Table 7: Aspect Keyphrases Reviewed

ASPECT	SYMBOL	KEYPHRASE
Conjunction	☌	unites or joins with
Sextile	⚹	facilitates the expression of
Square	□	creates dynamic tension with, conflicts with
Trine	△	harmonizes with, flows with
Quincunx	⚻	forces adjustment with
Opposition	☍	opposes, needs to balance with

Table 8: Natal Planet Keyphrases

PLANET	KEYPHRASE
Sun	My basic identity and conscious purpose
Moon	My emotions, feelings and daily habits
Mercury	My capacity to think, speak, learn and reason
Venus	My capacity to attract people and things that I love and value
Mars	My capacity to initiate, act and assert myself based on personal desire
Jupiter	My search for meaning, truth, and ethical values
Saturn	My capacity to create order, form, and discipline in my life
Uranus	My capacity to be unique and to liberate myself from past restrictions
Neptune	My capacity to transcend the finite self through expressing unity with a greater whole
Pluto	My capacity to transform and renew myself
Chiron	My capacity for holistic understanding
Ceres	My capacity to unconditionally love and nurture myself and others
Pallas	My capacity for creative wisdom and original perceptions
Vesta	My capacity to integrate and focus my energies
Juno	My capacity for meaningful relationships

Exercise 7: I Interpret My Transits

Now you will interpret the aspect relationships in the same way as you did in the Aspect Exercise 3, page 165, by combining keywords! (Isn't that how we have done it for the entire workbook?) First, let us summarize the keywords for the transiting planets, the aspects and the natal planets.

Table 6 summarizes the themes of the transiting planets.

Table 7 briefly reviews the keywords for the aspects.

Table 8 reviews the keyphrases (and keywords) for the natal planets and asteroids. It is these dimensions of your personality that are awakened and activated by the transiting planets.

Now let's look at the aspect sentence that you will be completing and interpreting. Do not fill these sentences out, as you will be provided with blank forms later on.

My Transit Interpretation

Date of the Transit: Month _____ Day _____ Year _____.

During this period, the **transiting planet** _____

is forming a _____ **aspect** with my **natal planet** _____

in my _____ **house**.

Fill in the **transiting planet's keyphrase** from Table 6

_____.

Fill in the **aspect keyphrase** from Table 7 _____.

Fill in **natal planet's keyphrase** from Table 8

_____.

The transit directly activates **this area of my life.** Fill in the natal planet's **house keywords** from Appendix B _____.

Because this exercise may at first appear involved, let us complete two examples, taken from our clients' experiences, to show you how simple it really is. During 1971, transiting, the planet Neptune was traveling through the sign of Sagittarius. While doing so, it formed a square to David's natal Pisces Sun in the fourth house.

Now we will fill out the aspect-interpretation sentence, and see if we can discern the meaning of the transit.

Date of the Transit: Month ___*May*___ Day ___*26*___ Year ___*1971*___.

During this period, the **transiting planet** _____*Neptune*_____

is forming a ___*square*___ **aspect** with my **natal planet** ___*the Sun*___

in my ___*4th*___ **house**.

Fill in the **transiting planet's keyphrase** (Neptune) from Table 6

___*The opportunity to experience a greater spiritual perspective*___.

Fill in the **aspect** (square) **keyphrase** from Table 7 ___*creates dynamic tension with*___.

Fill in **natal planet's** (the Sun's) **keyphrase** from Table 8

my basic identity and conscious purpose
_____ .

The transit directly activates **this area of my life.** Fill in the natal planet's **house keywords** position (4th house) from Appendix B _____ _My home and family_ _____ .

Does this transit interpretation accurately portray the events that occurred during the period?

During this time, David truly experienced the influence of Neptune. He began to open up to his spirituality, read the holy books of a number of religions, questioned his old secular belief system, and eventually replaced it with a new and more "mystical" one. This transit also affected his home life, for he decided to leave his home in New York, never to return. His old heritage and roots dissolved (a Neptune keyword) away.

Let's look at a _second example_. During September and October of 1985, transiting Jupiter passed over Diana's Mercury in Aquarius in her third house. Let's fill in the aspect sentence to see what occurred.

Date of the Transit: Month _____ _October_ _____ Day _____ _10_ _____ Year _____ _1985_ _____ .

During this period, the **transiting planet** _____ _Jupiter_ _____

is forming a _____ _conjunction_ _____ **aspect** with my **natal planet** _____ _Mercury_ _____

in my _____ _3rd_ _____ **house.**

Fill in the **transiting planet's keyphrase** (Jupiter) from Table 6

The opportunity to expand my horizons and to experience abundance
_____ .

Fill in the **aspect** (conjunction) **keyphrase** from Table 7 _____ _unites or joins with_ _____ .

Fill in **natal planet's** (Mercury) **keyphrase** from Table 8

my capacity to think, speak, learn, and reason
_____ .

The transit directly activates **this area of my life.** Fill in the natal planet's **house keywords** position (3rd house) from Appendix B _____ _My learning and knowledge_ _____ .

Our transit sentence once again makes perfect sense, for it was during this period that with the help of an astrologer, Diana expanded her horizons (Jupiter) by studying (Mercury in the third house) the subject of astrology (Aquarius is the sign most often associated with astrology). This she did through taking a class and reading a number of books (the third house).

Are you getting the hang of it? How about trying it yourself? Go back to step 1 of this exercise and find the transits to your own planets that you wrote down. Then one by one, interpret them by filling in the aspect sentences, as we have in the preceding examples.

To insure that you don't run out of transit forms, take a blank transit interpretation page and make a number of extra photocopies for yourself.

My Transit Interpretation

Date of the Transit: Month_____ Day_____ Year_____.

During this period, the **transiting planet** _____ is forming

a _____ **aspect** with my **natal planet** _____ in

my _____ **house.**

Fill in the **transiting planet's keyphrase** from Table 6:

_____.

Fill in the **aspect** keyphrase from Table 7: _____.

Fill in **natal planet's keyphrase** from Table 8:

_____.

The transit directly activates **this area of my life.** Fill in the natal planet's **house keywords** from Appendix B:

_____.

Journal Entry

In your own words, describe how this particular transit has affected or is affecting your life. As a result of this transit, have any fundamental changes occurred in your values, attitudes, or philosophical outlook?

_____

_____

_____

_____

_____

_____

_____

_____

_____

_____

_____

_____

_____

_____

_____

_____

_____

_____

_____

_____

_____

My Transit Interpretation

Date of the Transit: Month_____ Day_____ Year_____.

During this period, the **transiting planet** _____ is forming

a _____ **aspect** with my **natal planet** _____ in

my _____ **house.**

Fill in the **transiting planet's keyphrase** from Table 6:

_____.

Fill in the **aspect** keyphrase from Table 7: _____.

Fill in **natal planet's keyphrase** from Table 8:

_____.

The transit directly activates **this area of my life.** Fill in the natal planet's **house keywords** from Appendix B:

_____.

Journal Entry

In your own words, describe how this particular transit has affected or is affecting your life. As a result of this transit, have any fundamental changes occurred in your values, attitudes, or philosophical outlook?

_____

_____

_____

_____

_____

_____

_____

_____

_____

_____

_____

_____

_____

_____

_____

_____

_____

_____

_____

_____

My Transit Interpretation

Date of the Transit: Month_____ Day_____ Year_____.

During this period, the **transiting planet** _____ is forming

a _____ **aspect** with my **natal planet** _____ in

my _____ **house.**

Fill in the **transiting planet's keyphrase** from Table 6:

_____.

Fill in the **aspect** keyphrase from Table 7: _____.

Fill in **natal planet's keyphrase** from Table 8:

_____.

The transit directly activates **this area of my life.** Fill in the natal planet's **house keywords** from Appendix B:

_____.

Journal Entry

In your own words, describe how this particular transit has affected or is affecting your life. As a result of this transit, have any fundamental changes occurred in your values, attitudes, or philosophical outlook?

_____

_____

_____

_____

_____

_____

_____

_____

_____

_____

_____

_____

_____

_____

_____

_____

_____

_____

_____

My Transit Interpretation

Date of the Transit: Month_____   Day_____   Year_____ .

During this period, the **transiting planet** _____ is forming

a _____ **aspect** with my **natal planet** _____ in

my _____ **house.**

Fill in the **transiting planet's keyphrase** from Table 6:

_____ .

Fill in the **aspect** keyphrase from Table 7: _____ .

Fill in **natal planet's keyphrase** from Table 8:

_____ .

The transit directly activates **this area of my life.** Fill in the natal planet's **house keywords** from Appendix B:

_____ .

Journal Entry

In your own words, describe how this particular transit has affected or is affecting your life. As a result of this transit, have any fundamental changes occurred in your values, attitudes, or philosophical outlook?

_____

_____

_____

_____

_____

_____

_____

_____

_____

_____

_____

_____

_____

_____

_____

_____

_____

_____

_____

_____

My Transit Interpretation

Date of the Transit: Month_____ Day_____ Year_____.

During this period, the **transiting planet** _____ is forming

a _____ **aspect** with my **natal planet** _____ in

my _____ **house.**

Fill in the **transiting planet's keyphrase** from Table 6:

_____.

Fill in the **aspect** keyphrase from Table 7: _____.

Fill in **natal planet's keyphrase** from Table 8:

_____.

The transit directly activates **this area of my life.** Fill in the natal planet's **house keywords** from Appendix B:

_____.

Journal Entry

In your own words, describe how this particular transit has affected or is affecting your life. As a result of this transit, have any fundamental changes occurred in your values, attitudes, or philosophical outlook?

_____

_____

_____

_____

_____

_____

_____

_____

_____

_____

_____

_____

_____

_____

_____

_____

_____

_____

_____

My Transit Interpretation

Date of the Transit: Month_____   Day_____   Year_____ .

During this period, the **transiting planet** _____ is forming

a _____ **aspect** with my **natal planet** _____ in

my _____ **house.**

Fill in the **transiting planet's keyphrase** from Table 6:

_____ .

Fill in the **aspect** keyphrase from Table 7: _____ .

Fill in **natal planet's keyphrase** from Table 8:

_____ .

The transit directly activates **this area of my life.** Fill in the natal planet's **house keywords** from Appendix B:

_____ .

Journal Entry

In your own words, describe how this particular transit has affected or is affecting your life. As a result of this transit, have any fundamental changes occurred in your values, attitudes, or philosophical outlook?

_____

_____

_____

_____

_____

_____

_____

_____

_____

_____

_____

_____

_____

_____

_____

_____

_____

_____

_____

_____

Conclusion

Hopefully, we have been able to introduce you to the fascinating subject of astrological timing. By studying how these principles work in your own chart, you will be better able to take advantage of future opportunities when they occur, and thereby more effectively express the many potentials contained in your natal birth chart.

Answer Key to Exercise 4

1. Sun's Position—17 degrees Aquarius, 24 minutes, 8 seconds
2. Moon's Position—14 degrees Capricorn, 15 minutes, 50 seconds
3. Mercury's Position—21 degrees Aquarius, 28 minutes
4. Venus' Position—21 degrees Aquarius, 41 minutes
5. Mars' Position—2 degrees Sagittarius, 30 minutes
   (Notice that on February 2, Mars left the sign of Scorpio and entered Sagittarius.)
6. Jupiter's Position—26 degrees Aquarius, 36 minutes
7. Saturn's Position—8 degrees Sagittarius, 20 minutes
8. Uranus' Position—21 degrees Sagittarius, 21 minutes
9. Neptune's Position—4 degrees Capricorn, 51 minutes
10. Pluto's Position—7 degrees Scorpio, 22 minutes

Answer Key to Exercise 5

TRANSITING PLANET	ASPECT FORMED	NATAL PLANET
3. Mars	Square	Sun in Pisces
4. Mars	Square	Mars in Pisces
5. Mars	Opposition	Pallas in Gemini
6. Jupiter	Conjunct	Venus in Aquarius
7. Jupiter	Trine	Uranus in Gemini
8. Saturn	Square	Sun in Pisces
9. Saturn	Square	Mars in Pisces
10. Saturn	Square	Saturn in Virgo
11. Saturn	Opposition	Pallas in Gemini
12. Uranus	Sextile	Venus in Aquarius
13. Uranus	Opposition	Uranus in Gemini
14. Neptune	Sextile	Sun in Pisces
15. Neptune	Trine	Saturn in Virgo
16. Pluto	Sextile	Moon in Capricorn
17. Pluto	Trine	Sun in Pisces
18. Pluto	Trine	Mars in Pisces

(You may have found other aspects not listed above.)

Further Reading

If you wish to learn more about the topics covered in this chapter, we recommend the following books.

Transits

Davison, Ronald, *The Technique of Prediction*
Forrest, Steven, *The Inner Sky*
Freeman, Martin, *Forecasting By Astrology*
Hand, Robert, *Planets in Transit*
Lundsted, Betty, *Transits: The Time of Your Life*
Riotte, Louise, *Planetary Planting*
Robertson, Marc, *The Transit of Saturn*
Ruperti, Alexander, *Cycles of Becoming*

Planetary Aspects

Carter, Charles, *The Astrological Aspects*
Pelletier, Robert, *Planets in Aspect*
Tierney, Bil, *Dynamics of Aspect Analysis*

Additional resources are located in the bibliography.

Chapter 7

—*The Applications of Astrology*—

Multa renascentur, quae jam cedidere cadentque, Quae nunc sunt in honore.
Much will rise again that has long been buried,
and much become submerged which is held in honor today.

Horace

ABOUT TEN YEARS AGO, an astrological friend of ours decided to teach a beginning class on astrology at a local university. In order to do so, he had to offer the class through a specific department. The options were abundant—psychology, philosophy, religious studies, history, comparative religion, etc.—each of these disciplines fell under the umbrella of astrology. Yet, as he met with the department heads and presented the course proposal, each of them responded in the identical manner—"*Sorry, but astrology does not apply to our field!*"

Irony of ironies! Here was one of the most universal languages known to humankind, one that touched on ALL of these subjects, and the professors saw no possible application. Their response, however, was not surprising. In the past two centuries, astrology has been shunned by academia as an unproven "pseudoscience." Moreover, it has also been put down by most religious groups who associate astrology with fortune telling, divination, and even witchcraft!

As a result of these and other misperceptions, most individuals are quite unaware of astrology's *true nature* and the benefits that it has to offer. Consequently, we would like to present a brief overview of the many ways in which astrology is being used to help people better understand themselves and the world around them. In so doing we hope that you will receive a better understanding and appreciation of this divine art and science.

Below we have listed some of the **major branches** of the astrological science.

Astro-Psychology, Vocational Astrology, Synastry—The Astrology of Relationships, Medical Astrology, Astrology and Child Rearing, Electional Astrology—The Timing of Events, Mundane or Political Astrology, Historical Astrology, Astro-Economics, Horary Astrology.

As you can see, the range of application is amazingly broad. Let us briefly review each branch of astrology and explore its beneficial effects on human affairs.

Astro-Psychology

As I am a psychologist, I am particularly interested in the particular light the horoscope sheds on certain complications in the character. In cases of difficult psychological diagnosis, I usually get a horoscope in order to have a further point of view from an entirely different angle. I must say that I have very often found that the astrological data elucidated certain points which I otherwise would have been unable to understand.

Carl Gustav Jung

Essentially, people seek out astrologers for the same reasons they go to any other guide or consultant—to receive guidance on some important aspect of their lives. Because the astrological language describes the workings of the human psyche, the problems that clients bring to astrologers are usually personal—work, love, finance, health, creative fulfillment, etc. Serving in this capacity, the astrologer functions as a personal counselor to his or her client. Hence, the terms **astro-therapist, astro-psychologist,** and **astro-analyst** are used to describe the astrologer's parallel function to that of the psychotherapist, psychologist or psychoanalyst.

Although only a handful of psychologists and psychiatrists incorporate astrology into their practices, astrology has always had a natural affinity with its hundred-year-old sister social science. For example,

psychologists have developed a number of tests, which, like astrology, measure and describe specific personality types. Most notable among these is the Meyers Briggs Type Inventory, whose four basic types of Intuition, Sensation, Thinking and Feeling loosely parallel the astrological elements of Fire, Earth, Air and Water.

Indeed, the major use of astrology to psychologists lies in its diagnostic capabilities. Carl Jung, upon whose work the Meyers Briggs test is based, computed the charts of many of his clients. Because the chart reveals a blueprint of the psyche, Jung found that he could gain immediate access to information that would otherwise take months to uncover. The examples below show how normal psychological complexes can show up in the birth chart.

Because it provides an instant snapshot of the workings of the human psyche, astrology is a valuable therapeutic tool that can be used as an *adjunct* to traditional psychotherapy. Hence, not only astrologers, but all mental health professionals (psychiatrists, psychologists, social workers, marriage and family counselors, pastoral counselors) can use astrology as an awareness tool to facilitate the analysis of their clients. We recommend that these professionals use astrologers as consultants, calling upon them to help evaluate and diagnose the important psychological elements of their cases. In this way, the process of therapy can be made both more efficient and more effective.

PSYCHOLOGICAL COMPLEX	ASTROLOGICAL DESCRIPTION
He has a high achievement need	His Sun is in Capricorn
She is an impulsive person	Her Mars is in the sign of Aries
Her emotional needs were denied in early childhood	Her Moon is squaring Saturn
His thinking is confused and disordered	His Mercury opposes Neptune
He tends to intellectualize his feelings	His Moon is in Gemini

Vocational Astrology

"What is the secret of success? To fall in love with your work. I don't think I would have been very happy selling felt hats."

Comedian George Burns
on his 90th birthday

The field of vocational astrology is a division of natal astrology in that it applies the information provided by the natal birth chart to the study of career. We gave you an introduction to this subject in part one of Chapter Four.

Recent studies have determined that two out of three American workers are dissatisfied with their jobs. Vocational counselors tell us that this is due to the fact that people choose careers because of pressures that come from *outside* themselves—e.g. what the parents want (based on what Mommy or Daddy did with their lives), what is practical, what will make the most money, what the new "in" career is (computers, etc.). Rarely, however, do high school or college students look within themselves and ask, "What is my passion? What is it that I most enjoy doing?" If more people looked within to discover their true vocations (from the Latin *vocare*—inner calling), then the level of job frustration would decrease dramatically.

The beauty of astrology is that it describes, through its symbolic language, the exact nature of a person's vocational needs and loves. Therefore, we believe that in addition to the traditional "guidance counseling," every graduating high school student should be given a vocational chart interpretation. If this occurred, then the students would enter college with a much clearer vision of their career directions and much of the current confusion and malaise would surely decrease.

Synastry—The Astrology of Relationships

During the 1970 s, the traumatic passage of Pluto, planet of death and rebirth, through Libra, sign of marriage, signaled the end of traditional marriage structures in Western culture. Throughout this transitional period (1968–1983), old marriage values were challenged and divorce rates shot to a new high. What Pluto was telling us was that no longer could a marriage survive simply on the basis of the traditional marital roles (husband as breadwinner, wife as homemaker; husband rules, wife obeys). Now, relationships had to be based on the true Libran principle of **equality** and give and take. Thus, for marriages to survive today, they must exist on a more conscious level than those of previous generations.

There is no better tool to meet this challenge than astrology. For as we saw in Chapter Four, the birth chart provides many clues as to what you need and what you can offer in a relationship. The authors have engaged in a number of long-term studies of couples who had their charts compared as they initiated their relationships. Time after time, our clients have told us that learning how their birth charts were interacting enabled them to better understand the dynamics of their relationships, and thus helped them to fulfill each other's wants and needs.

Based on these experiences, we highly recommend that all individuals entering into a relationship—whether for love or in business—should first consult an astrologer for a chart comparison. If this were done on a consistent basis, we believe that the quality of relationships in business, marriage, and the family would greatly improve.

Medical Astrology

The discipline of medical astrology is the science and art of obtaining scientific knowledge of disease and its causes through a study of the birth chart. Although the use of astrology in modern medicine is rare indeed, the two disciplines have been connected since their inception. Hippocrates, the father of modern medicine, made extensive use of astrology in his practice and urged his students to do likewise. In the following centuries, physicians such as Galen, Culpepper, and Paracelcus carefully observed the physical influences of stellar phenomena. Similarly, medical astrology can be used by today's holistically–minded physician in three important ways.

First, when a physical illness occurs, it doesn't happen randomly, but at the individual's vulnerable points. These weaknesses, which may arise through heredity, childhood illnesses, and learned neurotic behaviors, are also portrayed in the horoscopic pattern. In some instances, these tendencies may remain latent throughout the life if the person does not strain them through poor health habits. If a chain has a weak link and no stress is placed on it, the chain remains whole. But if sufficient stress does occur, then the previously latent problem will manifest into a definite illness.

Tables 1 and 2 show the correspondences between the signs and planets and certain bodily parts and functions. Each of these correspondences represents a potential problem area. Hence, Geminis are predisposed to respiratory ailments, Capricorns to knee injuries, Pisces to foot problems, etc.

Secondly, astrology can assist doctors by pointing out the psychic imbalances that may manifest as physical maladies. Research in psychosomatic medicine has clearly demonstrated the essential unity of mind and body. Researchers now acknowledge that many physical maladies result from mental or emotional stress— psychic disharmonies that are also depicted in the birth chart. For example, a person with Mars (assertion) in a water sign such as Cancer (self–repression) will have difficulty directly expressing his or her anger. If the anger continues to turn inward, stomach ulcers (Cancer rules the stomach) could result.

A third application of medical astrology involves the use of planetary transits to signal the times when physical/emotional crises are most likely to occur. For example, astrologers have traditionally advised against having operations on the full moon. Recently, medical researchers have confirmed that the risk of hemorrhaging dramatically increases at this time. In addition to the lunar cycle, medical astrologers monitor planetary transits to the client's sixth (health) and eighth (transformation) houses. Invariably, these periods are associated with physical or psychological crises that can manifest as a specific health problem. If the transiting planet is Uranus, Neptune, or Pluto, then the illness will have major significance.

An example of such a transit occurred in the life of Richard Nixon. Figure 1 portrays his birth chart, revealing a number of stress patterns that aptly describes his history of physical infirmities. His knee vulnerability is depicted by the stressful aspects to his Sun, Mercury and Jupiter in Capricorn (knees). Secondly, Nixon's lung weakness is depicted by Mars (inflammation) conjunct Mercury (respiration) and opposing Pluto (tissue destruction) in Gemini (the lungs). True to form, Nixon contracted pneumonia as a child. Finally, circulation problems are indicated by the Moon in Aquarius (circulation) squaring Saturn (restriction).

The transit that brought these latent weaknesses to the surface occurred during Watergate as transiting Saturn first passed over Pluto–Mars opposition and then opposed his Sun (his vitality and will). Thus, in September of 1974, at a low psychological ebb after having resigned from the presidency, Nixon experienced a blood clot that originated in his knees and traveled to his lungs, nearly killing him.

The relationship between astrology and human health is a subject that warrants further study. Although more research is needed to fully understand its applications, physicians can still use medical astrology to improve the quality of their clients' health as well as their own.

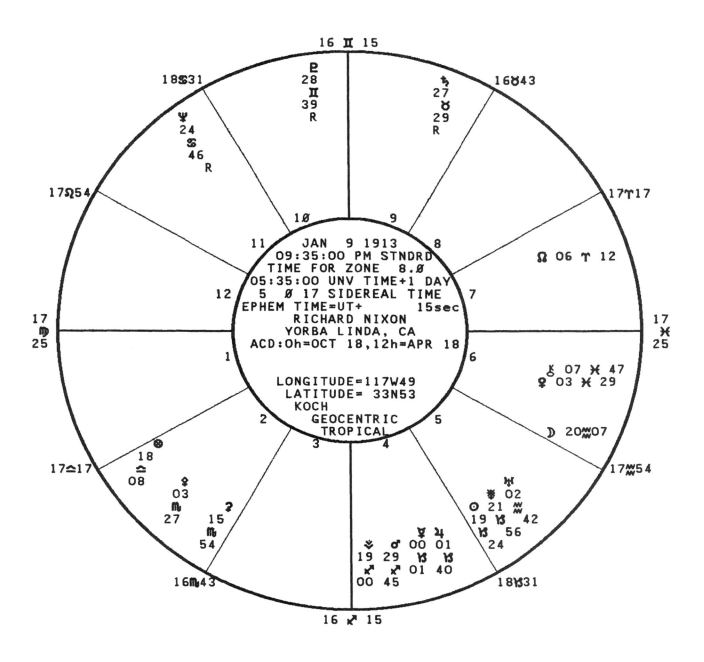

JAN 9 1913
09:35:00 PM STNDRD
TIME FOR ZONE 8.Ø
05:35:00 UNV TIME+1 DAY
5 Ø 17 SIDEREAL TIME
EPHEM TIME=UT+   15sec
RICHARD NIXON
YORBA LINDA, CA
ACD:0h=OCT 18,12h=APR 18

LONGITUDE=117W49
LATITUDE= 33N53
KOCH
GEOCENTRIC
TROPICAL

Table 1: Physiological Correspondences of the Signs

SIGN	EXTERNAL REGION	INTERNAL REGION	SYSTEM
Aries	Head	Blood, Brain	Muscular
Taurus	Neck	Throat	Metabolic
Gemini	Shoulders, Arms, Lungs, Hands	Nerves	Central Nervous
Cancer	Breasts	Stomach, Uterus	Upper Alimentary
Leo	Upper Back	Heart, Upper Spine	Cardiac
Virgo	Abdomen	Intestines	Lower Alimentary
Libra	Small of the Back	Kidneys	Endocrine
Scorpio	Genitals	Colon, Sex Organs	Urogenital
Sagittarius	Hips, Thighs	Lower Spine	Autonomic Nervous
Capricorn	Knees, Skin	Bones, Teeth, Joints	Skeletal
Aquarius	Ankles	Electrical Impulses of the Nerves	Circulatory
Pisces	Feet	Body Fluids	Lymphatic

Cardinal sign disorders are acute in nature, manifesting in fevers, infections, and inflammations.

Fixed sign disorders are chronic and are caused by excessive inertia or rigidity. Common afflictions include congestion, cysts, tumors, calcification of the joints and hardening of the arteries.

Mutable sign disorders are mental and result from the dissipation of energy. Resulting illnesses manifest as nervous disorders, fatigue, anemia, and mental and physical exhaustion.

Table 2: Physiological Correspondences of the Planets

PLANET	PHYSIOLOGICAL PROCESS
Sun	The Heart and the circulation
Moon	Digestion and lactation
Mercury	Respiration and the nervous system
Venus	Glandular activity, Female sex organs, Venous circulation
Mars	Muscular activity, Male sex organs, Arterial circulation
Jupiter	Growth and assimilation
Saturn	Maturation and aging
Uranus	The transmission of electrical impulses through the nervous system
Neptune	The reception of supersensible or psychic impulses
Pluto	Anabolism and catabolism; the body's regenerative processes

These tables are taken from *Astrology: The Divine Science* by Mark Douglas and Marcia Moore.

Astrology and Child Rearing

Nobody has to be reminded that parenting is hard work, one of the most challenging jobs we face. Many years ago, I asked a mother of five who loved her parenting role to summarize what she had learned from her experience. "I can tell you in two words," she replied. "Patience and sacrifice."

Unfortunately, the stresses put upon today's family (both parents working, single parent households, etc.) are making parenting even more difficult, especially for the children. This is clearly evidenced by the unprecedented increase in child abuse, child kidnappings (symbolized by the asteroid Ceres), runaway children, depression in children, and teenage suicides. Clearly, growing up in today's society is a difficult and hazardous occupation.

While astrology cannot provide a panacea for these social ills, it can help the sincere parent to better understand and support the genuine nature of his or her child. For astrology teaches us that children do not come into the world as a "tabula rasa" (a blank slate), but with predisposed character structures that include specific wants and needs, strengths and weaknesses. Thus, it becomes the parent's job to *guide* that growing being along its natural course, to provide the right environment for the seed to grow into a healthy and mature plant.

The prescription for what the child needs to fulfill his or her unique set of requirements is provided by the birth chart. Your child's personality needs can be described by using the exercises in this book, just as you used them to describe your own. Thus, we recommend that you as a parent learn about your child's birth chart by using *Astrology for Yourself* or by consulting a professional astrologer. In so doing you will learn to accept your child as he or she is, and not try to force him or her to become somebody else. Instead of projecting your expectations onto your child, you will be supporting his essential and unique nature. And ironically, by accepting your children as they are, they will become more attuned to their natural flow and thus be far easier to parent.

Thus, astrology can help the process of child rearing in three ways. First, it teaches us that children are themselves from the outset, that they come with their own unique packages and sets of instructions.

Secondly, if this is so, then parents can be relieved of the burden of guilt that comes from believing that every aspect of their children's personalities is their doing. Astrology depicts parents as guides, not gods.

Finally, by comparing charts of parent and child, the nature of the karmic relationship can be discerned. It has often been said that children are our greatest teachers. The exact nature of these teachings and lessons may be revealed by a chart comparison. And, if we can understand exactly why we and our children have come together and what we have to learn from each other, then the task of parenting will be seen as a continual learning experience, one which can only further the growth and evolution of both parent and child.

Electional Astrology—The Art of Timing Events

Misses! the tale that I relate this lesson seems
to carry;
Choose not alone a proper mate but a proper
time to marry.

William Cowper

In our study of transits, we described the importance of astrological cycles in chronicling human growth and development. Using these same principles, we can choose to initiate certain events according to the astrological times that will be most favorable to their success.

One such ancient practice is planting by the moon. Throughout history, amateur gardeners and commercial farmers have used nature's cosmic rhythms to enhance the health and productivity of their crops. Thus, whether you maintain a vegetable garden in lower Manhattan or raise tomatoes in the Sacramento Valley, you can learn to plant by the moon. Table 3 provides an introduction to the principles of Moon planting.

The Signs

The most fertile signs are the water signs Cancer, Scorpio and Pisces and the earth sign Taurus. The earth sign Capricorn and the air sign Libra are also fertile but less so than the water signs and Taurus. The barren signs are the fire signs Aries, Leo and Sagittarius, the air signs Gemini and Aquarius and the earth sign Virgo.

Most seeds, plants, trees, cuttings and transplants should be set out in the most fertile signs. The fertile signs are best for starting compost piles, harvesting seeds to be replanted, as well as roots and bulbs to be replanted later. Organic fertilizers should be applied in fertile signs and crops are best irrigated in the fertile water signs.

The barren signs should be used for plowing, cultivating, pulling weeds, pruning trees (to discourage growth), getting rid of pests, cutting firewood and lumber, and for cutting lawns to discourage growth. The dry barren signs can be used for harvesting herbs, fruits and vegetables for drying and storage.

Moon in Aries: Dry and barren—best for cultivating, plowing, pulling weeds, getting rid of pests, cutting firewood and lumber, and harvesting crops to dry.

Moon in Taurus: Moist and fertile—best for planting roots, leafy crops, and producing hardiness in plants. Also for grafting, budding, and taking cuttings.

Moon in Gemini: Dry and barren—good for cultivating, weeding, getting rid of pests, cutting wood, and harvesting crops for drying and storage.

Moon in Cancer: Moist and fertile—good for planting anything. Good for viny plants, peas, beans, melons, cucumbers, etc. and irrigating crops.

Moon in Leo: Dry and barren—best for cultivating, weeding, cutting wood, getting rid of pests and harvesting crops for drying and storage.

Moon in Virgo: Moist and barren—cultivate, prune, cut wood, harvest crops to be dried or stored.

Moon in Libra: Moist and semi-fruitful—good for planting flowers for beauty, root crops, viny crops, hay and fodder crops, harvest seeds and roots to be replanted later.

Moon in Scorpio: Moist and fertile—good for vine growth and sturdiness, planting anything, harvesting seeds and roots to replant, irrigating, grafting.

Moon in Sagittarius: Dry and barren—cultivate, weed, cut firewood, get rid of pests, harvest crops for drying and storage.

Moon in Capricorn: Moist and semi-fertile—good for roots and tubers, for harvesting seeds and roots to replant, and for fertilizing.

Moon in Aquarius: Dry and barren—best for cultivating, weeding, cutting wood, getting rid of pests, and harvesting crops for drying and storage.

Moon in Pisces: Moist and fertile—good for planting roots (except potatoes), irrigating, grafting, layering, and taking cuttings.

Plant in *Cancer* for abundance, *Taurus* for hardiness, *Libra* for beauty, and *Scorpio* for sturdiness.

Phases of the Moon

The First Quarter: Plant *annual* crops that bear their fruits, leaves, etc. above ground, especially the leafy crops. Also plant cereals, grains, melons, cucumbers, celery, cabbage, spinach, etc. Graft, layer and take cuttings.

The Second Quarter: Plant *annuals* that yield their crops above ground, especially the viny crops—peas, beans, melons, squash, tomatoes, peppers, cereals, grains, hay, garlic, and cucumbers. Take cuttings, graft, and harvest above ground crops for storage and drying. (Also harvest for drying in the first quarter.)

The Third Quarter: Plant *biennials, perennials,* bulbs, roots, trees, grapes, berries, potatoes, shrubs; pull weeds, cut trees for firewood and lumber, plow, cultivate, prune trees and vines, get rid of pests, and harvest below–ground crops for drying and storage.

The Fourth Quarter: Fertilize, cultivate, cut trees for lumber and firewood, prune trees, get rid of pests, plant roots, trees, perennials, biennials, plow, and harvest below–ground crops to eat, dry and store.

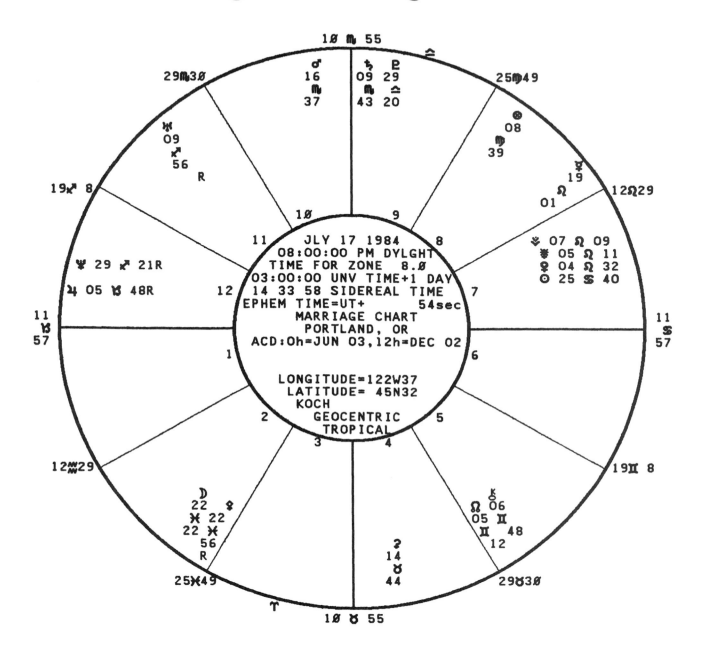

Another common timing practice alluded to by Mr. Cowper's quotation is that of choosing event charts for marriage. Figure 2 is one such marriage chart chosen for a wedding between a Pisces and Scorpio. A marriage chart is analyzed in two ways: by looking at the chart itself and by comparing it to the birth charts of the marital partners. In the first case, note that the chart itself contains certain marital elements—the Sun, Venus, and Juno in the seventh house of marriage. The Sun in Cancer also reinforces the issues of home and family that are important to the couple. Secondly, the watery Cancer sun favorably blends with the man's Pisces and woman's Scorpio Sun sign. Moreover, the Capricorn rising blends with the wife's own Capricorn rising and husband's Capricorn moon.

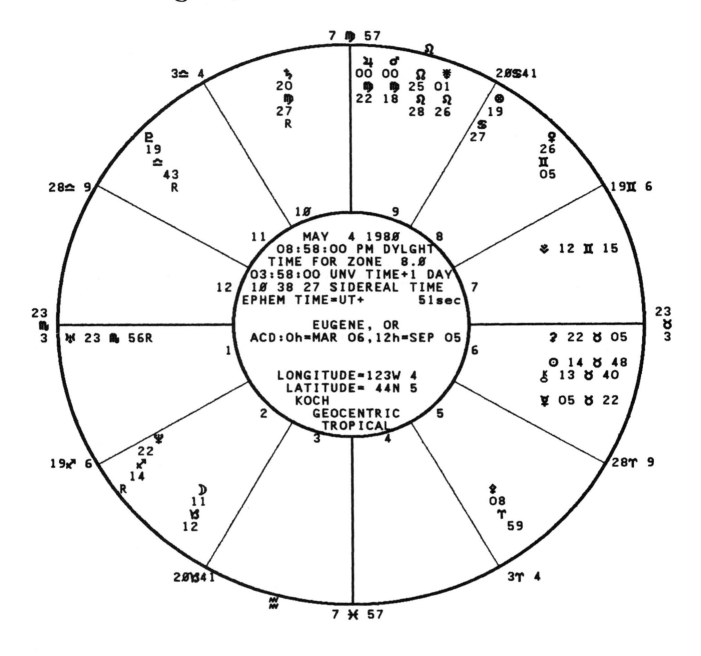

Finally, Figure 3 shows an event chart that was chosen for a successful graphics art business. Besides the favorable aspects between the earth signs in the earth houses, the chart has positive connections to the charts of the business partners.

Finally, the *Wall Street Journal* has reported how realtors are successfully using astrology to pick the most auspicious times for the listing and selling of homes.

Though we have only touched upon the subject of electional astrology, its benefits should be clear. The next time you plan to initiate a major project, use astrological timing to help insure its successful outcome.

Wall Street Journal,
October 10, 1986

Thinking of Buying Or Selling a House? Ask Your Astrologer

* * *

Mercury May Be Retrograde, And That Means Trouble, Feng Shui and a Lamppost ◇

By KATHLEEN A. HUGHES

Staff Reporter of THE WALL STREET JOURNAL

LOS ANGELES—After deciding to sell his home in Upland, Calif., novelist Whitney Stine pounded a "For Sale" sign into his front yard. But he deliberately waited to do so until 2:22 p.m. one Thursday.

The house sold three days later for his asking price—$228,000. And Mr. Stine credits the quick sale to the advice of his astrologer, John Bradford, whom he has consulted for 12 years in the sale of five houses.

"He always tells me the exact time to put out the sign according to the phases of the moon, and the houses have always sold within a few months," Mr. Stine says.

Such behavior isn't odd in California real estate. "Getting advice from fortune-tellers, astrologers and religious advisers is commonplace," says Lynn Borland, a vice president of Fred Sands Realtors in Los Angeles. Sometimes the advice nips a deal in the bud, delays a closing or keeps a house off the market for months.

A Crystal Ball

Perhaps one shouldn't be surprised that people seek out a little omniscience before buying and selling. Says Lee Siegel, a professor of religion at the University of Hawaii: "It's a vulnerable feeling to write a big check. If you can find someone who has a crystal ball, that's very reassuring."

Consider Joyce Chupack, a vice president of Wings Travel in Beverly Hills. After she and her husband separated last year, she says he wanted to sell their Beverly Hills house right away. Before she did, however, Ms. Chupack took it up with a psychic, James Watson. "He said, 'you're going to move your home, but I suggest you wait a year to get a better price,'" she recalls. Something told him interest rates were going down.

So she waited—despite a lot of pressure from her husband, whom she never told about the psychic. Meanwhile, a booming housing market and declining rates have indeed done wonders for the market value of the house. Ms. Chupack says an appraisal last year valued the house at $700,000 to $800,-000; a recent appraisal came in at $900,000. "I'm so glad I listened to him" (the adviser, not her husband), says Ms. Chupack, who now does have the house on the market.

Good News and Bad

Real-estate agents say they frequently encounter a completely different set of advisers and superstitions when selling homes to Asians, particularly to Chinese customers. Certain beliefs have been passed along from antiquity and reflect a blend of chinese astrology and *feng shui,* an ancient custom with roots in nature worship, Taoism and yin and yang. Buyers' demands often leave your average real-estate salesmen perplexed, to say the least.

After searching for a house for two-and-a-half years, Nelson Moy, the president of United Poultry in Los Angeles, found a four-bedroom place in Beverly Hills that he and his wife liked. But, then, he consulted a feng shui adviser, who told him: "In this house you will have a son, but your wife will die," recalls Mr. Moy. "My wife said we're not living here, for sure."

The couple eventually found another house to love, this one with pool and a tennis court. To be on the safe side, Mr. Moy flew in an additional feng shui adviser from Arizona, and both gurus gave the deal the go-ahead. Indeed, one said, "You will prosper and get very wealthy," Mr. Moy recalls.

Mr. Moy says he doesn't know what the advisers based their recommendations on, but he says he relies on such advice because his parents did. "I'm old-fashioned," he says, "What's it going to hurt?"

Some people simply adhere to old superstitions—maybe read a book—and skip the advisers. To do so can mean having to relocate a lamppost or tree.

When Lily Lowe, the owner of a Los Angeles sweater company moved to Pasadena three years ago, she had a huge palm removed from the front of the house, and that cost "quite a bit," she says. "They say you will fight a lot or you will be divorced [if there's a tree or pole in front of your house]," says Ms. Lowe, who wasn't even married at the time.

But Ms. Lowe knows from experience that a tree can mean trouble. When she lived in Glendale, her house faced a tree, and, she says, "I had a struggling few years in . . . my business and personal life." When she moved to the house, *sans* palm tree, in Pasadena, she started making money. "I used to think it was rotten superstition. Now, I know there's something to it," she says.

Adherents of feng shui are fearful of living in a house facing the end of a road at an intersection. The idea is that bad *ch'i,* or invisible forces, might flow down the road and cause harm by dispersing harmonious ch'i. A lamppost or tree is thought to have the same, arrow-like, divisive quality.

While the beliefs often mystify real-estate people, salesmen usually try to accommodate clients, if only to close a deal. Agent Natalie Gewertz said she appealed to city officials in Pasadena for permission to have a lamppost moved 20 feet—away from the front of a house she was trying to unload. The cost to her client: $2,000. "If I hadn't been creative, I wouldn't have sold the house," she says. "I explained to the city that it was a Chinese superstition. The city understood."

Astrologers, however, often keep agents cooling their heels. Last February, Susan Wallerstein told her neighbor, a new real-estate agent, that she planned to sell her house in Sherman Oaks. But when Ms. Wallerstein mentioned the plan to her astrologer, she told her, "Oh, my God! Don't!" according to Ms. Wallerstein. The astrologer suggested waiting a month (to ensure a speedier sale) and told Ms. Wallerstein to stick the sale sign in the ground on March 30, Easter sunday, between 5:20 a.m. and 6:41 a.m.

Ms. Wallerstein did as told. She set her alarm clock and, after a fitful night's sleep, rose in time to put up the sign at dawn. The house sold on the first day it was shown, for $270,000, some $5,000 more than the Wallersteins had planned to settle for. Still, the real-estate agent was a bit ruffled. "It was frustrating," the agent says. "I think it would have sold quickly in February, but who knows?"

Ms. Wallerstein's astrologer, Alice Q. Reichard, has a simple explanation: The moon rules property. And on Easter Sunday, between 5:20 a.m. and 6:41 a.m., the moon was in Sagittarius, a mutable sign that means motion—or a quick sale. "If the moon had been in a fixed sign, the property would have taken a long time to sell," says Ms. Reichard.

And that's not all. When the Wallersteins had first wanted to sell their house Mercury was about to go retrograde, a period during which Mercury's path appears to change direction because the planet has overtaken the Earth in its orbit. It happens 3.15 times a year. And Mercury rules sales contracts. "If you sell when Mercury is retrograde, there will be a slip-up in the contract, or the sale won't go through," says Ms. Reichard. But on Easter Sunday, Mercury was behaving itself, real-estate-wise.

Some who have ignored the position of the planets when buying a home cite dire consequences. Take, for instance, Stacey Dean, A Las Vegas astrologer. She bought a four-bedroom house two years ago for $93,500 as at a time hardly propitious for buying houses, as Ms. Dean learned, to her regret. "I wanted to exercise my free will," sighs Ms. Dean.

The first hint of trouble came when she discovered electrical switches reversed; the kitchen light turned on the dining-room fan. Then the shower leaked into the stairway. The clincher came last May when she found a legal notice tacked to her garage announcing that the property was to be auctioned off because of outstanding liens against it. Ms. Dean says the matter is in litigation.

Sometimes, strange things happen outside Southern California. Last March, Joy Lamberson, a property manger, checked with her astrologer before a group of investors she works for purchased a $3.5 million apartment complex in Lexington, Ky. The astrologer, Carolyn Dodson of Nashville, Tenn., said to stall them two weeks. But the investors wouldn't wait. "They said I worry too much," says Ms. Lamberson.

Now, she says, they haven't sold a single one of 125 units. Two-thirds of the units flooded when it rained. Tenants stopped paying their rents to protest water damage. And the Health Department closed the swimming pool. "We had six managers there for five-and-a-half months working on the problems," says Ms. Lamberson. "The investors are sorry now."

Mundane Astrology

Literally, "the astrology of the world," mundane astrology comprises the study of the birth charts of countries, states, world leaders, and the events that occur to them. Another name for this astrological discipline is Political Astrology.

"How," you may ask, "can astrology be applied to the political arena?" The answer is quite simple. Nations, like people, display their own drives, needs, and temperaments. For example, we think of the English as aloof with a dry sense of humor, the Germans as logical and precise, the French as artistic and sensual, and Americans as individualistic and self-reliant. Over the years, astrologers have researched the dates of birth of these nations, set up their birth charts, and correlated the celestial patterns to national temperaments. Of these birth charts, the most thoroughly investigated has been that of the United States. Figures 4 and 5 portray two commonly used versions of the U.S. birth chart. (Although we know that America celebrates its birthday on Independence Day, July 4, the exact moment of the signing of the Declaration of Independence has not yet been established.)

Many books have been written about this event chart. In the space allotted, we will cover the main points.

1. That the USA, "born" July 4, 1776 is a **Cancer Sun** sign is quite clear to any observer of the country. The Cancerian themes of home, family, Mom, apple pie, and love of country are deeply ingrained in the national psyche. That we have not only mothered ourselves, but also the world, is demonstrated by the way in which we have opened our doors to millions of immigrants searching for a new home. The words inscribed on the Statue of Liberty epitomize this nurturing, Cancerian concern:

"Give me your tired, your poor, your huddled masses yearning to be free; the wretched refuse of your teeming shore. Send these, the homeless tempest-tossed to me."

2. The **Aquarius Moon** symbolizes another aspect of the national psyche—our love of liberty and freedom (prime Aquarian themes). Moreover, our belief in the equality of human beings and government "by the people" (stated by the Aquarian president Lincoln) have led us to develop that most Aquarian of political institutions—democracy. It is also interesting to note that some of our most popular presidents (Lincoln, Roosevelt, and now Ronald Reagan) are all Aquarians. Evidently, they have found a way to tap into the unconscious needs and aspirations (the Moon) of the American people.

3. The conjunction on the Sun (one's purpose), Jupiter (expansion), and Venus (the power of attraction) in Cancer (sustenance) falls in the **second-eighth house axis** of material resources. This explains the abundance of natural resources endowed to us and the material prosperity we have created with it. Although our Cancerian insecurities have led to an overconsumption of material goods, we have also been generous (Jupiter) with our resources, helping to rebuild Europe after World War II and donating millions to the needy through foreign aid.

4. Finally, at the moment of our "birth," **Uranus,** planet of revolution, freedom, self-reliance, and scientific innovation, was on the **horizon** in the sign of Gemini. We have certainly made major scientific advances in the Gemini fields of transportation and communication. Moreover, Uranus rules constant change, making Americans, despite their love of home, a very mobile people. The average American uproots him- or herself every seven years.

Hopefully, this brief overview has demonstrated that nations, like people, have their own birth charts which contain the seeds of their characters and destinies.

Astro-Economics

Astro-economics applies the tools of astrology to the study of economic trends and cycles. Like historical astrology, the transits and cycles of outer planets correspond to the most important cycles.

For example, the planet Neptune corresponds to mass money. Thus when Neptune was transiting through the sign of expansion, Sagittarius, in the 1970 s, we experienced a time of high inflation. Now that Neptune is in the earth sign of restriction and limitation, Capricorn, we are in the midst of a long-term deflationary cycle. This is precisely what occurred when Neptune last transited through the earth sign Virgo, from 1929 to 1942.

Aside from the outer planets, astrologers also use sunspot activity to chronicle overall business cycles. In addition, many national newsletters exist that correlate astrological cycles to overall economic trends or to the movement of financial markets (especially the stock market). If you wish to gain more exposure to the realm of financial astrology, you might want to subscribe to one of these newsletters or attend a lecture at a local astrology conference. Again, our bibliography will provide you with the references you need.

Figure 4: U.S.A. Birth Chart 1

July 4, 1776   Philadelphia, PA   2:17 AM

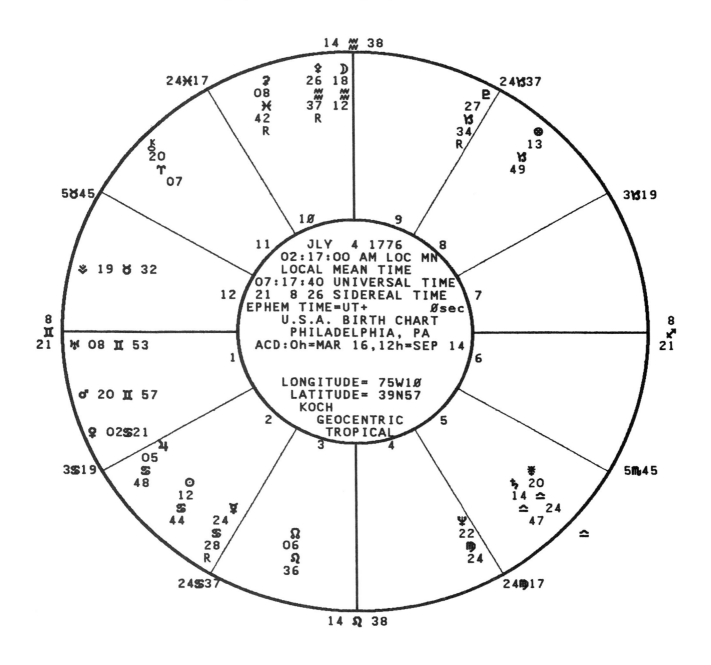

July 4, 1776   Philadelphia, PA   4:46 PM

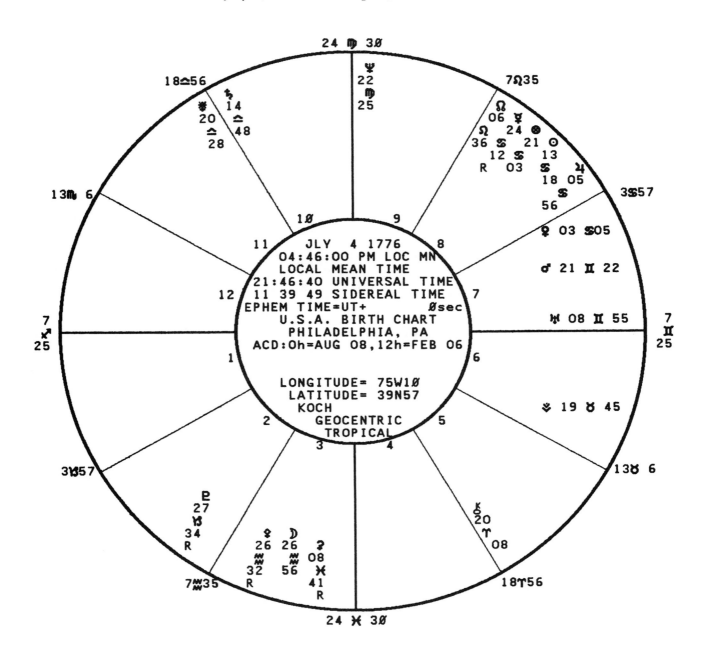

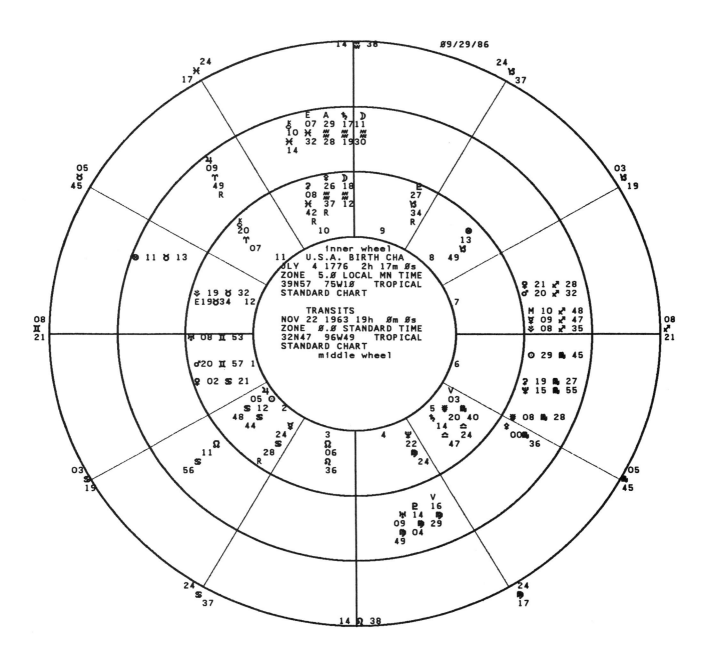

Historical Astrology

Historical astrology applies astrological principles to the interpretation of history. This is accomplished in a number of ways.

First and foremost, historical astrology correlates the cycles of the three outermost planets (Uranus, Neptune and Pluto) to major historical changes. For example, the discovery of Uranus corresponded to a host of political, scientific, and industrial revolutions and to an accelerated rate of change that remains with us today. Pluto's discovery ushered in the atomic age. Moreover, when Pluto became associated with the principle of death and rebirth, as it passed through a specific sign, the affairs of that sign underwent a permanent metamorphosis. For example, Pluto's movement through the sign of Libra in the 1970 s brought permanent changes in marital structures and basic human relationships.

Secondly, astrologers construct birth charts of important historical events in order to gain insight into their meanings. Examples include the dropping of the A-bomb (ushering in the atomic age), the first airplane flight at Kitty Hawk, the launching of the first satellite (initiating the space age), etc. In the first example, it is interesting to note that at the moment of the dropping of the first A-bomb, transiting Saturn, the great Timer had just passed through 17 degrees of Cancer, the same degree that Pluto occupied when it was discovered.

Thirdly, historical astrologers pay careful attention to major transits in the charts of nations and world leaders. For example, on November 22, 1963, the day that president Kennedy was assassinated, fourteen stressful aspects (squares, quincunxes and oppositions) were applying from the transiting planets to the chart of the U.S.A., most of which symbolized violence in some form. The transits are illustrated in Figure 6. Clearly, the predominance of such powerful aspects corresponds to the profound impact that this tragic event had on the national psyche.

Astrological cycles therefore chronicle not only our *personal* histories, but our **collective** history as well. Historical astrology promises to be even more useful as Pluto's passage through the sign of Scorpio mirrors the positive transformation that humanity must experience if we are to safely enter the twenty-first century.

Horary Astrology

Horary Astrology is the practice of casting a chart for a time when a question is asked and using the birth chart as a means of finding an answer. The chart erected for the time of the question is known as the horary chart.

The principle behind horary astrology is simple. Whenever a *question* is asked at a point in time, the *answer* to that question exists at that same moment in time. Virtually any type of question can be addressed to the horary astrologer: "Should I undertake this endeavor?", "Will I receive my promotion?", "Where did I place my lost earrings?", etc.

Once the question is asked, the astrologer draws up a birth chart for the exact moment of the inquiry and then interprets it according to a very structured set of rules. Some astrologers even construct a chart for the time of their client's appointment and interpret it to see what types of issues will be brought up in the session. If physicians applied this technique to their patients, they might be able to learn about a new patient's medical condition before he or she even enters the office.

The rules for interpreting horary charts are quite different from the chart interpretation techniques that you have learned in *Astrology for Yourself*. If you want to learn more about the subject of horary astrology, we would suggest that you read a book on the subject or enroll in a correspondence course.

We have just provided you with a brief overview of the ten major branches of astrology. By now, we hope that you realize that there is far more to this vast subject than the newspaper columns and mass market books let on.

Astrology touches on virtually every aspect of human endeavor and in each instance can be applied in some beneficial manner. As we approach the dawning of the Aquarian Age, astrologers are hopeful that astrology's **validity** and **value** will be recognized by science and academia so that its many beneficial social applications may be experienced throughout the planet Earth.

Further Reading

If you wish to learn more about the topics covered in this chapter, please check the bibliography where recommended books are listed by subject.

Chapter 8

Looking Inward

YOU ARE ABOUT TO CONCLUDE the initial phase of your astrological journey. As a result of your exploration, you should now have a deeper and more comprehensive understanding of yourself than you did when you first opened the pages of this book.

We hope that *Astrology for Yourself* has provided you with an enjoyable and informative introduction to the science and art of astrology. Should you desire to further pursue your astrological self-study, we suggest that you consult the excellent references that we have listed in the bibliography. Delving into astrology is a lifetime process that is limited only by the boundaries of your curiosity and your thirst for self-knowledge.

In our introduction, we stated that if you completed the exercises contained in this work, you would gain a knowledge of yourself that would transform the quality of your life. This brief chapter will give you the opportunity to document the exact nature of the changes that have occurred.

In addition, Appendix E will provide an overview of all that you have learned through a sample interpretation of the birth chart of Martin Luther King, Jr.

Exercise 1: Summing Up

In this exercise, you will be integrating all that you have learned from the exercises you have completed. Relax, take a deep breath, and allow yourself to review the new ideas, insights and changes that you have experienced while journeying through *Astrology for Yourself*. Every birth chart contains several **basic life themes**. All the astrological indicators, each in a different way, repeat and amplify the variations of these essential themes. Keep this in mind as you consider the following questions.

In completing this exercise, we ask that you pull out and write down the insights about yourself that *immediately* come to your mind. Do not censor or stop to analyze the flow of information. Just let it pour forth spontaneously.

1. Look back over the list of **exercises** in the Table of Contents. Do any stand out as having had a significant effect on you? Which ones are they, and what insights have you gained from them?

_____

_____

_____

_____

_____

_____

_____

_____

_____

_____

2. Were there any repeating or **re-occurring** astrological **themes** that happened over the course of the exercises? If so, what types of themes are they? What significance do they have in your life?

_____

_____

_____

_____

_____

_____

_____

_____

3. Can you locate your **major challenges** that repeated themselves in the exercises? If so, what are they? To what extent are you using unskillful qualities to maintain and augment these tensions? What changes and adaptations can you make to resolve these dilemmas?

_____

_____

_____

_____

_____

_____

_____

_____

_____

4. What areas do you perceive as your **major strengths**? How can you use these qualities in their most skillful applications? How might you use these strengths to overcome and resolve the important challenges that you listed above?

_____

_____

_____

_____

_____

_____

_____

_____

_____

5. In the space below, feel free to write down any additional **thoughts** or **insights** that come to you as you review the major life themes of your birth chart interpretation.

_____

_____

_____

_____

_____

_____

_____

_____

_____

_____

_____

_____

In the introduction, we asked you to choose which changes you would most like to occur in your life as a result of reading _Astrology for Yourself_. On the following page, we have reprinted those benefits. Look back over those you originally picked to see if your goals have been realized. Perhaps some new benefits arose that you were not expecting.

Now, read over the statements provided in Table 1 on the next page and check the benefits that you have received from participating in and completing _Astrology for Yourself_.

Table 1: Discovering What I Have Learned

CHECK HERE IF BENEFIT APPLIES | **BENEFITS THAT I HAVE RECEIVED FROM STUDYING *ASTROLOGY FOR YOURSELF***

_____ 1. I have gained a better understanding of my basic temperament and style of being in the world.

_____ 2. I have gained a fuller knowledge of my abilities, talents, strengths and potentials.

_____ 3. I have gained a better understanding of where my major challenges lie and how I can turn them into opportunities.

_____ 4. I see myself as connected to a larger order, one that is purposeful, meaningful and just.

_____ 5. Many of my feelings and hunches about myself have been confirmed and validated.

_____ 6. I have gained a clearer understanding of my needs and aspirations in my life work.

_____ 7. I have gained a clearer understanding of my overall relationship needs and of the relationship dynamics of an important partnership.

_____ 8. I have gained a knowledge and appreciation of individual differences as depicted by the fact that each person's birth chart has its own unique set of needs. I have also come to appreciate my own uniqueness and individuality.

_____ 9. I understand that astrological energies are by nature *neutral* and that I have the freedom to express them in a skillful or unskillful manner.

_____ 10. I see astrology giving me a way to view myself from a more objective and all-inclusive vantage point. Consequently, I have been able to gain a new perspective on my life.

_____ 11. I understand that the purpose of living is to grow and reach my highest potential, and that my birth chart is a road map that can guide me along this journey of transformation.

_____ 12. I understand that my evolution unfolds in an orderly and timely manner, and that I can use my birth chart to identify and support the major passages and transitions in my life.

Now that you are finished, look back over your choices. We hope that you have checked a majority of the benefits; but even if you chose just one, this signifies that a positive change has been affected in your life.

We hope that this change (or changes) heralds the beginning of a new era, one that will quicken the pace of your spiritual progress toward the ultimate goal of self-knowledge and self-realization.

Appendices

As filters that color the expression of planetary energies, the signs of the Zodiac symbolize twelve basic psychological needs that all of us experience in our lives. The keywords in this appendix describe the characteristics and tendencies of the signs of the Zodiac. As you complete the exercises in this book, you will be using these descriptions to paint a portrait of yourself.

Remember that the signs themselves are neutral. It is **how you apply them** that makes the difference. Thus, if you have been using a certain zodiacal energy in a way that is creating destructive or unhappy results in your life, you can also choose to express the very same sign in a more positive or constructive manner. It is not a matter of adding something that you do not have, but of learning how to better use **what is already available.**

The following pages contain **keywords** for the skillful and unskillful applications of the twelve signs of the Zodiac. You will be referring to these pages in many of your exercises, as well as to Appendix B which contains the house keywords.

Aries

Cardinal Fire, Yang, Personal
Initiating Identity Action
Relates to Mars
Corresponds to first house

Sign Keyphrase:
My need to be independent and develop self-awareness

Qualities of Aries

Skillful Application

initiating, starting, pioneering, innovative
giving birth, inspiring, daring, naive
spontaneous, childlike, direct
innocent

energetic, driving, eager, active, confident
forceful, assertive, headstrong
enthusiastic, exuberant, active
independent, courageous, fearless
competitive

Unskillful Application

rash, reckless, careless
starts but does not finish
impulsive, irresponsible, violent
self-centered, foolhardy, impatient

aggressive, overpowering, selfish
belligerent, brusque, uncontrollable
uncooperative, combative
overzealous, temperamental, argumentative
overbearing, headstrong, coarse

Taurus

Fixed Earth, Yin, Personal
Stabilizing Material Security
Relates to Venus
Corresponds to 2nd house

Sign Keyphrase:
My need to be resourceful, productive and stable

Qualities of Taurus

Skillful Application

earthy, practical, productive
prudent, conserving, sensual, physical
resourceful, industrious

steadfast, stable, reliable, dependable
loyal, trustworthy, persevering, patient
deliberate, persistent, enduring, consistent
determined

artistic, aesthetic, loves the beauty of nature

domestic, placid

Unskillful Application

materialistic, conservative
possessive, overcautious
acquisitive, too security oriented

stubborn, stuck in a rut
fixed in his/her ways, bull-headed
sluggish, torpid, lethargic

self-indulgent, lazy, passive

uncontrolled appetites

Gemini

Mutable Air, Yang, Personal
Adapting to Social and Intellectual Learning
Relates to Mercury
Corresponds to 3rd house

Sign Keyphrase:
My need to communicate with and learn from others

Qualities of Gemini

Skillful Application

mental, intelligent, bright, learns easily
witty, curious, inquisitive, alert
logical, rational, knowledgeable, literary
fluent, studious

communicative, verbal, talkative
articulate, sociable, linking

jack-of-all trades, adaptable, flexible, dual
versatile, clever, dexterous
lighthearted, inventive, changeable

Unskillful Application

superficial, spacy, shallow
overly abstract, intangible
over-intellectualizing, diffusive
unemotional

wordy, gossiping, nosy, imitative
fretful

master of none, inconsistent, scattered
noncommittal, indecisive, nervous
high-strung, capricious, fickle
restless, impatient, flighty

Cancer

Cardinal Water, Yin, Personal
Initiating Emotional and Soul Action
Relates to the Moon and Ceres
Corresponds to the 4th house

Sign Keyphrase:
My need to give and receive emotional warmth and security

Qualities of Cancer

Skillful Application

emotional, feeling, receptive
sensitive, psychic, gentle
tender, vulnerable, sympathetic

nurturing, providing, caring
sustaining, protective, maternal
feeding, domestic, patriotic

shy, retiring, collecting, tenacious
oriented toward the past, retentive

Unskillful Application

insecure, moody, defensive
over-emotional, non-trusting
hypersensitive, touchy, brooding

smothering, clinging, consuming
overprotective, dependent
fearful, timid, clannish

withdrawn, grasping
stuck in the past, afraid to let go

Leo

Fixed Fire, Yang, Interpersonal
Stabilizing Identity Security
Relates to the Sun and Pallas
Corresponds to the 5th house

Sign Keyphrase:
My need to creatively express myself and be appreciated by others

Qualities of Leo

Skillful Application

self-assured, self-confident, dynamic
powerful, authoritative, radiant, commanding

impressive, majestic, dignified, noble
honorable, regal, royal, proud
thrives on appreciation, a leader
courageous, loyal

self-expressive, creative, dramatic
performing, loving, giving, ardent
magnanimous, warm, big-hearted
generous, playful, flamboyant
romantic

Unskillful Application

prideful, self-centered, vain, selfish
bombastic, overbearing, conceited
stubborn

dictatorial, domineering, haughty
arrogant, pompous, patronizing
aristocratic, grandiose, snobbish
having a superiority complex

childish, egocentric, possessive
demands to be center of attraction
melodramatic, extravagant, spendthrift
flirtatious, heartbreaker, tease
doubts own creative abilities

Virgo

Mutable Earth, Yin, Interpersonal
Adapting to Material Learning
Relates to Vesta, Ceres, and Mercury
Corresponds to 6th house

Sign Keyphrase:
My need to analyze, discriminate, and function efficiently

Qualities of Virgo

Skillful Application

practical, efficient, clear, analytical
dividing, differentiating, minute

discriminating, discerning, precise
detailed, exacting, meticulous, dexterous
technical, fastidious, organized, economical

disciplined, skillful, helpful
serving, efficient, dutiful, humble
conscientious, health-conscious
ultilitarian, unselfish, sanitary

Unskillful Application

petty, picky, trivial
skeptical, nitpicking

can't see the forest for the trees
critical, fault-finding, judgmental
perfectionistic, worrisome, lacking confidence

obsessive-compulsive, workaholic
self-deprecating, neurotic
hypochondriacal, has germ-fetish
self-denying, prudish

Libra

Cardinal Air, Yang, Interpersonal
Initiating Social and Intellectual Action
Relates to Juno and Venus
Corresponds to 7th house

Sign Keyphrase:
My need to cooperate with others and to create beauty, balance and harmony

Qualities of Libra

Skillful Application

relating, sharing, cooperative, partner-oriented
social, agreeable, easygoing, gregarious
affable, considerate

balanced, weighing, just, fair
tactful, diplomatic, charming
mediating, impartial

aesthetic, artistic, refined
beautiful, harmonious, pleasing
well-proportioned, tasteful

Unskillful Application

dependent, can't act alone
gives away power to others

indecisive, hesitant, passive
vacillating, inactive, idle
indifferent, fence-straddler
over-compromising

superficial (beauty is only skin deep)
vain, overly delicate
imbalanced

Scorpio

Fixed Water, Yin, Interpersonal
Stabilizing Emotional Security
Relates to Pluto
Corresponds to 8th house

Sign Keyphrase:
My need for deep involvements and intense transformations

Qualities of Scorpio

Skillful Application

regenerating, transforming
cathartic, giving birth, complex
metamorphosizing, healing, renewing
musical

penetrating, probing, researching
joining, piercing, erotic, sexual
intense, magnetic, powerful, emotional

mysterious, occult, hidden
deep, complex, psychological

Unskillful Application

power-hungry, destructive
violent, annihilating, sarcastic
death-oriented, obsessive, fixed
extremist, excessive

overwhelming, lustful, desirous
jealous, possessive, resentful
revengeful, vindictive, cruel

secretive, nonrevealing, deceptive
paranoid, suspicious, distrustful, repressed

Sagittarius

Mutable Fire, Yang, Transpersonal
Adapting to Identity   Learning
Relates to Jupiter and Chiron
Corresponds to 9th house

Sign Keyphrase:
My need to explore and expand the horizons of my mind and world

Qualities of Sagittarius

Skillful Application

wise, understanding, sage-like
philosophical, aspiring, metaphysical
ethical, idealistic, religious, visionary
moral, truth-seeking, open minded

optimistic, hopeful, jovial, expansive
buoyant, generous, benevolent, philanthropic
merciful, tolerant

exploring, adventurous, wandering
seeking, freedom loving, frank
outspoken, truthful, speculative
loves animals, athletic

Unskillful Application

condescending, pompous
head too high in the clouds
ungrounded, self-righteous, zealous
opinionated, dogmatic

deluded, has blind faith, impractical
a false prophet, looks to Lady Luck
extravagant, indolent, wanderlust

scattered, exaggerating, excessive
seeking a free lunch, irresponsible
tactless, insensitive, wasteful, restless
gambling

Capricorn

Cardinal Earth, Yin, Transpersonal
Initiating Material Action
Relates to Saturn
Corresponds to 10th house

Sign Keyphrase:
My need for structure, organization, and social accomplishment

Qualities of Capricorn

Skillful Application

organized, practical, responsible
disciplined, dutiful, conscientious
structured, systematic, hardworking, mature
law-abiding, dependable, industrious

pragmatic, realistic, constructive
administrating, planning, patient
orderly, deliberate, methodical, efficient
cautious, prudent, frugal, reserved

striving, accomplishing, attaining, ambitious
achieving, successful, recognized

Unskillful Application

controlling, conservative
obsessed with order, compulsive
guarded, overcautious, rigid, fearful
miserly, materialistic, distrustful

restricted, inhibited, pessimistic
constricted, unemotional, undemonstrative
lacking spontaneity, cold, guilty, repressed
unimaginative, self-doubting, melancholy

opportunistic, calculating, over-ambitious
Machiavellian, manipulating, self-seeking

Aquarius

Fixed Air, Yang, Transpersonal
Stabilizing Social and Intellectual Security
Relates to Uranus
Corresponds to 11th house

Sign Keyphrase:
My need to be innovative, original, and to create social change

Qualities of Aquarius

Skillful Application

reforming, progressive, liberal
humanitarian, democratic, universal
philanthropic, altruistic, tolerant, friendly
social, gregarious, people-oriented

independent, freedom-loving, original, bohemian
eccentric, experimental, unorthodox, unusual
unconventional, innovative, revolutionary
futuristic, progressive, New Age

mental, intuitive, inventive
quick, brilliant, electric, scientific

Unskillful Application

disorganized, anarchistic, undisciplined
rebelling without a cause, fanatical
tearing down but providing no alternative
opinionated, unreasonable

deviant, overly eccentric, a crank
antisocial, impractical, strange
avoiding the here and now
negligent, thoughtless

erratic, unpredictable, inconsistent
impersonal, detached, aloof, unthinking

Pisces

Mutable Water, Yin, Transpersonal
Adapting to Emotional and Soul Learning
Relates to Neptune
Corresponds to 12th house

Sign Keyphrase:
My need to commit myself to a dream or ideal and work toward its realization

Qualities of Pisces

Skillful Application

unifying, dissolving, boundless, subtle
infinite, flowing, amorphous, refined

imaginative, dreamy, poetic, emotional
inspiring, idealistic, utopian
visionary, romantic, mystical, intuitive
spiritual, otherworldly, ethereal
universal, transcendental, atonement

impressionable, mediumistic, receptive
absorbant, sensitive, psychic, empathic

compassionate, empathetic, healing, gentle
sympathetic, sacrificing, surrendering, humble
unselfish, retiring, renouncing

Unskillful Application

nebulous, confused, chaotic
unconscious, vague, drifting, intangible

unreal, illusory, impractical, unrealistic
insubstantial, ungrounded, dual
fictitious, delusional, cloudy, indolent
chimerical, deceptive, secretive
reclusive, self-destructive, vulnerable

gullible, indiscriminate, passive, indecisive
procrastinating, escapist, vacillating

hypersensitive, misunderstood, martyred
melancholy, moody, suffering, victimized
lacks faith in self

The houses, as we have explained, represent twelve departments of life or fields of experience that all human beings share in common. In the birth chart, they tell us **where** the planetary action is taking place.

The houses are listed below with their essential meanings and keywords.

First House

Cardinal Fire, Yang, Personal
Relates to Mars
Corresponds to the sign Aries

Self Awareness: how others see you, personality, mannerisms, outer behavior, persona, mask, image, body, physical appearance, head and face, stature, attractiveness, complexion, general constitution, individuality, self-projection, life's beginnings, early childhood, home environment and impressions, health, vitality, self-expression, image presented to others.

Second House

Fixed Earth, Yin, Personal
Relates to Venus
Corresponds to the sign Taurus

Relationship to Substance: finances, possessions, personal resources, attachments, survival needs, material security, self-acquired wealth, savings and accumulations, financial vision, earning and spending habits, enjoyment of the material world, attitudes towards possessions, wealth.

Third House

Mutable Air, Yang, Personal
Relates to Mercury
Corresponds to the sign Gemini

Communication with the Environment: mental activity, routine interactions, transmitting and receiving information, intellectual endeavors, teaching, writing, conversation, messages, telegrams, correspondence, personal thoughts, journal keeping, letter writing, the day-to-day environment, acquaintances, short journeys, relatives, neighbors, siblings, intimate brotherhoods or sisterhoods—consciousness groups, covens, sanghas.

Fourth House

Cardinal Water, Yin, Personal
Relates to the Moon and Ceres
Corresponds to the sign Cancer

Establishing Foundations: personal integration, home, foundation, a protected and secure environment, family, traditions, your roots, heritage, and background.

The source of emotional security and wholeness, the private self, introversion, the parent who played the mother role, land, property, real estate.

Private life, later life conditions, circumstances and environment, end of life, subconscious, psychological foundation, intimate ties.

Fifth House

Fixed Fire, Yang, Social
Relates to the Sun and Pallas
Corresponds to the sign Leo

Creative Self-Expression: All creative extensions of yourself—children, child-bearing, the arts, dance, drama, theater, music, personal love, romance, affairs, play, recreation, pleasure, entertainment and relaxation, games, sports, hobbies, speculation, investments, gambling.

Sixth House

Mutable Earth, Yin, Social
Relates to Mercury and Vesta
Corresponds to the sign Virgo

Self Improvement: personal reorientation, growth through crisis or sickness, analytical introspection, readjustment, purification, general state of health, care of the body, hygiene, nutrition, physical therapy.

Daily work environment, employment, work and labor, employees, self-discipline, skills and craftsmanship, service as a means of healing self and others, love and kindness to animals.

Seventh House

Cardinal Air, Yang, Social
Relates to Venus and Juno
Corresponds to the sign Libra

Completion through Others: what you seek in others, one-to-one or small group relationships, marriage, personal attributes of the marriage partner, dealings with others, business partnerships, legal contracts, alliances, conflict with others, litigation, cooperation or competition, projection.

Eighth House

Fixed Water, Yin, Social
Relates to Mars and Pluto
Corresponds to the sign Scorpio

Transformation: the emotional consequence of a relationship, intense unions, sexual activities, death and rebirth, joint resources, investments, dowries, legacies, inheritance, wills and life insurance.

Delving into the unknown, psychic research, surgery, the world of the occult, sorcerers, nature's secrets, deeply felt peak experiences, after-death experiences, the door to the world beyond, any occupation connected with death.

Personal unconscious, psychology, attitudes towards growth and change, letting go, releasing attachments, dealing with your partner's attachments, counseling, depth interactions with others.

Ninth House

Mutable Fire, Yang, Universal
Related to Jupiter
Corresponds to the sign Sagittarius

Expansion of Awareness: the search for meaning, the "higher" or superconscious mind, collective thinking, abstractions, philosophy, metaphysics, religion, ecclesiastics, clergymen, religious rituals, philanthropic, philosophic and spiritual tendencies, your belief system, ethics and morals.

Travel to distant lands, interests in foreign countries and people, long journeys, voyages, exploration, distant discoveries, far-reaching communications, higher education, law, publishing, prophetic dreams, consciousness-expanding travels, "trips," teachers, gurus, places far removed from the place of birth.

Tenth House

Cardinal Earth, Yin, Universal
Relates to Saturn
Corresponds to the sign Capricorn

Social Integration: your standing in the community, public life, vocation, profession, career, business, status, societal recognition, achievements, accomplishments, reputation, honors gained, function in society.

The parent who played the father role, authority and authority figures, persons in power, influence of the law where you live.

Eleventh House

Fixed Air, Yang, Universal
Relates to Uranus
Corresponds to the sign Aquarius

Social Reform: group involvement, collective endeavors, clubs and organizations to which you belong, common links to others beyond time and space, social causes, ideals, and progress, the common good, humanitarianism, universal world citizenship, global awareness.

Impersonal love, altruism, your friendships, your hopes, wishes, dreams, and aspirations.

Twelfth House

Mutable Water, Yin, Universal
Relates to Neptune
Corresponds to the sign Pisces

Transcendence: the end of the cycle where you must take care of unfinished business and resolve past karma, and come to terms with unresolved issues.

The accumulated results of all the previous house activities and experiences.

"Ghosts" from the past, restraints, restrictions, places of confinement, prison, hospitals, asylum, psychological blocks, aloneness, isolation,

OR

Freeing yourself from past restrictions, transcending karma through grace, attaining inner peace, rendering compassionate service to humanity.

Retreats from the world, monasteries, seclusion, secret affairs, secret societies and mystical associations, institutions in general.

Inner realities, universal visions, introspection, self-examination, fantasies and dreams, sleep patterns, spiritual bliss,

OR

Psychological escapism, self-undoing, troubles, worries, sorrow, pain, bereavement, loss and suffering.

That aspect of yourself most hidden from conscious awareness and from others, the shadow.

Appendix C: Keywords for the Planets

In this last appendix, we have listed below the major concepts and keywords for the planets. Reading them over will give you a deeper understanding of the planetary functions as they operate in yourself and your birth chart.

The Sun

Relates to Leo and the 5th house

Keyphrase: My basic identity and conscious purpose.

Keywords for the Sun

1. Our **center,** source, essence, power, life-force, will, vitality, purpose, life's direction, what we really are.
2. Our ability to focus our talents to realize a **central purpose.**
3. The **creative potential** that resides within each individual.

The Moon

Relates to Cancer and the 4th house

Keyphrase: My emotions, feelings and daily habits.

Keywords for the Moon

1. The **female principle**—the woman within each of us.
2. Our **emotional responses,** moods, changes, fluctuations.
3. Our ability to give and receive **nurturance;** the nurturing parent, the home, how we seek security.
4. Our **habits,** conditioning and unconscious behavior, what we do instinctually.

Mercury

Relates to Gemini and the 3rd house

Keyphrase: My capacity to think, speak, learn and reason.

Keywords for Mercury

1. **Thought:** the intellect, rational mind, logic, reason, intelligence, versatility.
2. **Communication:** speech, language, symbols, words, writing, learning, teaching.
3. **Association:** travel, commerce, interaction with environment.

Venus

Relates to Taurus, Libra, 2nd and 7th houses

Keyphrase: My capacity to attract people and things that I love and value.

Keywords for Venus

1. **Attraction:** what we desire to join with, partnerships, relationships, our social urge, cohesion, co-operation.
2. **Beauty:** aesthetics, charm, good taste, refinement, the arts, elegance.
3. **Harmony:** balance, symmetry, melody, rhythm, grace.

Mars

Relates to Aries and the 1st house

Keyphrase: My capacity to initiate, act and assert myself based on personal desire.

Keywords for Mars

1. **Self-Projection:** activity, assertion, directness, aggression, pioneering energy, forging ahead, force, power, accomplishment, competition, conquest, impulse, impatience.
2. **Desire:** passion, sexuality, gratification, drive, energy, courage, unchecked emotion, anger, fury, violence, war.

Jupiter

Relates to Sagittarius and the 9th house

Keyphrase: My search for meaning, truth, and ethical values.

Keywords for Jupiter

1. **Expansion:** increase, growth, abundance, enlargement, prosperity, wealth, fortune, benevolence, generosity, joviality, overabundance, overexpansion, exaggeration, too-muchness.
2. **Understanding:** urge to find meaning, wisdom, philosophy, aspiration, religion, morals, ethics, con-

science, idealism, principles, beliefs.
3. **Optimism:** faith, hope, trust, positiveness, good will, improvement.

Saturn

Relates to Capricorn and the 10th house

Keyphrase: My capacity to create order, form and discipline in my life.

Keywords for Saturn

1. **Limitation:** form, structure, order, definition, boundary, mold, shape, focus, organization, crystallization, concentration, control, blockage, restriction, lack, insecurity, fear.
2. **Universal Law:** time, gravity, cycles, karma, maturation, old age.
3. **Tester of Life:** life's learning experiences, responsibility, patience, discipline, resoluteness, seriousness, purposefulness, caution, prudence, obstacle, difficulty, inhibition, frustration.

Uranus

Relates to Aquarius and the 11th house

Keyphrase: My unique individuality and capacity to liberate myself from past limitations.

Keywords for Uranus

1. **The Awakener:** illuminator, liberator, rebel, radical, revolutionary, shatterer of old forms, change, freedom, reform, inventiveness, altruism, impersonal love, platonic relations, independence, disruption, anarchy, fanaticism.
2. **Inspiration:** lightning, electricity, suddenness, illumination, revelation, originality, genius, invention, discovery.
3. **Deviation:** uniqueness, unorthodoxy, unconventionality, originality, eccentricity, nonconformist, unpredictable, erratic, peculiar, unusual, the anomalous.

Neptune

Relates to Pisces and the 12th house

Keyphrase: My capacity to transcend the finite self through expressing unity with a greater whole.

Keywords for Neptune

1. **Dissolver of Form:** cosmic solvent, unity, oneness, wholeness, the need to merge, disorder, disintegration, chaos.

2. **Intangibility:** nebulousness, vagueness, fantasies, understanding beyond reason, divinity, dreams, clouds, visions, ghosts, spirits, imaginings, confusion, illusion, unreality, deception, delusion.
3. **Refinement:** impressionability, sensitivity, clairvoyance, psychic abilities, the mediumship, chaotic mentality.
4. **Idealism:** the dreamer, utopian, visionary, healer, artist, savior or martyr, empathy, compassion, sacrifice, surrender, devotion, celestial music.

Pluto

Relates to Scorpio and the 8th house

Keyphrase: My capacity to transform and renew myself.

Keywords for Pluto

1. **Regeneration:** death, annihilation, destruction, black magic, breaking down, upheaval, terrorism, catabolism, elimination, release, purging, catharsis, cleansing, rebirth, creation, renewal, resurrection, rising from the depths, building up, anabolism, eruption, sex.
2. **Transformation:** metamorphosis, transmutation, alchemy, permanent alteration, irreversible change, mutation, reorganization, revitalization.
3. **Penetrating the Secrets of Life:** the unseen, the invisible planes, extrasensory perception, the underworld, subterranean, hidden power, atomic energy, laser beams, x-rays, genetic engineering.

Chiron

Related to Scorpio and Sagittarius

Keyphrase: My capacity for holistic understanding.

Chiron Themes

1. **Bridge or link between the known and the unknown:** links the tradition and stability of Saturn with the change and revolution of Uranus.
2. **Maverick:** an independent who does not conform to his/her group or align with any particular faction or belief.
3. **Healing and Wholemaking:** holistic health, education, and view; integrating instinct with intellect and body with mind.
4. **Personal Questing:** teacher/healer; wounded healer; the inner teacher of intuition (Uranus) and the outer teacher of tradition (Saturn).
5. **A Key:** opening new doorways, turning points in life direction.

Chiron Keywords

teaching, guiding, mentoring, healing, instructing, wise, learning, educating, sagacious, noble, free-spirited, a maverick, unorthodox, catalyzing, synthesizing, integrating, linking mind, body and spirit, bringing a new direction, awakening, dying and becoming, initiating, wounding, fragmented, ignorant.

Ceres

Relates to Cancer, Virgo, and Taurus-Scorpio

Keyphrase: My capacity to unconditionally love and nurture myself and others.

Ceres Themes

1. **Cancer:** giving and receiving nurturing; all kinds of family relationships—parents and children; providing and caring for others; self-acceptance and self-worth.
2. **Taurus-Scorpio:** attachment and letting go, loss and return, capacity for grief and sorrow, rejection, abandonment, separation, principle of sharing, death and renewal cycles.
3. **Virgo:** productivity, growth, self-reliance, work.

Ceres Rulerships

1. **Procreation:** proceative sexuality, childbirth, miscarriage, abortion, menarche and menopause, death and dying, children, all kinds of parenting relationships.
2. **Nourishment:** nurturing and helping vocations; nursing, social-service, food and hunger, nutrition, food-related services, food-related illnesses, agriculture and growing; cultivation of land and plants, harvest.
3. **Productivity:** labor, work, ecology, domestication, animals, adaptation and survival.

Ceres Keywords

nurturing, mothering, growing, caring for, sustaining, fertile, productive, nourishing, powerful, concerned, civilizing, domesticating, providing, feeding, nature, insecure, controlling, overprotecting, smothering, self-rejecting, rejecting self, rejecting others self-hating, critical, judgmental, fearful, self-hate, dependent, destructive, clinging, ferocious, tenacious, grasping, hungry, barren, deprived, neglected, abandoned.

Pallas

Relates to Leo, Libra, Aquarius

Keyphrase: My capacity for creative wisdom and original perceptions.

Pallas Themes

1. **Wisdom and Creativity:** learning, creativity, intelligence, creative visualization.
2. **Accomplishment and Success:** status, honor, competition, fears of success.
3. **Sexual Identity:** sexual imbalances, androgyny, father complexes, sublimated sexuality, sexual alienation in a relationship.

Pallas Rulerships

1. **Intelligence:** range of intelligence; learning and perceptual difficulties, whole pattern perception; gestalt integration, healing.
2. **Arts:** arts and crafts, handcraft skills, weaving, woolworking, embroidery, etc.
3. **Justice:** social concern, political involvements, government, public service, liaison between government and people, legal matters, diplomacy, mediation, militancy, martial arts, women's liberation, feminism.
4. **Vocation:** career training; responding to sexism in professional world.

Pallas Keywords

wise, perceptive, inventive, original, intuitive, creative, ingenious, intellectual, artistic, skillful, strategic, practical, rational, ambitious, technical, pragmatic, integrating, accomplished, professional, literary, organizing, resourceful, defending, protecting, fair, just, balanced, soldiering, ruthless, competitive, calculating, fearful, manipulative, cold, austere, sterile, unemotional, dry, retarded, dull, stupid.

Vesta

Relates to Virgo and Scorpio

Keyphrase: My capacity to integrate and focus my energies.

Vesta Themes

1. **Virgo:** personal integration, self-identification, renewal of virginity and separation, meaningful work, dedication to a cause, devotion to a spiritual path, personal commitment, sacrifice to reach goals, elimination of unessential.
2. **Scorpio:** sexual liberation or sexual inhibition.

Vesta Rulerships

1. **Personal Integration:** disciplined personal routines—health, exercise, meditation; focus on a goal, commitment to a path.
2. **Sexual:** sexual fears, guilt and inadequacies; denial and separation from personal relationships, sublimation of sexual energies to devotional-spiritual, scholastic, or service paths.
3. **Sanctuary:** safety, hospitality, tradition, secret orders and societies, ritual.

Vesta Keywords

pure, devoted, dedicated, committed, moral, dutiful, responsible, traditional, conservative, hard working, perfect, sacrifice, discipleship, service, simplicity, integrity, focused, centered, whole-in-oneself, intact, self-identified, self-contained, private, solitary, free spirited, individualistic, sexual, sexually liberated, sexually inhibited, chaste, unmarried mother, ascetic, celibate, frigid, impotent, barren, promiscuous, prostitute, workaholic, confined, limited, narrow-minded, bigoted, fanatic, zealous, martyr, unfocused, uncommitted.

Juno

Relates to Libra and Scorpio

Keyphrase: My capacity for meaningful relationships.

Juno Themes

1. **Relationships:** equal partnerships vs. power struggles; compatibility and trust, cooperation between equals; jealousy and possessiveness; sexual fidelity; psychological projection; emotional attachments; committed and spiritual relationships; cycles of leaving and returning.
2. **The Eternal Feminine:** women's predicament in marriage; feminine power.
3. **The Powerless:** minorities, the elderly, battered wives, abused children.

Juno Rulerships

1. **One-to-one Relationships:** business, mate, marriage, friend, employer-employee, teacher-student, etc.; marriage and compatibility counseling; receptivity to others.
2. **Ceremony and Rituals:** marriage, engagement, divorce; legitimate and illegitimate children, heirs; social protocol, social position.
3. **Women:** women's sexual cycles, women's arts, women's equal rights, beauty and adornment.
4. **Atmosphere:** weather, money (Juno was Goddess of the Mint).

Juno Keywords

wife, husband, partner, committed, supportive, equal, cooperative, compromising, sharing, trusting, refined, intimate, merging, joining, faithful, loyal, sexual, fertile, flirtatious, attracting, magnetic, jealous, possessive, revengeful, competitive, vindictive, unfaithful, barren, angry, quarrelsome, inferior, unequal, victimized, sado-masochism, seduction, rape, violation, abused.

The computer revolution has revolutionized astrology as well. Until recently, all chart calculations had to be done by hand. Now, anyone with a personal computer can obtain astrological software that will compute and print out complete birth charts. If you don't own a personal computer, you can use a chart casting service in your area.

If you wish to obtain a birth chart that matches the chart illustrations that appear in this book, then we suggest that you write the people who provided those charts—Astro Communications Services, Inc.

Essentially, you can obtain the following types of birth charts:

1. A **complete** *natal birth chart* and aspectarian (**including** Chiron and the four **asteroids**).
2. A **relationship comparison** in which the planetary aspects between two birth charts are calculated and printed out. Figure 2 on page 122 shows what the comparison will look like.
3. A report listing the **transiting** planets and their aspects to the natal chart.
4. The positions of the eleven **new asteroids** listed in Chapter Three.

If you wish to obtain these charts, either for yourself or for a friend, you can use the information below.

Astro Communications Services Order Form

Astrology for Yourself Computer Report

Natal Chart as you see illustrated in this book on page 26......................$7.95
Chart Comparison: Aspects between the planets of two charts **(CP2)** $3.95
Please provide the birth data (date, time, and place) for both people.
You must order the natal charts for both.
Personal Transit Calendar: Planets in the sky aspecting your natal planets
12 months without Moon **(CT-12)**......................$17.95
12 months with Moon **(CAT-12)**......................$24.95
Shipping & handling charge (per order) $3.00

Please provide birth place, birth date, and birth time for each individual. Specify **Astrology for Yourself** style charts so we can fill your orders to the specification of the authors.
You can use **AFY** as a simple code. We will know what you mean!
Call or write today!

Astro Communications Services, Inc., P.O. Box 1646, El Cajon, CA 92022-1646
www.astrocom.com
E-mail: astrosales@astrocom.com. Fax your order request to: (619) 631-0180

Finally, for those of you who wish to learn more about the asteroids and would like a *complete* asteroid Ephemeris (Ceres, Pallas, Vesta, Juno, Chiron and eleven new asteroids), we recommend our publication *Asteroid Goddesses.* You can write to us to obtain an autographed copy.

Moreover, if you are an astrologer who wishes to use *Astrology for Yourself,* either as a **textbook** for a class, or to give your clients as a tool to help them understand their charts, you can order copies from us at a 10% discount, provided your purchase five or more.

If you wish to order either of these books, photocopy the order form below and send it to us.

Ordering books by Douglas Bloch and Demetra George

Name _____

Address _____

City/State/Zip _____

Astrology for Yourself $19.95 x _____ copies = _____

Asteroid Goddesses $22.95 x _____ copies = _____
    Includes an ephemeris for 16 asteroids, including Ceres, Pallas, Vesta, and Juno.

Mysteries of the Dark Moon (George) Available from your local bookseller or on-line retailer.

I Am with You Always (Bloch) $12.95 x _____ copies = _____

Listening to Your Inner Voice (Bloch) $12.95 x _____ copies = _____

Positive Self Talk for Children (Bloch) $16.95 x _____ copies = _____

Healing from Depression (Bloch) $14.95 x _____ copies = _____

Words that Heal (Bloch) $12.95 x _____ copies = _____

Words that Heal the Blues (Bloch) $12.95 x _____ copies = _____

Subtotal   _____

Subtract 10% if you order five or more copies   _____

Postage and Handling ($5.00 for the first copy; $3.00 for each additional)   _____

Total cost $ _____

Please mail your order and payment to

Douglas Bloch   Demetra George
4226 NE 23rd Ave   **or**   PO Box 5431
Portland, OR 97211   Eugene OR 97405
(503) 284-2848   (541) 345-5680

Please allow 7-10 days for delivery

Appendix E: Sample Chart Interpretation
The Horoscope of Martin Luther King, Jr.

The purpose of this appendix is to give you, the reader, an overview of how to synthesize the many factors in a birth chart. Throughout the book we have discussed the various components of chart interpretation—the elements, the modalities, planets, signs, houses, aspects, moon phases, the nodes of the moon, etc. Now we bring them all together in the context of a single birth chart. The chart for this demonstration is that of the great civil rights leader and advocate of nonviolent resistance—Martin Luther King, Jr.

Guidelines for Chart Interpretation

The guiding principle of horoscope interpretation is, very simply, *pay attention to what stands out.* In the majority of cases the most obvious is the most essential. As an astrologer you must train your eye to discern the horoscope's salient themes and configurations. Ask "What gives this chart its mark of distinction?", and you will discover the unique attributes of the individual whose psyche is symbolically portrayed. The following outline provides you with a step-by-step procedure you can use to locate these highlights

1) Begin by determining **hemisphere emphasis.** Observe which hemispheres, if any, contain a significant weighting of planets (ten or more). For this and subsequent steps, the term "planets" will refer to the following bodies: the Sun, Moon, Mercury, Venus, Mars, Jupiter, Saturn, Uranus, Neptune and Pluto; Chiron, and the asteroids Ceres, Pallas, Vesta and Juno.

　Refer to the table below for a brief review of the four hemispheric patterns.

2) Second, examine the planets' sign placements to determine which of the **elements, modalities** or **orientations** is most emphasized. The key below the horoscope provides a summary of the planetary distributions.

　Note that King's water emphasis parallels the yielding dimension of his philosophy of nonviolent resistance. The transpersonal leaning depicts a strong spiritual and philosophical orientation that formed the foundation of his life and enabled him to pursue his ideals in the face of severe opposition.

3) Observe the element, modality and orientation of the **Sun, Moon** and **Ascendant.** What do they reveal about the individual's purpose (the Sun), his emotional responses (the Moon) and his outer expression (the Ascendant)?

　The Sun and Ascendant in cardinal signs show King's inclination to take action and initiate change.

　The Sun and Moon in transpersonal signs repeat the transpersonal emphasis indicated above.

　The elements of the Sun, Moon and Rising signs—earth, water and fire—blend the attributes of pragmatism, compassion and courage.

In particular, it is worth describing the uncanny astrological symbolism of King's Capricorn Sun, Pisces Moon and Aries Ascendant in greater detail.

Sun in Capricorn: King was born to a middle class family in Atlanta, and his early life was balanced, order-

Hemisphere Emphasis: Individual's Mode of Expression

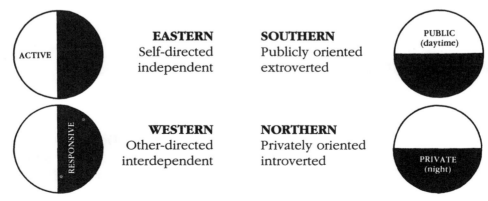

EASTERN
Self-directed
independent

SOUTHERN
Publicly oriented
extroverted

WESTERN
Other-directed
interdependent

NORTHERN
Privately oriented
introverted

Note that King's chart displays an Eastern hemisphere emphasis, symbolizing his role as pioneer and initiator.

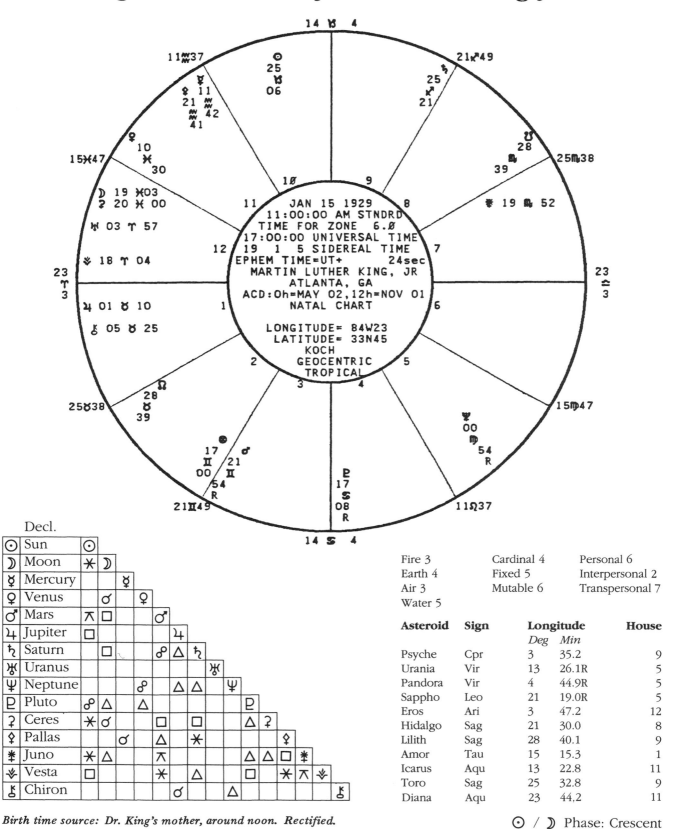

JAN 15 1929
11:00:00 AM STNDRD
TIME FOR ZONE 6.0
17:00:00 UNIVERSAL TIME
19 1 5 SIDEREAL TIME
EPHEM TIME=UT+ 24sec
MARTIN LUTHER KING, JR
ATLANTA, GA
ACD:0h=MAY 02,12h=NOV 01
NATAL CHART

LONGITUDE= 84W23
LATITUDE= 33N45
KOCH
GEOCENTRIC
TROPICAL

Decl.													
☉ Sun	☉												
☽ Moon	✶	☽											
☿ Mercury			☿										
♀ Venus		♂	♀										
♂ Mars	⊼	□		♂									
♃ Jupiter	□				♃								
♄ Saturn		□		☍	△	♄							
♅ Uranus							♅						
♆ Neptune			☍		△	△		♆					
♇ Pluto	☍	△	△						♇				
⚳ Ceres	✶	♂		□	□		△	⚳					
⚴ Pallas		♂		△	✶			♀					
⚵ Juno	✶	△		⊼			△	△	□	⚵			
⚶ Vesta	□		✶	△			□		✶	⊼	⚶		
⚷ Chiron				♂		△						⚷	

Birth time source: Dr. King's mother, around noon. Rectified.

Fire 3   Cardinal 4   Personal 6
Earth 4   Fixed 5   Interpersonal 2
Air 3   Mutable 6   Transpersonal 7
Water 5

Asteroid	Sign	Longitude		House
		Deg	*Min*	
Psyche	Cpr	3	35.2	9
Urania	Vir	13	26.1R	5
Pandora	Vir	4	44.9R	5
Sappho	Leo	21	19.0R	5
Eros	Ari	3	47.2	12
Hidalgo	Sag	21	30.0	8
Lilith	Sag	28	40.1	9
Amor	Tau	15	15.3	1
Icarus	Aqu	13	22.8	11
Toro	Sag	25	32.8	9
Diana	Aqu	23	44.2	11

☉ / ☽ Phase: Crescent

ly and conventional. His college classmates described him as dutiful, conscientious and mature beyond his years—classical traits of a Capricorn. In Capricornian style, King excelled at organizing and planning, qualities that he successfully applied in leading the American civil rights movement.

Moon in Pisces: If this were a book on Sun sign astrology, our portrayal of Dr. King would now be complete. But portraying King solely as a down-to-earth Capricorn would be doing him a grave disservice. For true to the Pisces Moon, King was also a dreamer and visionary. Who else but a Pisces could have given a speech called "I Have A Dream"? Throughout his life, King was able to meld the pragmatism of his Capricorn Sun with the idealism of the Pisces Moon. Perhaps this is why he referred to himself as the "practical dreamer" and the "idealist-realist."

Aries Rising: In contrast to the conservative Capricorn Sun, King's Aries rising gave him the courage and initiative to pioneer the civil rights movement. The Aries influence can be seen in his book *Why We Can't Wait* and his call for "Freedom now!" Driven by the forces of action (Aries) and restraint (Capricorn), he walked a fine line between evolution and revolution. Moreover, with Mars, ruler of the Aries Ascendant, placed in Gemini in the third house (language and communication), King delivered many fiery and moving orations. More than anything, King's spiritual power manifested through his gift of words, as exemplified by the "I Have a Dream" speech.

A wide conjunction between Pallas and Mercury in Aquarius also shows King's power and skill in the use of words and the communication media. Pallas-Mercury types are also adept in the arts of mediation, negotiation, affirmation and positive thinking.

4) Locate any planets that are **conjunct** any of the **four angles** (Ascendant, Descendant, M.C. and I.C.).

A planet on the Ascendant will be expressed through the individual's personality.

A planet on the Descendent will be expressed through the individual's relationships.

A planet on the M.C. will be expressed through the individual's public self—his career.

A planet on the I.C. will be expressed through the individual's private self—his family, roots, emotional foundation.

In King's chart, a number of these conjunctions are evident.

The prominence of the Sun close to the M.C. portrays the public standing which he attained as well as his natural leadership capacities.

Next, three bodies hover around the Ascendant—**Vesta**, keeper of the flame; the benevolent **Jupiter**,

ruler of religion and philosophy; and **Chiron**, the wounded healer, who although immortal, sacrificed his immortality to save the life of Prometheus. With this triple conjunction of planets ruling spirituality, is it any wonder that King obtained a degree in theology and found his calling in the ministry?

5) Fifth, note the **moon phase** and the placement of the **nodes of the moon**.

King was born under a **Crescent Moon Phase**, symbolizing the struggle away from the ghosts of the past and the need to establish a whole new social and economic identity for oneself (or in this case one's race) different from that given by parents. This person struggles against the forces of inertia, habit, patterns of failure and despair, and needs to mobilize his or her resources to overcome the limitations of the past and to forge ahead into the future. You can see how well this interpretation fits the life of this great leader.

In King's chart, the North Node in Taurus signifies the need to build a new set of values and develop self-sufficiency, which he did through the Civil Rights movement.

The South Node in Scorpio shows the potential to seek gratification of desires through relationships which can become self-destructive. This weakness manifested through his sexual affairs, which threatened his reputation and through which the FBI tried to discredit him.

6) Next, look to see if **three or more** planets are located in any one house or sign. If this is the case, then the meaning of that sign or house will play an important part in the life of the individual.

In King's chart, the eleventh and twelfth houses are given strong emphasis.

Venus, Mercury and Pallas in the **eleventh house** depict King as a social visionary who brought much-needed change to societal mores. The placement of Pallas, who fights for the underdog, in the revolutionary sign of Aquarius, contributed to this urge.

Pallas Athena in Aquarius is the political revolutionary, advocating and defending humanitarian causes and organizing grassroots protests. The wisdom of Pallas in Aquarius is the wisdom of the future—creating forms that will benefit generations to come.

Pallas Athena in the eleventh house can conceive and birth new social visions. It has a strong political nature that ardently works for social change. Its creative wisdom is expressed through becoming an advocate, spokesperson and orator.

Moon, Ceres, Uranus and Vesta in the **twelfth house** show that it was King's karmic destiny to engage in selfless service for the betterment of his people and humanity. The twelfth house also rules "secret enemies." Hence unbeknownst to King, the FBI covertly worked to discredit him.

Vesta in twelfth implies a dedication to selfless service and the pursuit of spiritual values. Vesta is a temple priest or priestess, here indicating many previous lifetimes following the devotional or spiritual path—in Aries as the "enlightened warrior". In this lifetime, King took these spiritual values, created a philosophical and political perspective, and externalized them in the real world (Jupiter in Taurus).

The twelfth house also corresponds to what the Buddhists call the bodhisattva—an enlightened being who is freed from cyclic rebirth but who chooses to continue being reborn in order to alleviate the suffering of others and guide them towards liberation.

Finally, Venus, Moon and Ceres in Pisces, the twelfth sign, gave King the sensitivity to human suffering that motivated him to spiritually nurture (Ceres keyword) his race and all humankind.

7) Next, observe any significant **aspects** in the chart. Begin by looking for close planetary aspects to the Sun or Moon. Conjunctions and oppositions are the most important. The closer the aspect, the more powerful the effect.

One of the most prominent aspects shows Mars, ruler of the Aries Ascendant, opposing Saturn. Mars stands for movement, Saturn for the status quo. Thus, a dynamic tension (the opposition) existed between King's drive to push ahead (Mars) and the natural resistance of the established order (Saturn). This struggle is stated again by contrasting King's Sun in the Saturn-ruled Capricorn with the martial sign of Aries rising.

Second, it is interesting to note the opposition of King's Sun (his purpose and mission) with Pluto (transformation, death and rebirth). A strong Pluto shows the desire to work for the good of society on a large level. It also indicates that the fruits of one's work may not be totally realized until after death. The night before he died, King prophetically stated, "I may not get there with you, but I want you to know that we as a people will get to the promised land."

Finally, a series of trines between Venus in Pisces, Pluto in Cancer and Juno in Scorpio showed the ease (keyword for the trine) with which King was able to enlist the help of others (Venus and Juno) for the purpose of transforming the foundation of society (Pluto in the fourth house).

8) The next step in your chart synthesis involves interpreting **each planet and asteroid** by its sign and house position as you did with your own chart on pages 54-86 of this book.

Remember, the planet tells us *what* is being expressed. Its sign position describes *how* that energy is being expressed. Its house position depicts *where* that energy is being expressed.

You will note that we have also included in the chart the twelve **"minor" asteroids** which were described on pages 88-100. It is not necessary that you include them in the major part of your interpretation. Nevertheless, if one happens to be prominently placed in the chart (by house position or aspect), it will also play a major role in the life.

For example: King has the asteroids **Toro** and **Hidalgo** conjunct Saturn and opposing Mars.

Toro, symbol of the Bull, is the principle of power and strength and how we confront or react to the onslaught of negative energies. Unconsciously used, Toro depicts brute force, retaliation and oppression. But on a more conscious level, it signifies the principle of *nonviolent resistance* and the capacity to transmute negatively to positively charged energy, by turning one's enemies into one's allies. This was King's exact philosophy—to win over his enemies by the transforming power of love.

Miguel Hidalgo was a Spanish priest born in Mexico who was assigned a parish of poor Indians. He became sympathetic to their plight of famine, poverty and illiteracy, and led an army of tens of thousands of Indians in revolt. Known as the Father of Mexican Independence, Hidalgo in the birth chart symbolizes the principle of political activism, standing up for what is right, fighting for individual beliefs, and being advocate for the poor and powerless. This is an uncanny description of Dr. King's life.

In addition, King has the asteroid Icarus conjunct Mercury. Icarus was the winged youth who flew into the Sun because he forgot—or ignored—his father's warning to follow the middle path. Icarus is the principle of liberation through risk-taking. Icarus' challenge is for self-discipline and control over one's free flight in order to successfully traverse the quick and narrow path.

King's message (Mercury) was one of liberation and risk-taking, and at the same time the need for moderation and non-extremism. He was no doubt viewed as extreme by the supporters of the status quo. In the eyes of many, however, he was doing what was necessary to transform an unjust system.

9) Finally, take note of any significant **transits** to the chart. On October 14, 1964, the day of the announcement that Dr. King had won the Nobel Peace Prize, the Moon in 23° of Capricorn passed directly over King's Sun in the tenth house (public recognition). Moreover, transiting Jupiter, which often brings good fortune, was also trining King's tenth house Sun.

Two months later, on December 10, 1964, King made his famous acceptance speech in Oslo. On that day, transiting Sun in 18° Capricorn conjuncted the natal M.C., while transiting Mars, Uranus and Pluto in 14-16° of Virgo and Jupiter in 18° of Taurus all trined the Midheaven! The spiritual lesson of earth signs is service, and five planets formed this amazing grand trine in earth signs. It surely was a day marking the culmination of King's life of public service.

Meanwhile, Venus and Neptune in 18° Scorpio sextiled the M.C. and made a conjunction to Juno. The transiting Moon in 22° Aquarius made a conjunction to Pallas, a trine to Mars and a sextile to Saturn. Transiting Saturn in 29° Aquarius sextiled its natal place.

Every planet in the sky made a positive aspect to the birth chart: a day of destiny for a great man.

A final note:
King and the Mountaintop ——

Throughout his life, the metaphor of the mountain played a prominent role in Dr. King's speeches. The night before his assassination, King told his supporters, "I'm not worried about anything now, because I have been to the mountaintop, and I've seen the promised land." In many spiritual traditions, the mountain signifies a place of spiritual consciousness, a meeting place between man and God. King, a highly spiritual person, was no doubt aware of this metaphysical correspondence.

The symbolism of the mountain appears three times in Dr. King's horoscope.

First, he was born under the sign of Capricorn, the sign of the goat which is often portrayed as steadily climbing to the top of a mountain.

Second, the planet Jupiter played a dominant role in King's birth chart. In classical mythology, Zeus/Jupiter was the supreme king of the heavens who ruled the world from lofty Mount Olympus, home of the gods.

Also, Chiron had his home on a cave at the top of Mt. Pelion from which he guided the Greek youths in achieving their destiny. In King's chart, Chiron is conjunct Jupiter close to the Ascendant. Thus, the horoscope portrays quite clearly why the symbol of the mountain became the focus and culmination of King's life and work.

We hope that this sample chart synthesis and the guidelines for interpretation will help in your own quest to interpret and understand the universal language of astrology. We wish you the best in your exploration of this most ancient and sacred science.

Note to the reader: The asteroid interpretations given for Dr. King were taken from from the book *Asteroid Goddesses*, by Demetra George (with Douglas Bloch). See Appendix D for information on how to obtain the book.

MARS THROUGH PLUTO: 1931–2000

1931	♂	♃	♄	♅	♆	♇
Jan 1	15♌35	16♋14	13♑42	11♈29	5♍38	20♋00
15	11 49	14 22	15 22	11 42	5 25	19 43
Feb 1	5 14	12 19	17 19	12 10	5 02	19 21
15	0 26	11 08	18 50	12 42	4 40	19 06
Mar 1	27♋47	10 31	20 11	13 21	4 16	18 54
15	27 41	10 33	21 21	14 05	3 54	18 45
Apr 1	0♌26	11 25	22 25	15 02	3 29	18 41
15	4 28	12 45	23 00	15 50	3 14	18 43
May 1	10 30	14 50	23 16	16 43	3 03	18 51
15	16 40	17 05	23 10	17 27	3 00	19 03
Jun 1	24 59	20 12	22 39	18 12	3 04	19 22
15	2♍21	23 01	21 55	18 43	3 15	19 41
Jul 1	11 14	26 25	20 52	19 08	3 35	20 06
15	19 21	29 29	19 50	19 20	3 57	20 28
Aug 1	29 35	3♌16	18 37	19 22	4 29	20 54
15	8♎17	6 21	17 45	19 13	4 58	21 15
Sep 1	19 11	9 59	17 00	18 51	5 36	21 37
15	28 25	12 49	16 41	18 25	6 07	21 52
Oct 1	9♏15	15 47	16 43	17 49	6 40	22 03
15	18 58	18 04	17 05	17 15	7 06	22 09
Nov 1	1♐03	20 19	17 57	16 35	7 32	22 09
15	11 14	21 40	18 58	16 06	7 48	22 04
Dec 1	23 07	22 31	20 24	15 42	7 57	21 53
15	3♑42	22♌35	21♑50	15♈29	7♍59	21♋39

1932	♂	♃	♄	♅	♆	♇
Jan 1	16♑45	21♌50	23♑45	15♈27	7♍52	21♋19
15	27 38	20 35	25 24	15 37	7 39	21 01
Feb 1	10♒58	18 31	27 25	16 02	7 18	20 39
15	22 01	16 40	29 01	16 32	6 56	20 24
Mar 1	3♓52	14 51	0♒36	17 12	6 31	20 10
15	14 54	13 33	1 55	17 55	6 08	20 02
Apr 1	28 13	12 42	3 15	18 51	5 43	19 57
15	9♈05	12 40	4 03	19 39	5 27	19 59
May 1	21 20	13 22	4 36	20 33	5 16	20 07
15	1♉55	14 34	4 46	21 17	5 12	20 19
Jun 1	14 31	16 39	4 31	22 05	5 16	20 38
15	24 42	18 47	4 00	22 37	5 26	20 57
Jul 1	6♊06	21 36	3 06	23 04	5 45	21 21
15	15 52	24 18	2 08	23 18	6 06	21 43
Aug 1	27 26	27 48	0 53	23 23	6 38	22 10
15	6♋43	0♍48	29♑54	23 17	7 07	22 31
Sep 1	17 42	4 30	28 55	22 57	7 45	22 53
15	26 27	7 31	28 22	22 32	8 16	23 08
Oct 1	6♌06	10 53	28 07	21 57	8 49	23 20
15	14 11	13 40	28 14	21 24	9 16	23 26
Nov 1	23 28	16 46	28 49	20 43	9 42	23 27
15	0♍32	18 59	29 38	20 13	9 58	23 22
Dec 1	7 48	21 03	0♒53	19 46	10 09	23 10
15	13♍10	22♍21	2♒13	19♈32	10♍11	22♋57

1933	♂	♃	♄	♅	♆	♇
Jan 1	18♍00	23♍11	4♒02	19♈27	10♍05	22♋36
15	20 04	23 11	5 39	19 34	9 53	22 18
Feb 1	19 30	22 22	7 41	19 57	9 32	21 57
15	16 16	21 05	9 20	20 25	9 10	21 41
Mar 1	11 10	19 25	10 55	21 00	8 47	21 28
15	5 51	17 36	12 23	21 42	8 24	21 19
Apr 1	1 39	15 34	13 56	22 37	7 59	21 14
15	0 55	14 16	14 58	23 25	7 42	21 16
May 1	2 52	13 26	15 50	24 20	7 29	21 23
15	6 31	13 19	16 16	25 05	7 24	21 34
Jun 1	12 43	13 59	16 22	25 55	7 27	21 53
15	18 54	15 07	16 06	26 29	7 36	22 12
Jul 1	26 51	16 59	15 26	26 59	7 53	22 36
15	4♎26	19 02	14 36	27 16	8 14	22 58
Aug 1	14 17	21 56	13 24	27 25	8 45	23 26
15	22 51	24 36	12 22	27 21	9 14	23 47
Sep 1	3♏43	28 03	11 12	27 05	9 51	24 10
15	13 01	1♎01	10 26	26 42	10 22	24 25
Oct 1	24 01	4 29	9 52	26 09	10 56	24 38
15	3♐56	7 29	9 43	25 35	11 23	24 44
Nov 1	16 19	11 03	9 58	24 54	11 51	24 45
15	26 45	13 49	10 32	24 23	12 08	24 41
Dec 1	8♑55	16 43	11 33	23 54	12 20	24 30
15	19♑44	18♎56	12♒42	23♈36	12♍23	24♋16

1934	♂	♃	♄	♅	♆	♇
Jan 1	3♒01	21♎06	14♒23	23♈28	12♍18	23♋56
15	14 03	22 21	15 56	23 32	12 07	23 38
Feb 1	27 29	23 08	17 56	23 51	11 47	23 17
15	8♓33	23 06	19 37	24 16	11 26	23 00
Mar 1	19 33	22 27	21 17	24 50	11 03	22 47
15	0♈29	21 16	22 52	25 30	10 40	22 37
Apr 1	13 36	19 19	24 37	26 25	10 14	22 32
15	24 15	17 31	25 51	27 12	9 57	22 33
May 1	6♉13	15 37	26 59	28 07	9 43	22 40
15	16 31	14 19	27 41	28 53	9 36	22 51
Jun 1	28 48	13 25	28 08	29 45	9 38	23 09
15	8♊43	13 18	28 09	0♉21	9 46	23 28
Jul 1	19 50	13 53	27 47	0 54	10 02	23 52
15	29 24	14 59	27 10	1 14	10 22	24 14
Aug 1	10♋46	16 56	26 06	1 26	10 52	24 42
15	19 58	18 58	25 05	1 26	11 21	25 03
Sep 1	0♌55	21 53	23 49	1 13	11 58	25 26
15	9 45	24 33	22 53	0 52	12 29	25 42
Oct 1	19 38	27 50	22 03	0 21	13 03	25 56
15	28 06	0♏49	21 37	29♈48	13 31	26 03
Nov 1	8♍04	4 31	21 31	29 07	13 59	26 05
15	16 00	7 34	21 49	28 34	14 17	26 01
Dec 1	24 39	10 57	22 33	28 03	14 30	25 50
15	1♎47	13♏45	23♒30	27♈43	14♍35	25♋37

1935	♂	♃	♄	♅	♆	♇
Jan 1	9♎42	16♏51	25♒00	27♈31	14♍31	25♋17
15	15 23	19 04	26 26	27 32	14 22	24 59
Feb 1	20 51	21 13	28 22	27 47	14 02	24 37
15	23 43	22 28	0♓03	28 10	13 42	24 21
Mar 1	24 36	23 10	1 45	28 41	13 19	24 07
15	23 05	23 16	3 25	29 19	12 56	23 57
Apr 1	18 09	22 34	5 19	0♉13	12 29	23 51
15	12 50	21 23	6 44	1 00	12 11	23 51
May 1	7 56	19 34	8 07	1 55	11 56	23 57
15	6 06	17 48	9 05	2 42	11 49	24 08
Jun 1	7 15	15 47	9 53	3 35	11 49	24 26
15	10 32	14 29	10 11	4 13	11 55	24 44
Jul 1	16 12	13 36	10 09	4 49	12 11	25 08
15	22 27	13 26	9 47	5 12	12 30	25 31
Aug 1	1♏14	14 02	8 57	5 28	12 59	25 58
15	9 16	15 08	8 02	5 31	13 27	26 20
Sep 1	19 47	17 07	6 46	5 21	14 04	26 44
15	28 58	19 11	5 44	5 03	14 35	27 01
Oct 1	9♐57	21 58	4 41	4 33	15 10	27 15
15	19 55	24 41	4 00	4 02	15 38	27 22
Nov 1	2♑24	28 14	3 33	3 20	16 07	27 25
15	12 57	1♐18	3 33	2 47	16 26	27 21
Dec 1	25 12	4 52	3 58	2 13	16 41	27 12
15	6♒04	7♐58	4♓41	1♉51	16♍46	26♋59

1936	♂	♃	♄	♅	♆	♇
Jan 1	19♒22	11♐39	5♓56	1♉35	16♍44	26♋39
15	0♓20	14 31	7 14	1 33	16 35	26 21
Feb 1	13 37	17 41	9 03	1 45	16 17	25 59
15	24 28	19 57	10 41	2 05	15 57	25 42
Mar 1	6♈00	21 58	12 30	2 36	15 33	25 27
15	16 38	23 20	14 13	3 13	15 10	25 16
Apr 1	29 20	24 17	16 14	4 05	14 43	25 10
15	9♉38	24 24	17 47	4 52	14 24	25 10
May 1	21 12	23 48	19 23	5 47	14 09	25 16
15	1♊08	22 41	20 33	6 35	14 01	25 27
Jun 1	13 00	20 47	21 39	7 29	14 00	25 45
15	22 37	19 01	22 14	8 09	14 06	26 03
Jul 1	3♋25	17 05	22 31	8 47	14 20	26 27
15	12 44	15 44	22 26	9 12	14 39	26 50
Aug 1	23 54	14 46	21 53	9 31	15 08	27 18
15	2♌58	14 36	21 08	9 36	15 35	27 40
Sep 1	13 51	15 14	19 58	9 28	16 12	28 04
15	22 43	16 22	18 54	9 13	16 43	28 21
Oct 1	2♍44	18 16	17 43	8 45	17 18	28 35
15	11 24	20 24	16 49	8 14	17 46	28 43
Nov 1	21 48	23 26	16 04	7 33	18 16	28 46
15	0♎14	26 15	15 48	6 59	18 36	28 42
Dec 1	9 42	29 42	15 54	6 24	18 51	28 33
15	17♎48	2♑51	16♓22	6♉00	18♍57	28♋20

1937	♂	♃	♄	♅	♆	♇
Jan 1	27♎21	6♑46	17♓21	5♉42	18♍56	28♋00
15	4♏53	9 58	18 28	5 37	18 48	27 42
Feb 1	13 31	13 45	20 08	5 46	18 30	27 20
15	20 01	16 43	21 42	6 04	18 11	27 03
Mar 1	25 48	19 27	23 21	6 31	17 48	26 48
15	0♐34	21 53	25 05	7 06	17 25	26 38
Apr 1	4 27	24 21	27 11	7 56	16 58	26 31
15	5 32	25 53	28 51	8 42	16 39	26 30
May 1	3 51	26 59	0♈37	9 37	16 22	26 36
15	29♏59	27 19	2 00	10 25	16 13	26 46
Jun 1	24 08	26 54	3 24	11 21	16 11	27 03
15	20 36	25 54	4 16	12 02	16 16	27 22
Jul 1	19 37	24 13	4 55	12 43	16 29	27 46
15	21 32	22 27	5 08	13 11	16 47	28 08
Aug 1	26 44	20 20	4 57	13 33	17 15	28 36
15	2♐48	18 53	4 27	13 41	17 42	28 59
Sep 1	11 44	17 45	3 30	13 38	18 18	29 23
15	20 05	17 29	2 29	13 25	18 49	29 41
Oct 1	0♑25	17 57	1 15	12 59	19 24	29 56
15	10 00	18 59	0 13	12 30	19 53	0♌04
Nov 1	22 07	20 59	29♓11	11 50	20 24	0 08
15	2♒23	23 08	28 36	11 15	20 44	0 05
Dec 1	14 20	26 02	28 21	10 39	21 00	29♋56
15	24♒54	28♑53	28♓30	10♉12	21♍08	29♋44

1938	♂	♃	♄	♅	♆	♇
Jan 1	7♓46	2♒38	29♓09	9♉51	21♍08	29♋24
15	18 21	5 53	0♈02	9 43	21 01	29 06
Feb 1	1♈06	9 54	1 29	9 48	20 44	28 43
15	11 30	13 13	2 54	10 03	20 25	28 26
Mar 1	21 47	16 28	4 29	10 28	20 04	28 11
15	1♉56	19 35	6 11	11 00	19 40	28 00
Apr 1	14 04	23 07	8 18	11 49	19 13	27 52
15	23 54	25 43	10 02	12 34	18 53	27 51
May 1	4♊59	28 17	11 57	13 28	18 35	27 56
15	14 32	0♓05	13 30	14 17	18 26	28 06
Jun 1	25 58	1 35	15 10	15 13	18 22	28 23
15	5♋15	2 11	16 18	15 57	18 26	28 41
Jul 1	15 46	2 07	17 17	16 40	18 38	29 05
15	24 52	1 23	17 50	17 10	18 54	29 28
Aug 1	5♌50	29♒48	18 03	17 36	19 21	29 56
15	14 49	28 05	17 51	17 47	19 48	0♌19
Sep 1	25 39	25 52	17 12	17 47	20 23	0 44
15	4♍32	24 15	16 22	17 37	20 54	1 01
Oct 1	14 40	22 57	15 11	17 15	21 30	1 17
15	23 31	22 25	14 06	16 47	21 59	1 26
Nov 1	4♎15	22 40	12 50	16 08	22 31	1 31
15	13 04	23 35	12 01	15 33	22 52	1 29
Dec 1	23 07	25 19	11 24	14 55	23 09	1 20
15	1♏54	27♒23	11♈14	14♉27	23♍18	1♌08

1939	♂	♃	♄	♅	♆	♇
Jan 1	12♏30	0♓26	11♈30	14♉02	23♍20	0♌49
15	21 10	3 17	12 06	13 51	23 14	0 31
Feb 1	1♐35	7 04	13 15	13 52	22 58	0 08
15	10 02	10 20	14 30	14 05	22 40	29♋51
Mar 1	18 20	13 42	15 57	14 26	22 18	29 35
15	26 26	17 05	17 34	14 57	21 55	29 23
Apr 1	5♑53	21 09	19 39	15 43	21 28	29 15
15	13 12	24 22	21 25	16 27	21 07	29 13
May 1	20 50	27 51	23 25	17 21	20 49	29 18
15	26 36	0♈40	25 06	18 09	20 38	29 27
Jun 1	1♒55	3 39	26 59	19 07	20 33	29 44
15	4 20	5 42	28 21	19 52	20 35	0♌01
Jul 1	4 17	7 28	29 39	20 37	20 46	0 25
15	1 47	8 26	0♉30	21 10	21 02	0 48
Aug 1	27♑14	8 47	1 07	21 39	21 28	1 16
15	24 29	8 22	1 16	21 53	21 54	1 39
Sep 1	24 21	7 03	0 59	21 58	22 29	2 05
15	27 05	5 27	0 25	21 51	23 00	2 23
Oct 1	2♒44	3 20	29♈25	21 31	23 35	2 40
15	9 17	1 33	28 22	21 06	24 05	2 50
Nov 1	18 37	29♓50	27 01	20 27	24 37	2 55
15	27 04	29 02	26 00	19 53	24 59	2 53
Dec 1	7♓17	28 56	25 04	19 14	25 18	2 46
15	16♓31	29♓34	24♈34	18♉44	25♍28	2♌34

1940	♂	♃	♄	♅	♆	♇
Jan 1	27♓58	1♈09	24♈26	18♉16	25♍31	2♌15
15	7♈29	3 03	24 43	18 02	25 26	1 57
Feb 1	19 04	5 57	25 31	17 59	25 12	1 34
15	28 35	8 43	26 32	18 08	24 54	1 16
Mar 1	8♉44	11 57	27 54	18 29	24 32	1 00
15	18 09	15 10	29 23	18 57	24 09	0 47
Apr 1	29 29	19 13	1♉23	19 42	23 41	0 39
15	8♊44	22 35	3 08	20 25	23 20	0 37
May 1	19 13	26 25	5 10	21 18	23 01	0 41
15	28 18	29 42	6 56	22 07	22 50	0 50
Jun 1	9♋16	3♉29	8 59	23 05	22 44	1 07
15	18 15	6 23	10 32	23 51	22 46	1 24
Jul 1	28 27	9 22	12 05	24 38	22 56	1 48
15	7♌21	11 37	13 11	25 13	23 11	2 11
Aug 1	18 09	13 47	14 11	25 45	23 36	2 40
15	27 02	14 59	14 39	26 01	24 02	3 03
Sep 1	7♍51	15 40	14 46	26 09	24 37	3 29
15	16 47	15 30	14 28	26 04	25 07	3 48
Oct 1	27 03	14 32	13 45	25 47	25 43	4 05
15	6♎04	13 06	12 51	25 23	26 13	4 15
Nov 1	17 06	10 54	11 32	24 46	26 46	4 20
15	26 15	9 02	10 25	24 12	27 08	4 19
Dec 1	6♏47	7 12	9 16	23 32	27 28	4 11
15	16♏04	6♉07	8♉29	23♉01	27♍38	4♌00

1941	♂	♃	♄	♅	♆	♇
Jan 1	27♏26	5♉41	7♉58	22♉31	27♍42	3♌41
15	6♐52	6 04	7 55	22 15	27 38	3 23
Feb 1	18 24	7 23	8 22	22 09	27 24	3 00
15	27 57	9 05	9 06	22 16	27 07	2 42
Mar 1	7♑34	11 15	10 09	22 32	26 46	2 26
15	17 13	13 47	11 27	22 58	26 24	2 14
Apr 1	28 58	17 15	13 18	23 40	25 56	2 04
15	8♒39	20 19	14 58	24 22	25 34	2 02
May 1	19 39	24 00	16 59	25 14	25 14	2 05
15	29 11	27 17	18 47	26 02	25 02	2 14
Jun 1	10♓31	1♊17	20 56	27 02	24 55	2 30
15	19 32	4 32	22 38	27 48	24 56	2 47
Jul 1	29 17	8 06	24 24	28 37	25 05	3 11
15	7♈05	11 03	25 46	29 14	25 19	3 34
Aug 1	15 11	14 20	27 07	29 49	25 43	4 03
15	20 13	16 41	27 55	0♊09	26 08	4 26
Sep 1	23 29	19 01	28 28	0 21	26 42	4 53
15	23 14	20 24	28 32	0 19	27 13	5 12
Oct 1	19 46	21 18	28 11	0 05	27 48	5 30
15	15 27	21 25	27 32	29♉44	28 19	5 40
Nov 1	11 39	20 40	26 24	29 09	28 52	5 47
15	11 13	19 24	25 17	28 35	29 15	5 46
Dec 1	13 42	17 26	24 00	27 55	29 36	5 39
15	17♈55	15♊32	23♉00	27♉22	29♍48	5♌28

1942	♂	♃	♄	♅	♆	♇
Jan 1	24♈50	13♊26	22♉06	26♉50	29♍53	5♌10
15	1♉32	12 09	21 42	26 31	29 50	4 52
Feb 1	10 27	11 25	21 42	26 21	29 37	4 29
15	18 14	11 32	22 07	26 24	29 21	4 10
Mar 1	26 18	12 18	22 52	26 38	29 01	3 54
15	4♊32	13 39	23 55	27 01	28 39	3 41
Apr 1	14 42	15 56	25 32	27 40	28 10	3 31
15	23 09	18 15	27 05	28 20	27 49	3 28
May 1	2♋53	21 16	29 01	29 11	27 28	3 31
15	11 27	24 10	0♊48	29 59	27 15	3 39
Jun 1	21 53	27 53	2 59	0♊59	27 06	3 54
15	0♌31	1♋02	4 46	1 47	27 06	4 12
Jul 1	10 25	4 41	6 43	2 37	27 14	4 35
15	19 08	7 51	8 17	3 16	27 27	4 58
Aug 1	29 47	11 36	9 56	3 55	27 50	5 27
15	8♍37	14 31	11 02	4 18	28 14	5 51
Sep 1	19 26	17 47	12 00	4 33	28 48	6 18
15	28 26	20 10	12 26	4 35	29 18	6 38
Oct 1	8♎50	22 26	12 30	4 25	29 54	6 56
15	18 02	23 56	12 10	4 06	0♎24	7 08
Nov 1	29 22	25 01	11 21	3 33	0 59	7 15
15	8♏50	25 14	10 23	3 00	1 23	7 15
Dec 1	19 47	24 41	9 06	2 20	1 44	7 09
15	29♏31	23♋33	7♊58	1♊46	1♎57	6♌58

1943	♂	♃	♄	♅	♆	♇
Jan 1	11♐29	21♋34	6♊46	1♊11	2♎04	6♌40
15	21 29	19 42	6 03	0 49	2 02	6 22
Feb 1	3♑47	17 33	5 37	0 36	1 51	5 59
15	14 02	16 11	5 39	0 36	1 35	5 40
Mar 1	24 24	15 22	6 04	0 46	1 16	5 24
15	4♒50	15 11	6 49	1 06	0 54	5 10
Apr 1	17 36	15 48	8 08	1 43	0 26	4 59
15	28 10	16 57	9 29	2 21	0 04	4 55
May 1	10♓14	18 51	11 16	3 10	29♍42	4 58
15	20 45	20 58	12 58	3 58	29 28	5 05
Jun 1	3♈25	23 57	15 08	4 57	29 18	5 20
15	13 40	26 41	16 57	5 46	29 17	5 37
Jul 1	25 08	0♌01	19 00	6 38	29 23	6 01
15	4♉50	3 03	20 42	7 19	29 35	6 24
Aug 1	16 05	6 48	22 36	8 01	29 57	6 53
15	24 46	9 54	23 58	8 27	0♎21	7 17
Sep 1	4♊22	13 33	25 18	8 46	0 54	7 45
15	11 13	16 26	26 04	8 51	1 24	8 05
Oct 1	17 28	19 28	26 34	8 44	2 00	8 24
15	21 01	21 51	26 36	8 28	2 30	8 36
Nov 1	22 08	24 15	26 11	7 58	3 05	8 44
15	19 56	25 45	25 28	7 27	3 30	8 45
Dec 1	14 36	26 47	24 21	6 47	3 53	8 39
15	9♊25	27♌04	23♊14	6♊12	4♎06	8♌29

1944	♂	♃	♄	♅	♆	♇
Jan 1	5♊25	26♌32	21♊51	5♊34	4♎14	8♌12
15	5 00	25 26	20 53	5 10	4 14	7 54
Feb 1	7 36	23 30	20 02	4 53	4 04	7 31
15	11 40	21 40	19 43	4 50	3 49	7 12
Mar 1	17 20	19 47	19 46	4 58	3 29	6 53
15	23 31	18 20	20 12	5 16	3 07	6 40
Apr 1	1♋48	17 16	21 10	5 49	2 39	6 28
15	9 06	17 02	22 17	6 26	2 17	6 24
May 1	17 48	17 32	23 51	7 15	1 55	6 26
15	25 39	18 33	25 26	8 01	1 40	6 33
Jun 1	5♌27	20 27	27 31	9 01	1 30	6 49
15	13 41	22 28	29 18	9 50	1 28	7 06
Jul 1	23 15	25 10	1♋23	10 43	1 33	7 29
15	1♍46	27 48	3 10	11 26	1 45	7 52
Aug 1	12 16	1♍14	5 14	12 10	2 06	8 21
15	21 04	4 12	6 47	12 38	2 29	8 46
Sep 1	1♎55	7 52	8 24	13 00	3 02	9 14
15	11 01	10 54	9 28	13 08	3 32	9 34
Oct 1	21 36	14 17	10 20	13 04	4 08	9 54
15	1♏01	17 07	10 44	12 51	4 38	10 06
Nov 1	12 40	20 18	10 43	12 23	5 13	10 15
15	22 26	22 37	10 19	11 52	5 39	10 16
Dec 1	3♐48	24 49	9 28	11 13	6 02	10 11
15	13♐56	26♍16	8♋27	10♊37	6♎16	10♌01

1945	♂	♃	♄	♅	♆	♇
Jan 1	26♐25	27♍18	7♋04	9♊58	6♎25	9♌43
15	6♑52	27 29	5 57	9 32	6 25	9 26
Feb 1	19 44	26 52	4 49	9 12	6 16	9 02
15	0♒27	25 44	4 10	9 06	6 02	8 43
Mar 1	11 15	24 10	3 51	9 11	5 44	8 26
15	22 06	22 23	3 54	9 25	5 22	8 11
Apr 1	5♓19	20 16	4 27	9 56	4 54	7 59
15	16 12	18 51	5 17	10 30	4 32	7 55
May 1	28 34	17 49	6 34	11 17	4 09	7 56
15	9♈19	17 32	7 56	12 03	3 54	8 03
Jun 1	22 10	17 58	9 51	13 02	3 42	8 17
15	2♉35	18 57	11 34	13 52	3 39	8 34
Jul 1	14 15	20 39	13 37	14 46	3 43	8 57
15	24 11	22 35	15 26	15 31	3 54	9 20
Aug 1	5♊53	25 23	17 36	16 17	4 14	9 49
15	15 08	27 59	19 17	16 48	4 36	10 14
Sep 1	25 52	1♎23	21 09	17 14	5 08	10 43
15	4♋09	4 19	22 29	17 25	5 38	11 04
Oct 1	12 54	7 46	23 41	17 26	6 13	11 24
15	19 44	10 47	24 26	17 15	6 44	11 37
Nov 1	26 39	14 23	24 52	16 50	7 20	11 46
15	0♌46	17 12	24 50	16 21	7 46	11 48
Dec 1	3 08	20 11	24 21	15 43	8 10	11 44
15	2♌32	22♎30	23♋35	15♊07	8♎26	11♌35

1946	♂	♃	♄	♅	♆	♇
Jan 1	28♋17	24♎49	22♋21	14♊27	8♎36	11♌18
15	22 53	26 13	21 12	13 58	8 37	11 00
Feb 1	16 56	27 12	19 52	13 35	8 29	10 37
15	14 24	27 21	18 57	13 25	8 16	10 17
Mar 1	14 25	26 53	18 18	13 27	7 59	10 00
15	16 36	25 51	17 59	13 38	7 37	9 45
Apr 1	21 25	24 00	18 04	14 05	7 10	9 32
15	26 41	22 14	18 33	14 37	6 47	9 27
May 1	3♌42	20 16	19 29	15 22	6 24	9 27
15	10 29	18 50	20 37	16 07	6 08	9 33
Jun 1	19 19	17 44	22 17	17 05	5 55	9 47
15	26 59	17 27	23 52	17 55	5 50	10 03
Jul 1	6♍06	17 51	25 49	18 51	5 53	10 26
15	14 22	18 47	27 36	19 36	6 03	10 49
Aug 1	24 41	20 34	29 48	20 26	6 22	11 19
15	3♎26	22 30	1♌34	20 59	6 43	11 44
Sep 1	14 19	25 19	3 36	21 29	7 15	12 13
15	23 31	27 55	5 08	21 44	7 44	12 34
Oct 1	4♏17	1♏09	6 38	21 48	8 19	12 55
15	13 54	4 07	7 40	21 40	8 50	13 09
Nov 1	25 53	7 49	8 32	21 19	9 26	13 20
15	5♐57	10 53	8 52	20 52	9 53	13 22
Dec 1	17 41	14 18	8 47	20 15	10 18	13 19
15	28♐09	17♏10	8♌21	19♊39	10♎34	13♌10

1947	♂	♃	♄	♅	♆	♇
Jan 1	11♑04	20♏22	7♌23	18♊57	10♎46	12♌53
15	21 51	22 41	6 21	18 27	10 48	12 36
Feb 1	5♒05	25 00	4 58	18 00	10 42	12 12
15	16 04	26 25	3 53	17 47	10 30	11 53
Mar 1	27 05	27 17	2 57	17 45	10 13	11 35
15	8♓07	27 34	2 18	17 53	9 53	11 19
Apr 1	21 27	27 05	1 57	18 17	9 25	11 06
15	2♈22	26 04	2 04	18 46	9 02	11 00
May 1	14 42	24 22	2 37	19 29	8 38	11 00
15	25 22	22 37	3 26	20 12	8 21	11 05
Jun 1	8♉06	20 31	4 48	21 10	8 07	11 18
15	18 23	19 06	6 11	22 00	8 02	11 34
Jul 1	29 54	18 02	7 58	22 56	8 04	11 57
15	9♊45	17 42	9 40	23 43	8 12	12 20
Aug 1	21 24	18 05	11 50	24 35	8 30	12 49
15	0♋44	19 01	13 37	25 11	8 50	13 15
Sep 1	11 42	20 50	15 46	25 45	9 21	13 44
15	20 25	22 49	17 25	26 02	9 50	14 06
Oct 1	29 56	25 30	19 08	26 10	10 25	14 28
15	7♌51	28 09	20 26	26 07	10 56	14 43
Nov 1	16 45	1♐39	21 39	25 49	11 32	14 54
15	23 22	4 42	22 19	25 24	12 00	14 57
Dec 1	29 49	8 16	22 40	24 48	12 26	14 54
15	4♍12	11♐24	22♌34	24♊13	12♎43	14♌46

1948	♂	♃	♄	♅	♆	♇
Jan 1	7♍15	15♐08	21♌59	23♊30	12♎56	14♌30
15	7 20	18 04	21 10	22 58	13 00	14 13
Feb 1	4 01	21 21	19 54	22 28	12 55	13 50
15	29♌00	23 44	18 46	22 12	12 44	13 30
Mar 1	23 15	25 54	17 37	22 07	12 26	13 10
15	19 27	27 27	16 43	22 12	12 06	12 54
Apr 1	18 08	28 37	15 59	22 33	11 38	12 41
15	19 39	28 56	15 46	23 00	11 16	12 34
May 1	23 35	28 34	15 56	23 40	10 52	12 34
15	28 28	27 37	16 26	24 23	10 34	12 39
Jun 1	5♍42	25 51	17 29	25 20	10 19	12 52
15	12 27	24 06	18 38	26 09	10 13	13 08
Jul 1	20 52	22 07	20 13	27 06	10 14	13 30
15	28 43	20 38	21 47	27 54	10 22	13 53
Aug 1	8♎45	19 27	23 50	28 48	10 39	14 23
15	17 24	19 06	25 36	29 26	10 59	14 49
Sep 1	28 18	19 30	27 46	0♋02	11 29	15 18
15	7♏36	20 28	29 30	0 23	11 58	15 41
Oct 1	18 33	22 12	1♍22	0 34	12 33	16 03
15	28 24	24 13	2 50	0 33	13 04	16 18
Nov 1	10♐41	27 10	4 20	0 18	13 40	16 30
15	21 02	29 55	5 16	29♊56	14 08	16 34
Dec 1	3♑06	3♑19	5 58	29 21	14 35	16 31
15	13♑51	6♑27	6♍12	28♊47	14♎53	16♌23

1949	♂	♃	♄	♅	♆	♇
Jan 1	27♑04	10♑22	6♍00	28♊03	15♎06	16♌08
15	8♒04	13 37	5 27	27 30	15 11	15 51
Feb 1	21 30	17 28	4 24	26 57	15 06	15 27
15	2♓34	20 29	3 20	26 39	14 56	15 07
Mar 1	13 37	23 19	2 13	26 31	14 40	14 48
15	24 36	25 53	1 09	26 33	14 21	14 32
Apr 1	7♈49	28 32	0 06	26 50	13 53	14 18
15	18 34	0♒14	29♌33	27 14	13 30	14 11
May 1	0♉40	1 34	29 19	27 52	13 06	14 09
15	11 05	2 07	29 29	28 32	12 48	14 14
Jun 1	23 30	1 58	0♍07	29 28	12 32	14 26
15	3♊32	1 11	1 00	0♋17	12 25	14 41
Jul 1	14 46	29♑39	2 18	1 15	12 25	15 04
15	24 24	27 57	3 41	2 04	12 31	15 26
Aug 1	5♋52	25 47	5 35	2 59	12 47	15 57
15	15 06	24 12	7 16	3 40	13 06	16 22
Sep 1	26 04	22 51	9 24	4 19	13 35	16 53
15	4♌53	22 22	11 09	4 43	14 03	17 16
Oct 1	14 42	22 35	13 07	4 58	14 38	17 38
15	23 03	23 26	14 43	5 01	15 09	17 54
Nov 1	2♍48	25 14	16 27	4 50	15 46	18 07
15	10 27	27 14	17 38	4 30	16 14	18 12
Dec 1	18 40	0♒02	18 40	3 58	16 42	18 10
15	25♍15	2♒49	19♍14	3♋25	17♎01	18♌03

1950	♂	♃	♄	♅	♆	♇
Jan 1	2♎13	6♒30	19♍26	2♋41	17♎16	17♌48
15	6 46	9 43	19 13	2 06	17 21	17 31
Feb 1	10 18	13 45	18 30	1 31	17 18	17 08
15	11 00	17 05	17 36	1 10	17 09	16 47
Mar 1	9 14	20 23	16 33	0 58	16 54	16 28
15	5 09	23 34	15 26	0 57	16 35	16 12
Apr 1	28♍40	27 12	14 11	1 09	16 08	15 56
15	24 16	29 56	13 22	1 31	15 45	15 48
May 1	22 03	2♓40	12 45	2 06	15 20	15 46
15	22 46	4 38	12 35	2 44	15 02	15 50
Jun 1	26 26	6 23	12 49	3 38	14 45	16 02
15	1♎11	7 13	13 23	4 27	14 37	16 17
Jul 1	8 02	7 26	14 23	5 24	14 35	16 39
15	14 57	6 56	15 32	6 14	14 40	17 01
Aug 1	24 18	5 34	17 13	7 12	14 55	17 31
15	2♏36	3 57	18 46	7 54	15 13	17 57
Sep 1	13 19	1 44	20 48	8 37	15 41	18 28
15	22 35	0 01	22 33	9 04	16 09	18 52
Oct 1	3♐37	28♒29	24 32	9 23	16 43	19 15
15	13 35	27 44	26 13	9 29	17 15	19 32
Nov 1	26 03	27 41	28 07	9 23	17 52	19 46
15	6♑35	28 23	29 30	9 06	18 20	19 51
Dec 1	18 50	29 54	0♎48	8 37	18 49	19 50
15	29♑42	1♓48	1♎39	8♋04	19♎09	19♌44

1951	♂	♃	♄	♅	♆	♇
Jan 1	13♒02	4♓42	2♎15	7♋21	19♎25	19♌29
15	24 03	7 27	2 21	6 46	19 31	19 13
Feb 1	7♓26	11 09	2 01	6 08	19 30	18 50
15	18 24	14 24	1 22	5 44	19 22	18 29
Mar 1	29 17	17 44	0 29	5 29	19 08	18 10
15	10♈04	21 08	29♍25	5 24	18 49	17 53
Apr 1	22 58	25 13	28 06	5 32	18 23	17 36
15	3♉25	28 30	27 06	5 50	18 00	17 28
May 1	15 10	2♈04	26 12	6 22	17 35	17 25
15	25 16	4 58	25 43	6 59	17 15	17 28
Jun 1	7♊18	8 07	25 33	7 51	16 57	17 39
15	17 02	10 20	25 47	8 39	16 48	17 54
Jul 1	27 59	12 19	26 27	9 36	16 45	18 15
15	7♋24	13 31	27 20	10 27	16 49	18 38
Aug 1	18 39	14 10	28 45	11 25	17 03	19 08
15	27 46	13 59	0♎08	12 10	17 20	19 34
Sep 1	8♌41	12 56	2 02	12 56	17 48	20 05
15	17 33	11 29	3 42	13 26	18 15	20 29
Oct 1	27 31	9 26	5 40	13 49	18 49	20 54
15	6♍07	7 35	7 23	13 59	19 20	21 11
Nov 1	16 22	5 40	9 24	13 56	19 57	21 26
15	24 38	4 39	10 55	13 43	20 26	21 32
Dec 1	3♎51	4 15	12 27	13 17	20 56	21 32
15	11♎38	4♈38	13♎32	12♋46	21♎16	21♌26

1952	♂	♃	♄	♅	♆	♇
Jan 1	20♎40	5♈57	14♎29	12♋03	21♎34	21♌13
15	27 37	7 40	14 54	11 27	21 41	20 57
Feb 1	5♏16	10 22	14 56	10 47	21 42	20 33
15	10 41	13 01	14 35	10 21	21 34	20 13
Mar 1	15 13	16 10	13 52	10 02	21 20	19 52
15	17 50	19 19	12 57	9 54	21 02	19 34
Apr 1	18 12	23 18	11 40	9 59	20 36	19 18
15	15 50	26 40	10 35	10 15	20 13	19 09
May 1	10 39	0♉31	9 30	10 44	19 48	19 06
15	5 40	3 49	8 46	11 18	19 28	19 08
Jun 1	1 44	7 40	8 16	12 09	19 09	19 19
15	1 19	10 39	8 13	12 56	19 00	19 33
Jul 1	3 52	13 45	8 32	13 53	18 56	19 55
15	8 12	16 08	9 10	14 44	18 59	20 17
Aug 1	15 28	18 30	10 18	15 44	19 12	20 48
15	22 40	19 55	11 30	16 30	19 29	21 14
Sep 1	2♐33	20 52	13 13	17 18	19 56	21 45
15	11 24	20 57	14 47	17 51	20 22	22 10
Oct 1	22 09	20 15	16 42	18 17	20 56	22 35
15	2♑00	19 00	18 24	18 30	21 27	22 53
Nov 1	14 23	16 55	20 27	18 31	22 05	23 08
15	24 50	15 01	22 04	18 20	22 34	23 15
Dec 1	7♒00	13 02	23 45	17 56	23 04	23 16
15	17♒45	11♉45	25♎01	17♋27	23♎25	23♌10

1953	♂	♃	♄	♅	♆	♇
Jan 1	0♓51	11♉01	26♎14	16♋45	23♎43	22♌57
15	11 38	11 08	26 54	16 09	23 52	22 41
Feb 1	24 39	12 11	27 17	15 28	23 52	22 18
15	5♈16	13 41	27 13	14 59	23 46	21 57
Mar 1	15 46	15 40	26 48	14 39	23 33	21 37
15	26 07	18 04	26 07	14 28	23 16	21 19
Apr 1	8♉31	21 24	24 58	14 28	22 51	21 02
15	18 33	24 23	23 55	14 40	22 28	20 52
May 1	29 49	28 00	22 43	15 06	22 02	20 48
15	9♊32	1♊15	21 47	15 38	21 42	20 50
Jun 1	21 09	5 14	20 58	16 26	21 22	21 00
15	0♋34	8 30	20 37	17 12	21 12	21 14
Jul 1	11 11	12 06	20 36	18 08	21 07	21 35
15	20 23	15 07	20 55	18 59	21 09	21 57
Aug 1	1♌25	18 29	21 44	20 00	21 20	22 27
15	10 26	20 57	22 42	20 48	21 36	22 54
Sep 1	21 17	23 27	24 11	21 39	22 02	23 26
15	0♍10	25 01	25 37	22 14	22 28	23 51
Oct 1	10 15	26 09	27 25	22 44	23 01	24 16
15	19 02	26 29	29 05	23 01	23 32	24 35
Nov 1	29 38	26 00	1♏08	23 06	24 10	24 51
15	8♎18	24 55	2 48	22 59	24 40	24 59
Dec 1	18 09	23 06	4 36	22 39	25 10	25 01
15	26♎41	21♊13	6♏01	22♋12	25♎32	24♌56

1954	♂	♃	♄	♅	♆	♇
Jan 1	6♏55	19♊01	7♏29	21♋32	25♎52	24♌43
15	15 13	17 34	8 24	20 55	26 01	24 28
Feb 1	25 02	16 34	9 07	20 13	26 03	24 05
15	2♐53	16 27	9 21	19 42	25 58	23 45
Mar 1	10 24	16 59	9 14	19 19	25 47	23 24
15	17 30	18 07	8 48	19 04	25 30	23 06
Apr 1	25 20	20 12	7 53	19 00	25 05	22 48
15	0♑50	22 22	6 56	19 09	24 42	22 37
May 1	5 40	25 16	5 43	19 31	24 16	22 32
15	8 06	28 04	4 42	20 00	23 56	22 34
Jun 1	8 05	1♋42	3 38	20 46	23 35	22 43
15	5 27	4 49	3 01	21 30	23 24	22 56
Jul 1	0 42	8 26	2 40	22 25	23 17	23 16
15	27♐03	11 36	2 42	23 16	23 19	23 38
Aug 1	25 38	15 22	3 10	24 18	23 29	24 09
15	27 25	18 20	3 53	25 07	23 43	24 35
Sep 1	2♑39	21 41	5 06	26 01	24 08	25 08
15	8 51	24 09	6 21	26 39	24 34	25 33
Oct 1	17 26	26 34	8 00	27 12	25 07	26 00
15	25 52	28 13	9 35	27 32	25 37	26 19
Nov 1	6♒54	29 31	11 36	27 42	26 15	26 37
15	16 26	29 56	13 17	27 39	26 45	26 45
Dec 1	27 39	29 37	15 09	27 22	27 16	26 48
15	7♓37	28♋41	16♏41	26♋58	27♎39	26♌44

1955	♂	♃	♄	♅	♆	♇
Jan 1	19♓49	26♋51	18♏20	26♋20	28♎00	26♌32
15	29 52	25 01	19 28	25 44	28 11	26 17
Feb 1	12♈01	22 48	20 30	25 00	28 14	25 55
15	21 57	21 18	21 00	24 28	28 10	25 34
Mar 1	1♉48	20 17	21 11	24 02	28 00	25 13
15	11 32	19 53	21 01	23 44	27 44	24 54
Apr 1	23 14	20 15	20 24	23 36	27 19	24 36
15	2♊44	21 12	19 37	23 41	26 57	24 25
May 1	13 28	22 55	18 30	23 59	26 31	24 18
15	22 45	24 53	17 27	24 25	26 10	24 19
Jun 1	3♋54	27 45	16 14	25 07	25 48	24 27
15	13 00	0♌23	15 25	25 50	25 36	24 40
Jul 1	23 20	3 39	14 46	26 44	25 29	25 00
15	2♌19	6 38	14 31	27 35	25 29	25 22
Aug 1	13 10	10 22	14 38	28 37	25 37	25 52
15	22 05	13 27	15 04	29 27	25 51	26 19
Sep 1	2♍55	17 08	16 00	0♌23	26 15	26 51
15	11 49	20 02	17 03	1 04	26 40	27 17
Oct 1	22 02	23 09	18 31	1 41	27 12	27 45
15	0♎59	25 37	19 59	2 04	27 43	28 05
Nov 1	11 53	28 09	21 55	2 19	28 21	28 23
15	20 54	29 47	23 34	2 19	28 51	28 33
Dec 1	1♏15	1♍02	25 28	2 06	29 23	28 37
15	10♏21	1♍29	27♏05	1♌45	29♎47	28♌34

1956	♂	♃	♄	♅	♆	♇
Jan 1	21♏26	1♍12	28♏53	1♌09	0♏09	28♌23
15	0♐35	0 17	0♐12	0 34	0 20	28 08
Feb 1	11 44	28♌29	1 29	29♋50	0 25	27 46
15	20 55	26 42	2 14	29 16	0 22	27 25
Mar 1	0♑46	24 45	2 42	28 45	0 12	27 03
15	9 56	23 12	2 48	28 25	29♎56	26 44
Apr 1	20 59	21 55	2 29	28 14	29 32	26 24
15	0♒01	21 30	1 54	28 15	29 10	26 13
May 1	10 08	21 46	0 56	28 30	28 44	26 06
15	18 44	22 37	29♏56	28 54	28 23	26 07
Jun 1	28 42	24 20	28 41	29 34	28 01	26 14
15	6♓16	26 13	27 44	0♌15	27 48	26 27
Jul 1	13 51	28 48	26 51	1 08	27 40	26 47
15	19 07	1♍21	26 22	1 58	27 39	27 08
Aug 1	23 01	4 42	26 10	3 01	27 47	27 39
15	23 32	7 38	26 21	3 52	28 00	28 05
Sep 1	20 48	11 17	27 00	4 49	28 23	28 39
15	17 02	14 19	27 50	5 32	28 48	29 05
Oct 1	13 45	17 44	29 06	6 12	29 20	29 33
15	13 17	20 37	0♐26	6 38	29 50	29 54
Nov 1	16 04	23 52	2 15	6 56	0♏28	0♍13
15	20 33	26 16	3 51	6 59	0 59	0 23
Dec 1	27 22	28 36	5 45	6 50	1 31	0 27
15	4♈21	0♎11	7♐24	6♌31	1♏55	0♍25

1957	♂	♃	♄	♅	♆	♇
Jan 1	13♈41	1♎26	9♐18	5♌57	2♏18	0♍14
15	21 50	1 48	10 44	5 23	2 30	0 00
Feb 1	2♉04	1 25	12 13	4 39	2 36	29♌38
15	10 42	0 26	13 11	4 04	2 33	29 17
Mar 1	19 24	28♍59	13 52	3 33	2 25	28 56
15	28 11	27 14	14 14	3 10	2 10	28 36
Apr 1	8♊52	25 05	14 15	2 54	1 47	28 16
15	17 40	23 33	13 55	2 52	1 25	28 04
May 1	27 43	22 20	13 11	3 03	0 59	27 57
15	6♋30	21 52	12 18	3 24	0 37	27 56
Jun 1	17 09	22 05	11 05	4 00	0 15	28 03
15	25 55	22 54	10 03	4 39	0 01	28 15
Jul 1	5♌57	24 27	9 00	5 30	29♎51	28 34
15	14 44	26 15	8 18	6 20	29 50	28 55
Aug 1	25 26	28 56	7 47	7 22	29 56	29 25
15	4♍17	1♎27	7 41	8 13	0♏08	29 52
Sep 1	15 06	4 47	8 00	9 13	0 30	0♍26
15	24 04	7 42	8 36	9 57	0 54	0 53
Oct 1	4♎25	11 08	9 38	10 41	1 25	1 21
15	13 33	14 10	10 47	11 10	1 56	1 43
Nov 1	24 46	17 47	12 26	11 33	2 34	2 03
15	4♏06	20 39	13 58	11 40	3 04	2 14
Dec 1	14 54	23 43	15 49	11 35	3 37	2 20
15	24♏27	26♎07	17♐28	11♌19	4♏02	2♍18

1958	♂	♃	♄	♅	♆	♇
Jan 1	6♐12	28♎35	19♐26	10♌49	4♏26	2♍08
15	15 59	0♏08	20 58	10 16	4 39	1 55
Feb 1	28 01	1 20	22 39	9 32	4 46	1 33
15	8♑02	1 40	23 48	8 56	4 45	1 12
Mar 1	18 08	1 23	24 43	8 24	4 37	0 51
15	28 19	0 31	25 21	7 58	4 24	0 31
Apr 1	10♒47	28♎49	25 42	7 37	4 01	0 10
15	21 05	27 05	25 37	7 32	3 40	29♌57
May 1	2♓52	25 04	25 10	7 39	3 14	29 49
15	13 09	23 32	24 28	7 55	2 52	29 47
Jun 1	25 30	22 15	23 22	8 29	2 28	29 53
15	5♈30	21 47	22 21	9 05	2 14	0♍04
Jul 1	16 37	21 58	21 12	9 54	2 03	0 23
15	25 57	22 44	20 19	10 42	2 00	0 44
Aug 1	6♉36	24 21	19 31	11 44	2 05	1 14
15	14 35	26 11	19 10	12 36	2 16	1 41
Sep 1	22 55	28 53	19 09	13 37	2 38	2 14
15	28 14	1♏25	19 29	14 24	3 00	2 42
Oct 1	1♊54	4 35	20 14	15 10	3 31	3 11
15	2 23	7 32	21 11	15 42	4 01	3 33
Nov 1	29♉10	11 14	22 39	16 09	4 39	3 55
15	24 19	14 18	24 04	16 20	5 10	4 07
Dec 1	19 06	17 46	25 50	16 20	5 43	4 13
15	16♉46	20♏41	27♐28	16♌08	6♏09	4♍13

1959	♂	♃	♄	♅	♆	♇
Jan 1	17♉26	23♏58	29♐28	15♌40	6♏34	4♍04
15	20 24	26 24	1♑05	15 10	6 48	3 51
Feb 1	26 05	28 53	2 53	14 27	6 57	3 30
15	1♊57	0♐27	4 13	13 50	6 57	3 09
Mar 1	8 33	1 29	5 20	13 16	6 50	2 48
15	15 39	1 58	6 12	12 47	6 37	2 27
Apr 1	24 47	1 43	6 52	12 23	6 16	2 06
15	2♋35	0 52	7 04	12 14	5 55	1 52
May 1	11 44	29♏19	6 54	12 16	5 29	1 43
15	19 53	27 37	6 26	12 30	5 06	1 40
Jun 1	29 56	25 29	5 31	12 59	4 42	1 45
15	8♌20	23 56	4 35	13 32	4 27	1 55
Jul 1	18 02	22 41	3 25	14 19	4 15	2 14
15	26 38	22 10	2 25	15 06	4 11	2 34
Aug 1	7♍11	22 20	1 24	16 08	4 15	3 04
15	15 59	23 06	0 49	17 00	4 25	3 31
Sep 1	26 49	24 45	0 28	18 02	4 45	4 05
15	5♎52	26 36	0 32	18 50	5 07	4 33
Oct 1	16 22	29 11	1 00	19 39	5 37	5 03
15	25 41	1♐46	1 44	20 14	6 06	5 26
Nov 1	7♏12	5 13	2 58	20 46	6 44	5 48
15	16 51	8 14	4 14	21 00	7 15	6 01
Dec 1	28 03	11 48	5 53	21 04	7 49	6 09
15	8♐01	14♐58	7♑28	20♌56	8♏15	6♍09

1960	♂	♃	♄	♅	♆	♇
Jan 1	20♐18	18♐44	9♑27	20♌32	8♏41	6♍02
15	0♑35	21 44	11 06	20 04	8 57	5 49
Feb 1	13 15	25 07	13 01	19 22	9 07	5 29
15	23 48	27 37	14 29	18 45	9 08	5 08
Mar 1	5♒12	29 55	15 51	18 08	9 02	4 45
15	15 56	1♑38	16 55	17 37	8 50	4 25
Apr 1	29 01	3 03	17 51	17 10	8 29	4 02
15	9♓49	3 34	18 18	16 58	8 08	3 48
May 1	22 07	3 26	18 25	16 57	7 42	3 38
15	2♈49	2 40	18 11	17 07	7 19	3 35
Jun 1	15 39	1 04	17 31	17 33	6 55	3 40
15	26 03	29♐23	16 42	18 05	6 39	3 50
Jul 1	7♉42	27 22	15 35	18 49	6 27	4 07
15	17 36	25 46	14 34	19 35	6 22	4 28
Aug 1	29 13	24 22	13 24	20 36	6 25	4 57
15	8♊21	23 50	12 37	21 28	6 34	5 25
Sep 1	18 48	23 59	12 00	22 30	6 53	5 59
15	26 44	24 46	11 49	23 20	7 15	6 27
Oct 1	4♋51	26 20	12 00	24 11	7 45	6 58
15	10 50	28 13	12 30	24 48	8 14	7 21
Nov 1	16 11	1♑02	13 30	25 23	8 52	7 44
15	18 26	3 43	14 37	25 41	9 23	7 58
Dec 1	17 54	7 04	16 08	25 48	9 57	8 07
15	14♋33	10♑11	17♑38	25♌43	10♏24	8♍08

1961	♂	♃	♄	♅	♆	♇
Jan 1	8♋07	14♑05	19♑35	25♌23	10♏50	8♍00
15	3 13	17 21	21 14	24 56	11 06	7 49
Feb 1	0 10	21 15	23 13	24 16	11 17	7 28
15	0 28	24 21	24 47	23 39	11 19	7 08
Mar 1	2 55	27 16	26 12	23 03	11 14	6 46
15	6 58	29 56	27 27	22 31	11 03	6 25
Apr 1	13 26	2♒46	28 40	22 00	10 43	6 02
15	19 38	4 38	29 22	21 45	10 22	5 47
May 1	27 25	6 12	29 48	21 39	9 56	5 36
15	4♌41	6 58	29 50	21 46	9 34	5 32
Jun 1	13 57	7 06	29 28	22 08	9 09	5 36
15	21 52	6 31	28 50	22 36	8 52	5 45
Jul 1	1♍11	5 11	27 52	23 18	8 39	6 02
15	9 33	3 34	26 52	24 02	8 33	6 22
Aug 1	19 57	1 23	25 38	25 01	8 35	6 51
15	28 43	29♑42	24 42	25 53	8 43	7 18
Sep 1	9♎36	28 08	23 49	26 56	9 01	7 53
15	18 45	27 26	23 22	27 47	9 21	8 21
Oct 1	29 26	27 24	23 15	28 40	9 50	8 52
15	8♏59	28 03	23 29	29 20	10 19	9 17
Nov 1	20 49	29 38	24 11	29 59	10 57	9 41
15	0♐47	1♒29	25 06	0♍20	11 28	9 56
Dec 1	12 23	4 09	26 26	0 32	12 03	10 06
15	22♐43	6♒50	27♑49	0♍31	12♏30	10♍08

1962	♂	♃	♄	♅	♆	♇
Jan 1	5♑28	10♒28	29♑41	0♍15	12♏57	10♍02
15	16 09	13 39	1♒19	29♌51	13 14	9 51
Feb 1	29 15	17 39	3 20	29 13	13 27	9 31
15	10♒09	21 00	4 58	28 37	13 29	9 11
Mar 1	21 06	24 20	6 30	28 00	13 26	8 49
15	2♓06	27 34	7 55	27 26	13 16	8 28
Apr 1	15 25	1♓18	9 22	26 52	12 56	8 04
15	26 21	4 08	10 18	26 34	12 36	7 48
May 1	8♈44	7 02	11 03	26 24	12 11	7 36
15	19 26	9 10	11 22	26 27	11 48	7 32
Jun 1	2♉15	11 09	11 19	26 44	11 23	7 34
15	12 36	12 12	10 56	27 09	11 05	7 42
Jul 1	24 12	12 41	10 11	27 48	10 51	7 58
15	4♊06	12 26	9 17	28 30	10 44	8 18
Aug 1	15 48	11 19	8 03	29 27	10 44	8 47
15	25 08	9 50	7 02	0♍18	10 51	9 14
Sep 1	6♋03	7 40	5 56	1 22	11 08	9 48
15	14 39	5 52	5 15	2 14	11 28	10 17
Oct 1	23 59	4 08	4 49	3 09	11 56	10 49
15	1♌35	3 10	4 47	3 51	12 24	11 14
Nov 1	9 56	2 50	5 11	4 34	13 02	11 40
15	15 50	3 17	5 51	4 59	13 33	11 56
Dec 1	21 08	4 34	6 58	5 15	14 08	12 07
15	24♌01	6♓17	8♒11	5♍18	14♏36	12♍10

1963	♂	♃	♄	♅	♆	♇
Jan 1	24♌35	9♓00	9♒56	5♍06	15♏04	12♍05
15	22 12	11 40	11 31	4 46	15 22	11 55
Feb 1	16 21	15 16	13 32	4 10	15 36	11 35
15	10 55	18 27	15 12	3 35	15 40	11 16
Mar 1	6 55	21 46	16 50	2 58	15 37	10 54
15	5 21	25 09	18 22	2 23	15 28	10 32
Apr 1	6 40	29 15	20 02	1 47	15 10	10 08
15	9 52	2♈34	21 11	1 25	14 51	9 52
May 1	15 11	6 12	22 13	1 11	14 25	9 39
15	20 55	9 12	22 48	1 10	14 03	9 33
Jun 1	28 52	12 29	23 06	1 22	13 37	9 34
15	6♍02	14 50	23 00	1 44	13 18	9 41
Jul 1	14 45	17 02	22 31	2 20	13 03	9 57
15	22 46	18 26	21 48	2 59	12 55	10 16
Aug 1	2♎56	19 22	20 40	3 55	12 54	10 44
15	11 36	19 26	19 38	4 45	13 00	11 11
Sep 1	22 30	18 40	18 24	5 49	13 15	11 46
15	1♏45	17 23	17 31	6 41	13 34	12 15
Oct 1	12 37	15 26	16 48	7 38	14 02	12 48
15	22 22	13 34	16 29	8 23	14 30	13 14
Nov 1	4♐31	11 30	16 32	9 08	15 07	13 40
15	14 45	10 15	16 57	9 37	15 38	13 57
Dec 1	26 42	9 34	17 48	9 58	16 13	14 09
15	7♑20	9♈42	18♒51	10♍04	16♏42	14♍14

1964	♂	♃	♄	♅	♆	♇
Jan 1	20♑26	10♈44	20♒25	9♍57	17♏11	14♍10
15	1♒22	12 15	21 54	9 40	17 30	14 01
Feb 1	14 44	14 46	23 52	9 08	17 45	13 42
15	25 48	17 16	25 33	8 34	17 50	13 23
Mar 1	7♓39	20 19	27 21	7 55	17 48	13 00
15	18 41	23 23	28 59	7 19	17 40	12 38
Apr 1	1♈58	27 19	0♓49	6 40	17 22	12 13
15	12 48	0♉39	2 09	6 16	17 03	11 56
May 1	25 01	4 29	3 25	5 59	16 38	11 43
15	5♉32	7 49	4 15	5 55	16 15	11 36
Jun 1	18 05	11 43	4 52	6 04	15 49	11 37
15	28 13	14 45	5 02	6 23	15 30	11 44
Jul 1	9♊34	17 58	4 50	6 56	15 14	11 59
15	19 17	20 28	4 20	7 33	15 06	12 17
Aug 1	0♋50	23 01	3 23	8 27	15 04	12 46
15	10 06	24 36	2 24	9 16	15 09	13 13
Sep 1	21 05	25 49	1 08	10 19	15 24	13 48
15	29 52	26 08	0 07	11 12	15 42	14 17
Oct 1	9♌35	25 41	29♒11	12 10	16 09	14 50
15	17 47	24 38	28 37	12 57	16 37	15 17
Nov 1	27 15	22 42	28 21	13 45	17 14	15 44
15	4♍34	20 50	28 30	14 16	17 45	16 02
Dec 1	12 13	18 45	29 04	14 40	18 20	16 15
15	18♍06	17♉17	29♒55	14♍50	18♏49	16♍20

1965	♂	♃	♄	♅	♆	♇
Jan 1	23♍49	16♉15	1♓17	14♍47	19♏19	16♍17
15	26 54	16 08	2 40	14 33	19 39	16 08
Feb 1	27 59	16 54	4 33	14 03	19 54	15 50
15	26 10	18 11	6 12	13 31	20 00	15 31
Mar 1	22 00	20 00	7 55	12 55	19 59	15 09
15	16 35	22 15	9 36	12 18	19 52	14 47
Apr 1	11 01	25 26	11 35	11 38	19 35	14 22
15	8 52	28 21	13 04	11 11	19 17	14 04
May 1	9 27	1♊53	14 34	10 50	18 52	13 49
15	12 11	5 05	15 39	10 42	18 29	13 42
Jun 1	17 37	9 03	16 37	10 46	18 03	13 42
15	23 22	12 19	17 05	11 02	17 44	13 48
Jul 1	0♎59	15 57	17 13	11 31	17 27	14 02
15	8 22	19 00	16 59	12 05	17 17	14 20
Aug 1	18 04	22 27	16 19	12 56	17 14	14 48
15	26 33	25 01	15 29	13 44	17 18	15 14
Sep 1	7♏23	27 40	14 15	14 47	17 32	15 49
15	16 41	29 24	13 11	15 40	17 49	16 19
Oct 1	27 42	0♋44	12 03	16 39	18 15	16 53
15	7♐38	1 17	11 15	17 27	18 42	17 20
Nov 1	20 03	1 04	10 38	18 19	19 19	17 49
15	0♑31	0 11	10 29	18 53	19 50	18 07
Dec 1	12 44	28♊31	10 44	19 21	20 26	18 22
15	23♑34	26♊42	11♓19	19♍35	20♏55	18♍28

1966	♂	♃	♄	♅	♆	♇
Jan 1	6♒53	24♊26	12♓26	19♍37	21♏26	18♍26
15	17 55	22 51	13 38	19 26	21 46	18 18
Feb 1	1♓21	21 35	15 22	19 00	22 03	18 01
15	12 23	21 15	16 58	18 30	22 10	17 42
Mar 1	23 21	21 34	18 39	17 55	22 10	17 21
15	4♈14	22 30	20 23	17 19	22 04	16 59
Apr 1	17 17	24 21	22 27	16 37	21 49	16 33
15	27 52	26 23	24 04	16 07	21 31	16 15
May 1	9♉46	29 08	25 46	15 43	21 07	15 59
15	20 00	1♋50	27 04	15 31	20 44	15 51
Jun 1	2♊11	5 23	28 21	15 31	20 17	15 49
15	12 03	8 28	29 06	15 42	19 57	15 54
Jul 1	23 06	12 03	29 36	16 07	19 39	16 07
15	2♋37	15 13	29 41	16 39	19 29	16 24
Aug 1	13 57	19 00	29 20	17 27	19 24	16 52
15	23 07	22 00	28 44	18 14	19 27	17 18
Sep 1	4♌03	25 25	27 40	19 15	19 40	17 53
15	12 54	27 58	26 38	20 08	19 56	18 23
Oct 1	22 50	0♌30	25 24	21 08	20 21	18 57
15	1♍20	2 18	24 25	21 58	20 48	19 25
Nov 1	11 25	3 48	23 29	22 52	21 24	19 55
15	19 29	4 25	23 02	23 29	21 55	20 15
Dec 1	28 22	4 20	22 56	24 01	22 31	20 30
15	5♎46	3♌35	23♓13	24♍19	23♏00	20♍38

1967	♂	♃	♄	♅	♆	♇
Jan 1	14♎07	1♌55	24♓01	24♍25	23♏32	20♍38
15	20 19	0 09	25 00	24 19	23 53	20 31
Feb 1	26 41	27♋54	26 32	23 57	24 12	20 15
15	0♏35	26 17	28 02	23 29	24 20	19 56
Mar 1	2 50	25 06	29 39	22 56	24 21	19 35
15	2 57	24 29	1♈22	22 20	24 16	19 13
Apr 1	29♎47	24 36	3 29	21 36	24 02	18 47
15	25 00	25 22	5 12	21 05	23 45	18 28
May 1	19 12	26 54	7 03	20 37	23 21	18 11
15	15 51	28 44	8 32	20 22	22 58	18 02
Jun 1	15 11	1♌27	10 06	20 17	22 31	17 58
15	17 18	4 00	11 08	20 25	22 11	18 02
Jul 1	22 02	7 11	11 58	20 46	21 52	18 15
15	27 43	10 08	12 22	21 14	21 41	18 31
Aug 1	6♏03	13 49	12 25	21 59	21 35	18 58
15	13 50	16 54	12 06	22 44	21 37	19 24
Sep 1	24 10	20 35	11 18	23 44	21 48	19 59
15	3♐15	23 32	10 23	24 36	22 03	20 29
Oct 1	14 10	26 43	9 10	25 37	22 28	21 04
15	24 07	29 15	8 05	26 28	22 53	21 33
Nov 1	6♑35	1♍55	6 54	27 24	23 29	22 03
15	17 07	3 41	6 10	28 04	24 00	22 24
Dec 1	29 21	5 07	5 43	28 40	24 36	22 41
15	10♒12	5♍45	5♈40	29♍01	25♏06	22♍50

1968	♂	♃	♄	♅	♆	♇
Jan 1	23♒26	5♍41	6♈06	29♍13	25♏38	22♍51
15	4♓22	4 57	6 50	29 10	26 01	22 45
Feb 1	17 34	3 20	8 07	28 52	26 20	22 30
15	28 22	1 36	9 27	28 27	26 29	22 12
Mar 1	9♈48	29♌38	11 04	27 54	26 32	21 50
15	20 21	27 59	12 44	27 18	26 27	21 28
Apr 1	2♉57	26 30	14 51	26 34	26 14	21 01
15	13 10	25 54	16 36	26 01	25 57	20 42
May 1	24 38	25 57	18 35	25 31	25 34	20 24
15	4♊30	26 38	20 12	25 13	25 11	20 14
Jun 1	16 16	28 09	21 59	25 05	24 44	20 10
15	25 49	29 55	23 15	25 09	24 24	20 14
Jul 1	6♋33	2♍22	24 24	25 27	24 04	20 25
15	15 50	4 50	25 06	25 52	23 53	20 42
Aug 1	26 57	8 08	25 31	26 35	23 46	21 08
15	5♌59	11 01	25 30	27 18	23 47	21 34
Sep 1	16 52	14 39	25 01	28 16	23 57	22 09
15	25 44	17 41	24 18	29 08	24 12	22 40
Oct 1	5♍47	21 07	23 12	0♎09	24 36	23 15
15	14 29	24 02	22 07	1 01	25 01	23 44
Nov 1	24 58	27 21	20 48	1 59	25 36	24 15
15	3♎29	29 51	19 51	2 41	26 08	24 37
Dec 1	13 06	2♎18	19 05	3 20	26 44	24 55
15	21♎22	4♎01	18♈44	3♎44	27♏14	25♍04

1969	♂	♃	♄	♅	♆	♇
Jan 1	1♏11	5♎27	18♈48	3♎59	27♏47	25♍06
15	9 01	6 00	19 15	3 59	28 09	25 01
Feb 1	18 07	5 51	20 14	3 45	28 29	24 47
15	25 11	5 03	21 22	3 23	28 39	24 29
Mar 1	1♐40	3 43	22 44	2 53	28 43	24 09
15	7 24	2 03	24 17	2 19	28 39	23 46
Apr 1	12 56	29♍52	26 20	1 34	28 27	23 19
15	15 51	28 14	28 06	1 00	28 11	22 59
May 1	16 41	26 51	0♉08	0 27	27 48	22 41
15	14 51	26 13	1 52	0 06	27 26	22 30
Jun 1	9 53	26 13	3 51	29♍53	26 59	22 25
15	5 18	26 51	5 19	29 54	26 38	22 27
Jul 1	2 04	28 14	6 46	0♎07	26 18	22 37
15	2 01	29 55	7 46	0 29	26 05	22 53
Aug 1	5 21	2♎29	8 35	1 08	25 57	23 18
15	10 20	4 55	8 55	1 49	25 57	23 44
Sep 1	18 23	8 12	8 51	2 46	26 06	24 19
15	26 13	11 04	8 25	3 36	26 20	24 50
Oct 1	6♑08	14 29	7 34	4 37	26 43	25 25
15	15 26	17 31	6 35	5 29	27 07	25 55
Nov 1	27 18	21 11	5 14	6 30	27 42	26 27
15	7♒23	24 05	4 08	7 14	28 13	26 50
Dec 1	19 09	27 14	3 04	7 56	28 49	27 09
15	29♒33	29♎43	2♉25	8♎23	29♏19	27♍20

1970	♂	♃	♄	♅	♆	♇
Jan 1	12♓14	2♏20	2♉04	8♎43	29♏53	27♍24
15	22 40	4 01	2 10	8 47	0♐17	27 19
Feb 1	5♈15	5 25	2 47	8 38	0 38	27 06
15	15 30	5 56	3 39	8 19	0 49	26 50
Mar 1	25 39	5 50	4 48	7 52	0 53	26 29
15	5♉40	5 09	6 12	7 19	0 51	26 07
Apr 1	17 39	3 36	8 07	6 35	0 40	25 39
15	27 23	1 56	9 50	5 59	0 25	25 19
May 1	8♊21	29♎55	11 52	5 24	0 03	24 59
15	17 49	28 17	13 40	5 00	29♏41	24 48
Jun 1	29 09	26 49	15 47	4 43	29 14	24 41
15	8♋23	26 11	17 25	4 40	28 52	24 42
Jul 1	18 49	26 09	19 07	4 49	28 32	24 52
15	27 53	26 46	20 23	5 07	28 18	25 06
Aug 1	8♌49	28 12	21 35	5 42	28 09	25 31
15	17 46	29 54	22 15	6 20	28 08	25 56
Sep 1	28 36	2♏29	22 37	7 15	28 15	26 31
15	7♍30	4 57	22 32	8 04	28 28	27 01
Oct 1	17 39	8 04	22 01	9 04	28 50	27 37
15	26 32	10 58	21 14	9 57	29 14	28 07
Nov 1	7♎20	14 39	20 00	10 59	29 48	28 41
15	16 13	17 44	18 53	11 45	0♐18	29 05
Dec 1	26 23	21 14	17 38	12 30	0 54	29 25
15	5♏17	24♏12	16♉42	13♎01	1♐25	29♍37

1971	♂	♃	♄	♅	♆	♇
Jan 1	16♏04	27♏35	15♉57	13♎25	2♐00	29♍42
15	24 55	0♐06	15 42	13 34	2 24	29 40
Feb 1	5♐37	2 44	15 54	13 29	2 46	29 27
15	14 22	4 27	16 27	13 13	2 58	29 12
Mar 1	23 01	5 41	17 20	12 49	3 04	28 52
15	1♑34	6 21	18 30	12 17	3 03	28 30
Apr 1	11 41	6 21	20 13	11 34	2 53	28 02
15	19 45	5 41	21 50	10 58	2 39	27 41
May 1	28 30	4 16	23 49	10 21	2 18	27 20
15	5♒34	2 39	25 37	9 54	1 56	27 07
Jun 1	13 03	0 30	27 48	9 33	1 29	26 59
15	17 54	28♏52	29 33	9 26	1 07	27 00
Jul 1	21 18	27 27	1♊26	9 31	0 45	27 08
15	21 52	26 45	2 55	9 46	0 31	27 21
Aug 1	19 21	26 41	4 27	10 17	0 20	27 45
15	15 46	27 16	5 26	10 52	0 18	28 10
Sep 1	12 22	28 44	6 14	11 44	0 24	28 44
15	12 05	0♐27	6 31	12 32	0 36	29 15
Oct 1	14 51	2 55	6 24	13 31	0 57	29 51
15	19 31	5 26	5 56	14 24	1 20	0♎22
Nov 1	27 10	8 49	4 57	15 27	1 54	0 56
15	4♓36	11 48	3 55	16 15	2 24	1 21
Dec 1	13 55	15 22	2 37	17 03	3 00	1 43
15	22♓32	18♐32	1♊31	17♎37	3♐31	1♎56

1972	♂	♃	♄	♅	♆	♇
Jan 1	3♈23	22♐21	0♊25	18♎05	4♐06	2♎03
15	12 30	25 24	29♉50	18 17	4 31	2 01
Feb 1	23 40	28 53	29 35	18 17	4 55	1 51
15	2♉55	1♑29	29 47	18 05	5 08	1 36
Mar 1	12 49	3 56	0♊23	17 42	5 15	1 15
15	22 01	5 48	1 18	17 12	5 14	0 53
Apr 1	3♊08	7 26	2 46	16 30	5 05	0 25
15	12 14	8 10	4 14	15 54	4 52	0 03
May 1	22 35	8 16	6 06	15 16	4 31	29♍42
15	1♋34	7 42	7 51	14 47	4 09	29 29
Jun 1	12 26	6 18	10 03	14 23	3 42	29 20
15	21 20	4 42	11 51	14 13	3 20	29 19
Jul 1	1♌28	2 40	13 52	14 14	2 58	29 27
15	10 20	0 59	15 30	14 26	2 43	29 39
Aug 1	21 06	29♐24	17 18	14 54	2 32	0♎03
15	29 58	28 39	18 32	15 26	2 29	0 27
Sep 1	10♍47	28 33	19 42	16 16	2 34	1 01
15	19 44	29 09	20 19	17 03	2 46	1 32
Oct 1	0♎01	0♑32	20 36	18 01	3 05	2 09
15	9 05	2 16	20 27	18 54	3 28	2 40
Nov 1	20 10	4 57	19 50	19 57	4 01	3 15
15	29 23	7 33	18 59	20 46	4 32	3 40
Dec 1	10♏01	10 50	17 46	21 36	5 08	4 03
15	19♏24	13♑55	16♊37	22♎13	5♐39	4♎17

1973	♂	♃	♄	♅	♆	♇
Jan 1	0♐54	17♑49	15♊18	22♎45	6♐14	4♎25
15	10 28	21 05	14 26	23 00	6 39	4 24
Feb 1	22 11	25 02	13 47	23 03	7 04	4 14
15	1♑55	28 11	13 38	22 54	7 18	4 00
Mar 1	11 44	1♒11	13 51	22 35	7 25	3 41
15	21 36	3 57	14 26	22 08	7 26	3 19
Apr 1	3♒38	6 56	15 34	21 28	7 18	2 51
15	13 35	8 58	16 48	20 52	7 05	2 29
May 1	24 56	10 45	18 29	20 12	6 45	2 07
15	4♓48	11 44	20 07	19 41	6 24	1 53
Jun 1	16 37	12 08	22 15	19 13	5 57	1 42
15	26 07	11 46	24 04	19 00	5 35	1 41
Jul 1	6♈32	10 39	26 08	18 57	5 12	1 47
15	15 07	9 10	27 54	19 05	4 56	1 58
Aug 1	24 30	7 01	29 54	19 28	4 44	2 21
15	1♉01	5 15	1♋22	19 58	4 40	2 44
Sep 1	6 47	3 30	2 52	20 44	4 44	3 18
15	9 05	2 35	3 49	21 29	4 54	3 49
Oct 1	8 22	2 18	4 31	22 26	5 13	4 25
15	4 56	2 44	4 45	23 19	5 35	4 57
Nov 1	29♈22	4 04	4 33	24 23	6 07	5 33
15	26 08	5 47	4 00	25 13	6 37	6 00
Dec 1	25 28	8 17	3 01	26 05	7 13	6 24
15	27♈32	10♒53	1♋56	26♎44	7♐44	6♎39

1974	♂	♃	♄	♅	♆	♇
Jan 1	2♉33	14♒25	0♋33	27♎20	8♐20	6♎49
15	8 08	17 33	29♊28	27 39	8 46	6 49
Feb 1	16 04	21 32	28 27	27 47	9 12	6 41
15	23 16	24 53	27 56	27 42	9 27	6 27
Mar 1	0♊52	28 14	27 47	27 26	9 35	6 09
15	8 45	1♓31	28 00	27 02	9 37	5 47
Apr 1	18 35	5 20	28 44	26 23	9 31	5 19
15	26 50	8 16	29 41	25 48	9 19	4 57
May 1	6♋22	11 17	1♋06	25 07	8 59	4 34
15	14 47	13 34	2 34	24 35	8 39	4 18
Jun 1	25 06	15 47	4 34	24 04	8 12	4 07
15	3♌39	17 03	6 19	23 47	7 49	4 04
Jul 1	13 29	17 48	8 24	23 40	7 26	4 08
15	22 09	17 47	10 12	23 44	7 10	4 19
Aug 1	2♍46	16 55	12 20	24 03	6 56	4 40
15	11 35	15 36	13 59	24 29	6 51	5 03
Sep 1	22 25	13 31	15 45	25 12	6 53	5 37
15	1♎26	11 41	16 59	25 55	7 02	6 07
Oct 1	11 51	9 48	18 03	26 51	7 20	6 44
15	21 06	8 38	18 39	27 42	7 41	7 16
Nov 1	2♏30	8 00	18 54	28 46	8 13	7 53
15	12 01	8 13	18 43	29 38	8 42	8 20
Dec 1	23 04	9 15	18 04	0♏32	9 18	8 46
15	2♐52	10♓47	17♋12	1♏13	9♐50	9♎02

1975	♂	♃	♄	♅	♆	♇
Jan 1	14♐58	13♓19	15♋52	1♏53	10♐26	9♎13
15	25 04	15 51	14 43	2 15	10 53	9 15
Feb 1	7♑29	19 20	13 27	2 28	11 19	9 08
15	17 51	22 28	12 37	2 26	11 35	8 56
Mar 1	28 19	25 45	12 07	2 14	11 45	8 38
15	8♒53	29 06	11 57	1 53	11 48	8 17
Apr 1	21 47	3♈13	12 14	1 17	11 43	7 49
15	2♓26	6 34	12 51	0 43	11 32	7 26
May 1	14 37	10 16	13 57	0 02	11 13	7 03
15	25 13	13 20	15 11	29♎28	10 53	6 46
Jun 1	7♈59	16 44	16 58	28 54	10 26	6 33
15	18 19	19 13	18 37	28 34	10 04	6 29
Jul 1	29 53	21 36	20 37	28 22	9 40	6 32
15	9♉43	23 11	22 25	28 23	9 23	6 42
Aug 1	21 10	24 23	24 37	28 38	9 08	7 02
15	0♊05	24 42	26 22	29 00	9 02	7 24
Sep 1	10 07	24 13	28 20	29 40	9 03	7 57
15	17 30	23 08	29 47	0♏21	9 11	8 27
Oct 1	24 40	21 20	1♌11	1 14	9 28	9 04
15	29 23	19 28	2 06	2 05	9 48	9 36
Nov 1	2♋27	17 17	2 48	3 09	10 19	10 14
15	2 09	15 51	2 59	4 01	10 48	10 42
Dec 1	28♊25	14 54	2 44	4 56	11 23	11 09
15	23♊12	14♈47	2♌09	5♏40	11♐55	11♎26

1976	♂	♃	♄	♅	♆	♇
Jan 1	17♊22	15♈32	1♌04	6♏23	12♐32	11♎40
15	14 57	16 51	29♋58	6 49	12 59	11 43
Feb 1	15 29	19 08	28 35	7 06	13 26	11 37
15	18 16	21 31	27 32	7 08	13 43	11 26
Mar 1	22 57	24 26	26 40	6 59	13 55	11 08
15	28 28	27 25	26 11	6 40	13 58	10 47
Apr 1	6♋10	1♉17	26 03	6 06	13 54	10 19
15	13 07	4 35	26 20	5 33	13 44	9 56
May 1	21 31	8 25	27 04	4 52	13 26	9 32
15	29 11	11 45	28 03	4 18	13 06	9 15
Jun 1	8♌48	15 41	29 34	3 42	12 39	9 01
15	16 55	18 47	1♌03	3 20	12 17	8 56
Jul 1	26 24	22 06	2 56	3 05	11 53	8 58
15	4♍52	24 42	4 41	3 02	11 35	9 07
Aug 1	15 20	27 25	6 52	3 13	11 20	9 26
15	24 07	29 11	8 39	3 33	11 13	9 48
Sep 1	4♎59	0♊38	10 45	4 10	11 13	10 20
15	14 06	1 10	12 21	4 48	11 20	10 51
Oct 1	24 43	1 00	13 59	5 40	11 36	11 27
15	4♏11	0 09	15 09	6 30	11 56	12 00
Nov 1	15 54	28♉24	16 13	7 33	12 26	12 38
15	25 44	26 35	16 43	8 26	12 55	13 07
Dec 1	7♐11	24 26	16 52	9 23	13 31	13 35
15	17♐23	22♉49	16♌36	10♏07	14♐02	13♎53

1977	♂	♃	♄	♅	♆	♇
Jan 1	29♐59	21♉32	15♌50	10♏53	14♐39	14♎07
15	10♑30	21 10	14 54	11 21	15 07	14 11
Feb 1	23 28	21 38	13 33	11 42	15 35	14 07
15	4♒15	22 43	12 25	11 47	15 52	13 56
Mar 1	15 07	24 21	11 24	11 42	16 04	13 40
15	26 01	26 27	10 37	11 26	16 09	13 20
Apr 1	9♓17	29 29	10 03	10 56	16 06	12 52
15	20 12	2♊18	9 58	10 24	15 57	12 29
May 1	2♈35	5 45	10 18	9 44	15 40	12 04
15	13 19	8 55	10 57	9 09	15 20	11 46
Jun 1	26 10	12 51	12 09	8 31	14 54	11 31
15	6♉35	16 06	13 24	8 06	14 31	11 25
Jul 1	18 13	19 46	15 05	7 47	14 07	11 25
15	28 09	22 51	16 43	7 41	13 48	11 33
Aug 1	9♊52	26 23	18 50	7 48	13 32	11 51
15	19 10	29 02	20 37	8 04	13 24	12 12
Sep 1	29 59	1♋50	22 47	8 37	13 23	12 44
15	8♋26	3 42	24 29	9 13	13 29	13 13
Oct 1	17 26	5 15	26 17	10 02	13 44	13 50
15	24 37	6 00	27 41	10 50	14 03	14 23
Nov 1	2♌09	6 03	29 04	11 53	14 32	15 02
15	7 04	5 22	29 54	12 46	15 00	15 32
Dec 1	10 41	3 53	0♍27	13 43	15 36	16 00
15	11♌32	2♋09	0♍32	14♏30	16♐07	16♎20

1978	♂	♃	♄	♅	♆	♇
Jan 1	9♌03	29♊52	0♍10	15♏19	16♐45	16♎36
15	4 24	28 10	29♌29	15 50	17 13	16 41
Feb 1	27♋47	26 41	28 20	16 15	17 42	16 39
15	23 48	26 07	27 14	16 24	18 00	16 29
Mar 1	22 17	26 12	26 07	16 22	18 13	16 14
15	23 12	26 56	25 06	16 10	18 19	15 54
Apr 1	26 54	28 34	24 11	15 43	18 17	15 27
15	1♌30	0♋26	23 45	15 13	18 09	15 03
May 1	7 59	3 03	23 41	14 34	17 53	14 38
15	14 26	5 39	23 59	13 59	17 34	14 19
Jun 1	22 59	9 07	24 48	13 19	17 08	14 03
15	0♍29	12 08	25 47	12 52	16 46	13 55
Jul 1	9 28	15 42	27 13	12 30	16 21	13 55
15	17 39	18 51	28 41	12 20	16 02	14 01
Aug 1	27 55	22 38	0♍39	12 22	15 44	14 18
15	6♎38	25 40	2 23	12 35	15 35	14 38
Sep 1	17 32	29 09	4 32	13 03	15 33	15 08
15	26 45	1♌47	6 17	13 36	15 38	15 38
Oct 1	7♏32	4 26	8 13	14 23	15 51	16 14
15	17 13	6 22	9 46	15 10	16 09	16 48
Nov 1	29 15	8 04	11 25	16 12	16 38	17 27
15	9♐22	8 52	12 31	17 04	17 06	17 57
Dec 1	21 11	9 01	13 25	18 03	17 41	18 27
15	1♑43	8♌27	13♍51	18♏51	18♐12	18♎48

1979	♂	♃	♄	♅	♆	♇
Jan 1	14♑42	7♌00	13♍54	19♏42	18♐50	19♎06
15	25 33	5 19	13 32	20 16	19 19	19 13
Feb 1	8♒51	3 04	12 40	20 45	19 49	19 12
15	19 52	1 20	11 42	20 58	20 08	19 03
Mar 1	0♓54	0 00	10 36	21 00	20 22	18 49
15	11 57	29♋12	9 30	20 51	20 29	18 30
Apr 1	25 17	29 04	8 19	20 28	20 29	18 03
15	6♈11	29 38	7 36	20 00	20 21	17 39
May 1	18 29	0♌58	7 08	19 22	20 06	17 14
15	29 07	2 39	7 06	18 47	19 49	16 54
Jun 1	11♉47	5 13	7 31	18 06	19 23	16 36
15	22 02	7 40	8 12	17 37	19 00	16 28
Jul 1	3♊30	10 46	9 20	17 11	18 35	16 26
15	13 19	13 40	10 35	16 59	18 16	16 31
Aug 1	24 56	17 19	12 21	16 56	17 57	16 46
15	4♋15	20 23	13 58	17 05	17 47	17 05
Sep 1	15 15	24 06	16 03	17 30	17 43	17 35
15	24 00	27 04	17 49	18 00	17 47	18 04
Oct 1	3♌37	0♍18	19 47	18 44	18 00	18 40
15	11 40	2 55	21 27	19 29	18 17	19 13
Nov 1	20 49	5 43	23 18	20 29	18 44	19 53
15	27 45	7 36	24 36	21 21	19 11	20 24
Dec 1	4♍44	9 12	25 48	22 20	19 46	20 55
15	9♍46	10♍02	26♍33	23♏09	20♐17	21♎18

1980	♂	♃	♄	♅	♆	♇
Jan 1	13♍58	10♍12	26♍59	24♏03	20♐55	21♎37
15	15 20	9 39	26 58	24 39	21 25	21 45
Feb 1	13 44	8 12	26 28	25 12	21 55	21 46
15	9 42	6 33	25 43	25 29	22 16	21 39
Mar 1	3 54	4 36	24 40	25 34	22 31	21 24
15	29♌04	2 52	23 35	25 28	22 39	21 06
Apr 1	26 03	1 14	22 16	25 08	22 40	20 39
15	26 19	0 26	21 21	24 43	22 33	20 15
May 1	29 11	0 16	20 35	24 06	22 19	19 49
15	3♍24	0 46	20 14	23 32	22 01	19 29
Jun 1	10 05	2 06	20 16	22 50	21 36	19 11
15	16 31	3 43	20 40	22 19	21 13	19 01
Jul 1	24 41	6 03	21 29	21 52	20 48	18 58
15	2♎23	8 25	22 30	21 36	20 28	19 03
Aug 1	12 19	11 38	24 03	21 30	20 09	19 17
15	20 55	14 28	25 32	21 36	19 59	19 35
Sep 1	1♏48	18 05	27 30	21 57	19 54	20 04
15	11 06	21 06	29 12	22 25	19 57	20 33
Oct 1	22 04	24 33	1♎11	23 06	20 09	21 09
15	1♐57	27 30	2 54	23 50	20 25	21 42
Nov 1	14 16	0♎53	4 51	24 49	20 52	22 23
15	24 40	3 27	6 19	25 40	21 19	22 54
Dec 1	6♑47	6 02	7 45	26 40	21 54	23 26
15	17♑34	7♎53	8♎43	27♏30	22♐25	23♎49

1981	♂	♃	♄	♅	♆	♇
Jan 1	0♒50	9♎30	9♎30	28♏25	23♐03	24♎09
15	11 51	10 14	9 46	29 03	23 33	24 18
Feb 1	25 18	10 18	9 38	29 39	24 04	24 20
15	6♓22	9 41	9 08	29 58	24 25	24 14
Mar 1	17 24	8 30	8 21	0♐06	24 40	24 02
15	28 21	6 55	7 23	0 04	24 49	23 44
Apr 1	11♈31	4 45	6 04	29♏48	24 51	23 18
15	22 13	3 03	5 01	29 25	24 46	22 54
May 1	4♉16	1 30	4 00	28 51	24 33	22 28
15	14 37	0 41	3 22	28 17	24 16	22 07
Jun 1	26 58	0 28	3 01	27 35	23 51	21 47
15	6♊57	0 56	3 05	27 02	23 28	21 37
Jul 1	18 07	2 08	3 33	26 32	23 03	21 32
15	27 43	3 41	4 18	26 14	22 43	21 35
Aug 1	9♋08	6 07	5 34	26 03	22 22	21 48
15	18 21	8 28	6 51	26 06	22 11	22 05
Sep 1	29 19	11 40	8 39	26 23	22 05	22 33
15	8♌09	14 30	10 16	26 47	22 07	23 01
Oct 1	18 01	17 54	12 12	27 25	22 18	23 37
15	26 25	20 56	13 55	28 07	22 33	24 10
Nov 1	6♍18	24 36	15 57	29 04	22 59	24 51
15	14 07	27 33	17 32	29 54	23 25	25 23
Dec 1	22 37	0♏46	19 09	0♐54	23 59	25 56
15	29♍31	3♏20	20♎21	1♐44	24♐31	26♎20

1982	♂	♃	♄	♅	♆	♇
Jan 1	7♎03	6♏04	21♎27	2♐41	25♐09	26♎42
15	12 17	7 54	22 01	3 22	25 39	26 52
Feb 1	16 59	9 30	22 15	4 01	26 11	26 56
15	18 59	10 12	22 03	4 23	26 33	26 51
Mar 1	18 45	10 18	21 32	4 35	26 49	26 40
15	16 03	9 47	20 45	4 37	26 59	26 23
Apr 1	10 09	8 25	19 32	4 25	27 03	25 57
15	4 59	6 51	18 28	4 05	26 58	25 34
May 1	1 08	4 49	17 18	3 33	26 46	25 07
15	0 27	3 08	16 27	3 00	26 30	24 46
Jun 1	2 46	1 30	15 45	2 18	26 06	24 25
15	6 44	0 41	15 30	1 45	25 44	24 13
Jul 1	12 58	0 27	15 38	1 12	25 18	24 07
15	19 32	0 53	16 05	0 51	24 57	24 09
Aug 1	28 35	2 08	17 01	0 36	24 36	24 20
15	6♏45	3 41	18 05	0 35	24 24	24 36
Sep 1	17 21	6 08	19 40	0 48	24 17	25 03
15	26 34	8 31	21 10	1 09	24 18	25 30
Oct 1	7♐34	11 34	23 01	1 44	24 27	26 05
15	17 33	14 26	24 42	2 23	24 41	26 39
Nov 1	0♑02	18 06	26 45	3 18	25 06	27 19
15	10 34	21 11	28 24	4 07	25 32	27 52
Dec 1	22 49	24 42	0♏10	5 06	26 05	28 26
15	3♒41	27♏43	1♏32	5♐58	26♐36	28♎51

1983	♂	♃	♄	♅	♆	♇
Jan 1	17♒00	1♐11	2♏54	6♐56	27♐15	29♎14
15	28 00	3 47	3 44	7 39	27 45	29 26
Feb 1	11♓20	6 34	4 19	8 21	28 18	29 32
15	22 15	8 25	4 26	8 46	28 41	29 28
Mar 1	3♈04	9 48	4 12	9 02	28 58	29 18
15	13 46	10 40	3 39	9 07	29 09	29 03
Apr 1	26 35	10 54	2 39	8 59	29 14	28 38
15	6♉58	10 25	1 38	8 42	29 11	28 15
May 1	18 37	9 12	0 26	8 12	29 00	27 48
15	28 39	7 40	29♎26	7 41	28 45	27 26
Jun 1	10♊36	5 33	28 28	6 59	28 21	27 04
15	20 17	3 50	27 57	6 25	27 59	26 51
Jul 1	1♋09	2 16	27 43	5 51	27 33	26 43
15	10 32	1 23	27 52	5 27	27 12	26 44
Aug 1	21 44	1 05	28 29	5 09	26 50	26 53
15	0♌50	1 30	29 18	5 04	26 37	27 08
Sep 1	11 45	2 45	0♏38	5 12	26 29	27 33
15	20 37	4 20	1 58	5 30	26 28	28 00
Oct 1	0♍37	6 40	3 40	6 01	26 36	28 35
15	9 16	9 06	5 17	6 38	26 50	29 08
Nov 1	19 36	12 24	7 20	7 30	27 13	29 49
15	27 58	15 21	9 00	8 19	27 38	0♏22
Dec 1	7♎20	18 54	10 51	9 17	28 11	0 56
15	15♎19	22♐04	12♏21	10♐09	28♐42	1♏23

1984	♂	♃	♄	♅	♆	♇
Jan 1	24♎40	25♐55	13♏56	11♐08	29♐21	1♏47
15	1♏59	29 00	15 00	11 53	29 51	2 01
Feb 1	10 14	2♑34	15 54	12 38	0♑25	2 08
15	16 19	5 16	16 18	13 06	0 48	2 06
Mar 1	21 52	7 50	16 22	13 26	1 08	1 56
15	25 46	9 51	16 04	13 34	1 20	1 41
Apr 1	28 13	11 42	15 18	13 29	1 25	1 17
15	27 47	12 37	14 26	13 14	1 23	0 54
May 1	24 20	12 58	13 16	12 47	1 13	0 27
15	19 32	12 36	12 13	12 17	0 58	0 05
Jun 1	14 05	11 24	11 04	11 36	0 35	29♎42
15	11 51	9 54	10 20	11 02	0 13	29 29
Jul 1	12 32	7 54	9 49	10 26	29♐47	29 20
15	15 39	6 10	9 42	10 00	29 26	29 19
Aug 1	21 53	4 24	9 59	9 39	29 03	29 28
15	28 32	3 29	10 34	9 32	28 50	29 42
Sep 1	7♐56	3 08	11 38	9 37	28 41	0♏07
15	16 33	3 32	12 47	9 52	28 40	0 33
Oct 1	27 05	4 42	14 21	10 20	28 47	1 07
15	6♑48	6 18	15 52	10 54	28 59	1 40
Nov 1	19 04	8 50	17 51	11 45	29 23	2 21
15	29 26	11 20	19 31	12 32	29 47	2 54
Dec 1	11♒30	14 33	21 24	13 30	0♑20	3 29
15	22♒09	17♑35	22♏59	14♐22	0♑51	3♏56

1985	♂	♃	♄	♅	♆	♇
Jan 1	5♓08	21♑27	24♏44	15♐22	1♑29	4♏22
15	15 49	24 44	25 58	16 07	2 00	4 36
Feb 1	28 42	28 42	27 08	16 55	2 34	4 44
15	9♈12	1♒54	27 46	17 25	2 58	4 43
Mar 1	19 36	4 58	28 05	17 46	3 17	4 36
15	29 51	7 50	28 05	17 57	3 30	4 22
Apr 1	12♉06	10 57	27 38	17 57	3 37	3 58
15	22 02	13 08	26 57	17 46	3 35	3 36
May 1	3♊12	15 06	25 55	17 22	3 26	3 09
15	12 50	16 17	24 53	16 54	3 13	2 46
Jun 1	24 21	16 56	23 38	16 14	2 50	2 22
15	3♋42	16 48	22 44	15 39	2 29	2 08
Jul 1	14 16	15 54	21 57	15 02	2 03	1 58
15	23 24	14 34	21 34	14 34	1 41	1 56
Aug 1	4♌24	12 29	21 30	14 10	1 18	2 02
15	13 24	10 41	21 48	13 59	1 03	2 15
Sep 1	24 15	8 46	22 34	14 00	0 53	2 38
15	3♍08	7 40	23 30	14 11	0 51	3 03
Oct 1	13 15	7 08	24 51	14 36	0 57	3 37
15	22 04	7 21	26 15	15 07	1 08	4 09
Nov 1	2♎44	8 27	28 07	15 55	1 30	4 51
15	11 30	9 59	29 45	16 41	1 54	5 24
Dec 1	21 27	12 20	1♐39	17 38	2 26	6 00
15	0♏08	14♒49	3♐17	18♐29	2♑57	6♏28

1986	♂	♃	♄	♅	♆	♇
Jan 1	10♏34	18♒15	5♐10	19♐30	3♑35	6♏55
15	19 05	21 20	6 33	20 17	4 06	7 11
Feb 1	29 15	25 18	7 57	21 07	4 41	7 21
15	7♐27	28 38	8 50	21 40	5 06	7 21
Mar 1	15 26	2♓00	9 25	22 04	5 25	7 14
15	23 08	5 19	9 41	22 18	5 39	7 02
Apr 1	1♑56	9 12	9 34	22 22	5 48	6 40
15	8 32	12 13	9 08	22 14	5 48	6 17
May 1	15 05	15 21	8 18	21 53	5 40	5 51
15	19 33	17 46	7 22	21 27	5 27	5 27
Jun 1	22 43	20 11	6 07	20 49	5 05	5 03
15	22 53	21 38	5 07	20 14	4 44	4 47
Jul 1	20 13	22 38	4 07	19 36	4 18	4 36
15	16 17	22 51	3 29	19 07	3 56	4 32
Aug 1	12 18	22 16	3 06	18 39	3 33	4 37
15	11 28	21 07	3 07	18 26	3 17	4 48
Sep 1	14 00	19 10	3 34	18 22	3 05	5 10
15	18 34	17 19	4 15	18 30	3 02	5 35
Oct 1	25 46	15 20	5 23	18 51	3 07	6 07
15	3♒20	13 58	6 36	19 19	3 17	6 39
Nov 1	13 34	13 04	8 20	20 04	3 38	7 20
15	22 36	13 03	9 54	20 48	4 01	7 54
Dec 1	3♓19	13 50	11 46	21 44	4 32	8 31
15	12♓56	15♓10	13♐26	22♐34	5♑03	8♏59

1987	♂	♃	♄	♅	♆	♇
Jan 1	24♓45	17♓31	15♐23	23♐36	5♑41	9♏28
15	4♈32	19 55	16 53	24 24	6 13	9 45
Feb 1	16 24	23 17	18 29	25 16	6 48	9 56
15	26 07	26 21	19 35	25 51	7 13	9 58
Mar 1	5♉46	29 35	20 25	26 18	7 34	9 53
15	15 21	2♈55	20 57	26 36	7 49	9 42
Apr 1	26 51	7 02	21 10	26 44	7 59	9 20
15	6♊13	10 24	20 59	26 39	8 00	8 59
May 1	16 49	14 09	20 25	26 22	7 53	8 32
15	26 00	17 16	19 38	25 58	7 41	8 09
Jun 1	7♋04	20 48	18 29	25 21	7 20	7 43
15	16 06	23 24	17 27	24 48	7 00	7 27
Jul 1	26 21	25 56	16 19	24 09	6 34	7 14
15	5♌18	27 42	15 30	23 38	6 12	7 09
Aug 1	16 07	29 09	14 48	23 07	5 47	7 12
15	25 01	29 41	14 33	22 51	5 31	7 22
Sep 1	5♍50	29 29	14 40	22 43	5 18	7 43
15	14 46	28 37	15 06	22 48	5 14	8 06
Oct 1	24 59	26 58	15 58	23 05	5 17	8 38
15	3♎59	25 10	17 00	23 30	5 26	9 09
Nov 1	14 57	22 54	18 33	24 12	5 46	9 50
15	24 02	21 19	20 01	24 54	6 08	10 24
Dec 1	4♏29	20 08	21 49	25 48	6 39	11 01
15	13♏41	19♈46	23♐28	26♐38	7♑09	11♏30

1988	♂	♃	♄	♅	♆	♇
Jan 1	24♏55	20♈14	25♐28	27♐40	7♑47	12♏00
15	4♐14	21 20	27 03	28 29	8 19	12 18
Feb 1	15 36	23 25	28 49	29 22	8 55	12 32
15	25 00	25 39	0♑05	0♑00	9 21	12 35
Mar 1	5♑06	28 27	1 12	0 32	9 43	12 31
15	14 33	1♉21	1 57	0 52	9 59	12 20
Apr 1	26 01	5 08	2 28	1 02	10 10	12 00
15	5♒26	8 24	2 32	1 00	10 11	11 39
May 1	16 06	12 13	2 14	0 46	10 06	11 12
15	25 17	15 33	1 39	0 24	9 54	10 49
Jun 1	6♓07	19 31	0 39	29♐49	9 34	10 23
15	14 37	22 40	29♐39	29 16	9 13	10 05
Jul 1	23 36	26 03	28 29	28 37	8 48	9 52
15	0♈32	28 46	27 32	28 05	8 25	9 46
Aug 1	7 10	1♊37	26 36	27 33	8 01	9 48
15	10 32	3 33	26 07	27 14	7 44	9 57
Sep 1	11 16	5 13	25 56	27 03	7 30	10 17
15	8 55	5 59	26 08	27 05	7 25	10 39
Oct 1	4 24	6 04	26 44	27 19	7 28	11 10
15	1 02	5 26	27 34	27 42	7 36	11 41
Nov 1	29♓58	3 53	28 55	28 22	7 55	12 22
15	1♈52	2 09	0♑16	29 02	8 17	12 56
Dec 1	6 30	29♉59	1 59	29 54	8 47	13 33
15	12♈05	28♉15	3♑35	0♑44	9♑17	14♏03

1989	♂	♃	♄	♅	♆	♇
Jan 1	20♈12	26♉44	5♑36	1♑45	9♑55	14♏34
15	27 36	26 08	7 14	2 35	10 27	14 53
Feb 1	7♉10	26 20	9 06	3 30	11 03	15 07
15	15 21	27 12	10 31	4 09	11 29	15 11
Mar 1	23 43	28 38	11 43	4 40	11 52	15 08
15	2♊13	0♊35	12 42	5 03	12 08	14 59
Apr 1	12 37	3 28	13 32	5 18	12 20	14 40
15	21 14	6 11	13 53	5 19	12 23	14 19
May 1	1♋07	9 33	13 53	5 08	12 18	13 53
15	9 47	12 40	13 32	4 49	12 08	13 30
Jun 1	20 19	16 34	12 46	4 17	11 49	13 03
15	29 01	19 49	11 53	3 45	11 29	12 45
Jul 1	8♌58	23 29	10 44	3 06	11 03	12 30
15	17 43	26 36	9 43	2 33	10 41	12 23
Aug 1	28 23	0♋12	8 36	1 58	10 15	12 23
15	7♍13	2 56	7 53	1 37	9 58	12 31
Sep 1	18 02	5 52	7 23	1 22	9 43	12 49
15	27 02	7 53	7 19	1 21	9 37	13 10
Oct 1	7♎24	9 37	7 37	1 31	9 38	13 41
15	16 34	10 33	8 13	1 51	9 46	14 11
Nov 1	27 50	10 52	9 19	2 27	10 04	14 51
15	7♏15	10 24	10 30	3 05	10 24	15 25
Dec 1	18 08	9 07	12 05	3 56	10 54	16 03
15	27♏46	7♋29	13♑37	4♑44	11♑23	16♏33

1990	♂	♃	♄	♅	♆	♇
Jan 1	9♐39	5♋13	15♑36	5♑45	12♑01	17♏05
15	19 33	3 26	17 15	6 35	12 33	17 25
Feb 1	1♑44	1 44	19 13	7 32	13 09	17 41
15	11 53	0 58	20 45	8 13	13 37	17 47
Mar 1	22 08	0 50	22 07	8 47	13 59	17 45
15	2♒28	1 21	23 18	9 12	14 17	17 37
Apr 1	15 07	2 46	24 25	9 31	14 31	17 20
15	25 34	4 29	25 01	9 35	14 34	17 00
May 1	7♓32	6 57	25 20	9 28	14 31	16 34
15	17 58	9 27	25 15	9 12	14 22	16 11
Jun 1	0♈31	12 49	24 46	8 42	14 03	15 44
15	10 41	15 47	24 04	8 11	13 44	15 24
Jul 1	22 01	19 18	23 01	7 33	13 19	15 08
15	1♉36	22 26	22 00	6 59	12 56	15 00
Aug 1	12 39	26 14	20 46	6 23	12 30	14 59
15	21 06	29 18	19 53	5 59	12 12	15 05
Sep 1	0♊15	2♌50	19 06	5 41	11 56	15 21
15	6 35	5 32	18 46	5 36	11 49	15 41
Oct 1	11 54	8 18	18 45	5 43	11 49	16 11
15	14 19	10 21	19 06	5 59	11 55	16 40
Nov 1	13 38	12 15	19 55	6 32	12 12	17 20
15	10 03	13 13	20 55	7 07	12 32	17 54
Dec 1	4 11	13 36	22 19	7 56	13 00	18 32
15	29♉50	13♌14	23♑45	8♑43	13♑29	19♏03

1991

	♂	♃	♄	♅	♆	♇
Jan 1	27♉45	11♌59	25♑40	9♑44	14♑07	19♏36
15	28 51	10 25	27 19	10 34	14 39	19 57
Feb 1	2♊54	8 11	29 20	11 31	15 16	20 15
15	7 48	6 24	0♒56	12 14	15 44	20 22
Mar 1	13 41	4 55	2 26	12 50	16 07	20 22
15	20 16	3 56	3 47	13 19	16 26	20 15
Apr 1	28 56	3 33	5 09	13 41	16 41	19 58
15	6♋26	3 55	6 00	13 49	16 46	19 40
May 1	15 20	5 03	6 38	13 45	16 44	19 14
15	23 19	6 35	6 50	13 32	16 35	18 51
Jun 1	3♌13	9 00	6 40	13 05	16 18	18 24
15	11 31	11 21	6 11	12 35	15 59	18 04
Jul 1	21 08	14 22	5 20	11 58	15 34	17 46
15	29 41	17 12	4 23	11 24	15 12	17 37
Aug 1	10♍12	20 49	3 08	10 46	14 45	17 34
15	18 59	23 52	2 08	10 20	14 27	17 39
Sep 1	29 49	27 35	1 07	9 59	14 09	17 54
15	8♎53	0♍35	0 31	9 51	14 01	18 12
Oct 1	19 25	3 52	0 12	9 54	14 00	18 40
15	28 47	6 33	0 16	10 07	14 05	19 10
Nov 1	10♏22	9 27	0 48	10 36	14 20	19 49
15	20 04	11 28	1 34	11 09	14 39	20 22
Dec 1	1♐21	13 14	2 46	11 55	15 07	21 01
15	11♐24	14♍14	4♒03	12♑41	15♑35	21♏32

1992

	♂	♃	♄	♅	♆	♇
Jan 1	23♐47	14♍38	5♒51	13♑41	16♑13	22♏06
15	4♑09	14 16	7 28	14 31	16 45	22 28
Feb 1	16 55	13 01	9 29	15 29	17 22	22 47
15	27 34	11 29	11 09	16 14	17 50	22 56
Mar 1	9♒04	9 33	12 52	16 54	18 16	22 57
15	19 52	7 46	14 21	17 25	18 36	22 51
Apr 1	3♓02	5 58	15 55	17 50	18 51	22 35
15	13 53	5 01	16 59	18 00	18 57	22 17
May 1	26 14	4 38	17 52	17 59	18 56	21 52
15	6♈58	4 56	18 20	17 48	18 48	21 29
Jun 1	19 50	6 04	18 29	17 23	18 31	21 01
15	0♉15	7 32	18 15	16 55	18 13	20 41
Jul 1	11 55	9 44	17 37	16 19	17 48	20 23
15	21 51	12 01	16 48	15 45	17 26	20 13
Aug 1	3♊32	15 08	15 37	15 06	16 59	20 09
15	12 45	17 56	14 34	14 39	16 40	20 13
Sep 1	23 23	21 30	13 23	14 15	16 22	20 26
15	1♋33	24 30	12 36	14 04	16 14	20 45
Oct 1	10 05	27 58	12 01	14 04	16 11	21 12
15	16 36	0♎56	11 49	14 15	16 21	21 40
Nov 1	22 56	4 23	12 02	14 41	16 30	22 19
15	26 22	7 01	12 34	15 12	16 49	22 52
Dec 1	27 36	9 43	13 33	15 56	17 16	23 31
15	25♋50	11♎41	14♒41	16♑41	17♑44	24♏02

1993

	♂	♃	♄	♅	♆	♇
Jan 1	20♋25	13♎29	16♒21	17♑40	18♑21	24♏37
15	14 56	14 23	17 53	18 30	18 53	25 00
Feb 1	10 00	14 41	19 53	19 29	19 31	25 20
15	8 41	14 21	21 34	20 14	19 59	25 29
Mar 1	9 46	13 13	23 14	20 54	20 24	25 31
15	12 49	11 44	24 50	21 27	20 44	25 27
Apr 1	18 23	9 36	26 36	21 55	21 01	25 13
15	24 05	7 51	27 52	22 08	21 08	24 55
May 1	1♌27	6 11	29 02	22 11	21 08	24 31
15	8 27	5 12	29 46	22 03	21 01	24 08
Jun 1	17 28	4 45	0♓15	21 41	20 46	23 40
15	25 15	5 03	0 19	21 16	20 28	23 19
Jul 1	4♍28	6 03	29♒59	20 40	20 04	23 00
15	12 45	7 28	29 23	20 07	19 41	22 49
Aug 1	23 07	9 45	28 21	19 27	19 14	22 43
15	1♎52	12 01	27 20	18 58	18 55	22 46
Sep 1	12 45	15 08	26 03	18 31	18 36	22 58
15	21 55	17 56	25 06	18 18	18 26	23 15
Oct 1	2♏38	21 17	24 15	18 14	18 23	23 41
15	12 14	24 19	23 47	18 21	18 26	24 08
Nov 1	24 08	28 00	23 39	18 44	18 39	24 46
15	4♐09	0♏59	23 54	19 12	18 57	25 19
Dec 1	15 50	4 15	24 36	19 54	19 23	25 58
15	26♐14	6♏54	25♒32	20♑37	19♑51	26♏30

1994

	♂	♃	♄	♅	♆	♇
Jan 1	9♑04	9♏46	27♒00	21♑35	20♑28	27♏05
15	19 48	11 43	28 26	22 24	20 59	27 29
Feb 1	2♒59	13 30	0♓21	23 24	21 37	27 50
15	13 56	14 22	2 02	24 10	22 06	28 01
Mar 1	24 55	14 39	3 44	24 52	22 32	28 04
15	5♓56	14 20	5 24	25 27	22 53	28 01
Apr 1	19 16	13 10	7 20	25 58	23 11	27 49
15	0♈12	11 42	8 46	26 14	23 19	27 32
May 1	12 34	9 42	10 11	26 21	23 21	27 09
15	23 15	7 58	11 10	26 16	23 15	26 46
Jun 1	6♉01	6 11	12 00	25 58	23 00	26 18
15	16 21	5 12	12 21	25 34	22 43	25 57
Jul 1	27 54	4 46	12 21	25 00	22 20	25 37
15	7♊47	5 01	12 01	24 27	21 57	25 24
Aug 1	19 28	6 04	11 13	23 47	21 30	25 17
15	28 49	7 30	10 19	23 16	21 10	25 18
Sep 1	9♋47	9 48	9 04	22 47	20 50	25 28
15	18 27	12 06	8 01	22 31	20 40	25 44
Oct 1	27 55	15 04	6 56	22 23	20 34	26 09
15	5♌43	17 54	6 13	22 28	20 37	26 35
Nov 1	14 25	21 32	5 44	22 46	20 49	27 12
15	20 45	24 37	5 42	23 12	21 05	27 45
Dec 1	26 46	28 09	6 05	23 51	21 31	28 24
15	0♍34	1♐12	6♓46	24♑32	21♑58	28♏56

1995

	♂	♃	♄	♅	♆	♇
Jan 1	2♍39	4♐44	7♓59	25♑28	22♑34	29♏32
15	1 42	7 26	9 16	26 17	23 06	29 56
Feb 1	27♌11	10 20	11 04	27 17	23 44	0♐19
15	21 45	12 19	12 42	28 04	24 13	0 31
Mar 1	16 45	13 52	14 23	28 47	24 40	0 36
15	13 46	14 54	16 06	29 24	25 02	0 34
Apr 1	13 29	15 23	18 09	29 59	25 21	0 23
15	15 40	15 06	19 43	0♒18	25 30	0 08
May 1	20 11	14 04	21 21	0 28	25 33	29♏45
15	25 25	12 40	22 34	0 26	25 28	29 23
Jun 1	2♍55	10 35	23 44	0 11	25 15	28 55
15	9 51	8 50	24 22	29♑50	24 59	28 33
Jul 1	18 22	7 07	24 44	29 18	24 36	28 12
15	26 16	6 04	24 41	28 46	24 13	27 59
Aug 1	6♎21	5 32	24 13	28 05	23 46	27 50
15	14 59	5 33	23 31	27 34	23 25	27 50
Sep 1	25 52	6 49	22 22	27 02	23 05	27 58
15	5♏08	8 15	21 19	26 43	22 53	28 12
Oct 1	16 01	10 27	20 06	26 32	22 47	28 36
15	25 49	12 47	19 11	26 33	22 48	29 02
Nov 1	8♐01	16 01	18 22	26 48	22 58	29 38
15	18 19	18 55	18 02	27 11	23 14	0♐10
Dec 1	0♑19	22 26	18 04	27 47	23 38	0 48
15	11♑00	25♐36	18♓28	28♑26	24♑05	1♐21

1996

	♂	♃	♄	♅	♆	♇
Jan 1	24♑10	29♐29	19♓24	29♑21	24♑41	1♐57
15	5♒08	2♑37	20 28	0♒09	25 12	2 23
Feb 1	18 32	6 16	22 06	1 09	25 51	2 47
15	29 37	9 03	23 38	1 57	26 21	3 00
Mar 1	11♓28	11 44	25 24	2 44	26 49	3 06
15	22 28	13 54	27 08	3 23	27 12	3 05
Apr 1	5♈44	15 56	29 14	4 00	27 32	2 55
15	16 31	17 03	0♈54	4 21	27 42	2 41
May 1	28 40	17 38	2 42	4 34	27 45	2 19
15	9♉09	17 29	4 06	4 34	27 41	1 57
Jun 1	21 38	16 31	5 32	4 22	27 29	1 29
15	1♊15	15 09	6 27	4 03	27 13	1 07
Jul 1	13 00	13 13	7 08	3 32	26 50	0 45
15	22 41	11 26	7 23	3 01	26 28	0 31
Aug 1	4♋11	9 32	7 15	2 20	26 01	0 21
15	13 26	8 25	6 48	1 48	25 40	0 20
Sep 1	24 25	7 50	5 52	1 14	25 18	0 28
15	3♌13	8 02	4 53	0 54	25 06	0 41
Oct 1	13 01	8 59	3 38	0 41	24 59	1 04
15	21 18	10 25	2 35	0 39	25 00	1 29
Nov 1	0♍56	12 48	1 31	0 51	25 09	2 04
15	8 28	15 12	0 55	1 11	25 24	2 36
Dec 1	16 28	18 20	0 37	1 45	25 48	3 14
15	22♍46	21♑19	0♈44	2♒23	26♑14	3♐47

1997

	♂	♃	♄	♅	♆	♇
Jan 1	29♍14	25♑10	1♈20	3♒16	26♑50	4♐23
15	3♎13	28 26	2 11	4 04	27 21	4 50
Feb 1	5 46	2♒26	3 36	5 04	28 00	5 14
15	5 25	5 41	5 00	5 52	28 30	5 28
Mar 1	2 33	8 48	6 35	6 37	28 57	5 35
15	27♍41	11 45	8 16	7 17	29 20	5 35
Apr 1	21 19	15 01	10 23	7 57	29 42	5 27
15	17 47	17 20	12 08	8 21	29 53	5 13
May 1	16 48	19 30	14 03	8 37	29 57	4 52
15	18 27	20 53	15 38	8 40	29 55	4 31
Jun 1	22 56	21 49	17 20	8 32	29 43	4 03
15	28 09	21 54	18 28	8 15	29 28	3 41
Jul 1	5♎22	21 15	19 31	7 47	29 06	3 18
15	12 30	20 05	20 06	7 17	28 44	3 03
Aug 1	22 00	18 06	20 22	6 37	28 17	2 52
15	0♏24	16 18	20 13	6 04	27 55	2 50
Sep 1	11 09	14 15	19 36	5 28	27 33	2 56
15	20 26	12 58	18 47	5 05	27 20	3 07
Oct 1	1♐27	12 11	17 38	4 49	27 12	3 29
15	11 24	12 10	16 32	4 44	27 11	3 53
Nov 1	23 51	13 01	15 15	4 52	27 20	4 27
15	4♑21	14 22	14 24	5 09	27 33	4 59
Dec 1	16 35	16 33	13 45	5 40	27 56	5 36
15	27♑27	18♒55	13♈32	6♒16	28♑21	6♐09

1998

	♂	♃	♄	♅	♆	♇
Jan 1	10♒46	22♒15	13♈45	7♒07	28♑57	6♐46
15	21 48	25 16	14 19	7 54	29 28	7 13
Feb 1	5♓13	29 11	15 26	8 53	0♒07	7 39
15	16 13	2♓31	16 40	9 42	0 37	7 54
Mar 1	27 09	5 53	18 06	10 28	1 05	8 02
15	7♈58	9 14	19 41	11 10	1 29	8 03
Apr 1	20 57	13 11	21 46	11 52	1 51	7 56
15	1♉28	16 16	23 32	12 19	2 04	7 44
May 1	13 17	19 32	25 33	12 38	2 10	7 24
15	23 27	22 05	27 15	12 44	2 08	7 03
Jun 1	5♊34	24 41	29 09	12 40	1 58	6 35
15	15 21	26 21	0♉33	12 25	1 44	6 13
Jul 1	26 21	27 35	1 53	12 00	1 22	5 50
15	5♋48	28 03	2 46	11 31	1 01	5 34
Aug 1	17 06	27 45	3 26	10 51	0 33	5 21
15	26 15	26 49	3 38	10 18	0 11	5 18
Sep 1	7♌11	25 01	3 24	9 41	29♑49	5 22
15	16 02	23 12	2 51	9 16	29 34	5 33
Oct 1	26 00	21 08	1 54	8 56	29 25	5 52
15	4♍33	19 36	0 51	8 49	29 23	6 15
Nov 1	14 45	18 26	29♈30	8 53	29 30	6 49
15	22 56	18 10	28 28	9 07	29 43	7 20
Dec 1	2♎00	18 41	27 30	9 35	0♒05	7 57
15	9♎38	19♓49	26♈58	10♒08	0♒29	8♐30

1999

	♂	♃	♄	♅	♆	♇
Jan 1	18♎23	21♓56	26♈46	10♒57	1♒04	9♐07
15	25 02	24 12	27 01	11 43	1 35	9 35
Feb 1	2♏10	27 27	27 47	12 42	2 13	10 02
15	6 59	0♈26	28 45	13 31	2 44	10 17
Mar 1	10 27	3 36	0♉00	14 18	3 13	10 27
15	12 08	6 55	1 27	15 01	3 37	10 30
Apr 1	11 04	11 01	3 26	15 45	4 01	10 24
15	7 33	14 23	5 10	16 14	4 14	10 13
May 1	1 46	18 11	7 12	16 37	4 22	9 54
15	27♎11	21 22	8 59	16 46	4 21	9 33
Jun 1	24 31	24 59	11 03	16 45	4 12	9 06
15	25 11	27 42	12 37	16 34	3 59	8 43
Jul 1	28 42	0♉24	14 13	16 11	3 38	8 20
15	3♏37	2 21	15 23	15 44	3 17	8 03
Aug 1	11 21	4 03	16 27	15 05	2 49	7 49
15	18 49	4 49	16 59	14 32	2 27	7 44
Sep 1	28 52	4 54	17 11	13 53	2 04	7 47
15	7♐49	4 16	16 57	13 26	1 49	7 56
Oct 1	18 38	2 49	16 18	13 04	1 38	8 15
15	28 31	1 06	15 26	12 53	1 35	8 36
Nov 1	10♑55	28♈49	14 09	12 54	1 41	9 09
15	21 25	27 06	13 01	13 05	1 52	9 39
Dec 1	3♒36	25 41	11 50	13 30	2 13	10 16
15	14♒24	25♈04	11♉01	14♒00	2♒37	10♐49

2000

	♂	♃	♄	♅	♆	♇
Jan 1	27♒35	25♈14	10♉24	14♒47	3♒11	11♐27
15	8♓26	26 06	10 18	15 31	3 41	11 54
Feb 1	21 33	27 57	10 39	16 29	4 20	12 22
15	2♈15	0♉01	11 20	17 18	4 51	12 39
Mar 1	13 36	2 40	12 24	18 09	5 22	12 51
15	24 03	5 28	13 41	18 53	5 47	12 54
Apr 1	6♉32	9 11	15 30	19 40	6 12	12 49
15	16 40	12 24	17 10	20 10	6 25	12 39
May 1	28 02	16 10	19 11	20 35	6 33	12 20
15	7♊11	19 30	20 59	20 47	6 34	12 00
Jun 1	19 30	23 30	23 08	20 48	6 26	11 33
15	28 59	26 41	24 51	20 39	6 13	11 11
Jul 1	9♋40	0♊09	26 39	20 18	5 53	10 47
15	18 53	2 56	28 02	19 53	5 32	10 30
Aug 1	29 58	5 57	29 25	19 15	5 04	10 15
15	8♌59	8 01	0♊16	18 42	4 42	10 10
Sep 1	19 51	9 55	0 52	18 02	4 18	10 11
15	28 44	10 53	0 58	17 34	4 02	10 20
Oct 1	8♍48	11 14	0 40	17 10	3 51	10 37
15	17 33	10 50	0 03	16 57	3 47	10 58
Nov 1	28 06	9 31	28♉57	16 54	3 52	11 30
15	6♎43	7 54	27 52	17 03	4 03	12 00
Dec 1	16 27	5 45	26 34	17 25	4 23	12 36
15	24♎53	3♊56	25♉32	17♒54	4♒46	13♐09

Progressions represent the second method that depicts how the potential of a birth chart unfolds. Unlike transits, which measure the *actual* changing positions of planets in the sky, progressions work on a *symbolic* level.

There are many ways to progress a chart. The most commonly used method is known as **secondary progressions**. The astrological technique of secondary progressions measures the continuing movements of the planets in the sky in the days after one's birth and symbolically relates them to a larger time period. It is based on the formula that *one day* of time in the ephemeris can be equated with the passage of *one year* in a person's life.

For example, let's say that you were born on June 6, 1949. The movement of the planets during the first day of life corresponds to the experiences of your first year of life; the movement during the second day corresponds to the second year, and so on. Thus, the position of the planets on June 7, 1949 represents your progressed horoscope when you are one year old (see Figure 6). If you wanted to know what your progressed chart looked like on your thirteenth birthday, you would look at the Ephemeris for June 20, thirteen days after the birth. (See Figure 6). Note that by June 20, the Moon, Venus, Mars, and Uranus have each changed their sign position. Since signs act as media for the expression of planetary energies, these planets are now manifesting through different frequencies that were not available at birth.

Although progressions work with purely symbolic relationships, they have proven to be valid in astrological practice. This implies some kind of parallel between the transits of the days of the first several months after birth and the remainder of our life. That is to say that the first ninety days after our birth correspond to, and in some way are a blueprint for, the following ninety years of our life.

As we described with Figure 6, an easy way to approximate the positions of your progressed planets is to look in the ephemeris for your birth date. Count down one day for each year of your age, beginning with the day after your birth as year one. Then read the positions of the progressed planets. For example, if you want to know the progressed positions for your twentieth year of life, count twenty days after your birth.

You will notice that the motions of the slower moving outer planets—Jupiter, Saturn, Uranus, Neptune, Pluto—are generally too slight to be of any consequence. However, the inner planets—Mercury, Venus, Mars, and the asteroids, along with the Sun and Moon—move much faster. In the course of several weeks they show clear changes in their house and sign positions and aspects to other planets.

These inner planets are called the personal planets as they describe the more personal qualities in our personality makeup. We tend to experience the movements of the inner planets, as well as the Ascendent and Midheaven, via

Figure 6: Determining Progressions

LONGITUDE **JUNE 1949**

DAY	SID.TIME	☉	☽	TRUE ☊	☿	♀	♂	♃	♄	♅	♆	♇
	h m s	° ' "	° ' "	° '	° '	° '	° '	° '	° '	° '	° '	° '
1 W	16 36 35	10♊ 10 4	29♋ 39 41	24♈R39.1	14♊R35.0	22♊ 5.6	23♉ 30.3	1♒R58.1	0♍ 7.4	29♊ 28.0	12♎R32.0	14♌ 25.8
2 Th	16 40 31	11 7 34	13♌ 19 29	24 34.3	14 3.1	23 19.2	24 13.7	1 55.8	0 10.5	29 31.4	12 31.3	14 26.8
3 F	16 44 28	12 5 2	27 9 40	24 31.3	13 30.2	24 32.8	24 57.0	1 53.4	0 13.8	29 34.9	12 30.6	14 27.8
4 Sa	16 48 25	13 2 30	11♍ 9 13	24D 30.3	12 56.7	25 46.3	25 40.2	1 50.8	0 17.1	29 38.3	12 30.0	14 28.8
5 Su	16 52 21	13 59 56	25 17 10	24 30.7	12 23.2	26 59.9	26 23.3	1 48.0	0 20.5	29 41.8	12 29.4	14 29.8
6 M	16 56 18	14 57 20	9♎ 32 17	24 31.7	11 50.3	28 13.4	27 6.4	1 45.0	0 24.0	29 45.3	12 28.8	14 30.8
7 Tu	17 0 14	15 54 44	23 52 41	24R 32.3	11 18.5	29 27.0	27 49.5	1 41.9	0 27.6	29 48.8	12 28.3	14 31.9
8 W	17 4 11	16 52 6	8♏ 15 36	24 31.5	10 48.5	0♋ 40.5	28 32.5	1 38.6	0 31.3	29 52.3	12 27.7	14 32.9
9 Th	17 8 7	17 49 28	22 37 11	24 28.6	10 20.6	1 54.0	29 15.4	1 35.1	0 35.1	29 55.8	12 27.3	14 34.1
10 F	17 12 4	18 46 48	6♐ 52 44	24 23.4	9 55.4	3 7.4	29 58.3	1 31.4	0 39.0	29 59.4	12 26.8	14 35.2
11 Sa	17 16 0	19 44 8	20 57 13	24 16.0	9 33.3	4 20.9	0♊ 41.1	1 27.6	0 42.9	0♋ 2.9	12 26.4	14 36.3
12 Su	17 19 57	20 41 27	4♑ 45 54	24 7.2	9 14.6	5 34.4	1 23.9	1 23.6	0 46.9	0 6.5	12 26.0	14 37.5
13 M	17 23 54	21 38 45	18 15 13	23 57.8	8 59.8	6 47.8	2 6.6	1 19.4	0 51.1	0 10.0	12 25.6	14 38.7
14 Tu	17 27 50	22 36 3	1♒ 23 11	23 48.8	8 48.9	8 1.2	2 49.3	1 15.1	0 55.3	0 13.6	12 25.3	14 39.9
15 W	17 31 47	23 33 21	14 9 43	23 41.0	8 42.2	9 14.6	3 31.9	1 10.6	0 59.5	0 17.2	12 25.0	14 41.1
16 Th	17 35 43	24 30 37	26 36 31	23 35.3	8D 40.0	10 28.1	4 14.5	1 5.9	1 3.9	0 20.7	12 24.7	14 42.4
17 F	17 39 40	25 27 54	8♓ 46 44	23 31.6	8 42.2	11 41.4	4 57.0	1 1.1	1 8.3	0 24.3	12 24.5	14 43.7
18 Sa	17 43 36	26 25 10	20 44 40	23D 30.0	8 49.0	12 54.8	5 39.4	0 56.1	1 12.8	0 27.9	12 24.3	14 45.0
19 Su	17 47 33	27 22 26	2♈ 35 18	23 29.8	9 0.5	14 8.2	6 21.8	0 51.0	1 17.4	0 31.5	12 24.1	14 46.3
20 M	17 51 29	28 19 41	14 23 57	23R 30.2	9 16.6	15 21.6	7 4.1	0 45.7	1 22.1	0 35.1	12 24.0	14 47.6
21 Tu	17 55 26	29 16 57	26 15 58	23 30.4	9 37.3	16 34.9	7 46.4	0 40.3	1 26.8	0 38.7	12 23.9	14 48.9
22 W	17 59 23	0♋ 14 13	8♉ 16 20	23 29.4	10 2.7	17 48.3	8 28.7	0 34.7	1 31.7	0 42.3	12 23.8	14 50.3
23 Th	18 3 19	1 11 28	20 29 26	23 26.4	10 32.6	19 1.6	9 10.8	0 29.0	1 36.6	0 45.9	12D 23.7	14 51.7
24 F	18 7 16	2 8 42	2♊ 58 42	23 20.9	11 7.1	20 14.9	9 53.0	0 23.2	1 41.5	0 49.5	12 23.7	14 53.1
25 Sa	18 11 12	3 5 57	15 46 17	23 13.0	11 46.0	21 28.2	10 35.0	0 17.2	1 46.6	0 53.0	12 23.8	14 54.5
26 Su	18 15 9	4 3 12	28 52 52	23 3.0	12 29.4	22 41.5	11 17.0	0 11.1	1 51.7	0 56.6	12 23.8	14 56.0
27 M	18 19 5	5 0 27	12♋ 17 31	22 51.8	13 17.1	23 54.8	11 59.0	0 4.9	1 56.9	1 0.2	12 23.9	14 57.4
28 Tu	18 23 2	5 57 41	25 57 56	22 40.6	14 9.1	25 8.1	12 40.9	29♑ 58.5	2 2.1	1 3.8	12 24.0	14 58.9
29 W	18 26 58	6 54 55	9♌ 50 44	22 30.4	15 5.2	26 21.3	13 22.7	29 52.1	2 7.5	1 7.4	12 24.2	15 0.4
30 Th	18 30 55	7♋ 52 8	23♌ 52 9	22♈ 22.4	16♊ 5.6	27♋ 34.6	14♊ 4.5	29♑ 45.5	2♍ 12.9	1♋ 11.0	12♎ 24.3	15♌ 1.9

progression as the subtle inner forces—our feelings, instincts, insights, and attitudes—that create a gradual shift in how we perceive and react to the outer conditions of our lives.

When analyzing the significance of progressed planets, here are some general guidelines to keep in mind.

1. Note when a progressed planet or progressed angle changes sign or house. The sign change indicates a fundamental shift in *attitude* or *psychological need*. A house change indicates a shift in the *circumstances* of expressions.

The positions of the progressed planets are entirely personal for each individual. When transiting Mercury is in 15 degrees of Leo, it is in 15 degrees of Leo for everyone. But note that when your *progressed* Mercury is in 15 degrees of Leo, it is unique to your individual chart.

2. Notice when a progressed planet makes an aspect to a natal or other progressed planet within a one degree orb. Remember that one degree is approximately one year of time.

3. Note when a progressed planet turns retrograde or direct by motion. This will indicate a subtle shift in the expression of the planet's energies (see page 147 for the meaning of retrograde motion).

Now let's take a brief look at the meanings of the progressed personal planets.

The Progressed Sun: The progressed Sun will move through not more than three signs during the course of an average life span. The Sun represents our basic life purpose and our urge toward conscious self-expression. The progressed Sun's movement shows the dynamic aspect of that urge as it unfolds through time. The aspects that the progressed Sun makes and its sign and house changes point to the changing circumstances that provide opportunities for growth, maturity, and deepening in our quest to fully actualize who we really are as individuals. The progressed Sun acts as a spotlight of consciousness illuminating and developing the other parts of our personality that it contacts. We will always identify with the qualities of our Sun sign at birth, but the progressed Sun allows us to modify our character in our evolutionary development.

For example, a person born with his Sun in 10 degrees of Gemini will always exhibit the typical Gemini qualities of mental inquisitiveness and urge to communicate; when he reaches the age of twenty, however, and the Sun progresses into Cancer, he may be able to use his mental and communicative skills in a way that emotionally nurtures others. At the age of fifty, with a progressed Leo Sun, he can give form to some kind of creative or dramatic self-expression with his words and ideas.

A person born with a 12th house Sun may be a natural recluse or have difficulty in externalizing the self, but when the Sun by progression crosses the Ascendent and moves into the 1st house, this person may be able to exhibit more personal strength and power of self-expression. The development of this self-confidence can enable the person to actualize his inherent talents in order to better generate material and financial resources when the progressed Sun enters the second house

The Progressed Moon represents your changing emotional responses and needs over the course of your life. Unlike the Sun, which takes thirty years to progress through a sign, the Moon does so in a little less than 2¼ years, progressing through all twelve signs in about 27½ years. This roughly corresponds to the 29-year Saturn cycle. While transiting Saturn is the great timer, chronicling changes in the *outer structures* of your life, the progressed Moon measures the emotional changes in your *inner* life, letting you know how you can best get your emotional needs met at different life stages.

For example, one client described the following changes as his progressed Moon changed signs. Notice how the different activities in each cycle are described by the keywords of the progressed Moon's sign position.

Progressed Moon enters **Pisces**—he goes to live in a spiritual community.
Progressed Moon enters **Aries**—he gets a job as self-employed salesperson working 100% on commission,
Progressed Moon enters **Taurus**—he switches his sales career to selling stocks, bonds, and other financial securities
Progressed Moon enters **Gemini**—he decides to become a full-time writer. To promote his books, he begins to lecture and teach seminars.
Progressed Moon enters **Cancer**—he enters therapy to work on his family of origin issues and to heal the inner child.
Progressed Moon enters **Leo**—he writes a book on children and starts volunteer teaching at an elementary school.

We recommend that you likewise find out when the progressed Moon changed sign and house positions in your birth chart and reflect upon what shifts occurred during those transitional periods in your life. At the end of this section we will show you how you can determine when the Moon changes sign and house.

A final note. As your Sun and Moon progress through the signs, their angular relationship naturally changes; hence the Moon Phase also changes. Once you know the exact position of your progressed Sun and your progressed Moon, you can calculate the position of your progressed Sun/Moon phase. Please refer to pages 137-145 for keywords for the eight Moon Phases.

Progressed Mercury shows our mental and intellectual development over the course of our life—perhaps through writing, art or music, teaching, or public speaking. If a person is born with retrograde Mercury, this *may* indicate that their mind is more inwardly turned or that they have difficulty in communicating their thoughts. At some point in the person's life Mercury will go direct by progression and there will be an opportunity for mentally opening out. By contrast, a person born with Mercury direct may become more introspective and reflective if Mercury turns retrograde by progression.

Progressed Venus shows the development of our values, of the feminine principle, creativity, and urge toward relationship and intimacy. Changes in house and sign positions show how and where these changes will take place.

Progressed Mars shows the unfolding of our initiative, assertiveness, energy, drive, and sexuality. Like Mercury, Venus and Mars also have progressions where they go retrograde and direct by motion.

How do you determine the exact positions of your progressed planets? The method we described earlier is only an approximate way to determine the position of your progressed planets. This is because the typical ephemeris shows the planets' positions for midnight or noon Greenwich Mean Time. Since hardly anyone is born *exactly* at midnight or noon, an astrological interpolation is needed to determine the time that must elapse for your planets to correspond to those listed in the

ephemeris. Rather than try to describe this involved procedure, we recommend that you send away for the "Day by Day" progressions report, calculated by Astro Communications. You can get this report for a 5-year, 10-year or 85-year period. Refer to Appendix D for ordering information or call 1-800-888-9983.

Figure 7 shows a sample page of this progression report. We have progressed the chart located on Figure 1, page 26, for the person's forty-first year. Note that the Sun has progressed from Pisces to Aries, the Moon is now in Gemini, Mercury is in Aries, etc. In addition, the report shows the exact date when the progressed Sun went from the fifth to the sixth house (February 4, 1990) as well as when the progressed Moon moved from Gemini to Cancer (April 13, 1990).

Once you know your progressed planetary positions, you can place them on the outside of the wheel of your natal horoscope as we show in Figure 8 (page 252). This will help you to clearly visualize how your birth chart has progressed over time.

Further Reading

Arroyo, Stephen, *Astrology, Karma and Transformation.*
Davison, Ronald, *The Technique of Prediction.*
Forrest, Steven, *The Changing Sky.*
Freeman, Martin, *Forecasting by Astrology.*
March, Marion and McEvers, Joan, *The Only Way to Learn About Tomorrow.*

Figure 7: Progressed Planets; Progressed Aspect

```
** 41 YEARS OLD IN 1990**
Sun  14-AR-54    5-N-52    5
Moo  26-GE-22   28-N- 1    8
Mer   6-AR-19    0-N-52    5
Ven  11-AR-49    3-N-27    5
Mar  10-AR-55    3-N-40    5
Jup  29-CP- 4   20-S-32    3
Sat  29-LE-55R  13-N-10   10
Urn  26-GE-56   23-N-37    8
Nep  13-LI-47R   3-S-56   11
Plu  14-LE-15R  24-N- 1    9
Asc   7-SG-40   21-S-36    2
Mc   25-VI-26    1-N-49   11
Nod  25-AR-41    9-N-56    6
Chr   8-SG-54R  17-S-33    2
Cer  11-LE-46   29-N-58    9
Pal  24-GE-47    5-S-54    8
Jun  28-TA-43   10-N- 4    7
Ves  24-SG-16   16-S-25    2
```

```
Jan 06  Moo  X    0  Urn  R
Jan 06  Sun  X  135  Sat  P
Jan 12  Moo  X   45  Cer  P
Jan 15  Sun  X  120  Plu  R
Jan 16  Sun  X  C-P  Pal  P
Jan 16  Moo  X    0  Urn  P
Jan 25  Moo  X   60  Nod  R
Feb 04  Sun  HOUSE 5 to 6
Feb 12  Jun  X  135  Nep  P
Feb 15  Mc   E   90  Urn  R
Feb 22  Jun  X  135  Nep  R
Mar 11  Moo  X   30  Jun  P
Mar 15  Ven  L    0  Mar  P
Mar 19  Moo  X  150  Jup  P
Mar 23  Moo  X   45  Plu  P
Apr 03  Moo  X   45  Cer  R
Apr 04  Mc   X  150  Nod  P
Apr 06  Asc  X   60  Mer  R
Apr 06  Moo  X   45  Mc   R
Apr 10  Moo  X   60  Sat  P
Apr 11  Moo  X   45  Plu  R
Apr 13  Moo  GEMI to CANC
Apr 14  Mer  E   60  Mer  R
Apr 16  Mer  L   60  Pal  R
Apr 18  Mer  E  120  Asc  P
Apr 23  Ven  X  120  Ves  R
```

Above: Progressed planets. Right: Progressed planets for 1990. E=entering 1 degree orbit; X=exact; L=leaving 1 degree orbit.

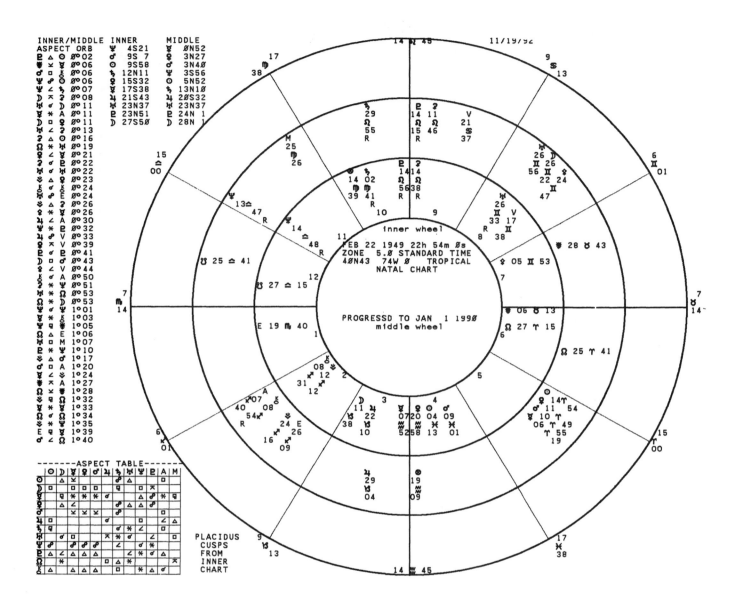

Over the past 50 years, the growth of astrological literature has been nothing short of astronomical. At the turn of the century, most of the available astrological literature had been written during the fatalistic Middle Ages and was no longer relevant to contemporary humanity. Fortunately, with the birth of modern person-centered astrology, a number of fine astrological authors have come forth and put their ideas in print.

What follows is a list of the most helpful and instructive books that we have employed during our professional experience. We have arranged them by topic so that you can refer to the literature according to your area of interest.

Introductory Books ————————————

Bacher, Elman, *Studies in Astrology V 1–4,* Rosicrucian Fellowship

Carter, Charles, *The Principles of Astrology,* Theosophical Publ. Hs. 1978; *The Zodiac and the Soul,* Gordon Pr., 1973.

Hall, Manly P., *Astrological Keywords,* Littlefield, 1975.

Hodgson, Joan, *Reincarnation through the Zodiac* (also published as *Wisdom in the Stars*), CRCS Publ., 1973.

Lewi, Grant, *Astrology for the Millions,* Llewellyn Publ., 1978.

March, Marion and McIvers, Joan, *The Only Way to Learn Astrology,* ACS Publ., 1976.

Mayo, Jeff, *Teach Yourself Astrology,* McKay, 1980; *The Planets and Human Behavior,* CRCS Publ., 1985.

Moore, Marcia, *Astrology, The Divine Science,* Arcane Publ., 1978.

Oken, Alan, *Complete Astrologer,* Bantam, 1980.

Pottenger, Maritha, *Complete Horoscope Interpretation,* ACS Publ., 1986.

Rudhyar, Dane, *The Astrology of Personality,* Aurora, 1978; *The Pulse of Life,* Shambhala, 1978; *The Astrological Houses,* CRCS Publ., 1986.

Medical Astrology ————————————

Bailey, Alice, *Esoteric Healing,* Lucis Trust, 1978.

Cornell, H.L., *Encyclopedia of Medical Astrology,* Llewellyn Publ., 1972.

Davidson, Dr. William, *Lectures on Medical Astrology,* Astrological Bureau, 1973.

Garrison, Omar, *Medical Astrology,* University Books, 1971.

Heindel, Max, *Astro-Diagnosis: Guide to Healing,* Rosicrucian Fellowship, 1929.

Jansky, Robert Carl, *Astrology, Nutrition and Health,* Whitford Press, 1977.

Naumann, Eileen, *American Book of Nutrition and Medical Astrology,* ACS Publ., 1982.

Stark, Marcia, *Astrology: Key to Holistic Health,* Seek It Publ., 1982.

Child-Rearing ————————————

Burmyn, Lynne and Baldwin, Christina, *Sun Signs for Kids: An Astrological Guide for Parents,* St. Martin's, 1985.

Edmands, Dodie and Allan, *Child Signs,* CRCS Publ., 1983.

Hand, Robert, *Planets in Youth,* Whitford Press, 1977.

Chart Interpretation ————————————

Greene, Liz, *The Outer Planets and Their Cycles,* CRCS Publ., 1983; *Saturn: A New Look at an Old Devil,* Weiser, 1976.

Hand, Robert, *Horoscope Symbols,* Whitford Press, 1980.

Leo, Alan, *The Art of Synthesis,* Inner Traditions, 1979.

Marks, Tracy, *The Art of Chart Synthesis,* Sag. Rising, 1979.

Planetary Aspects ————————————

Pelletier, Robert, *Planets in Aspect,* Whitford Press, 1974.

Rael, Leyla and Rudhyar, Dane, *Astrological Aspects,* Aurora, 1980.

Tierney, Bil, *Dynamics of Aspect Analysis,* CRCS Publ., 1983.

Moon Phases ————————————

Rudhyar, Dane, *The Lunation Cycle,* Aurora, 1967.

Astrology and Psychology ————————————

Arroyo, Stephen, *Astrology, Psychology and the Four Elements,* CRCS Publ., 1975; *Astrology, Karma and Transformation,* CRCS Publ., 1978.

Cunningham, Donna, *An Astrological Guide to Self-Awareness,* CRCS Publ., 1978.

Hebel, Doris, *Celestial Psychology,* Aurora, 1985.

Mayo, Jeff, *The Planets and Human Behavior,* CRCS Publ., 1985.

Pottenger, Maritha, *Healing With the Horoscope,* ACS Publ., 1983.

Rosenblum, Bernard, *The Astrologer's Guide to Counseling,* CRCS Publ., 1983.

Tyl, Noel, *Astrological Counsel,* Llewelyn Publ., 1975.

Moon's Nodes

Schulman, Martin, *Karmic Astrology: The Moon's Nodes and Reincarnation, Vol. 1,* Weiser, 1977.

Vocational Astrology

Wickenburg, Joanne, *In Search of a Fulfilling Career,* Search, 1977.

Relationship Astrology

Arroyo, Stephen, *Relationships and Life Cycles,* CRCS Publ., 1979.

Davidson, Ronald, *Synastry,* Aurora, 1983.

Goodman, Linda, *Linda Goodman's Love Signs,* Fawcett, 1985.

Greene, Liz, *Relating,* Weiser, 1978; *Star Signs for Lovers,* CRCS Publ., 1980.

Sargent, Lois H., *How to Handle Your Human Relations,* Am. Fed. Astrologers, 1958.

Townley, John, *Planets in Love,* Whitford Press, 1978.

Transits

Forrest, Steven, *The Changing Sky: The Dynamic New Astrology for Everyone,* Bantam, 1984.

Hand, Robert, *Planets in Transit,* Whitford Press, 1976.

Lundsted, Betty, *Transits: The Time of Your Life,* Weiser, 1980.

Riotte, Louise, *Planetary Planting,* ACS Publ., 1982.

Robertson, Marc, *The Transit of Saturn,* Am. Fed. Astrologers, 1980.

Ruperti, Alexander, *Cycles of Becoming,* CRCS Publ., 1978.

Mundane

Baigent, Campion and Harvey, *Mundane Astrology: An Introduction to the Astrology of Nations and Groups,* Aquarian Press, 1984.

Dodson, Carolyn, *Horoscopes of US States and Cities,* Am. Fed. Astrologers, 1976.

Lerner, Mark, *Mysteries of Venus,* Great Bear, 1980.

Lynes, Barry, *The Next Twenty Years.* Self-published.

Moore, Moon, *The Book of World Horoscopes,* Seek It Publ., 1980.

Penfield, Mark, *Horoscopes of the Western Hemisphere,* ACS Publ., 1984.

Historical Astrology

Rodden, Lois, *The American Book of Charts, Profiles of Women,* Am. Fed. Astrologers, 1979.

Economic Astrology

Lynes, Barry, *Astro-Economics.* Self-published.

Williams, Dr. David, *Astro-Economics: A Study of Astrology and the Business Cycle,* Llewellyn Publ., 1974.

Horary Astrology

Jacobson, Ivy M., *Simplified Horary Astrology.* Self-published.

Simmonite, Dr. W.J., *Horary Astrology,* Am. Fed. Astrologers, 1976.

Stone, Diana, *Correspondence Course in Horary Astrology* (8665 SW Canyon Road, Portland, OR 97225).

Watters, Barbara, Horary Astrology, Am. Fed. Astrologers, 1982.

Asteroids

Bach, Eleanor, *Ephemerides of the Asteroids,* Celestial Communications, 1973.

George, Demetra and Bloch, Douglas, *Asteroid Goddesses,* ACS Publ., 1986.

Lantero, Ermine, *The Continuing Discovery of Chiron,* Weiser, 1983.

Stein, Zane, *Interpreting Chiron,* Assoc. for Studying Chiron, 1982.